$$\frac{.*\alpha\beta *\gamma\delta \quad \vee\alpha\gamma}{\vee\beta\delta} \quad \text{Constructive Dilemma (CD}$$

$$\frac{.*B\alpha B\beta *B\gamma B\delta \quad \vee B\beta B\delta}{\vee B\alpha B\gamma} \quad \text{Destructive Dilemma (DD)}$$

$\dfrac{\Pi}{\beta}$ is valid if $\dfrac{\Pi \, -\beta,}{.\,\alpha-\alpha}$ is valid,   Reductio (R)

where we substitute for Π one or more consistent premisses.

$$\frac{*\alpha *\beta\gamma}{*.\alpha\beta\gamma} \quad \text{Exportation (Exp)}$$

$$\frac{\alpha}{\vee\alpha\alpha} \quad \frac{\alpha}{.\alpha\alpha} \quad \text{Tautology (Taut)}$$

$$\frac{B.B\alpha B\beta}{B\vee B\alpha B\beta} \quad \text{DeMorgan (DeM)}$$

$$\frac{*B\alpha\beta}{\vee B\alpha\beta} \quad \text{Ast}$$

$$\frac{*B\alpha B\beta}{*B\beta B\alpha} \quad \text{Transposition (Trans)}$$

$$\frac{\vee B\alpha B\beta}{|B\alpha B\beta} \quad \text{Stroke (St)}$$

$$\frac{-\alpha}{|\alpha\alpha} \quad \text{Nobarsatall (Nob)}$$

$$\frac{\vee\alpha\beta}{||\alpha\alpha|\beta\beta} \quad \text{Handy}$$

Logic: A Dialogue

A. K. Bierman *Department of Philosophy*
San Francisco State College

LOGIC: A DIALOGUE

I would raithair speak Logik wyth eny wun than eat, or ewen than cutte a kapur.—Fanebius Perlyng

HOLDEN-DAY, INC: San Francisco, London, Amsterdam

First printing June 1964
Second printing May 1966

Library of Congress Catalog Card No. 64-16572

Printed in the United States of America

Contents

This book is dedicated to Susan, Megan, and Benjamin*

* For further remarks see pages 395 and 396.

Letters of Introduction

Mr. Max Penny
San Francisco, Calif.

Dear Mr. Penny:

My name is Emory Nickel.   I am a student who would like to learn logic.   I understand that you teach logic and wondered if you would teach it to me this summer.   Naturally, I expect to pay you.

I realize that you like to have your summers free, but since we are to be caught in a cultural desert together this summer—which, according to one of the professors here, you are going to spend, as I am, in the mountains near town D—I thought you would not mind having someone who is interested in philosophy to talk with.

I will work hard, and although I have not had any philosophy, I think I am intelligent enough to be interesting.

Thank you for your consideration.

Respectfully yours,

/s/ Emory Nickel

Mr. Emory Nickel
Lincoln, Nebr.

Dear Mr. Nickel:

You are right about my wanting summers free, but in your letter to me you have touched upon one thing that makes me seriously consider your request, namely, the desire to talk with someone interested in philosophy while in the, as you put it, "cultural desert."

We can work out a course of instruction for you that should prove profitable for both of us. Let me tell you what I have in mind so you can decide if you want to go through with the course.

First of all, I'd like to indicate briefly what you cannot expect in the way of a logic course from me. If we were to use a current logic text, we would have to select from two kinds of books. One kind is what I'll call a rule-book. It is usually broken down into three parts: theory of meaning, deductive logic, and scientific method. I call it a rule-book because the most prominent part, deductive logic, consists mainly of giving rules for finding the validity of arguments expressed in natural languages, such as English. The rule-book text is designed mainly as a practical tool giving logical recipes for persons who need or desire more rigor in their reasoning.

Our course will follow the rule-book program only in part. I intend to cover just the first two topics: theory of meaning and deductive logic. Further, I do not conceive of our course primarily as a practical one, though we will apply what we learn of deductive logic to arguments in natural languages. I conceive of our course as being primarily theoretical.

The other kind of book we could choose is one which I call manipulative. The manipulative logic text is designed to train the student as quickly as possible in the techniques of manipulating the symbolic language of modern logic. It, too, is a practical book, though its practical value is greatest for those students who intend to make logic, mathematics, or the exact sciences their field of study.

Our course will follow the manipulative program only in part. You will learn how to manipulate a portion of the symbolic language of logic, but, as I'll explain in a bit, we'll use a different technique for learning it than is usual in manipulative logic books. Although my technique is initially not as fast as the other, it gives students a more self-conscious grasp of the symbolism because it doesn't tend to induce in them a rote-hypnosis. Except for historical precedent, logic taught the manipulative way could be taught as well in the mathematics department as in the philosophy department, and it sometimes is.

Now let me indicate more fully what you can expect in a logic course from me.

First, as I said, I do not want to use either the rule-book text or the manipulative text. They don't bear down on philosophy as I'd like to do. I want to consider some philosophic issues in such a way that a discussion of them will generate the need of and the demand for logic. A central philosophic issue in our course will be the nature of philosophic argument and its relation to a theory of linguistic concepts.

Secondly, most current rule-book texts handle theory of meaning in terms of traditional concepts, such as connotation, denotation, and Aristotelian definition. I plan to bring in more recent issues and concepts in theory of meaning and philosophy of language, particularly those found in Ordinary Language philosophy.

Thirdly, I want to integrate theory of meaning and deductive logic more than is usually done in introductory logic books. I'm going to use the symbolism of logic as a linguistic model for investigating the character of natural languages. Each time we come to grips with a philosophic issue about language, we'll turn to the logical symbolism to illustrate and clarify our point. The symbolism may also suggest the next line of inquiry. This will provide a philosophic setting for your exercises in logic.

The integration of theory of meaning and deductive logic will reach its apex with a sense logic, a logic of conceptual meaning. We will develop a formal symbolism which will enable us to know when we have and when we don't have the basic materials for a meaningful English subject-predicate sentence.

Fourthly, I want you to learn the symbolism of logic as you learned your native tongue. Generally, the symbolism of logic is interpreted for the reader by the writer at the beginning of the book, the interpretation being given in the tongue familiar to the student; the writer also usually gives the reader rules and directions for manipulating the logical symbolism. I'll not give you an interpretation until near the end of our course (I urge other instructors to do likewise, and enjoin students to let the pleasures of anticipation outweigh the pain of impatience), and, as to the rules and directions, you'll have to complete the formulation of them yourself on the basis of an examination of sample expressions of the symbolism.

By using this inductive teaching technique, you should, at the end of the course, have no more worries that you will lose your mastery of the symbolism while being examined on it than you have that you will forget the English language. In addition, if you are one of those who has always had a fear of symbolism, you can shed it; that fear has probably been caused by having been taught mathematics by a technique which encourages rote memorizing rather than understanding.

Let me reassure you. I will not be experimenting on you with this inductive technique. I have used it to teach many students, and with better results than those obtained by the usual method where you are given an interpretation of the symbolism and rules for their manipulation.

By learning logic in my fashion, I expect you will learn something from it other than rule applications and manipulatory skills.

If you wish to take a chance with these departures from recent logic texts, I shall be delighted to engage you in conversations this summer.

Cordially yours,

/s/ Max Penny

P.S. I am amused by the coincidence of our names. Any teacher worth his salt should be able to produce a student five times his own worth.

Mr. Max Penny
San Francisco, Calif.

Dear Mr. Penny:

I am anxious to chance the departures you outlined and look forward to seeing you this summer. I can hardly wait for this semester to be over.

Yours truly,

/s/ Emory Nickel

First conversation

LOGIC IN THE WIDE SENSE

*Everyman, I will go with thee, and be thy guide
In thy most need to go by thy side.*

I TOOK a bus to the town nearest where Mr. Penny was staying for the summer. He had written that he would meet me at the drug store which also served as the bus station. My relatives were there as well, and they had become acquainted with Mr. Penny while waiting for my bus to arrive.]

[He was younger and more informal than I had anticipated; also more aggressive, pressing me to explain why I thought Tolstoy's *The Kreutzer Sonata*, which I had been reading on the bus, was a philosophical novel. He could see that my relatives were not interested in our conversation and were anxious to get home, so we didn't have a chance to talk further. We agreed to meet the next day at his house to begin my course.]

[I found him the next day in an airy gazebo in the yard, behind his rented house. It was cool there and isolated, and that's where we philosophized that summer.]

PENNY: Hello, Mr. Nickel. I'm awfully glad to see you. Your relatives' attitude toward our short talk about *The Kreutzer Sonata* is, I'm afraid, typical of the intellectual interest in this town.

NICKEL: I know. I've spent several summers here. It will be wonderful to have some contrast.

Before we begin, I have a request to make.

PENNY: What is it?

NICKEL: Do you mind if I write down our conversations? I don't mean just what you say, but also what I say. My guess is that learning logic is like learning any other subject involving new ideas. If my friends try to learn something from the notes, it might be more useful to have a record of my discovery rather than of your achievement.

PENNY: Writing it down seems to make our conversation as irrevocable as . . . as history. The nice thing about free conversation is that we can always revise and so hold off the tyranny of time. There is security in impermanence, my friend.

NICKEL: Yes, but there's too much privacy, too. If logic is worth teaching to me, it's worth teaching to others. And since you can't talk privately to everybody, the next best thing is to let me make a permanent record, in writing, of all our conversations.

PENNY: It's a novel suggestion. Logic isn't usually presented in dialogue style, though this method does have a virtue if I'm right in believing that in the best presentation of a subject there is a genetic ordering of its concepts. I don't know of any "science" of genetic order that discovers the way in which concepts develop out of one another, showing that Concept *B* should be taught *after* Concept *A* because it fulfills the promise of *A*, and *before* Concept *C* because it facilitates the grasp of Concept *C*, and suggests *C*, nay, even makes the learner demand *C*.

6

In the absence of such a science, we can only hope to produce a genetically ordered logic "course" if I am guided by your responses, the virtue of the dialogue style then being that it captures this genesis.

Of course, we run the risk of producing and recording only your genetic order! And isn't the possibility of this private record the vice of the dialogue style? As contrasted with the ideal of a public, scientific discovery? Everyman, canst thou go with us?

NICKEL: Maybe there can't be any such thing as a "science of genetic order."

PENNY: What makes you say that?

NICKEL: Because from what you just said, the teacher doesn't discover an order, but produces one, or induces one in the student.

PENNY: Ah. So you think the genetic order isn't something inherent in the concepts, not an entity patiently awaiting discovery, but is an effect of the way in which they are presented. And if we're clever enough our dialogue will so present the subject that it will produce the same genetic order for everyman?

NICKEL: It seems worth a try to me.

PENNY: Your confidence and enthusiasm fire me. They also frighten me, for I may not have wit and art enough to help produce such an order.

I hope you also realize how against the spirit of the times this view of genetic order is. Don't you know that art is supposed to be an interim practice, something to be suffered until the scientific breakthrough? It's clear that impiety is our only shield and the love of talk our only weapon, Mr. Nickel. Are you ready?

NICKEL: Ready, Mr. Penny.

PENNY: In the same spirit in which Plato said that philosophy is the love of wisdom I shall say that *logic is the love of form.* This is admittedly poetical, a statement that sums up my experience of the subject, rather than describes it, but it may come to mean something to you after you have gone through a course in logic.

More prosaically, logic finds its subject matter in language; specifically, it is concerned with the *regularity* required in the combinations of linguistic elements. This regularity is a necessary feature of anything we would be willing to call a language. Suppose someone handed you a sheet of paper on which appeared some marks arranged either something like Example A or like B. (See page 8.)

If someone handed you Example A, how do you think you would react to the sheet?

NICKEL: First I would turn it over, so the marks would look more like English letters.

PENNY: And you would do the same thing with Example B?

NICKEL: I'm not sure. I can see that Example B looks pretty haphazard; even if I turned it over it wouldn't make much sense. Example B gives me the impression that some child has been playing on a typewriter. But it occurs to me that Example A might possibly make sense; it might be a coded message. If it were, then perhaps it should be read from left to right upside down rather than left to right right side up.

PENNY: Why do you think Example A suggests a coded or enciphered message while Example B does not?

NICKEL: Example A looks more like our ordinary writing than Example B; with Example B there seems no way of deciding which marks are combined. Oh. I see your point—the first shares some of the usual kind of order, hence some regular combinations.

Example A	*Example B*
)V∧&* 5(O⅄ Lu	⅄ ⅄ &∀)
	ᴚ U ⊥
	(�5 *
	∧
	S n
	N
ꜱ%NᴚU⊥ ⱸFꜱꜱ	s% E
	Oᴜ
	ⱸ

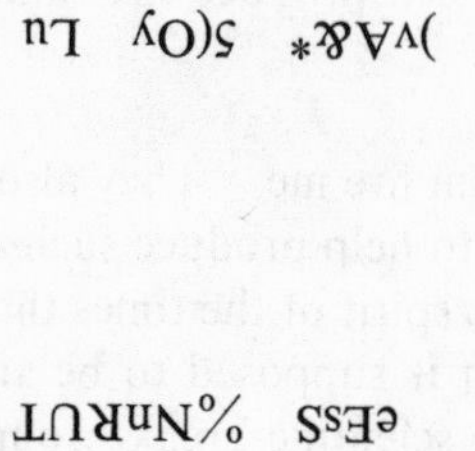

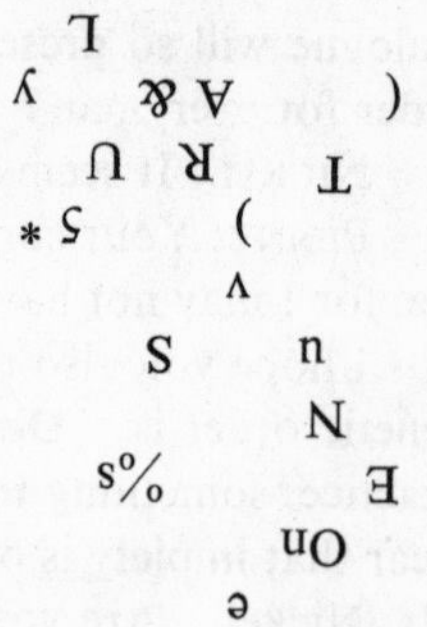

PENNY: Right. Now suppose Example A is an enciphered message.

NICKEL: Well . . . we say a message is "enciphered" when its usual linguistic order is hidden. If the message "Bring the pontoons with you," were written simply "Bring the pontoons with you," we would understand it immediately.

PENNY: Sure. Usually a person who sends an enciphered message does not want it understood or deciphered. To prevent someone from deciphering a message, wouldn't it be a good idea to make it look as little like a message as possible?

NICKEL: Because if no one suspects a hidden message, no one will even try to decipher it. Example B is like that all right; my first thought was that a child had been playing on a typewriter! I didn't suspect any regular combinations at all. I guess that proves you're right about our not calling anything a language that doesn't exhibit regularity.

PENNY: So if someone handed you Example B you might be inclined to toss it away as meaningless. Now suppose that someone in a dark

8

cloak slipped you a sheet of paper with twenty-one numbered holes cut in it, such that when you laid the paper over Example B one of the marks appeared through each of the holes. What would you think?

NICKEL: I would think you had put on a dark cloak to clinch your point. By the way, does Example A or Example B contain a message?

PENNY: I am the enemy and I am not talking. I am a private; my serial number is GO-7-123456.

NICKEL: Really. I want to know.

PENNY: Whining will not break my resolve. May I suggest an alternative?

NICKEL: I'll suggest one myself. I'll try to decipher it.

PENNY: Into English or Swahili?

NICKEL: Give me a hint.

PENNY: My serial number is GO-7-123456. My rank is private. War is hell.

NICKEL: Say, there could be a lot of different regularities disguised in Example A, couldn't there?

PENNY: If you tried to decipher Example A you would either succeed in extracting the message or you would fail.

NICKEL: That seems fairly obvious.

PENNY: But by confining your attention to Example A alone, you won't be able to tell whether your deciphering efforts have succeeded or failed.

NICKEL: That doesn't seem obvious.

PENNY: Consider this then. Suppose after trying very hard you didn't extract any blood from a turnip. Would you conclude that you had *failed* to extract the blood?

NICKEL: Of course not, for the turnip doesn't have any blood.

PENNY: And after trying very hard to extract a message, but being unable to do so, would you conclude that you had failed?

NICKEL: I can't be said to have *failed* to extract a message if it doesn't contain one.

PENNY: Do you have any way of telling, merely from a study of the regularities of Example A, that it does *not* contain a message?

NICKEL: I believe the most I can conclude after not extracting a combination of marks that makes sense is either that Example A does not contain a message *or* that I have failed. But I can't conclude either alternative alone. The only advantage I can see here is that at least I don't have to conclude I am a bad cryptographer.

PENNY: But you do admit, don't you, that you can't tell whether your deciphering efforts have failed or succeeded?

NICKEL: Since I can't tell whether or not I've failed and since I certainly haven't succeeded in coming up with any intelligible sentences, I have to admit that.

However, if I succeeded in extracting a new combination of marks which did make sense to me, I could conclude that I had succeeded in extracting the message *and* that I was a good cryptographer.

PENNY: That seems doubtful to me. Imagine that you are at a cocktail party at the Italian Consulate. Do you know the Italian language?

NICKEL: No.

PENNY: Under the influence you could jokingly be imitating Italian speech sounds. And now a flushed member of the staff walks up to you and insists that his honor can be satisfied only on the dueling mat. Choose your weapons. How would you get out of the fix you so innocently fell into?

NICKEL: I would explain that apparently I accidentally said something in Italian. I could not intend what I said, for I know no Italian.

PENNY: In other words, you uttered a combination of sounds that constitutes a *sentence*, but you did not send a message with that combination.

NICKEL: Because a sentence is a message only if I *intend* the sentence.

PENNY: That's right. The distinction between a sentence and a message is the only thing that will get you out of the dueling match. I might have written down Example A in the same spirit in which you uttered the Italian speech sounds. The fact that you extract from Example A a combination of marks that is a sentence for *you* doesn't mean it was *my* message. We can accidentally send a sentence as you did at the Consulate, but we can't accidentally send a message.

Do you think this distinction helps in the following case also? I am the enemy. You and a friend have worked very hard on Example A; in fact, so hard that you both come up with a ————; but each ———— has a different sense. The question now is: which one, if either, contains the ————? In five minutes or less fill in the blanks.

NICKEL: I take it with the words "sentence" or "message." Hmmm. I think that "sentence" should go in the first two blanks and "message" in the last one.

PENNY: Good. Now how would you decide which one was the message, if either?

NICKEL: There doesn't seem to be any way now except to start pulling your fingernails.

PENNY: I weaken and say: Mr. Nickel, he got it!

NICKEL: But you might be lying. Like I might have lied to the Italian. So now the only way to identify the message is to find out if you are lying.

PENNY: Determining that I was lying would not be sufficient to insure identification of the message. It would be sufficient if Example A yielded two and only two sentences. But you and I could dream up any number of ciphers that would force Example A to yield as many sentences.

NICKEL: I guess the only way of determining which sentence, if any, expresses the message is to check them all against the facts. For example, my interpretation of Example A might be: "Bridge K-2 will be blown up at 0400." If the bridge were blown up at that time, then I would know my sentence expressed the message.

PENNY: Nickel, you're infernally confident! Checking against the facts isn't always sufficient either. Sentences don't always state facts. Some of the sentences yielded by Example A might be like this one: "Blow up the K-2 bridge." How are you going to check that kind of sentence against the facts?

There's another difficulty. Suppose your friend's sentence was: "The white cliffs of Dover are gray." It is logically possible for both sentences to be true; and were they both to be true we would have to suppose according to your "factual" test that both express the message. It's logically possible to have 500 true sentences, hence, 500 messages.

NICKEL: It does seem an extreme view, all right. But isn't there any sure-fire way of finding the message?

PENNY: There is no method that can lead us with mathematical certainty to the message. However, there is another method you haven't mentioned of deciding which sentence expresses the message.

NICKEL: Does it involve additional messages?

PENNY: It does. For every different way we deciphered a set of characters we must have had a different cipher or system by which we converted the unintelligible set of characters into an intelligible set.

NICKEL: Am I right in thinking that a cipher consists of a set of rules or directions?

PENNY: Yes. They are rules for transposition or substitution of letters or both. A simple transposition cipher could consist of a single rule, for example: Reverse the order of the numbers and letters. If we encipher your sentence according to this rule, it then becomes: "0040 ta pu nwolb eb lliw 2-K egdirb." An equally simple substitution cipher could consist of the following single rule: Substitute for each letter and number the third letter and number that occurs after it in the alphabet and natural number system respectively. Then your sentence becomes: "Eulgjh N-5 zloo eh eoryq xs dw 3733."

NICKEL: I guess it's fairly obvious that Example B would probably be a combination of transposition and substitution rules.

PENNY: That would seem like a fair guess. Since every different sentence or set of sentences we get out of a set of characters has some corresponding cipher, the problem of deciding which sentence or set of sentences expresses the message can be seen to have a corresponding problem, the problem of deciding which cipher allows us to decipher the message.

NICKEL: And the correct cipher is the one which the sender used to encipher his message, right?

PENNY: That one or its equivalent.

NICKEL: Well, then, we should direct our efforts to selecting the right cipher. If we can do that, we automatically know which sentence expresses the message. It will be that sentence deciphered by means of the correct cipher.

PENNY: Very good, Nickel. And what method do you suggest we use to select the cipher?

NICKEL: I don't have a name for it, but I can describe it. Although a cipher hides a message by altering the familiar regularity of sentences, it actually imposes a new regularity. I imagine that generally the inventors of ciphers use them on more than one message. Is that so?

PENNY: I think that's generally true.

NICKEL: If he does use it on several messages, then they all share the new regularity. That's the key. For in case a person finds a cipher that works on several sets of characters, that makes them all intelligible, it is probable, but not certain—see how I've lost my infernal confidence—that he has found the correct cipher.

PENNY: Why is it probable?

NICKEL: It's unlikely that two different sets of characters produced by two different ciphers will both be made intelligible by one of the ciphers. Take my sentence for example, "Bridge K-2 will be blown up at 0400." You used two different ciphers to encipher it, producing (1) and (2). The application of one of them, e.g., the reverse-order cipher, to both encipherments will show you that's so. Just look at (1′) and (2′).

(1) 0040 ta pu nwolb eb lliw 2-K egdirb.

(1′) Bridge K-2 will be blown up at 0400.

(2) Eulgjh N-5 zloo eh eoryq xs dw 3733.

(2′) 3373 wd sx qyroe he oolz 5-N hjglue.

The application of the reverse-order cipher to the set of characters produced by the third-letter-after cipher, (2), produces (2′), which is nonsensical.

PENNY: Do you see what cryptography has to do with logic in the wide sense?

NICKEL: It is part of logic in the wide sense, because it is a search for hidden regularity.

PENNY: Nicely done, Nickel. What about grammar? Is it part of logic in the wide sense too?

NICKEL: Grammar can't be. There are too many exceptions to the rules.

PENNY: Are they *regularly* exceptions?

NICKEL: I think you have me there, though I'm not sure I should give up so easily.

PENNY: It occurs to me that part of literary criticism is swallowed by logic also.

NICKEL: That seems odd to me.

PENNY: Daren't a rose bloom in logic? Here is a passage from John Stuart Mill's *Autobiography* where he comments on Thomas Carlyle's writings.

> I have already mentioned Carlyle's earlier writings as one of the channels through which I received the influences which enlarged my early narrow creed; but I do not think that those writings, by themselves, would ever have had any effect on my opinions. What truths they contained, though of the very kind which I was already receiving from other quarters, were presented in a form and vesture less suited than any other to give them access to a mind trained as mine had been. They seemed a haze of poetry and German metaphysics, in which almost the only clear thing was a strong animosity to most of the opinions which were the basis of my mode of thought. . . . Instead of my having been taught anything, in the first instance by Carlyle, it was only in proportion as I came to see the same truths through media more suited to my mental constitution, that I recognized them in his writings . . . but the good his writings did me, was not as philosophy to instruct, but as poetry to animate. Even at the time when our acquaintance commenced, I was not sufficiently advanced in my new modes of thought, to appreciate him fully; a proof of which is, that on his showing me the manuscript of *Sartor Resartus*, his best and greatest work, which he had just finished, I made little of it; though when it came out about two years afterwards in *Fraser's Magazine* I read it with enthusiastic admiration and the keenest delight.*

Do you think Mill should feel so confident of the "proof" of the incorrectness of his earlier estimate of *Sartor Resartus*? Perhaps Carlyle's message was a haze. Although Mill later may have extracted some sentences that yielded sense to him, how was he to know they were the intended sentences?

* John Stuart Mill, *Autobiography*, Oxford University Press, New York, 1955, pp. 148–149.

NICKEL: *Sartor Resartus* is a book made up of sentences. Aren't they the sentences Carlyle intended?

PENNY: They may be, but that was not sufficient for Mill. Carlyle's sentences had a "form and vesture" that yielded no sense for him. What Mill says he had to do to get Carlyle's purported message was to have it presented in a different set of sentences, sentences whose "form and vesture" did yield sense to him. Mill is in the position typical of anyone who finds a poem, essay, or novel obscure as it stands. It is not sufficient in the teaching of literature that the teacher merely repeat the sentences put down by the author. The student himself can do that as well as the teacher. What the student needs is to have the work decoded, to have it interpreted, to have it restated in sentences whose regularity is familiar to him.

NICKEL: Besides that, works of literature are often supposed to have "depth" meanings as well as literal meanings.

PENNY: Depth meaning plus literal meaning equals?

NICKEL: Two meanings. The same questions that came up about Example A and a code could come up again with regard to literature.

PENNY: They not only could, they have and do. On first looking at a poem, for example, it often seems to be such a jumble that we could swear the author had violated every rule of regularity. It seems senseless. Just as Carlyle seemed senseless to Mill on first reading. But as moral beings we give him the benefit of the doubt and assume that he has substituted some regularities of his own, and that a diligent study will reveal them. But has he? Has the author really got a message? How much time should you spend trying to figure out *Finnegan's Wake*? When will you give it up as hopeless, deciding that it is all too random and irregular to possibly contain a message?

Or again. You are a literary critic; at last you've found *the* interpretation of *Finnegan's Wake*. You rush into print. But alas, the very week that your interpretation is published another comes out. Assuming that both interpretations are logically impeccable, that is, every item in the work is treated consistently and no items are omitted, what hue and cry may we expect?

NICKEL: Which one is *the* correct interpretation?

PENNY: And what can be meant by *the* interpretation?

NICKEL: The one the author intended.

PENNY: Indeed. Author's intentions—cocktail party duels—secrets of war—these are strange times, Nickel. Upon being asked which was the correct interpretation, an author, figuring to put all the salt in the bag he can, confesses to a double meaning. Both were intended—a rich work!

Or again. A work of literature whose surface or literal meaning is quite transparent give us a feeling that we have not grasped its true significance, or that feeling may be induced in us by a professor whose cleverness saves us all from boredom, and so we search for depth meaning.

Realize, sir, that the search for regularity lies at the base of all this.

NICKEL: I can see the moral of this tale. Never study literature, declare war, nor go to cocktail parties without having studied logic.

Let me try to sum up our discussion now, and then see if I can anticipate what bearing this has on what we'll be doing in this course. We started off with the notion of coded messages and then likened literary works to them; we assume that coded messages need decoding because their unfamiliar regularities yield no sense, and the passage from Mill shows that the same thing may hold for literature. Both coded messages and works of literature (or some at any rate), though they must consist of regular combinations of marks if they are to be decoded and interpreted, are contrasted with the combinations of marks that are the results of decoding and interpreting; the former are opaque; the latter are transparent, their sense being more easily grasped.

As for anticipating: If logic is the study of linguistic regularities, then I suppose that the aim or end of logic is the explicit formulation of a set of rules which, if followed when we combine marks, guarantee the formation of transparent sentences. It's as if the aim of logic were to establish an ideal language, one which could serve as a test of the meaningfulness of any combination of marks. If a combination, such as a poem, can be translated into this ideal language, then it is meaningful and we know what its meaning is; if it's not so translatable, then it's meaningless.

PENNY: You're hot on the trail, but I'd like to put in a demurrer. The business of logic may be to establish a transparent language, but I'm not so sure that such a language has any usefulness as a test of the meaningfulness of unfamiliar combinations of marks. First of all, that puts us right back where we just came from. We just saw that there is no guarantee that a combination of marks contains *no* meaning, for you may simply be a bad cryptographer who has failed to translate; nor is there a guarantee that you are a good cryptographer and have found the meaning which a combination of marks has for persons who habitually write or speak the combination, for it may admit of an alternative translation.

NICKEL: Of course. How could I forget so soon!

PENNY: In the second place, are you sure the ideal language can express everything which can be said?

NICKEL: No, I'm not. And I can see that it would have to be as rich as any possible language if it is to be a measure of meaning.

PENNY: Maybe for Carlyle the combinations of marks composing *Sartor Resartus* are quite regular and produce no haze. Had Mill studied it at greater length he might have come to see its regularity, grasped it, and realized that the "poetry" was richer than English, and was not a synonym for obscurity.

Kant, in the Preface to the *Critique of Practical Reason*, makes somewhat the same point about his first *Critique*, the *Critique of Pure Reason*.

> I have no fear, with respect to this treatise [*Critique of Practical Reason*], that I wish to introduce a new language, since the kind of thinking it deals with is very close to the popular way of thinking. This objection, moreover, could not have been made even to the first *Critique* [*of Pure Reason*] by anyone who had really thought his way through it instead of merely turning the pages. To make up new words for accepted concepts when the language does not lack expressions for them is a childish effort to distinguish one's self not by new and true thoughts but by new patches on old clothes. If any reader of that work can show that he knows more common expressions which are as adequate to the thoughts as the ones I used seemed to me, or can demonstrate the nullity of the thoughts themselves and therewith of the terms used to express them, he should do so. The first would greatly oblige me, for I only want to be understood; the second would be a service to philosophy itself. But, as long as those thoughts stand, I very much doubt that expressions both more suitable to them and more common can be found.*

To put it more generally, could you possibly find out if any ideal language was rich enough unless you knew independently of each other both the ideal language and the other language?

NICKEL: Knowing both independently does seem to be a necessary condition. But now, if I know without the aid of the ideal language that the "coded" combination of marks yields a sense, that is, has its own regularity, then the usefulness of the ideal language as a criterion of meaning disappears.

What happens to the superior transparency of the ideal language? Doesn't that hold up either?

PENNY: The image that suggests itself is that of two window panes, one dirty and one clean.

NICKEL: Are both to frame the same scene?

* Immanuel Kant, *Critique of Practical Reason*, trans. Lewis White Beck, copyright 1956 by The Liberal Arts Press, reprinted by permission of The Liberal Arts Press Division of The Bobbs-Merrill Company, Inc.

PENNY: How much better the clean pane; how much better the ideal language!

NICKEL: Is there an alternative image?

PENNY: We have not yet said enough about regularity to know if we should rid ourselves of an old myth and establish a new one. This is an introduction only, friend. It is meant to tantalize, not satisfy. For the moment we will have to be content with the promise that following explicit formation rules will at least guarantee regularity and sense, and protect us from senselessness.

To start us on the way to either replacing or retaining the myth of the clean and dirty window panes let's devote your energies to learning an ideal language. We can't intelligently decide about the superior transparency of an ideal language unless we have a look at one.

NICKEL: That seems reasonable enough. Will it be hard to learn?

PENNY: Like learning any language it will require practice. You wouldn't expect to learn German unless you tried speaking or writing it, would you?

NICKEL: No.

PENNY: You can't expect to learn the ideal language either unless you work with it. For that reason I have provided some exercises. Do them. Do them. Do them.

You needn't worry about having brains enough to learn the language, for it will be far simpler to learn than the English language, which you obviously were capable of learning.

NICKEL: Will I start to learn the ideal language soon?

PENNY: Today. At the end of every conversation I'll provide you with material designed to throw new light on what we've talked about after you've mastered it. Today's material will include an exercise involving not one ideal language, but two. I think two will be easier to master than one, and an exercise involving two will bear more obviously on today's conversation.

In effect, today we have been concerned with a translation problem, the structure of which is shown in the following diagram.

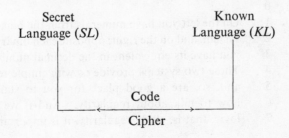

The code or cipher allows us to go between the two languages, to find the equivalent expressions in each.   Here is a more complex example.

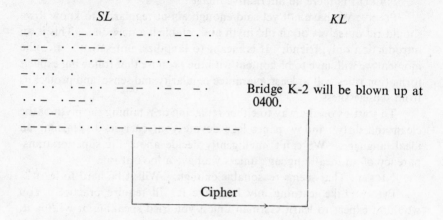

SL   KL

Bridge K-2 will be blown up at 0400.

Cipher →

1. Read *SL* left to right.
2. Each line of characters contains a separate word.
3. The top line contains the first word, the second line contains the second word, etc.
4. Two spaces between bars and/or dots isolates a letter or numeral from others.
5. b = − · · ·
6. r = · − ·
7. etc.

NICKEL: I take what you've just written is a model I am to follow in the exercises you are about to give me.
PENNY: You're off and running.   Here is your first exercise.

1.1:

0	0	On the left you have numerals from the binary number
1	1	system, and on the right, opposite each binary numeral,
10	2	you have its equivalent in the decimal number system.
11	3	These two systems provide us with simple regularities,
100	4	and, so, are a good place for you to start learning
101	5	how to talk about regularity. And if we are to do
110	6	logic, that is, study regularity, it is important to learn
111	7	

18

1000	8
1001	9
1010	10
1011	11
1100	12

how to talk well about regularity.   The fastest way to
learn how to do it well is to work on ciphers.

⠇   ⠇

Cipher
?

Since you're probably unfamiliar with the binary system, the problem
here is to know how to write numerals in the binary notation; for this
you need a cipher to go from the decimal to the binary numerals.   Here
are three samples of student attempts at such a cipher.

First Sample:

1. The binary equivalent of decimal numbers in sequence beginning
   with zero is found by adding the number one.
2. The second number is found by adding 9 to the first number.
3. The third number is found by adding 1 to the second number.
4. The fourth number is found by multiplying the second number by
   ten.
5. The fifth number and all successive numbers are found by following
   the same rules, beginning with adding 1 to the fourth number.

Second Sample:

1. The binary value is read from right to left.
2. 1 represents the existence of a value.
3. 0 represents the non-existence of a value.
4. Each decimal value is increased by one each line as you progress
   down, and each line is a single value.
5. If there is a zero in the rightmost column of the binary value
   replace it with a one.
6. If there is a one in the rightmost column, change it to a zero, and
   examine the number in the next column to the left.   If it has a
   zero, replace it with a one; but if it has a one, change it to a zero
   and continue doing this until you come to a column which contains
   a zero; then replace the zero with a one.

Third Sample:

1. Using a number in the decimal system, divide it by 2.
2. Record the remainder as the last digit (to the right) of the new number in the binary system.

    (a) If this quotient is a 0, the remainder is the dividend. There-fore, record the same number in the binary system as you had in the decimal system. (Note: This will occur only when the decimal number is 1 or 0.)

    (b) If this quotient is a 1, record the remainder and then go on to step 7.

    (c) If this quotient is more than 1, record the remainder and then go to step 3.

3. Divide the resultant quotient from step 2 by 2.
4. Record the remainder as the next to last digit of the binary number.
5. Continue to divide by 2 into the previous quotient, recording remainders, until a quotient of 1 is reached.
6. Record the remainder of this division as usual.
7. Record the quotient 1 as the first digit of the binary number.

NICKEL: In just scanning over the copies, the third one looks different from the first two.

PENNY: It is different, and it has an advantage over the other two. In order to translate a decimal numeral, for example, 76, into a binary numeral, the method of the first two samples requires that you first translate all the decimal numerals that precede 76. The third sample, on the other hand, permits you to translate any decimal numeral independent-ly of any other decimal numeral. Let's call the first two ciphers "sequen-tial ciphers" and the third a "nonsequential cipher."

NICKEL: What am I supposed to do with the sample ciphers?

PENNY: List all the errors, if any, in the steps in each sample. That's exercise 1.1.

I presume you'll allow that the elegance of brief and transparent directions is a goal for which every civilized person should strive when writing ciphers.

1.2: Presuming on your allowance, I want you to write your own cipher for the binary number system. It can be either sequential or nonsequential.

NICKEL: Does it have to be modeled on one of the above three samples?

PENNY: No, it doesn't. You can be original as long as you're elegant.

I want to warn you not to confuse a description with a cipher. Students frequently make the mistake of describing the relations between all the binary numerals and all the decimal numerals I've given you. They take each decimal numeral in turn and give directions for producing its equivalent binary numeral. That method ignores the very factor needed to select the correct cipher. Do you remember what that factor is?

NICKEL: Repetition?

PENNY: Sure; you can't test the correctness of a cipher without utilizing repetition.

What would you do with the twelve numerical samples you're given to provide yourself with repetition?

NICKEL: Without adding any more samples to them?

PENNY: Yes.

NICKEL: I'd divide them into at least two groups. Then, I suppose, I'd have to produce a cipher for one of the groups and use the other as a repetition group against which to check my cipher.

If the cipher I make up for the first group, when applied to the decimal numerals in the second group, doesn't produce the same binary numerals that appear in the second group, then I don't have a correct cipher. The same cipher should apply to all the members of the sample, providing, of course, they were all enciphered with a single cipher.

I think this is right since it's consistent with what we said about Example A and repetition.

PENNY: That is right. Why do you look doubtful?

NICKEL: You said a cipher is not a description. I don't see how I'm going to get started laying down rules unless I simply say what I see. For example, one thing I see is that the binary equivalents of odd numbers always have a one at the extreme right; when I say that I have described what I've seen.

PENNY: Good. That shows us why we have to cut the samples into at least two groups; one of them we can look at and describe; the other we can't look at.

It's essential that we keep ourselves in the dark about the other group; if we don't, it will lose its power to prove us wrong.

NICKEL: That last remark puzzles me.

PENNY: First of all, in order for a second group to falsify a proposed cipher, the cipher has to be stated generally enough to apply to the second group as well as to the group we've picked to describe. If I divide all the apples in the world into two groups, Winesaps and non-Winesaps, and say, "Winesaps are sour," the taste of the non-Winesap apples won't prove my statement false, will it?

NICKEL: Of course not, since the statement didn't apply to them.

PENNY: Right. That's why the description of the first group has to be general enough to cover the second group, the one you won't let yourself see.

Secondly, to explain why you mustn't let yourself see the second group, let's consider two situations in relation to a general description, "All Winesaps are sour." One situation is your having tasted all Winesaps and the other is having tasted only some of the Winesaps. Under which situation is it still possible to falsify "All Winesaps are sour"?

NICKEL: Under the situation where I haven't tasted all the Winesaps, only some of them.

I see now what a cipher is and how it's related to description, I think. A cipher is a general description of the seen and of the unseen. Only if it applies to the unseen can it be shown to be wrong.

PENNY: Strictly speaking, what you just said about ciphers is true only of proposed ciphers, sets of rules formulated in an attempt to extract the message. These rules are candidates for acceptance. Before they are accepted, they must be tested for their correctness, for they may not in fact enable us to extract the message. This doesn't apply to invented ciphers.

NICKEL: Can't invented ciphers be correct or incorrect?

PENNY: No. Only proposed ciphers are. An invented cipher can't be proven correct or incorrect, because it's not proposed as a description of something unseen; it's a set of directions for producing something not yet in existence.

Your remark about the seen and the unseen—a very nice one, by the way—applies to those cipher candidates we have formulated in an attempt to extract from a set of samples. It doesn't apply to ciphers we have invented.

And, not so incidentally, your remark applies not only to cipher candidates but to all rule candidates. Every attempt to extract a set of rules from a string of marks or sounds requires a general description of a portion seen and a portion unseen.

1.3: Next, I want you to utilize the cipher you come up with. Do this by translating the decimal numbers 13-25 into binary numbers, and do nothing that isn't explicitly allowed by the rules contained in your cipher.

NICKEL: Excuse me for interrupting, but we've been using the terms "code" and "cipher" interchangeably. Do they mean the same thing?

PENNY: Technically, a cipher gives us rules about the arrangement or substitution of letters, while the rules in a code provide for the arrangement or substitution of words, phrases, or even whole sentences. A bilingual dictionary is a good example of a code-book, though it doesn't provide rules for whole sentences, of course.

1.4: We speak English and we read English, but we learned to speak it before we learned to read it. When children enter school, do you think the following diagram correctly represents their situation?

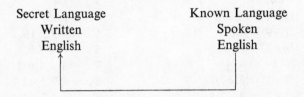

Secret Language   Known Language
Written   Spoken
English   English

NICKEL: Haven't you left "cipher" out of your diagram? Or maybe you've left out "code." Which one?

PENNY: That's the problem. How do we pass from spoken English to written English? Which way are we taught? By code or cipher or both? (a) I want you to answer that question. (b) For the second part of 1.4, you are to give some of the code and/or cipher rules for passing from spoken to written language. I don't expect all of them; I'm a good guy. I don't even expect most of them. But do enough to show you know what you're doing.

1.5: Then I want you to (a) make two different ciphers, C_1 and C_2, that allow us to decipher intelligible sentences from Example A. That will be relatively easy because no characters recur in Example A and they can be assigned any arbitrary substitution. For example, my first rule could be to turn Example A upside down; my second rule could be to read from left to right; and my next four rules could be substitution rules, substituting, for example, "T" for "e," "a" for "E," "I" for "s," and "k" for "S," thus producing "Talk."

(b) Next, select some sentence and encipher it with cipher C_1.

(c) Lastly, try to decipher the string of characters produced by step (b) by using cipher C_2.

NICKEL: Can I let two different characters from Example A stand for the same "English" letter?

PENNY: I believe I pointed out that substitution was arbitrary.

I want to shift our conversation and your exercises now to the two ideal languages I said you were going to learn. Because they will probably look unfamiliar, and, therefore, unnecessarily forbidding to you, I think it would be a good idea to sidle up to them through a more familiar symbolism, namely, arithmetic.

There are two ways of writing arithmetical expressions; you're used to A but not to B.

A.	B.
1. $(9+3)$	1'. $+9\ 3$
2. (4×7)	2'. $\times4\ 7$
3. (7×4)	3'. $\times7\ 4$
4. $(18\div3)$	4'. $\div18\ 3$
5. $[(7+9)=16]$	5'. $=+7\ 9\ 16$
6. $[16=(7+9)]$	6'. $=16+7\ 9$
7. $[(-4+6)=2]$	7'. $=+-4\ 6\ 2$
8. $[(7\times2)=(2\times7)]$	8'. $=\times7\ 2\times2\ 7$
9. $[(2\times3)=(4+2)]$	9'. $=\times2\ 3+4\ 2$
10. $\{[(2+3)+4]=9\}$	10'. $=++2\ 3\ 4\ 9$
11. $\{(7+8)=[5+(5+5)]\}$	11'. $=+7\ 8+5+5\ 5$

NICKEL: B is strange, all right.   But I can see that each expression in B might be equivalent to an expression in A; that 9', for example, might be equivalent to 9.

I say that because they have the same numerals in the same order; and they have the same operations; both have a $+$, a $\times$, and an $=$.

PENNY: Very sharp, Nickel.   They are equivalent.   It will facilitate your grasp of the regularity of B if you try to work out a cipher enabling you to translate from the familiar A expressions to the unfamiliar B expressions and *vice versa*.

1.6: For the following five A arithmetical expressions you are to write the equivalent B arithmetical expressions; and for the five B arithmetical expressions you are to write the equivalent A arithmetical expressions.

A.	B.
1. (15×9)	1'. $\div4\ 2$
2. $[(4\times3)+6]$	2'. $\times7+4\ 2$
3. $[(5\times4)=(40\div2)]$	3'. $=9\times3\ 3$
4. $\{[(2+3)\times5]=25\}$	4'. $=+15\ 2+9\ 8$
5. $\{(7\times2)=[6+(4\times2)]\}$	5'. $=9++3\ 3\ 3$

After you've done 1.6, I want you to look at this list of equivalent expressions from our two ideal languages which we'll call Polish, on the left, and Principia, on the right.   Polish (abbreviated "Po") owes its form to a Polish logician, Jan Łukasiewicz.   The Principia symbolism

("Pr") is taken from *Principia Mathematica*, by Alfred North Whitehead and Bertrand Russell.

Polish	Principia
1. *pq	1'. (p ⊃ q)
2. –*pq	2'. –(p ⊃ q)
3. *–qp	3'. (–q ⊃ p)
4. –*p–r	4'. –(p ⊃ –r)
5. vrq	5'. (r∨q)
6. •p–p	6'. (p•–p)
7. –⁑rp	7'. –(r ≡ p)
8. v*qrp	8'. [(q ⊃ r)∨p]
9. *qvpr	9'. [q ⊃ (p∨r)]
10. v–vrqp	10'. [–(r∨q)∨p]
11. vvrp–q	11'. [(r∨p)∨–q]
12. –vvpr–q	12'. –[(p∨r)∨–q]
13. v•pq*qr	13'. [(p•q)∨(q ⊃ r)]
14. –v–•qp*q–r	14'. –[–(q•p)∨(q ⊃ –r)]

PENNY: Which set of expressions looks more like the A arithmetical expressions and which more like the B?

NICKEL: The Polish expressions look more like B and the Principia more like A.

PENNY: You're right. Now try to analyze the resemblances of each pair.

1.7: (a) Which characters in Polish and Principia are analogous to the numerals? (b) Which characters are analogous to the arithmetical operations? (c) How are the rules for the arrangement of numerals and operations in A and B analogous to the rules for the arrangement of analogous characters in Principia and Polish?

It will be easier to state your answers to 1.7 if you have a vocabulary for talking about Polish and Principia. I'll give you one, and it will be the first of several sets of rules that we'll have before we finish your course.

NICKEL: Will I have to memorize all the sets of rules?

PENNY: Let's put it this way: I don't want you to memorize them, I want you to know them. It will be possible for you to do that because I'm designing our course in such a way that you'll have to figure out most of the rules yourself. That way you won't merely be memorizing rules of regularity that I give you, but you'll be thinking them through for yourself.

NICKEL: That sounds good to me, for I've always been frightened by symbolisms; your method might give me some self-confidence.

PENNY: Since there will be several sets of rules, I will label this first set Po-1 and Pr-1. I've also provided a pronunciation cipher, so that we can speak the expressions.

Po-1: Vocabulary			Pr-1: Vocabulary	
Letters:	p		p	
	q		q	
	r		r	
Functors:				
Binary	*	"ast"	⊃	"horseshoe"
	v	"vee"	v	
	.	"dot"	.	
	**	"double ast"	≡	"triple bar"
Monary	–	"bar"	–	
Punctuation marks			( )	"left and right parens"
			[ ]	"left and right brackets"

Now I want you to try translating from Polish to Principia and *vice versa*, using the fourteen equivalent expressions I gave you.

NICKEL: That seems like a pretty tough exercise. How am I to know why expressions are equivalent? I don't even know the meaning of either the Polish or the Principia expressions. In the Morse code example, I knew the English; and my sentence, "Bridge K-2 will be blown up at 0400" is in English; and I knew the numerals from the decimal number system.

PENNY: Not knowing the meaning of expressions won't prevent you from doing the exercise. You have all the information you'll need.

You should proceed in the following way: Cover the Principia expressions and translate from the Polish; then uncover the Principia expressions to check your answer. And, of course, *vice versa* to translate from Principia to Polish.

You have to extract the information; it's an exercise and is supposed to exercise you. Whenever you do not know what to do with some part of the vocabulary, look at a similar example among the fourteen equivalences. You have to *look* for the regularity; you literally have to train your eye to *see* a regularity. You must become a child again. After all, the child understands nothing of the sounds he hears; furthermore, since he knows no language whatsoever, it is impossible for us to inform him of the regularities in the sounds. Yet he learns the regularities; you did this once with English and you are only being asked to do it again with Polish and Principia. For example, by simply looking at the characters, not their meaning, you'll see that equivalent Polish and Principia expressions contain the same letters in the same order.

We can put the fourteen pairs of expressions into a familiar setting, if that helps. Consider each pair as a conversation, a short conversation to be sure, between two people, Polish and Principia. Polish says, "Ast pee cue," to which Principia replies, "Left parens pee horseshoe cue right parens," or *vice versa*. From such conversations you, as the child who overhears conversations, must sooner or later extract enough regularity to take part in such a conversation yourself.

NICKEL: I am ashamed but not confident. In that order.

PENNY: Perhaps I can help your confidence by working out an example.

I'll work the example in steps. Each step will subtract some vocabulary item from the left-hand column and that item will be added to the middle column, while the right-hand column will describe what I did.

$-v-pq$

(1) $-v-$ pq (Letters are in the same order.)
(2) $-v$ $-pq$ (The bar to the left of a letter stays with it.)
(3) $-$ $(-pvq)$ (The functor moves to the right, between the letters.)
(4) $-(-pvq)$ (The bar to the left of the functor goes to the left of the whole expression within parens.)

We can't make any enciphering move unless there is a similar move in one of the fourteen pairs of Polish-Principia expressions, for our moves must be governed by the rules of regularity embedded in the fourteen pairs. I want you to tell me in which pair or pairs we can find a move similar to (1), (2), (3), and (4).

NICKEL: All the pairs make a move similar to (1).

I see pairs 3, 4, 6, 11, 12, and 14 make moves similar to (2).

As to move (3): If v as a binary functor is representative of other binary functors, all the pairs exhibit a similar move. And 1–7 all have two letters and a binary functor enclosed in parens. That seems to be consistent in the larger expressions, 8–14, also.

Pairs 2, 4, and 7 show the bar to the left of the parens for move (4).

PENNY: Do 12 and 14 also exhibit move (4)?

NICKEL: I guess you'd have to say so, though the bar is to the left of a bracket instead of a parens.

PENNY: Here's one more piece of advice. This applies to expressions containing more than two letters, v*q**rp*, for example.

In translating that expression into Principia, it's best to break it down into parts. You see the **rp* part; you know how to translate that into Principia. We're shown how by 1 and 1'. You translate **rp* the same way, namely, ($r \supset p$), even if it is part of a larger expression. So far, that gives you v*q*($r \supset p$). Now simply treat ($r \supset p$) as if it were a letter and finish the translation.

NICKEL: *q*v($r \supset p$)?

PENNY: Correct. All you need to do now is add the brackets, [*q*v($r \supset p$)]. Try translating this expression one part at a time: **.qpvrq*.

NICKEL: *(*q.p*)v*rq*
      *(*q.p*)(*rv*q*)
      [(*q.p*) $\supset$ (*rv*q*)]

PENNY: Perfect. Now this should be easy.

1.8: You are to match the equivalent expressions. Each Polish expression has an equivalent Principia expression.

1. v.*pqr*	a. [*p*v(*q.r*)]
2. .*pv*qr*	b. [(*p*v*q*).*r*]
3. v*p.qr*	c. [*p*.(*q*v*r*)]
4. .v*pqr*	d. [(*p.q*)v*r*]

You can practice for the next exercise by going through the whole list of fourteen expressions, covering up one side and translating.

1.9: To the following seven Polish expressions you are to write the seven equivalent Principia expressions; and to the seven Principia expressions, you are to write the seven equivalent Polish expressions.

1. .−*pq*	1'. ($p \supset q$)
2. *q.pr*	2'. −[(*p.q*)v*r*]
3. *−.qpr*	3'. [(*p.q*) $\equiv$ (*q.p*)]
4. −.*qpr*	4'. −(*p*v−*q*)
5. **pq*qp*	5'. [−*p* $\equiv$ (*q.p*)]
6. v−v*pq*.−*pq*	6'. {[($p \supset q$).($q \supset r$)] $\supset$ ($p \supset r$)}
7. .v*pq*.*qrp*	7'. {(*p*v*q*).[*r*v(*pv*q*)]}

Before you go, I have something else for you to think about. It involves two poems.

LOGIC: A DIALOGUE

I Felt a Funeral in My Brain

I felt a funeral in my brain,
  And mourners, to and fro,
Kept treading, treading, till it seemed
  That sense was breaking through

And when they all were seated,
  A service like a drum
Kept beating, beating, till I thought
  My mind was going numb.

And then I heard them lift a box,
  And creak across my soul
With those same boots of lead, again.
  Then space began to toll

As all the heavens were a bell,
  And Being but an ear,
But I and silence some strange race,
  Wrecked, solitary, here.

—Emily Dickinson

Jabberwocky

'Twas brillig, and the slithy toves
  Did gyre and gimble in the wabe:
All mimsy were the borogoves,
  And the mome raths outgrabe.

—Lewis Carroll

There is a marked difference between these two poems; Carroll's contains combinations of letters which are unfamiliar to us while Dickinson's apparently contains no unfamiliar vocabulary. It's hard to believe we could grasp the full "message" of *Jabberwocky* without a code; "brillig," "slithy," etc., are not part of the known language; they seem more appropriate to some secret language. For I daresay most of us feel less confident than Humpty Dumpty about the meaning of these strange words. (See Lewis Carroll's *Through the Looking Glass.*)

I Felt a Funeral in My Brain seems less obviously in need of a code due to the familiarity of all its words; still we can't take all the words literally and entertain any confidence that the sentences then express the message, because it seems unlikely that Miss Dickinson was under the rather gross misapprehension that last rites were being performed inside her skull. I doubt that she was trying to write false sentences. We seem caught in a dilemma by this poem.

1.10: What are we to say? For our understanding of the poem, do we need to devise a code, and so treat some apparently familiar words as really belonging to a secret language, or can we consider all the words and sentences as being part of a known language, English, and so not in need of a code? Would a dictionary be of help in understanding Carroll's or Dickinson's poems?

1.11: Now that I have posed the question about the help we expect from a dictionary in understanding a poem, I might as well pose the same question about the following example, part of a poem by Pat Rose. She wrote this for a publicity release publicizing Random House's updating of *The American College Dictionary*.

> 'Twas fungo, and the sickle
> schmo
> Did granuloma in the jam.
> All flutter was the coolant
> snow,
> And winterize the nomogram.
>
> Go read the ACD, my son,
> To know what means the
> rance and rem.
> Go read the entry on Orlon
> To case a ploy and BEV a
> Zen.
>
> —Pat Rose*

NICKEL: I think I should have been rude and just gone. Good-bye.

PENNY: One moment more. This is an age of teachers, not learners. Do not deal too harshly with me if I perpetuate it. In order to "help" you check your comprehension of our conversation, I'll give you Review Questions.

NICKEL: Don't feel bad, Mr. Penny. We students are used to being considered lazy, and as a result have become so for the most part.

PENNY: We all have such a portion of crime that we shouldn't expect others to share ours with us. *Alors.*

* *San Francisco Chronicle*, January, 1959.

Review Questions

1. What feature is necessary for any collection of marks or sounds to be considered a language?

2. What linguistic distinction emerged from the Italian consulate story?

3. Why isn't checking sentences yielded by ciphers against the facts a foolproof method of selecting the sentence that expresses the message?

4. In a set of coded characters, why is it necessary to have a repetition of the characters in order to find the concealed message?

5. How is the notion of familiar regularity related to the points made by Mill and Kant?

6. What is the difference between a code and a cipher? What is the similarity?

Second conversation

A MODEL DREAM

Mannikinns are no kinn o' mann's.
Coo.   I have allweys thawt betr of
pynky, gaim-pleyng modells.—Fanebius Perlyng

PENNY: Good morning, Nickel. Why the large yawn?

NICKEL: I had a dream last night, a rather disturbing one, so I'm a little tired. But I'm game for today's session.

PENNY: Come here and tell Joseph all about it.

NICKEL: I don't think it has anything to do with logic.

PENNY: Have you interpreted it?

NICKEL: No, I don't know its meaning.

PENNY: Then for all you know, it may well be pertinent to logic.

NICKEL: In the beginning I was in an artist's studio. The sunlight streaming through the slanted window fell on me as I sat in an easy chair; it also fell on a lovely nude model who was standing on a pedestal. Soon a door opened and a man, his hands filled with clay, walked in and began to sculpt the model's head. When he finished, he placed the clay head in the air across the room from the model's head, turned around and left the studio, and the clay remained in the air unsupported!

When I turned from it to look at the model to see if she was as surprised as I, I was even more surprised. Her body was as before, but her head was gone, and floating in its place, unattached to her body, was a store window manikin's head, with its usual stiff stare.

PENNY: Were there two heads, or am I confused?

NICKEL: You're not confused. There were two heads, the clay head made by the artist and the manikin head that replaced the model's head.

I hadn't recovered from my shock when the door opened again, and a different artist, his hands filled with clay, walked in and began to sculpt the model's arms and hands. The same thing happened! The artist left; the clay arms stayed unsupported in the air where he placed them; where the nude model's arms had been there now were manikin arms and hands with their characteristic high-fashion twist. Like her manikin head, her manikin arms and hands were floating next to but detached from her body.

The same thing was repeated for the upper torso, the lower torso, the legs, and finally, the feet. The clay figure was all of a piece; all the sculpted parts had been joined; and the figure stood quite firmly on the floor now. But my living model was no more; her place was occupied by a disjointed manikin, its parts severally and disconnectedly afloat.

By this time I was shaking violently and I awoke. My friend, who is a medical student, had stopped by to visit me and was shaking me, trying to wake me up.

PENNY: He hasn't been telling you about his anatomy classes and cadavers has he?

NICKEL: Why, yes. Do you think that is the meaning of my dream?

PENNY: No, that is probably only an immediate incident causing

LOGIC: A DIALOGUE

your dream to take the form it did. I think it has a more profound interpretation than that. You had a lot of logic exercises to do. Your dream could be a fulfillment of a wish you entertained while doing them.

NICKEL: Let me tell you what went through my head while I was exercising. The thoughts were more disjointed than my telling of them will be, though.

We spent a lot of time on ciphers and codes, and all the exercises were built around them. Although they are interesting, I kept thinking we were giving them more attention than their intrinsic value deserved. I figured you must have other work for them in mind.

PENNY: We already have made them do a lot of work. They served to instruct and convince you of regularity's role as the basis for meaning.

NICKEL: Of course. And that's what started my thinking. In addition, our conversation suggested decoding was a useful way of finding the meaning of literary works. This reminded me of the similarity of familiar questions. "What does this coded set of characters mean?" "What does this poem mean?" "What does my dream mean?" "What does the music mean?" "What does this sentence, or this word, mean?"

I have often wished, and I did again last night, for a single way to find the meanings of such different things. And then it came to me, like a flash through the window, that you spent a lot of time on ciphers because the procedure we use to find the message in an enciphered set of characters might be a model procedure for finding meaning anywhere.

PENNY: There! You've found the interpretation of the nude model. The light streamed into your studio-study showing you a model; an idea was no longer covered, but nude, exposed for inspection.

NICKEL: It was a lovely thing!

PENNY: No doubt. But now the essential thing to lay bare is the meaning of other aspects of your dream.

NICKEL: Yes, why did the model turn into a disjointed manikin?

PENNY: Perhaps you were uneasy about this model; perhaps you were afraid that what appeared to you as a possible single procedure would turn out to be inapplicable to such diverse forms as music and dreams and poems. This fear and wish that it should not turn out so led you to project the creation of a new unity, the clay figure. You did not know how it could be created, so it involved miraculous events.

NICKEL: The miracle being the clay parts floating unsupported. I suppose, had my medical friend not awakened me, that next the clay figure would have come to life and—

PENNY: Snap! The dream is supposed to be over, Nickel. I can see you have a disposition to day-dream as well.

NICKEL: So it appears. I'm curious about the identity of the disjointed parts, if they have any.

PENNY: I shouldn't think it would be hard to identify them. How about this: The head would be logic in the wide sense; the arms and hands are codes and ciphers; poetry is the upper torso, while the lower torso represents dreams; the legs stand for (Why not "dance for"?) music; and, of course, the feet are words and sentences.

NICKEL: I don't know if this is important, but I just remembered that in my dream the sculptor who made the feet was a giant.

PENNY: That figures. The different artists signified different practitioners of the arts, and language's looms above them all, for everyone practices speech.

NICKEL: So, the model became a disjointed, dead manikin in my dream because I was afraid the single, cipher method would be inadequate. Is it inadequate?

PENNY: Inadequate for what?

NICKEL: Inadequate for finding the meaning of all those diverse things such as poems, music, and dreams. As I understand the cipher method of finding meaning, what we do is say that something, such as a poem or a piece of music, has such and such a meaning if we succeed in finding a cipher with which to translate the poem or music into standard, literal English.

PENNY: How would you go about showing it's inadequate?

NICKEL: That's pretty obvious. The cipher method would be an inadequate way of finding the meaning of a dream if we couldn't find its meaning by means of a cipher.

PENNY: There are two things about your reply that bother me. The first thing is this: If the dream, or a piece of music, didn't have a meaning, certainly the cipher method might fail to yield a meaning. How can you be sure which is the case, that the cipher method is inadequate or that the music doesn't have any meaning?

NICKEL: Hmmm. I couldn't decide on the cipher method's inadequacy unless I knew that every dream, every poem, every piece of music, etc., had a meaning, could I?

PENNY: You're so right. The second thing about your reply that bothers me is this: In the event that the meaning you assume the music has isn't forthcoming, how can you be sure it's the cipher method that's failed rather than you that's failed?

NICKEL: Maybe it's not possible to show that the cipher method is inadequate. Still I have some doubts about it.

PENNY: Let me try to re-create your state of mind in order to expose the root of your doubts.

Poems, music, and dreams are human products. We attribute intentions to their makers, intentions which involve other humans; consequently, though the products may appear opaque on first sight or sound, we suspect they contain a lonely cry, or a plea, or a whispered exhortation, or a challenge, or a declaration of love, or an artful, complex sigh of resignation addressed to a listener or reader or dreamer. And critics of all kinds reinforce our suspicion. They couldn't write without the word "expresses." They tell us, for example, that this piece of music "expresses compassion," this one "expresses anguish," implying that the music, the combination of notes, carries the author's intentions and has a meaning.

These considerations lead you to ask, "What does the music mean?" "What does the poem mean?" etc. At this point you are unquestionably committed to the belief that the music *does* mean something, that the dream *does* have a meaning. Now, enter Doubt, from the left wing: Will the cipher method be able to uncover the author's or the composer's or the dreamer's intended meaning despite the varied forms of the author's, composer's, and dreamer's products?

You are prepared to judge the cipher method a failure if it can't be applied successfully to all those forms.

NICKEL: You know my mind better than I do. But have you already exposed the root of my doubts?

PENNY: I have. The root is an assumption, which, like most roots, lies beneath the surface: You assume that music, and so forth, does have a meaning. I suggest you should entertain a doubt, not about the cipher method, but about the meaningfulness of music, etc.

When you saw Example A and B, you suspected that Example A contained a message and that Example B did not. But you exercised more caution with respect to Example A than you have with music and poems and dreams; you didn't assume that it certainly did contain a message; nor did you say what it was. You weren't and aren't prepared to say that failure to turn up a message for Example A showed the cipher method is inadequate to reveal that a set of characters has a meaning.

NICKEL: You're right.

PENNY: Then you can't say the cipher method is inadequate just because its use doesn't always produce a meaning.

NICKEL: That's true.

PENNY: What is the cipher method specifically designed to do?

NICKEL: It's designed to show a hidden regularity is present.

PENNY: And we have agreed that without regularity there is no meaning. And that when we find the hidden rules of regularity as stated by the cipher, we have found the message, the meaning intended by the author.

NICKEL: Yes, to both points.

PENNY: Then I don't see how one can show that an instrument designed to show the presence of regularity can be inadequate for showing the presence of meaning.

NICKEL: Are you saying, Mr. Penny, that music has no meaning?

PENNY: I haven't said that. I have said that if we continually fail to find a regularity in music, we should doubt if it has any meaning; and I will say that the cipher method is adequate as a test of the meaningfulness of all the different things you mentioned. After all, the sounds of music do not differ any more from English than the dots and dashes of Morse code do; further, it is immaterial to meaning whether it is the dots and dashes or notes in the octave scale that are regular.

NICKEL: I realize that doubt of the cipher method can depend upon assuming that every piece of music, for example, does have a meaning, but I don't think that's the only root of *my* doubt.

PENNY: Then it's your turn to know your own mind.

NICKEL: Ah. What do I see in the opaque ball? I see that I wonder. This is what I wonder: The cipher method is designed to reveal a hidden, though familiar, regularity. But why should we think that music, dreams, or poems must contain a regularity in order to have meaning? Why should we suppose they are *like* enciphered messages?

We take enciphered messages and translate them into words and sentences. Neville Cardus doesn't think music is like that, for he doesn't think we can put the meaning of music into words.

PENNY: Hold on, Nickel. You've asked me two different questions, not one as you seem to think.

First, you asked me if music, etc., must have any regularity to have meaning. You realize, don't you, that this is backtracking on something you just admitted; namely, that meaning depends on regularity?

NICKEL: I do. For better or for worse.

PENNY: Secondly, you asked me if music must have the kind of regularity that language has if it is to have meaning; that is, if it must be translatable into some natural language such as English.

Your doubt appears to have more than one root, and it sounds as if this Cardus person is watering them both liberally. Out with it! Give me Cardus.

NICKEL: Neville Cardus is a music critic. I copied something he said in one of his essays. It's from a collection of his essays, entitled, *Talking of Music*. I'll read it to you.

> A correspondent fourteen years old asks, "How should I listen to music? Should I feel anything, or see pictures? My teacher tells me that music means nothing but the notes." Out of the mouths of babes.

The teacher, of course, is wrong aesthetically and metaphysically. He is mistaken if he imagines he has broken free of his skin of sensation and penetrated to the Thing-in-Itself, the *Ding an Sich*. When somebody asked Beethoven to explain the "meaning" of the *Appassionata Sonata* . . . he said, "Read *The Tempest*." . . .

The meaning of music, we need hardly remind ourselves, cannot be put into words; for that matter, the "meaning" of a poem cannot be conveyed except in the words and rhythms chosen by the poet for a special purpose. . . .

Obviously, it is absurd to listen to Beethoven as an "objective pattern," and to attend to him as if he were a sort of monstrous spider spinning a web of tone by instinct. Music is no more "abstract" than poetry; it is a language in and through which composers have expressed themselves, their conceptions and visions of the world, precisely as Shakespeare, Goethe, Dante, Cervantes, and Lewis Carroll have expressed theirs.*

PENNY: No wonder you ran the two different questions together. Confusion abounds! First Cardus quotes Beethoven with approval when somebody is told to "Read *The Tempest*," which contains nothing if not words, in order to find the meaning of the sonata. Then he says the meaning of music cannot be put into words, after which he reverses himself again by telling us that music is a language. How *does* Cardus want to answer your second question?

NICKEL: Maybe he isn't expressing himself very clearly, but at least I think I know what he's aiming at. Will that do?

PENNY: I think we'd better take your hints.

NICKEL: Well, I think it's possible that music is a language, one which communicates emotions and feelings. However, since we can't put feelings and emotions into words, we can't expect to find linguistic regularity in music.

PENNY: Pray, how does music communicate feelings and emotions?

NICKEL: The sounds, and their combinations and rhythms, cause us to have feeling reactions; they arouse images and emotions associated with them in our past. Poetry has the added feature that words have many associations, most of which are peculiar to each of us.

PENNY: That is a strange notion of "meaning," even for music and poetry.

NICKEL: Don't forget, it is non-linguistic meaning. It doesn't rely on regularity for meaning; instead, it relies on the causal effects sounds have on us. That's why I asked you the first question, whether there might not be meaning without regularity.

* Neville Cardus, *Talking of Music*, Collins, London, 1957, pp. 212–213.

PENNY: I realize that. I see how you connected the two questions in your mind. Linguistic meaning depends on linguistic regularity; musical meaning depends on causal effects; hence, music has meaning, but it is not linguistic meaning.

I also realize that "meaning," like any word, can have several meanings, but I want to call your attention to a strange implication of this sense of "meaning."

Consider the Clever Chemist. The Clever Chemist was of a literary and musical turn of mind. He was a first-rate chemist, but what he longed for most of all was to write good poetry and to compose good music. Unfortunately, his efforts at both continually met with critical failure. He grew more and more despondent and frequently threatened suicide, which no one took seriously until the day they found him in his laboratory lying supinely on the floor with a starey, strangely ecstatic look on his face. Naturally, they rushed about seeing what they could do to save his life. He struggled mightily against their life-saving efforts. "Quit! Quit!" he shouted.

Presently he revived, and, in spite of their efforts, dashed excitedly to a hypodermic vial and showed it all around, proclaiming it as his greatest discovery. It's true, he did try to commit suicide as they supposed, but by accident he made the wrong solution; instead of being killed by the injected solution, he experienced Beethoven's *Appassionata Sonata*. He said, that is, he had the same feelings and associated images and emotions he normally has when he hears the piece played. He had struggled against their life-saving efforts so he could feel the sonata to the end. Later in the day he succeeded in chemically duplicating Emily Dickinson's *I Felt a Funeral in My Brain*.

But that is not the end of our story. The best part is that at last our Clever Chemist had found a way of writing and composing for which he was excellently trained and temperamentally suited. He filled his whole laboratory full of vial-poetry and vial-music.

NICKEL: Very funny.

PENNY: He marketed them and married a du Pont. Today when people visit the great man in his laboratory, they will often point to a vial and ask, "What does that vial mean?" He will answer with the name of that particular creation, for example, "Oh, that; it's 'Needle in the Haystack'." Of course you can't tell if it's music or poetry, not even after your injection—there are no sounds—just feelings.

I conclude that if you can say poetry and music "mean" without reliance on regularity because they *cause* feelings, emotions, and associations, we can with as much reason say it of the chemical solutions, for they too cause feelings and emotions.

40

Now, don't misunderstand me. You and the Clever Chemist can use "mean" that way, but when we started talking about the cipher model as an adequate test of meaning, and when I suggested music mightn't have any meaning, I took us to be using "meaning" in a more conventional way.

NICKEL: I thought I was using it in a conventional way until you dropped the Clever Chemist on me.

PENNY: We do sometimes speak of causal regularities; this might have induced some confusion. Whenever I drop a heavy metal object on a cement floor, it regularly causes a crashing sound. But do we ordinarily say that the object said something?

NICKEL: No, we don't.

PENNY: Thus, we must distinguish between causal regularities and linguistic regularities. Causal regularities aren't rules followed by nature in order to be understood, while linguistic regularities are rules generally followed by us so people will understand what we are saying. We don't say we understand what the typewriter is saying when it crashes to the cement floor, even though because of a causal regularity we expect the crashing sound.

NICKEL: That would be an odd way of talking, all right.

PENNY: It would be at that. The more usual way of talking about such a familiar crash is to say that we infer from the sound that a heavy, metal object fell on cement. We infer that the typewriter fell; the typewriter doesn't tell us it fell.

Now, what did the Clever Chemist discover when he attempted to commit suicide?

NICKEL: He discovered a causal regularity; he discovered that the injection of a certain chemical caused the same emotions and feelings in him as the sounds of the *Appassionata Sonata*. Since causal regularities are different from linguistic regularities, he had not discovered the linguistic meaning of the music.

PENNY: As I said before, you can say the music "means" such and such feelings in place of the music "causes" such and such feelings, but that use of "means" isn't relevant to my aim. My aim is to get as clear as possible about that sense of "means" which requires linguistic regularity, not that sense which requires causal regularity.

NICKEL: Let me take another crack at defending Cardus's statement that music has a meaning that can't be put into words. I admit your Clever Chemist incident destroyed my other defense; I'm assuming now that meaning does depend on linguistic regularity and not on regular causal effects.

Suppose that we lost all of the English language except that usually spoken by four-year-old children. In that case we couldn't translate all

French scientific literature into English; there would be some French regularity that had no English counterpart. But the surplus French would still have regularity, hence, still have meaning.

PENNY: We made the same point when we discussed Mill's attempts to understand Carlyle.

NICKEL: At any rate, I'm saying it's perfectly possible to liken a musical surplus to the French surplus, with the added point that the musical regularity might be surplus to any language. That would imply music could have a meaning that can't be put into words.

PENNY: A well-wrought argument, Nickel.

NICKEL: Having said that, I'm again inclined to believe my fears about the disintegrating model may have been well justified. The cipher method again strikes me as an inadequate way of finding all regularity.

I don't think the cipher method would be of any help in finding the surplus regularity of music, because this is how I think the method works. When we are faced with a set of characters or sounds whose meaning is unknown to us, we set about finding its regularity, but we do so in relation to another regularity which is familiar to us. For example, in case I want to find the meaning of an enciphered set of characters I try to find its regularity in relation to the language known by me and its sender, which might be English or French or Japanese. When I find a cipher that translates the characters into a known language, it's possible I've found the meaning; I test the cipher by trying it out on other sets which repeat characters of the first set to see if it continues to produce meaningful sentences in the known language.

A cipher, thus, is simply a set of rules coordinating an unknown regularity with a known regularity. Has my description been accurate?

PENNY: It's a fine summation. Continue.

NICKEL: Now if music has no linguistic counterpart, it is impossible to carry out the procedure of finding its regularity in relation to a linguistic regularity. Since that procedure is the essence of the cipher method, we have to conclude that the cipher model is inadequate for finding all regularity.

There! Do I have you stumped? How do you like manikins?

PENNY: You think you have me stumped because the cipher method requires two regularities before it can be employed, and since music has no non-musical counterpart, we are left with a single regularity.

NICKEL: Exactly.

PENNY: Permit me to give you an even greater feeling of triumph.

Consider learning a language without the aid of another language, something which happened to all of us when we learned our native tongue. Every human had to do this without knowing any counterparts.

You learned English; no one taught you what English words and sentences meant by referring you to another linguistic regularity; they couldn't for you knew no other regularity.

The cipher method was of no use to you when you learned the meaning of English either.

NICKEL: That's true! Bye, bye, Model; hello, Manikin.

PENNY: Here's another feather. Do you know any other language besides English?

NICKEL: No, I don't.

PENNY: You do know the meaning of some English sentences and words, though?

NICKEL: Oh yes, I'm sure of that.

PENNY: Earlier today you wondered if the cipher method was adequate for finding the meaning of sentences and words. Since you know no other linguistic regularity than English, it would appear that the model cannot play a role in helping you to know the meaning of English sentences and words either.

NICKEL: I must say I admire you. I've never seen anyone as cooperative as you are in refuting your own theory.

PENNY: What theory is that?

NICKEL: The theory that we can always decide some set of marks or sounds has a meaning by finding a cipher which translates its regularity into a familiar regularity.

PENNY: Yes, we certainly can't hold that theory. We have to find out on occasion that something has a meaning without being able to make use of another language. The two-language method of determining the presence of linguistic regularity in a set of sounds or marks is not universally applicable; we have to devise a one-language method as well. Until we do devise such a method, we won't be able to decide if music has linguistic meaning nor, obviously, if you and Cardus are right.

The fact that the cipher, or two-language, method, might not be applicable to music doesn't give you and Cardus the palm of victory. In order to prove that music has meaning in the linguistic sense, you still have to show that it has linguistic regularity.

How do you account for two English-speaking people understanding one another when they converse?

NICKEL: When I utter an English sentence, I know what it means; if it means the same to the person who heard me, then we have understood one another. Two minds must have the same thought.

PENNY: Is a meaning a thought?

NICKEL: They're not identical; a meaning is known by a thought. Meanings are what we think about when we talk.

PENNY: Just as I predicted.

NICKEL: Naïve?

PENNY: Yes. Tell me, Nickel, do you think the other person's thoughts and does he think yours?

NICKEL: Of course not.

PENNY: Then how do you know you're thinking about the same meaning? You've tried to explain that persons understand one another because they possess a common meaning; consequently, we don't know we have a common understanding unless we know we have a common meaning. Now that you've ruled out thinking one another's thoughts, we have to look for other clues which show we have a common meaning. What other clues do we have?

NICKEL: I'm ashamed to say my corner pocket is empty.

PENNY: Maybe the following quotation will get some action. I knew when I saved this clipping it would come in handy some day. It's from a column on jazz by Ralph Gleason in the *San Francisco Chronicle*.

> The two Adderleys, for instance, on certain numbers sound like the same man playing different horns, if you follow me. In other words, in statement and response situations they function with the same concept so that what Julian plays on the alto and Nat plays on the cornet might have come from the same imagination.*

NICKEL: Gleason's saying that when two people play alike they have the same concept. According to that, sounds would be a clue to a common meaning. That can't be!

PENNY: When you converse on the telephone, what other clues do you have but the word-sounds the other person makes? And what does he have but the sounds you make? We *have* to account for our knowing we have a common meaning on the basis of the sounds, or on the basis of shapes in the case of written regularities.

Your familiarity with English blinds you; your explanation of a common understanding of English is naïve because you take the meaning of its sentences for granted; you forget you have to find out *if* they have the same meaning for another person as they have for you; you forget that when someone else speaks, all you can experience are his sounds; and since you can't experience his thoughts, they must play no role in finding out if a sentence has the same meaning for him as it does for you.

NICKEL: Your accusation is perfectly correct; I did take meanings for granted. But I didn't forget the other person's thoughts play no

* *San Francisco Chronicle*, October 25, 1959.

44

role in explaining how we communicate; I didn't forget, because I didn't realize until just now that they play no role.

PENNY: Come home, Nickel. All is forgiven.

I want now to introduce some ideas that we need in order to see how the one-language method is used to learn and test for a common meaning in the sounds and shapes of a native tongue.

Gleason's second sentence suggests the place to begin: "in statement and response situations." Thus far we've been dealing with only one kind of statement and response situation, the kind I will call an equivalence conversation.

NICKEL: An equivalence conversation? Was exercise 1.8, the Polish-Principia translation exercise, about equivalence conversations? You used the word "equivalence" in it.

PENNY: Yes, it was. Any deciphering or decoding is an equivalence conversation. If a German says, "Der Hund ist rot" and I reply with, "The dog is red," or *vice versa*, we have had an equivalence conversation.

Of the two sentences comprising an equivalence conversation we often say, "They mean the same thing," or, "They have a common meaning."

NICKEL: Then in equivalence conversations, at least, the cipher method does give a way of finding out whether two people understand one another, of finding out whether they have a common meaning. This is what we established yesterday.

PENNY: Right. Because I'm going to introduce non-equivalence conversations next, for purposes of contrast, we'll need to be somewhat more precise about verifying common meaning in equivalence conversations. When someone utters a sentence, I say that I understand it, that he and I have a common meaning, only after I verify that the expression comprising my half of the conversation is equivalent to it. And equivalence, of course, is verified when a cipher or code continues to transform unfamiliar expressions into familiar ones.

But in non-equivalence conversations no two differing expressions with the same meaning occur; consequently, we have to verify that two people give a common meaning to an expression without verifying that two expressions have the same meaning.

Non-equivalence conversations have an additional contrasting feature: To any statement there is more than one correct response.

When I say "correct" response, I do not mean "true" response, but "appropriate" response. The following non-equivalence conversation should illustrate that.

Odd: How many pennies do you have in your pocket?
Even: Five.

Supposing that Even does have exactly five pennies in his pocket; he has then answered truly and appropriately. If he had answered, "Seven," he would have answered falsely and appropriately.

NICKEL: I always have a choice of responses in non-equivalence conversations?

PENNY: Yes; there are always at least two non-equivalent, appropriate responses from which to choose.

NICKEL: The name "non-equivalence conversation" is cumbersome. Do you mind if I replace it with the name "choice conversations," indicating I have a choice of responses? No pun is intended.

PENNY: An excellent suggestion, and no offense taken.

NICKEL: Let me see if I've got this straight. A choice conversation is one in which to any statement there is more than one correct response, and none of the responses has the same meaning as the statement or any other response, unless, of course, the same sentence recurs.

PENNY: Straight. Although the notion of "appropriate response" is important, we can't give a full analysis of it now. Fortunately, all we need for our present purpose is an intuitive, common sense grasp of the idea. The following choice conversation will show you already have that.

Odd (a): I have a yellow pencil.
Even (a): Did you buy it?
Odd (b): My mother gave it to me.
Even (b): Do you expect it will grow without fertilizer?

NICKEL: How ridiculous!

PENNY: What? The Even (b) response?

NICKEL: Sure. Even must not have heard what Odd said.

PENNY: There. You immediately and intuitively recognized an inappropriate response. You recognize inappropriate responses all the time; it's nothing out of the ordinary.

NICKEL: By gosh, you're right. It happens most frequently to me at parties; when I'm talking to some fellow and it gets too loud or he's concentrating too feverishly on some girl, and gives me a cock-eyed reply. That's the clue he hasn't heard me.

PENNY: Suppose you get that kind of answer when you know very well the other fellow heard you, and you know he isn't playing the joker.

NICKEL: In that case, I'd say he didn't understand what I'd said.

PENNY: That is, that you and he didn't have a common meaning?

NICKEL: You slipped that one in very quietly—but effectively. Did I use the one-language method, though?

PENNY: You did. There's nothing mysterious or new about it.

It utilizes two regularities just as the cipher method did; in addition, one of the regularities is known to you and the other is unknown.

NICKEL: You'll have to explain that to me.

PENNY: Consider the nature of choice conversations. In a choice conversation to any statement, *S*, you can always choose between several appropriate responses. The regularity known to you is the class of responses you consider appropriate.

NICKEL: And the unknown regularity is the class of responses someone else considers appropriate?

PENNY: Sure. What you listen for is his regularity. If he always responds with sentences you consider appropriate, then your regularity and his are similar.

NICKEL: If our regularities are similar, we give the sentences spoken in the choice conversation a common meaning?

PENNY: Exactly. And in case the other person responds with a sentence not included in your class, you know that his regularity does not jibe with yours, that is, that you two don't give a common meaning to *S*.

NICKEL: That's what happened with the Even (b) response! To the statement, "My mother gave it [the pencil] to me," Even's class of appropriate responses would include, "Do you expect it will grow without fertilizer?" while my class would not include it.

Why do you call this the one-language method instead of the cipher, or two-language, method? Two regularities are involved in each.

PENNY: We know that there are two kinds of linguistic regularities: one involves the elements of a language, such as an alphabet or a set of phonemes; the other involves the arrangements of the elements. We distinguish one language from another because they differ with respect either to one kind of regularity or both. A cipher is a correlation of two languages, that is, two regularities, the substitution rules correlating the variant elements and the transposition rules correlating the variant arrangements.

We use the cipher, or two-language, method to verify a proposed translation from one language to another; we make no attempt to amalgamate the two sets of regularities into a single set. You and I, on the other hand, endeavor to use the same elements, English letters and phonemes, in similar arrangements; we endeavor to speak and write the same language. We can, thus, speak of using the one-language method to find out how far we have succeeded in adopting a single identical set of regularities; and we can speak of using the two-language method to find out how far we have succeeded in correlating two sets of regularities.

Despite that difference, we should notice that both methods fall under a more general one, what we might call the inductive method. In the inductive method we form an hypothesis about an initially unknown regularity and test the hypothesis by matching the hypothesized regularity against one which is known by us.

Let's apply this to some familiar examples to be sure you have it clearly in mind, taking the two-language method first. Remember "Bridge K-2 will be blown up at 0400," and the reverse cipher?

NICKEL: Very well. Reversed, the sentence reads, "0040 ta pu nwolb eb lliw 2-K egdirb."

PENNY: Suppose we have discovered and used the reverse cipher successfully on the reversed sentence. But we still wonder if it is *the* cipher which gives the sender and me a common meaning. To decide, we then use the inductive method and form the following hypothesis:

If "Bridge K-2 will be blown up at 0040" and "0400 ta pu nwolb eb lliw 2-K egdirb" have a common meaning, then every sentence of his when reversed will yield a meaningful English sentence.

A hypothesis can be confirmed or disconfirmed. Disconfirmation is always shorter and more definite than confirmation.

NICKEL: Because it only takes one instance to disconfirm the hypothesis? For instance, if I am in possession of this set of characters from the sender, "Opr mirf stle llivr," the reversal of them, "Rvill elts frim rpo," disconfirms my hypothesis.

PENNY: That's the reason. Confirmation, to win our confidence, requires several instances of success; several sets of characters when reversed must yield meaningful English sentences.

NICKEL: Let me try to show the application of the inductive method to choice conversations. I'll use the Odd-Even conversation and pretend I'm Odd.

If Even and I give a common meaning to "I have a yellow pencil," then Even will respond with a sentence contained in my response class, which would contain, for example, "The Greeks used yellow pencils," and "I have a red one," and "Did you buy it?" and "Are you going to use it?"

In case Even doesn't respond with one of the sentences I would consider an appropriate response, then, providing he has heard me accurately, I could conclude we don't have a common meaning.

I suppose the confirmation of a common meaning in choice conversations takes more instances for disconfirmation than it did for equivalence conversations, but I don't see how to use more instances.

PENNY: More instances are required all right, and the structural relations they bear to one another makes the process of confirmation an interesting one.

NICKEL: What kind of structural relations are you referring to?

PENNY: The best way of specifying them is to construct a visual model. Since the "instances" we're talking about are sentences, the elements of the model will be sentences. I like to call the model a cornucopia. You'll understand why when you see it.

We can make the cornucopia more compact and general if we give a name to every sentence that can enter into it. Let's name the first sentence in a conversation S. Since there may be many conversations, each with a different first sentence, we'll distinguish their first sentences from each other by giving them subscripts, S_1, S_2, etc.

NICKEL: We could let R with subscripts be the names for correct responses to the S's.

PENNY: And because to every sentence there is more than one appropriate response, it will be handy to have names for the groups of appropriate responses, such as RG_1 for the name of the response group to S_1, and RG_9 for the name of the response group to S_9. The response group will always have a subscript matching the S's subscript.

NICKEL: But conversations can go on and on. We'll have to think of an easy way of naming all the re-responses and the groups of re-responses, and so on.

PENNY: That shouldn't be hard to handle. We'll just keep adding on another R as you did when you said "re-response." Since every response has a group of re-responses, we'll simply name the group of re-responses "RRG_n", and the re-responses themselves "RR_n", where the "n" subscript is any number. And so forth.

A conversational cornucopia will have a structure that looks like this:

$$
S_1 : RG_1 \begin{cases} R_1 : RRG_1 \begin{cases} RR_1 : RRRG_1 \begin{cases} RRR_1 \\ \cdot \\ RRR_5 : RRRRG_5 \begin{cases} RRRR_{41} \\ \cdot \\ \cdot \\ \cdot \\ RRRR_{50} \end{cases} \\ \cdot \\ RRR_{10} \end{cases} \\ \cdot \\ RR_{10} \end{cases} \\ \cdot \\ \cdot \\ R_{10} : RRG_{10} \begin{cases} RR_{91} \\ \cdot \\ RR_{100} : RRRG_{100} \begin{cases} RRR_{991} \\ \cdot \\ \cdot \\ \cdot \\ RRR_{1000} \end{cases} \end{cases} \end{cases}
$$

NICKEL: I can see why you called the conversational model a cornucopia, all right. Starting at the small end, the basket of language grows longer and larger and spills its fruit. There are 1000 pieces already.

PENNY: You must realize that the subscripts above are an arbitrary choice. We've supposed each group of responses contains ten sentences. That probably is not so.

NICKEL: Yes, I realize that. I also realize that our model only partially represents a cornucopia, for many of the entries are left out.

Does the cornucopia represent a conversation?

PENNY: No. It represents the possibilities for conversation when you start with S_1. Here's one possible conversation: S_1 R_1 RR_1 RRR_5 $RRRR_{50}$. Here's another possible conversation: S_1 R_{10} RR_{100} RRR_{991}. You can imagine two or more persons taking turns saying the sentences.

NICKEL: Boy! There're a lot of possible conversations packed in every cornucopia.

PENNY: There certainly are. Before you answer the next question I'm going to ask you, we should note that any two sentence utterances which are similar will have the same name. For example, "The rag is damp" and "The rag is damp" will both have the same name, such as RR_{27}. Further, each such utterance will have one and only one name.

Now, is this a possible conversation within the cornucopia we've just made? S_1 R_1 RR_{10} RRR_{1000}.

NICKEL: I don't think so. RRR_{1000} probably isn't contained in $RRRG_{10}$, the re-response group to RR_{10}.

PENNY: Very good. A cornucopia, then, is a criterion for deciding that a string of sentences is not a conversation as well as for deciding that a string of sentences is a conversation.

What do you say to this? If two persons mean the same thing by a sentence, their response classes will be identical. That is, they'll contain the same sentences.

NICKEL: I agree with that.

PENNY: And what if their response classes are identical throughout? No matter how long the conversation.

NICKEL: In that case, they will mean the same thing by all the sentences.

PENNY: They will have identical cornucopias.

NICKEL: Does each person have a cornucopia?

PENNY: They do. Each person has many cornucopias, for there are a great many different sentences with which one may start a conversation.

NICKEL: Then there will be as many cornucopias as there are sentences.

PENNY: We have to qualify that. In one sense that is true; in another sense it is not. If you'll look at our model cornucopia, you'll notice that there are cornucopias within cornucopias. For example, a conversation might be started with RR_1 as the opening sentence; you'll notice that what follows is also a cornucopia. In that sense every sentence has a cornucopia (unless there is a peculiar class of "final" sentences). But the sense in which there are not as many cornucopias as there are sentences comes from the fact that within larger cornucopias are smaller cornucopias. We need fewer large cornucopias than sentences to represent conversational structures.

This is what we must remember about cornucopias: They are pictures of a person's conversational regularities.

NICKEL: Then the problem of finding out if someone gives the same meaning to a sentence that I do is the problem of finding out if his cornucopia is the same as mine. If it is, we share a regularity. My cornucopia is the known regularity and the other person's is the unknown regularity.

PENNY: You've put the point squarely before us.

NICKEL: I doubt that we ever know if our cornucopias are identical.

PENNY: Why do you say that?

NICKEL: I've never sat down with someone and compared cornucopias. I've never compared response groups with anyone. In fact, the way I see it, in actual conversations we usually respond with only a single sentence, or maybe two or three sentences, from a response class. This jeopardizes any confidence we might have in confirming our inductive hypotheses about sharing a common meaning. And that's what started this whole discussion about cornucopias.

PENNY: Lacking a complete cornucopia, we certainly can't be positive about the confirmation of a common meaning, even supposing it were possible to make a complete cornucopia, but at least we can increase our confidence.

NICKEL: I don't see how that's possible.

PENNY: Our confidence increases with an increase in the length of our conversation. The longer we converse, the greater the number of samples we have from his cornucopia. If the conversation remains a possible one according to your cornucopia, the more likely it is you two do mean the same thing by the sentences.

In addition, you must remember that there are two persons checking. If you utter a sentence that results in a string of sentences that is not a possible conversation according to the other person's cornucopia, you've both found out that your cornucopia regularities are not identical.

NICKEL: That reassures me somewhat.

PENNY: Before you grow complacent, we should note a special factor that is intrinsically interesting and also shows that the cornucopia as we've drawn it to this point is somewhat over-simplified.

The same sentence can occur in more than one response group. Here are a couple of partial cornucopias in both of which R_2 occurs. We can suppose they are Odd's cornucopias.

S_1 : Haakon plays the tuba. RG_1
$\begin{cases} R_1 : \text{What orchestra} \\ \quad\ \ \text{does he play with?} \\[6pt] R_2 : \text{That takes} \\ \quad\ \ \text{good lungs.} \quad RRG_2 \\[6pt] R_3 : \text{But he only has} \\ \quad\ \ \text{two fingers on} \\ \quad\ \ \text{each hand.} \end{cases}$
$\Big\{ RR_6 : \text{But it takes less practice to play well than the violin.}$

S_2 : Haakon is a distance runner. RG_2
$\begin{cases} R_2 : \text{That takes} \\ \quad\ \ \text{good lungs.} \\[6pt] R_4 : \text{Has he set} \quad RRG_4 \\ \quad\ \ \text{any records?} \\[6pt] R_5 : \text{But he only} \\ \quad\ \ \text{has one leg.} \end{cases}$
$\Big\{ RR_3 : \text{He ran the mile in 3:40.}$

Imagine that Odd tries to talk to Even about Haakon, and that Even responds in both cases with R_2.

First Conversation	Second Conversation
Odd: S_1	Odd: S_2
Even: R_2	Even: R_2

Can Odd tell from these two conversations whether or not he and Even give a common meaning to S_1? Or to S_2?

NICKEL: I don't think so, for with this limited sampling of Even's cornucopia Odd can't rule out the possibility that Even's response group to S_1 is the same as his response group to S_2. If they were the same, then for Even S_1 and S_2 would be equivalent in meaning. Of course, they're not equivalent for Odd, so Odd and Even won't have a common cornucopia.

PENNY: Nor can Odd rule out the possibility that Even exchanges the meanings of S_1 and S_2, so that Even means by S_2 what Odd means by S_1, and by S_1 what Odd means by S_2.

NICKEL: I can think of another possibility: That R_2 doesn't mean to Even what it means to Odd, so that it wouldn't even begin to confirm a common meaning as we might ordinarily assume it did.

PENNY: That's correct. I'd like to leave this topic now. We can take it up again more profitably in an exercise.

NICKEL: Let me ask you one question about cornucopias before we leave them.

PENNY: Go ahead.

NICKEL: Why is it that there are several responses to sentences? What accounts for response groups?

PENNY: Probably the main factor is what I call response dictors. There are a lot of things you can do to a sentence. Here are some such dictors. You can deny a sentence, or entertain it, or doubt it, or amplify it, or assent to it, or repeat it, or infer from it, or believe it. Each of these dictors calls for a different sentence. A response sentence denying another sentence is different from the response sentence which amplifies it.

NICKEL: A person can also verify, interpret, analyze, retract, contrast, or emphasize a sentence. I get it. Thanks.

Whither now?

PENNY: Back to your nude, for I have restored her unto you.

NICKEL: I don't mind. She is a comely thing, and much to be preferred to a manikin.

PENNY: I owe it to you to make the model better known. I should explain why I'm trying so hard to clarify that particular sense of "meaning" and "language" which depends on regularity, and why I think that that sense of the words is more important than other senses they have.

I have picked on that sense because meaning and language considered as such are what make human cooperation possible.

Think of all the linguistic cooperation we engage in. We are given a sales pitch, we resist and then we say "Yes." We tell jokes. We confide. We promise to say nothing, and then we say and break the promise. We organize meetings. We order our meal.

NICKEL: Why, most of our life consists of just this kind of activity, of linguistic cooperation!

PENNY: It does indeed. Without regularity we could no more co-operate in these things than we could cooperate in playing games.

NICKEL: Games? But games aren't cooperative. We try to beat one another when we play games, when we play most games, anyway.

PENNY: To beat another at a game depends upon some cooperation.

I can't beat you at chess if you play according to checker rules. If we don't both follow the rules of a game, that particular game won't go. The rules of a game set the limits of behavior; they set down the conditions that make the game go.

In an equivalence conversation the rules are quite simple; our behavior is limited to the production of a single equivalent response. In such conversations we operate under the equivalence dictor alone.

NICKEL: But choice conversations are much more complex.

PENNY: Yes, they are. For in choice conversations we operate under many dictors.

In effect, we choose a sentence to accomplish a purpose, for the dictors introduce the purposive element into language. We don't always state our purpose because we don't always need to do so. The other person who is acquainted with the same linguistic regularity as we are doesn't need to be told after he's said "A is B" that now I intend to deny what he's said. He knows that when I say "A is not B."

NICKEL: The "not" is the tip-off.

PENNY: Sure. Being acquainted with the regularity governing "not," he knows that "A is B" has been denied.

Sometimes a person may doubt a sentence you've uttered, that is, he may utter a response sentence falling under the doubt dictor. What is likely to be your response to his doubt?

NICKEL: My response could be a proof. In that case my response falls under the proof dictor. I guess that could take more than one sentence.

PENNY: If you are to know whether you've accomplished your purpose of proving a sentence, one of the things you should learn is the linguistic regularity required of a set of sentences falling under the proof dictor, just as you had to learn that "not" accomplishes the purpose of denying a sentence.

NICKEL: I look forward to that, but at the moment I'm terribly tired.

PENNY: And I have to meet a visiting philosopher at the Buena Vista in an hour. We'd better get to your exercises, all right.

You'll recall that the occurrence of similar sentences in more than one response group caused special difficulties in ascertaining the identity or dissimilarity of two persons' cornucopias.

NICKEL: I guess you're referring to our R_2 example, the one about Haakon having good lungs.

PENNY: That's the one. The fact that Even responds with R_2 to S_1 and to S_2, and that R_2 appears in Odd's S_1 cornucopia and in his S_2 cornucopia makes it possible for Odd to frame at least three alternative hypotheses about Even's cornucopia. (1) For Even, S_1 and S_2 could

54

have equivalent meanings, (2) for Even, S_1 and S_2 could exchange meanings; (3) for Even, R_2 doesn't have the same meaning as it does for Odd.

2.1: The following portions of some possible cornucopias of Even's are to be considered. The notation for their mapping is derived from one of Odd's cornucopias.

NICKEL: Let me make sure I get your point about notation before you give me the portions. When we map Even's cornucopias, are you saying we should use the names of the sentences as they are given in Odd's cornucopia? So that, if "That takes good lungs" is named R_2 in Odd's cornucopia, that sentence when uttered by Even should also be named R_2?

PENNY: I do. The names have to name the same sentences or we won't be able to see how two persons' cornucopias differ when we look at them. It's the different location of the names of the sentences in the cornucopias that show us the cornucopias are not identical.

The situation is no different here than with any unit of measurement. Making a measurement is making a comparison. For example, measuring the length of a table is comparing the table length to the length of a ruler. The statement that a table is two feet in length is a comparison of the table length to two lengths of a 12 inch ruler.

It will be impossible to agree on the measurement of anything if we don't agree on units of measurement, that is, if we don't select some units as standard. Once we have a standard, we can state a common measurement with respect to the standard unit, whether it be a standard foot, or a standard centimeter, or a standard cornucopia. In the present instance, we are simply making Odd's cornucopia the standard one. Using his names for sentences, we see how other cornucopias compare with it and each other. This gives us a measure for difference of meaning.

Here are the portions of some possible cornucopias of Even's.

(1) $S_1 — RG_1$
    $S_2 — RG_1$

(2) $S_1 — RG_1 \begin{cases} R_2 — RRG_3 \end{cases}$

(3) $S_1 — RG_2$
    $S_2 — RG_1$

(4) $S_1 — \begin{cases} RG_1 \\ RG_2 \end{cases}$

    $S_2 — \begin{cases} RG_1 \\ RG_2 \end{cases}$

Odd and Even might not give S_1 the same meaning because of any one of the following circumstances.

(a) For Even, R_2 doesn't have the same meaning as it does for Odd;
(b) For Even, S_1 and S_2 have equivalent meanings;
(c) For Even, S_1 and S_2 exchange meanings.

Which cornucopia or cornucopias of the above would Even possess if (a) were the case? If (b) were the case? If (c) were the case?

This next exercise turns on the fact that most words have several meanings; we say these words are multivocal. Words with a single meaning we say are univocal. It is generally the case that when we use a multivocal word in a sentence we mean to be using it in only one way, even though it could mean something else. We can usually tell which meaning is intended, can't we?

NICKEL: Yes. You're hinting that because of multivocal words we continually test for a common meaning; I have to keep checking to see if I know which meaning the speaker has in mind before I can understand him. This is another circumstance the cipher method has to cope with.

PENNY: You've got a hint in the hand. It sometimes happens that multivocal words are ambiguous, that is, one can't tell which meaning is intended.

2.2: Though multivocality may annoy us when it results in ambiguity, it may also delight us. A pun makes use of a term's multivocality. (i) How does a pun do this? (ii) What must be the structure of a cornucopia if it is to be possible to pun during a conversation?

Odd (c): I'd like a date with that mannequin.
Even (c): Bad choice, Odd. She's green.
Odd (d): Ah, love. How green was my sally!
Even (d): No. No. Her name is Monique.

Before going on to the next exercises we'll have to add to the Principia symbolism. You can add these monary functors to your Pr-1 vocabulary list.

{} left and right braces
[[ ]] left and right open brackets

In doing the Polish-Principia equivalence exercises last time you probably noticed that there are two differences between Polish and Principia. First the components they share exhibit a different sequence; secondly, Principia contains punctuation marks, which Polish does not contain.

NICKEL: I take it Polish accomplishes with the relative position of its functors what Principia accomplishes with the use of parentheses and brackets.

PENNY: That's a good observation. Exercise 1.8 shows how punctuation allows us to write different Principia expressions; although a and b have exactly the same letters and functors in the same sequence, we can make two different expressions by adding punctuation marks. Polish accomplishes the equivalent differentiation with the aid of a change in functor sequence alone, exhibited by 3 and 4.

This next exercise today is designed to help you see the relations between Principia's punctuation marks and Polish's functor sequences. In addition, it will help you later to formulate the cipher rules for the Polish-Principia translation.

NICKEL: I've been expecting that exercise to rear its lovely head sooner or later.

PENNY: By requiring some other exercises, such as the next two today, and others scheduled to follow our next conversation, we'll build a terminology enabling us to simplify our cipher rules.

You will notice that numerals are written above each vocabulary item in the following expressions. The numerals indicate expression strength, and the larger the numeral, the stronger the expression. You'll observe also that the Polish and Principia expressions opposite one another are equivalent.

100	10 1 01
1. $*pq$	1'. $(p \supset q)$
100	10101
2. vpr	2'. $(p \lor r)$
1100	110 1 01
3. $-{*\atop *}pq$	3'. $-(p \equiv q)$
1000	101001
4. $vq-p$	4'. $(q \lor -p)$
21000	210101202
5. $v.pqr$	5'. $[(p.q) \lor r]$
2201100	220 2 1101012
6. $-*r-.pq$	6'. $-[r \supset -(p.q)]$
2001100	20021101012
7. $v-r-.qp$	7'. $[-r \lor -(q.p)]$
20100	202101012
8. $vr.pq$	8'. $[r \lor (p.q)]$
210000	2100101202
9. $v.-prq$	9'. $[(-p.r) \lor q]$
3210000	3210 1 01202 3 03
10. $*.{*\atop *}pqrp$	10'. $\{[(p \equiv q).r] \supset p\}$

310021000
11. ..pq..rpp

33321001000
12. --*.*qpvrpr

322100010010000
13. *-.vqp*rr.-q-r

32100021000
14. *.vpqr.*prq

4321000210000
15. v*.vpqr.*prqp

4100321001000
16. v.pq**.qrvprp

6543210000000
17. ******pqqqrrq

7060504030020 01000
18. *q*p*r*p*-r*-p*-qr

310101321010120 23
11'. {(p.q).[(r.p).p]}

333210 1 01210 1012 3 03
12'. --{[(q≡p).(rvp)]⊃r}

322101012210 1 0123 10010013
13'. {-[(qvp).(r≡r)]≡(-q.-r)}

3210101202 3 210 1 012023
14'. {[(pvq).r]⊃[(p⊃r).q]}

43210101202 3 210 1 012023404
15'. ⟦{[(pvq).r]⊃[(p⊃r).q]}vp⟧

41010143210101 2 101012 3 034
16'. ⟦(p.q)v{[(q.r)⊃(pvr)]⊃p}⟧

6543210 1 01 2 02 3 03 4 04 5 05 6 06
17'. [(⟦{[(p⊃q)⊃q]⊃q}⊃r⟧⊃r)⊃q]

70 7 60 6 50 5 40 4 300 3 200 2 100 1 01234567
18'. {q⊃[p⊃(r⊃⟦p⊃{-r⊃[-p⊃(-q⊃r)]}⟧)]}

It might help you to see what's going on if I were to give you some applications of numerical strength to a symbolism with which you're acquainted.

NICKEL: As you did when you gave me the A and B arithmetical expressions?

PENNY: Yes, but to avoid confusion from too many numerals, I'll give you algebraic expressions.

10 1 01
1. (a+b)

10 1 01
2. (b×a)

210 1 01 2 02
3. [(a÷b)=c]

20 2 10 1 012
4. [c=(a+b)]

210 1 01 2 10 1 012
5. [(a+b)=(b+a)]

1 00
1'. +ab

1 00
2'. ×ba

2 1 000
3'. =÷abc

2 0 1 00
4'. =c+ab

2 1 00 1 00
5'. =+ab+ba

58

3210 1 01 2 10 1 012 3 10 1 013   3 2 1 00 1 00 1 00
6. $\{[(a\times b)+(c\times d)]=(e\times f)\}$ 6'. $= + \times ab \times cd \times ef$

2.3: I want you to write the number of the expression strength above all the vocabulary items in the arithmetical expressions and in the 14 equivalent Polish and Principia expressions I gave you last time.*

2.4: Write the simplest rules you can for the assignment of numeral strength to the vocabulary items in both Polish and Principia expressions. These two sets of rules will be Po-2 and Pr-2.

You'll have to have three kinds of rules for Polish and four for Principia. For Polish you'll need rules (1) for letters, (2) for binary functors, and (3) for the monary functor, bar.

NICKEL: For Principia I'll need those three plus (4) a rule for the punctuation marks.

PENNY: That's correct. I'm going to give you the same advice now that I gave you for doing 1.9. Remember that no matter how long an expression may become, it always consists of smaller parts which are treated in the larger expression the same way they were treated when they stood alone. For example, it's obvious from the first sample that the vocabulary items in $*pq$ are assigned this numeral strength: $\overset{100}{*pq}$. If that expression, which, in general, consists of a binary functor and two letters, appears in a larger expression, it receives the same numeral strength assignment: $\overset{100}{.r*pq}$.

Similarly for that last expression: $\overset{20100}{.r*pq}$. If it appears in a larger expression, it will receive the same numerical assignment: $\overset{20100}{v.qr.r*pq}$.

NICKEL: Your advice, then, is to start with smaller parts and build up, the same advice holding for both Polish and Principia.

PENNY: Exactly. I'm going to be freer than a Kwakiutl with my advice today. Clearly it is a functor's neighbors which determine its strength. These two examples show us that the vee and dot exchange their strength after exchanging neighborhoods: $\overset{20100}{vr.qp}$ and $\overset{20100}{.rvqp}$. Your problem is to state the rules of the way the neighbors determine a functor's strength.

NICKEL: Here's one piece of advice you won't have to give me. In order to produce a set of rules, I won't try to describe the whole set of

* Reader: See pages 24–25.

Second conversation   59 examples. I'll try to work out rules for some of the samples and then apply them to the remaining samples as a repetition check on my rules. I say this because the search for a set of numerical rules seems similar to the search for a cipher for the binary rules.

PENNY: Clever fellow. Generalizing on his past experience!

NICKEL: I notice that the highest numeral in the sample expressions is 7. Do my rules have to provide for no greater strength?

PENNY: Nowhere have I seen any evidence that there is a limit to the length of expressions.

NICKEL: My rules will have to be given without respect to any particular numeral strength then, for strength seems to be correlated with length.

PENNY: Not always. $\frac{20100}{vqvrp}$ is shorter than $\frac{2100100}{v.qqvrp}$, but their main functors have the same strength. However, an addition to the second expression would increase the strength of the resulting expression. There being no limit to the additions we can make, there are an indefinite number of occurrences of punctuation marks required for Principia. Don't fall into the error of describing the numeral strength of the ones I've given in the samples.

2.5: After doing these exercises you are capable of more complex Principia-Polish equivalence conversations. Here are some longer expressions for you to translate.

1. $.v*prq .-.pqr$
2. $****pqqrp$
3. $-*q*r*p*-pq$
4. $-.p-v-*-.*_*pqrpq$
5. $.v*pv-qrv.*_*qr-*qqvp-r*pq$
1′. $\{[(p \supset q) \supset -(q \equiv q)] \supset p\}$
2′. $-\{-p \supset [(q \supset p) \supset (p \supset r)]\}$
3′. $[[(q \supset p)vr] \supset \{p.[(q \equiv r).p]\}]$
4′. $-[\{[(pvq)v-q] \supset r\}vp]$
5′. $([-\{-[(p \supset q)vr] \supset -[rv(q \supset p)]\} \supset -p]vq)$

NICKEL: Are you going to give me any exercises involving the application of the cipher method to music, poetry, and dreams?

PENNY: A more appropriate place for that kind of exercise would seem to be in the music, literature, and psychology departments, respectively. The role of the logician is to clarify the general procedure rather than to make specific applications. Besides, there is an important linguistic matter that we have to discuss before we can begin to discuss poetry adequately, namely, metaphor.

I do have a question about procedures in dream interpretation, however.

To lead up to the question on dreams I want to give you some quotations from Freud.

> We find ourselves in the full daylight of a sudden discovery. Dreams are not to be likened to the unregulated sounds that rise from a musical instrument struck by the blow of some external force instead of by a player's hand; they are not meaningless, they are not absurd; they do not imply that one portion of our store of ideas is asleep while another portion is beginning to wake. On the contrary, they are psychical phenomena of complete validity—fulfillments of wishes; they can be inserted into the chain of intelligible waking mental acts; they are constructed by a highly complicated activity of the mind.
>
> The question whether it is possible to interpret *every* dream must be answered in the negative. . . . It is always possible to go *some* distance: far enough, at all events, to convince ourselves that the dream is a structure with a meaning, and as a rule far enough to get a glimpse of what that meaning is. Quite often an immediately succeeding dream allows us to confirm and carry further the interpretation we have tentatively adopted for its predecessor. A whole series of dreams, continuing over a period of weeks or months, is often based upon common ground and must accordingly be interpreted in connection with one another. In the case of two consecutive dreams it can often be observed that one takes as its central point something that is only on the periphery of the other and *vice-versa*, so that their interpretations too are mutually complementary. I have already given instances which show that different dreams dreamt on the same night are, as a quite general rule, to be treated in their interpretation as a single whole.
>
> When we have become familiar with the abundant use made of symbolism for representing sexual material in dreams, the question is bound to arise of whether many of these symbols do not occur with a permanently fixed meaning, like the "grammalogues" in a shorthand; and we shall feel tempted to draw up a new "dream-book" on the decoding principle. . . . Dreams make use of this symbolism for the disguised representation of their latent thoughts. . . . They frequently have more than one or even several meanings, and, as with Chinese script, the correct interpretation can only be arrived at on each occasion from the context.*

2.6: Each of the three distinct paragraphs deals with a separate aspect of what we've talked about so far. I want you to identify them.

* Sigmund Freud, *The Interpretation of Dreams*, trans. James Strachey, Basic Books, New York, 1955, p. 122; pp. 524–525; pp. 351–353, respectively.

2.7: While we're on quotations, here's an interesting one from Lewis Carroll's *Through the Looking Glass*, which bears on our conversations.

"It is a very inconvenient habit of kittens" (Alice had once made the remark) "that, whatever you say to them, they *always* purr. If they would only purr for 'yes' and mew for 'no,' or any rule of that sort," she had said, "so that one could keep up a conversation! But how *can* you talk with a person if they *always* say the same thing?"

(a) Answer Alice's question by reference to our distinction between types of conversations.

(b) Could a person carry on a choice conversation with someone who uttered only "yes" and "no"?

NICKEL: That instantly strikes me as being improbable.

PENNY: It probably strikes you as being even more improbable that a person could tell someone how to spell a word by purring for "yes" and mewing for "no."

NICKEL: It certainly does.

PENNY: It's quite possible. Suppose someone wanted to spell "yep." He would first have to indicate that "y" is the first letter. He can do this merely by purring and mewing. Of course, the right questions must be asked.

Q_1: Is the letter in the first half of the alphabet?

A_1: No. abcdefghijklm/nopqrstuvwxyz

Q_2: Is it in the first half of the remaining letters? (When the number of letters is odd, the first half will be one greater than the second half)

A_2: No. nopqrst/uvwxyz

Q_3: Is it in the first half of the remaining letters?

A_3: No. uvw/xyz

Q_4: Is it in the first half of the remaining letters?

A_4: Yes. xy/z

Q_5: Is it in the first half of that set of letters?

A_5: No. x/y

It's clear that there is another way of saying "y." In this new regularity, "y" is "no, no, no, yes, no."

2.8: Spell "yep" using the purr-mew technique.

NICKEL: But what is the connection between using "yes-no" for spelling and using it for carrying on a conversation?

PENNY: The purr-mew technique is merely a selecting technique.

NICKEL: But in spelling I have the alphabet from which to select; and you know what I'm spelling with my "yes-no" for we both agree on the letters that are in the alphabet and the order in which they appear.

PENNY: Then all you need to do is find something from which to select sentences that satisfies those regularity requirements.

NICKEL: Cornucopias?

PENNY: I've just thought of another question for you to worry about.

2.9: I gave you earlier a quote where Ralph Gleason used the terms "statement" and "response" to describe the Adderley brothers playing.* Can you think of any sentential response dictors that apply literally to musical responses? If you can't, Gleason's description, like most descriptions of music, is metaphorical. The consequence is that we can't say music has meaning in the same sense in which we say sentences have meaning.

NICKEL: Does this mean that the one-language method of verifying the presence of a common regularity shows that music doesn't have any linguistic regularity?

PENNY: The statement-response way of isolating the segments in a flow of conversational sound was necessary for testing the existence of a common cornucopia, an isomorphic regularity. I leave you to draw your own conclusions about the existence of a "musical" cornucopia.

2.10: I can't forbear adding a statement about painting as a human product with meaning. This was written by John C. Oglesby.

> What is the content of his paintings? What, in other words, do they have to say? Well, they are certainly not probing the meaning of life or the universe, and they are rarely symbols for something else. The meaning of these paintings resides in the non-verbal world of visual experience just as the meaning of music resides in the world of sound and the emotional responses it causes.†

Review Questions

1. How is Nickel's dream as interpreted related to his worries about the cipher method?

2. What are the two arguments Nickel gives for his view that though music has a meaning it can't be put into words?

3. Distinguish between a cipher and the cipher method.

* Reader: See page 44.   † *Sacramento Bee.*

4. Distinguish between an equivalence conversation and a choice conversation.

5. Why are a person's thoughts useless in finding out if he understands what you say?

6. Why is a cornucopia like a yardstick?

7. How are the one-language and the two-language methods of determining common meaning related to the inductive method?

Third conversation

LOGIC IN THE NARROW SENSE

Ther wyll nevr bee anoother Arystotel—unles ther bee anoother Sokrotas.—Fanebius Perlyng

PENNY: Did you dream last night, Nickel?
NICKEL: No. You really must have reassured me.
PENNY: In that case, I'd better give you some more anxieties. I'd not like to be the one responsible for the disappearance of your dream model.
NICKEL: I do feel as if I have a pretty good conception of logic in the wide sense. After our last session I don't think I'll ever forget that rule-governed linguistic regularity, the subject matter of logic in the wide sense, plays such an important role in our cooperative lives. I can see that the study of logic is a study of man.
PENNY: This also holds for today's topic, logic in the narrow sense; we can expect a study of logic thus qualified to be a study of man qualified, a study of some aspect of man. After a brief description of logic in the narrow sense, you'll soon be able to figure out which property of man provides the pertinent aspect.
The word "logic" is much more commonly used in the narrow, traditional sense than in the wide sense. This narrower, more traditional use of the term "logic" does not involve a shift away from the study of regularity, but only a decrease of scope; instead of being a study of all linguistic regularity, it is a study of the regularity exhibited and required in that part of language which we use to make inferences.
NICKEL: I suppose you mean it's about what we call reasoning? That would make logic in the narrow sense a study of the rational aspect of man.
PENNY: We have to be careful here; it would be easy to confuse two subject matters when we use the term "reasoning." "Reasoning" is sometimes used to refer to mental processes, which are traditionally thought to be the subject matter of psychology, and must be distinguished from the subject matter of logic, which is linguistic regularity. From the perspective of logic in the narrow sense, the proper study of rational man is a study of linguistic inferential regularity.
NICKEL: Will we try to develop an ideal language that will cover inferential regularity?
PENNY: Principia and Polish are ideal languages specifically designed to cover that aspect of language. I think our future conversations about them will be clearer if we explicitly acknowledge an important distinction. It is a distinction with which you are already familiar and one which is easily made. By being explicit about it, we may be encouraged to honor it. The following argument supplies us with a nice violation of the distinction.

> John is brave.
> Brave has exactly five letters.
> Therefore, John has exactly five letters.

66

NICKEL: The conclusion of that argument certainly doesn't follow.

PENNY: Can you locate the difficulty?

NICKEL: I think the trouble lies in the word "brave." It seems to mean two different things in this one argument. It strikes me as being what you called yesterday a multivocal word; the first time it means a character trait and the second time it means a word.

PENNY: Good. When a multivocal word is used in at least two of its ways within a single argument, we say the fallacy of equivocation has been committed. This particular kind of equivocation is of special interest to us, for it turns upon a violation of the distinction I wish to make explicit. Let us call it the use-mention distinction.

Take the word "brave." It can either be used or it can be mentioned, that is, talked about. In "John is brave" it is used to refer to a character trait; in "Brave has exactly five letters" it is mentioned and something is said about it.

NICKEL: That seems clear enough. We sometimes use language to talk about things, and sometimes we want to talk about language itself.

PENNY: That means we shall have to teach you more names.

NICKEL: I don't follow that remark.

PENNY: We wish to be able to talk about, mention, any word, but the dictionary contains few words that are names for other words. It contains few words whose definitions say that the word defined refers to a specific word. Thus, we'll need to develop a whole new vocabulary if we are to be able to talk about any word.

NICKEL: That doesn't seem like a problem. We can just use a word to mention itself. We do it all the time.

PENNY: But maybe we shouldn't do it all the time. You have already seen that equivocation is a possible consequence of letting a word mention itself in the "John is brave" argument.

Allowing a word to mention itself may have another unwanted consequence, one that can occur outside as well as inside an argument. I'll illustrate the consequence by asking you a question I want you to answer. How is it you spell well?

NICKEL: That's an ambiguous question. I don't know whether to answer "By practice" or by spelling the word "well."

PENNY: Thus, ambiguity can be a consequence of allowing a word to mention itself.

NICKEL: Self-mentioning has to be avoided sometimes, doesn't it?

PENNY: That's right.

NICKEL: But how can we avoid it?

PENNY: By using names of words we wish to mention, permitting no word to be its own name.

NICKEL: But where will we get all the names we'll need?

PENNY: They won't be hard to obtain if we adopt a new spelling rule. We can invent the name of a word, or phrase, or sentence for that matter, that we wish to mention by adding a " z " at the beginning and end of the expression. With the new name, we can refer to, that is, mention, any expression that resembles the collection of letters lying between the z's. The ambiguous question I asked you to answer need no longer be ambiguous: How is it you spell zwellz?

NICKEL: Zoundz: w-e-l-l.

PENNY: Actually, there is a familiar device which serves the same purpose as " z " which has long been used for written language. That device is quotation marks. In news stories, when the reporter wants to mention what a person said, he puts the sentence or word within quotation marks. Using that device, my question looks like this: How is it you spell "well"?

We might call these expressions with the quote marks or z's in front and back quote-names.

NICKEL: Ciphers could make use of quote-names very handily, for in stating cipher rules we continually mention expressions from two regularities.

PENNY: Surely. Liberal use of quote-names may make discourse about language less confusing, though failure to use them doesn't always lead to confusion. Suppose I had said the following: That formula contains a +. Though the " + " in that sentence is used to mention itself, you're not likely to misunderstand that sentence.

In writing up your notes of our conversations, don't feel you have to use quote-names in contexts where there is no danger of ambiguity or equivocation.

NICKEL: You know, adding quote-names to a language is almost like inventing another language, a "quote-language" especially designed to talk about languages.

PENNY: Other people have remarked on the need for such a language; they usually call it a meta-language. If we had a meta-language available and always used it, need we worry about use-mention ambiguity or equivocation, the kind of equivocation we got in the "brave" argument or the kind of ambiguity we got in the "well" question?

NICKEL: I don't think so. For if we always used a quote-name whenever we mentioned an expression, the other person would always have a way of telling when we're mentioning and when we're using an expression. That will prevent use-mention ambiguity.

We won't have use-mention equivocation either, for a quote-name and the expression it refers to will be different expressions; being different, we'll see right off that in one sentence an expression is being mentioned and that in another sentence an expression is being used.

PENNY: Very good, Nickel. Frequently persons who want a meta-language want one which contains not only quote-names but also expressions for talking about the meaning and truth of expressions in the object-language.

NICKEL: What's an object language?

PENNY: Any language you're talking about as a whole, for example, "Urdu is spoken by Mohammedans in India"; or any language some part of which is being talked about, for example, "All English verbs possess a tense"; or any language containing a specific expression which is being mentioned, as in "The German word 'Gemütlichkeit' is a comfortable word."

NICKEL: Then Urdu, English, and German could all be object-languages?

PENNY: Sure, and any one of them, when augmented with quote-names and expressions such as "is true" and "is false" enabling us to talk about the truth value of sentences, and with expressions enabling us to talk about the meaning of expressions, becomes a meta-language.

NICKEL: Meta-languages are just languages we can use to talk about other languages then.

PENNY: That's right, though we should note that a language may serve the purpose of a meta-language even though it contains no quote-names and though no words are used to mention themselves.

NICKEL: How is that possible? Can you give me an example?

PENNY: The last word in the sentence immediately preceding this one contains seven letters. To which word have I referred?

NICKEL: "Example." You can refer to specific expressions by description, I see, providing that the description applies to only one thing, as it seems to me "The last word in the sentence immediately preceding this one" does.

I can see why a meta-language to be a meta-language must contain quote-names or descriptions of expressions in the object-language, but I don't see why it also must contain expressions for talking about the truth or meaning of them.

PENNY: One reason some people give for saying this is that they don't think an object-language should contain such expressions.

But if the object-language doesn't contain, for example, the expression "is false," or any synonyms of it, then we can't say in the object-language that any of its sentences are false. Right?

NICKEL: Right.

PENNY: Still, we may want to speak of the falsity of object-language sentences. If we can't do it in the object-language, we have to do it in the meta-language. And we can't do it in the meta-language unless it contains——

NICKEL: ——the expression "is false."

PENNY: Now you see why a meta-language must contain "is false" and "is true."

NICKEL: Yes, but before I can be convinced that we need such a meta-language, I'll have to be shown why an object-language shouldn't contain "is false" and "is true."

PENNY: I'm not sure I can convince you of the need for a meta-language, because the argument I'm about to give you hasn't convinced all philosophers and logicians.

NICKEL: Has it convinced you?

PENNY: The issue is so complicated that it would be useless to talk of conviction without considering all the complications. And I don't want to consider them now.

NICKEL: Then why bring up the whole idea of a meta-language?

PENNY: Because we might find a meta-language useful even though we haven't been shown it is necessary. I notice you're wearing a sleeveless shirt. Do you have to be shown it is necessary to wear it before you feel justified in wearing it, or is it enough that it is useful to wear it?

NICKEL: Let me slip into my hair shirt while I ask this question. Why do some people think an object-language shouldn't contain such an expression as "is false"?

PENNY: They think that an object-language which did, would contain paradoxical sentences, for if in that language we can apply "is false" to its declarative sentences then the following sentence is a sentence in the object-language: This sentence is false.

NICKEL: Which sentence is false?

PENNY: "This sentence is false" is the sentence which is supposed to be false, interpreting "This sentence" as referring to the sentence in which it occurs.

NICKEL: Then "This sentence is false" is the sentence which is supposed to be paradoxical?

PENNY: That's right.

NICKEL: By a "paradoxical sentence" do you mean one that is odd and seemingly false, but, nevertheless, true?

PENNY: That's one common use of the word. I have another use in mind, however. "Paradoxical" describes a sentence that is contradictory; it's a sentence which is true if and only if it is false.

NICKEL: That's too odd to be possible.

PENNY: Let's see whether that's so. You'll admit, won't you, that

"This sentence is false," being a sentence in the object-language, must itself be true or false?

NICKEL: I believe so, if it's a sentence.

PENNY: Let's grant that it is a sentence, and let's abbreviate it to "S." Now tell me: Is "S" true or false?

NICKEL: I don't know. What would make it true?

PENNY: What makes the sentence "The apple is red" true?

NICKEL: The apple's being what the sentence says it is, that is, red.

PENNY: That's what makes our paradoxical sentence "S" true; it's being what it says it is, that is, it's being false.

NICKEL: But if it's being false is what makes it true, then "S" can't be false; it must be true.

PENNY: I'm not so sure, for if it is true, then it is what it says it is. And what it says is that it is false. So it's being true makes it false.

NICKEL: Pretty odd, all right. That sentence can't be true unless it's false and it can't be false unless it's true.

PENNY: To put it in another but equivalent way, if "S" is true then "S" is false, and if "S" is false then "S" is true.

Or, to put it in still another and equivalent way, "S" is true if and only if "S" is false, which, again, is the same as saying "S" is false if and only if "S" is true.

Doesn't that seem contradictory to you?

NICKEL: Yes, it does.

PENNY: Supposing that you thought it was unsatisfactory for a language to contain such sentences, do you see why you wouldn't want "is false" or any synonyms for it in the object-language?

NICKEL: Sure. With "is false" out of the object-language, you'd eliminate such paradoxical sentences. You couldn't form the sentence "S," "This sentence is false," where "S" is the object-language sentence to which "is false" applies.

PENNY: Good. Now whether or not that is a good argument, whether or not the object-language-meta-language distinction is necessary, we may still find the distinction a useful one. For using that distinction, we can be clearer about logic in general. It has at least two aims: (1) to create a transparent, ideal object-language; (2) to formulate explicitly the rules of regularity governing the formation of expressions in that language. The rules will be in the meta-language because the rules have reference to the object-language.

Since logic in both the wide and narrow sense shares those aims, we can get at the narrower sense only by specifying the particular narrower scope of its subject matter. We have to specify that part of linguistic regularity of which logic in the narrow sense aims to give an account. In order to do this we shall have to develop some linguistic categories. I think we need only three of them to specify the subject matter of logic in the narrow sense: expression, proposition, and argument.

From my use of "expression" you have probably already grasped its sense; it is used to cover every kind of linguistic item, such as letters, syllables, phrases, words, sentences, and any other units composed of sentences. We can think of a language as a sum total of all its possible expressions, and logic in the wide sense as concerned with the regularity governing all those expressions.

NICKEL: And propositions and arguments——

PENNY: ——are types of expressions. Logic in the narrow sense studies the regularity of that part of language composed of argument expressions. Our next step is to regularize the term "proposition" and relate it to the concept of *truth* and to regularize the term "argument" and relate it to the concept of *validity*. Let's start by reflecting on sentence expressions.

Sentence expressions serve many functions. They may be imperatives used to get someone to do something. "You are to share with your sister." They may be normatives used to remind someone of their obligation, "You ought to share with your sister." They may be used to warn our daughters, "You can't trust the water, dear, nor tall, dark men." Or to persuade the reluctant, "The mayor bought one just like this several days ago." Sentences may be used to evaluate, "The picture is beautiful." Or to grade, "This sow is the best in her class."

NICKEL: I catch on. They can be used to express, "I feel so happy!" Or to ask questions, "How much did you say it was?" Or to express doubt, "But my hair must be mussed."

PENNY: Our list could get quite long. Let me end it with the assertive use, "My fingers are broken." An assertive sentence is one which is true or false. Let's call such sentences propositions. So far as sentence expressions are concerned, the scope of logic in the narrow sense is confined to a study of the relations between assertive sentences.

NICKEL: Logic in the wide sense, being interested in all linguistic regularity, would consider *all* the above kinds of sentences in its scope, wouldn't it?

PENNY: That's right. And there could be uses of the term "logic" whose scope falls between the two extremes we have indicated here. For example, it might include, besides propositions, the study of the regularity exhibited by relations between sentences used to express obligations and prohibitions, and there are such logical systems. They are called *deontic* logics.

Or there could be a logic of questions. There have been attempts at this; it is known as *erotetic* logic.

Now we are ready to turn to argument expressions. By an argument expression I shall mean an expression made up of propositions, some of which we ordinarily call premisses and at least one of which we call the conclusion.

An argument is always an inference, but an inference is not always an argument. We can have inference expressions though the premisses and conclusions are not propositions. But in order to have an argument expression, all the premisses as well as a conclusion must be propositions, sentences used assertively.

NICKEL: That's not fixed in my mind very well. There are too many words. I have a tempest in my head-pot.

PENNY: Perhaps examples will help. Let me first give you an example of an inference that is also an argument. Imagine the following context. You have been to the Blue Fox for dinner; it has been splendid food, in fact so good that it has seduced you into an embarrassing situation. The bill is $30.00 and you have brought only $20.00 with you. Dish-washing is out, for at this price surely they must simply throw the dishes away.

Give me what you think is the inference and tell me why it is an argument.

NICKEL: I infer that I can't pay the bill from the fact that the check is for a greater amount of money than I possess. Is this an argument because the premiss, "The check is for a greater amount of money than I possess," and the conclusion, "I can't pay the bill" are both propositions?

PENNY: Right. Now tell me whether or not the next inference is an argument. Oedipus, King of Thebes, husband of Jocasta, who was the wife of the late King Laius, has sworn that the murderer of Laius shall be banished from Thebes forever. Oedipus discovers in his search for the murderer that he himself has killed Laius. Thus he falls under the judg-ment that he himself earlier passed on the yet unknown murderer. Should Oedipus allow the judgment to stand or make an exception of himself? As you know, Oedipus does not make an exception of himself.

We might phrase Oedipus' inference as follows:

I have sworn to banish the murderer.
We ought to do that which we have sworn to do.
I am the murderer.
Therefore, I ought to banish myself.

NICKEL: This is not an argument, because the second premiss and the conclusion are not propositions. They express an obligation rather than state a fact. I take it that so far as inference expressions are concerned, logic in the narrow sense has confined itself principally to argument expressions.

PENNY: Yes. And the chief interest in arguments is in their validity.

Let me give some more examples of contexts in which we would use arguments. They should make it fairly obvious why arguments have been thought important to study. After I give them to you I want you to give a definition of "valid argument" that shows the intimate relationship between truth and validity. Ready?

NICKEL: Maybe you should just tell me the definition.

PENNY: This is supposed to be a record of your discovery, not my achievement. Remember?

NICKEL: Ready.

PENNY: *Problem solving:* My car won't start and I have to be at the train station in twenty minutes to meet a friend who has to make a quick transfer to another station.

Constructing theories: Nature exhibits a wonderful order of events and adjustment of parts. How is one to account for this? Is it due to a divine Being whose intelligence and power surpass our understanding, or is it due to the mechanical necessity which governs atoms in their interaction?

Finding the significance of facts: The Boss didn't seem quite as cordial this morning. Did he fight with his wife? Did he have some pressing difficulty in mind? Or am I losing the inside track to Dempster?

Plausible lies: You can't tell your husband where you were last night, and yet you have to give an account that will not permit him to infer that it is composed of false propositions.

Identifying objects: I find lying on the floor beneath my desk a small object. It is chromed, metal, and slightly oily, and of such complex shape that it is surely an important part of some machine. My typewriter? Our sewing machine? Perhaps use of the machine without this part will harm the machine.

Making predictions: I have only recently come into some money and, in my desire to increase the sum, have made an investment in some stocks. To my dismay the stocks have steadily declined in value since I purchased them. Will they continue to go down, or will their present trend be reversed as my broker assures me it will? The company will soon merge with a large corporation whose reputation for high earnings is well-known.

Gambling: Should you take the even money bet that the man trying to make his point will roll a seven before he rolls a six?

Proving a theorem in mathematics: It has been taken as a postulate that

$$\text{If } \quad a \neq 0 \quad \text{and} \quad b \neq 0, \quad \text{then} \quad a.b \neq 0.$$

Can it be proven that

$$\text{If } \quad a.b = 0, \quad \text{then either} \quad a = 0 \quad \text{or} \quad b = 0 \quad \text{or both equal zero?}$$

After proper reflection on these you may proceed at will.

NICKEL: The sample contexts do show me why arguments, at least reliable arguments, and the study of arguments are important. In all those examples we had to increase our knowledge. So reliable arguments are important because by using them we can add to the number of propositions we know are true.

We want to know if they are reliable because only reliable arguments will give us true conclusions and new knowledge.

PENNY: *If* the premisses are true.

NICKEL: And unreliable arguments could lead us to false conclusions.

PENNY: Even if the premisses are true.

From that you should be able to get a definition of "validity," which expresses the intimate relation between validity and truth.

NICKEL: I could substitute "valid" for "reliable." I think I've got it. An argument is valid——

PENNY: If and only if——

NICKEL: An argument is valid if and only if it is impossible that its premisses are true and its conclusion false.

PENNY: I thought that once we got the concepts of proposition, argument, and validity clearly in mind we would have sufficient vocabulary to qualify the two aims of logic in general so as to obtain a succinct expression of the aims of logic in the narrow sense, but I see that we need one more concept.

An argument is formed by combining propositions. A proposition is formed by combining words. Not every combination or form of words is a meaningful combination. There are some forms whose words are so combined that they violate the rules of regularity governing the formation of meaningful sentence expressions, for example, "Clips groan it find is."

NICKEL: So we could say a parallel thing for arguments?

PENNY: Yes. Not every combination or form of propositions is a valid combination.

NICKEL: Then we could also say there are some arguments which combine propositions so as to violate the rules governing the formation of valid arguments. And we call these "invalid" arguments.

PENNY: And the key concept here is——?

NICKEL: Form!

PENNY: Logic is the love of form.

NICKEL: That shapes our wit and guides our tongue . . .

PENNY: Yes?

NICKEL: Sorry, I am only a one-line poet.

PENNY: I think we now have all the concepts we need to relate the two aims of logic to the notions of truth and validity. I'll use our new conceptual distinctions to express the notion of logic in the narrow sense.

NICKEL: You mean the concepts of a proposition, an argument, an expression, validity, and form?

PENNY: Yes. (1) The first aim of logic is to create a transparent ideal language through which we can more readily see the form of proposition expressions and/or argument expressions.

(2) The second aim of logic is to formulate the rules of regularity governing the use of propositions in the formation of valid argument expressions.

NICKEL: Will most of the course be taken up with these two aims?

PENNY: Yes, it will absorb most of your energy and attention. But, my friend, we have still to speak of larger things.

NICKEL: What do you mean?

PENNY: The course will demand much of you and take a summer from the springtime of your life. Ought you not to consider whether you want to trade such a precious thing for a knowledge of logic? Why *do* you want to learn logic?

NICKEL: I don't believe, now that you mention it, I am any more clear about that than I was about the subject of logic. I'm still young, so time doesn't seem short enough to press me.

PENNY: It isn't just the shortness, it's also that this time will never come round again. Youth is the only time we prepare the regrets of middle age.

NICKEL: I am not the only one who has to decide if learning logic is worth my time.

PENNY: How so?

NICKEL: Do you not teach logic?

PENNY: I do.

NICKEL: Wouldn't you be morally to blame if you took up the springtime of all those students' lives without giving them a prize in return?

PENNY: But suppose I reply that I do not direct them to take it, that they come to me and ask for it, just as you did. The responsibility is theirs, not mine.

NICKEL: Maybe they come to you in ignorance, not knowing it is a waste of time. The very word "logic" makes the subject sound like the candy of subjects. Would you consider yourself blameless if you set up shop and sold wares that looked like candy, but were poison? Could you shrug your shoulders innocently and say that the people who purchased them in ignorance asked for the "candy" and that you are not to blame, because you didn't direct them to buy it?

I don't think you could. I think you have to decide, too, if logic is worth these people's time, for your moral status is at stake. If you can't justify learning logic, but continue teaching it, you're immoral.

PENNY: So now we both must face it. Press me to an answer, Nickel.

NICKEL: OK. Do you think it is valuable to study logic?

PENNY: My answer is "Yes." But I want to make an even stronger claim. I want to claim that it is the most valuable subject that a man can study.

NICKEL: If you can convince me of that, I will throw myself into logic with a fervor.

PENNY: You had better reserve yourself somewhat, or you may lose your life to logic.

NICKEL: That isn't good?

PENNY: Let us get on. Tell me, do you admire persuasive speakers?

NICKEL: Yes, I do.

PENNY: Because of their power to move their audience?

NICKEL: Yes, especially when they can move an audience that starts out being hostile to them. Maybe I envy them as much as I admire them.

PENNY: Then I think we ought to fear them. This power they have is dangerous if they can make the worse appear the better, and make us believe they have given us knowledge when they have only changed our convictions. No man should be allowed to speak for more than three minutes uninterruptedly; after that time anyone should have the right to interrupt and question him.

Plays, movies, radio and television programs, and college lectures are all dangerous. Their design gives the speaker or writer sufficient uninterrupted time to rob us of our critical, questioning faculties. They give no one the opportunity to pick at the net they weave from their strand of unsevered time.

Plays, movies, and professors who lecture are the worst offenders; not because their intent is any worse, but because they don't have to be interrupted by——

NICKEL: Commercials?

PENNY: Yes; how odd it is that commercials should turn out to have any merit at all.

NICKEL: But commercials won't keep us out of bondage to the persuaders.

PENNY: That seems safe enough to say.

NICKEL: Perhaps we need a Socrates, another gadfly to keep questioning us, someone to break the smug trance in which we live.

PENNY: The forces of persuasion long ago saw how to nullify a Socrates.

NICKEL: The hemlock does the trick all right.

PENNY: Not the hemlock. That was a mistake; the hemlock immortalized and made a hero. There is a much more effective means.

A Socrates can be effective only in a city state, a state small enough for a man to know all citizens, all speakers, and their teachers. *Size* will nullify a Socrates. Make the political unit the nation with millions of citizens; put up hundreds of radio stations and keep them going twenty-four hours a day; add a fascinating, unblinking eye to radio and make business spend so much money to buy time that the whole of business will close ranks against the suggestion that three minutes be the longest time a man may speak without interruption; encourage a multitude of little theatres to spring up everywhere, giving thousands more a chance to entrance; and institutionalize education, that is, build universities and make classes so large that guilt and fear keep us from interrupting—with all this going for them the forces of Persuasion can be sure there will not be enough " socrates " to break the spell.

Dost thou feel *free* Everyman?

NICKEL: How do you relate logic to this?

PENNY: Is it enough that Christ should love?

NICKEL: No, for we also should love.

PENNY: And is it enough that Socrates should question?

NICKEL: No, for I suspect if we wait for a Socrates we will condemn ourselves to bondage.

PENNY: Then the only way to freedom from the power of the persuaders is to make Socrates of ourselves.

NICKEL: The point being that the subject of logic is to make questioners of us all.

PENNY: Not quite. The subject of logic is to make *effective* questioners of us all. What makes us questioners is the possession of the critical attitude, the attitude that always, always drives us to question a claim.

NICKEL: Better free than polite?

PENNY: If it is the rational rather than the rationalizing society that you want.

You must realize that logic as a subject owes its very existence to impoliteness. At some time all of us have had our belly full of the tapeworm of persuasion, and would be free of it; but we cannot be free of it, we cannot effectively criticize, unless we can distinguish the genuinely reason-

78

able from the speciously reasonable.   Logic as a subject is the entity called into being as an Instrument Critique, not an Instrument Politique, to enable us to distinguish and expose the specious.   It is called into being to make our critical questioning effective, and as such, *logic*, Sir, *is a civic virtue.*

NICKEL: I can see now that though the subject of logic is necessary to our own freedom, in itself it is a mere skeleton.

PENNY: That's right.   It requires animation by the critical attitude. So, if a logic course is to succeed in making logic a civic virtue, it must make logic live in you; it must arouse the spirit of the critical attitude.

Hast thou spirit, boy?

NICKEL: I think aplenty.

PENNY: I bid thee then to join the dance of reason.   Arise and be a freeman.

NICKEL: You can surely rattle the sword of reason.

PENNY: I don't know about that; but I do see that we have another justification for dia-logic.

NICKEL: Dia-logic?

PENNY: Dialogue—two people interrupting each other, mutually reasoning to a conclusion to cut the possibility of seduction to a minimum. For to keep the topic moving, you have to keep your wits about you. And if you keep your wits about you, you are free.

NICKEL: Since it is all-important to be free, logic as our liberator is the most valuable subject one can study.

PENNY: That's why I made such a strong claim.

NICKEL: What if somebody made the claim that political science is more important as a means to being a freeman?   Or history?

PENNY: I would ask him if we can rest assured that it contains no persuasion.   If he said yes, then he must have used logic to decide that it didn't; if he said no, then in order to separate the science from the persuasion we would need logic.   In either case, we must presuppose logic.

NICKEL: Logic is *the* science of sciences?

PENNY: All hail, Logic!

Many introductory logic courses (and books) are organized from the civic-virtue point of view.   Others are organized more technically, for people who are going to take more courses in logic and whose ultimate aim is to do work primarily in the philosophy and foundations of mathematics or the formalized languages of the sciences.

NICKEL: I take it you do not want our conversations to be organized in either of those ways.

PENNY: That's right.   Let me give you my reasons for not making either of them my chief end.

Third conversation

The civic-virtue type course tries to score with the ideal language by using it to make arguments in ordinary language more transparent, and, thus, to make their validity more easily and definitely evaluated. We'll do this too, but I don't want to make this the only end of our course, for I know very well that this ideal language flounders and drowns in the river of Lethe.

NICKEL: The river of Lethe?

PENNY: The stream of forgetfulness spoken of in Plato's *The Republic*. In from one week to two months after such a course most people lose the manipulatory skills required for using the ideal language.

NICKEL: But a critical attitude might remain.

PENNY: Yes, that might not be lost. And that's the virtue of that type course. The technical type course is also subject to the Lethe criticism except for those people who go on to take more logic courses.

NICKEL: And I don't suppose there are many who take several logic courses. I don't have any friends who have.

PENNY: You're right; most people will take only one logic course, and for many it will also be the only philosophy course they will ever take.

NICKEL: Wait a minute. Are you hinting that you plan to organize our conversations as if they were an introduction to philosophy and not an introduction to logic? And as if it were the last philosophy course that I will take?

PENNY: Well, are you going to take any other philosophy courses?

NICKEL: I don't know for sure. But that wasn't the point of my question. After all, I asked for a course in logic, not an introduction to philosophy.

PENNY: Evidently you have a conception of what an introductory course in philosophy is like and it does not accord with your conception of what an introduction to logic is like.

NICKEL: That's right. A friend of mine took an introductory course in philosophy and he showed me the book they used. It had some sections on ethics, metaphysics, theory of knowledge, political philosophy, and things like that. Studying what philosophers have said about those fields does not seem to me to be the same as studying linguistic regularity.

PENNY: Before we go on, we'd better get our bearings. I have been trying to show you the high purposes that the study of logic in the narrow sense may serve.

NICKEL: You have argued that the study of logic is a civic virtue because it serves to promote rational freedom, and that prolonged study of logic leads to the philosophy of mathematics and a better understanding of the language of science.

PENNY: Right; and now I want to show how it can serve an additional purpose. I want to show how an introduction to logic can also be the best introduction to philosophy and promote the good of your soul.

NICKEL: Will we discuss that next time?

PENNY: I think not. It seems better to devote a couple of days to some logic in the narrow sense, of which you'll have to know something before we can proceed to show the importance of logic to philosophy.

NICKEL: I hope you have enough time left today to satisfy my curiosity about something that just occurred to me.

PENNY: What is that?

NICKEL: I might learn a lot of logic in the narrow sense, that is, learn the transparent ideal language through which I can see the form of arguments, and learn the rules of regularity governing valid argument formations; also, I might have the full critical spirit and be anxious to show that logic as a civic virtue lives in me; I might see the need for criticizing another fellow's argument; but if the other fellow, the one on whom I am generously using all my logic, doesn't know the logic I know, how much good will all my knowledge be? Unless I give him a whole course in logic, he won't know what I'm talking about.

PENNY: It's cumbersome if knowledge is not evenly distributed, all right. But if we don't have time to distribute what we know, we have to find other means of dealing civilly with our fellow citizens. You might deal with them the way the Hatter and the March Hare dealt with Alice when she was in Wonderland.

NICKEL: When Alice went to the Tea-Party?

PENNY: Yes. It's near the beginning of the tea party, after the Hatter has asked, "Why is a raven like a writing-desk?" I'll read it to you.

> "Do you mean that you think you can find out the answer to it?" said the March Hare.
>
> "Exactly so," said Alice.
>
> "Then you should say what you mean," the March Hare went on.
>
> "I do," Alice hastily replied; "at least—at least I mean what I say—that's the same thing, you know."
>
> "Not the same thing a bit!" said the Hatter. "Why you might just as well say that 'I see what I eat' is the same thing as 'I eat what I see'!"
>
> "You might just as well say," added the March Hare, "that 'I like what I get' is the same thing as 'I get what I like'!"
>
> "You might just as well say," added the Dormouse, which seemed to be talking in its sleep, "that 'I breathe when I sleep' is the same as 'I sleep when I breathe'!"
>
> "It *is* the same thing with you," said the Hatter . . .

Let's construe Alice's reply to the March Hare in this way: Because

I say, "I mean what I say," it follows that I say, "I say what I mean."
We can put this in another way.

I mean what I say.   (Premiss)

Therefore, I say what I mean.   (Conclusion)

Alice may be taken to claim that the truth of the conclusion follows from the truth of the premiss and that the premiss is true.

NICKEL: The March Hare, the Hatter, and the Dormouse are trying to show that the argument is invalid, right?

PENNY: Right.   And to explain how their refutation works we require the use of the concepts we discussed earlier: proposition, expression, argument, validity, and form.   Do you want to try your hand at explaining their refutation?

NICKEL: No, but I'll try anyway.   We have Alice concerned with propositions, because she claims the two expressions "I mean what I say" and "I say what I mean" are true.   She also claims the former is a premiss for the latter.

The March Hare, the Hatter, and the Dormouse are not claiming Alice doesn't have an argument.   They are claiming she doesn't have a valid argument.   If she doesn't have a valid argument, then, although the premiss may be true, the conclusion she draws from it is not necessarily true.

I get all that, but I'm not sure how form comes into the explanation. Nor do I see how to relate form to "I see what I eat" and "I eat what I see."

PENNY: That's probably because I was too vague before.   I'd better be more graphic, that is, literal, about form; then you'll probably be able to see the role of form and see how it is related to the refuters' statements. Here are two forms or shapes: ⎢⎯⎯⎯⎢, (⎯⎯⎯).   If I write down the following, what do you think I have produced?

I (⎯⎯⎯) what I ⎢⎯⎯⎯⎢.

NICKEL: I'd say you have made the form of a sentence.

PENNY: Very good.   Now, suppose I write down the following.

I (⎯⎯⎯) what I ⎢⎯⎯⎯⎢

⎯⎯⎯⎯⎯⎯⎯⎯

I ⎢⎯⎯⎯⎢ what I (⎯⎯⎯)

NICKEL: I think that must be the form of Alice's argument.

PENNY: It is also the form of other arguments.

NICKEL: Is it also a form for the March Hare, the Hatter, and the Dormouse's argument?

PENNY: It is.

NICKEL: Then they all have the same form!

PENNY: They do.   Do you love that form?

NICKEL: I do.

PENNY: Then you are a budding logician, for logic is the love of form. Let's see if we can bring that bud to flower.

An argument form is a combination of the forms of the propositions it contains.   Some argument forms are valid combinations of proposition forms while others are invalid.

Now, how do we show that an argument is invalid?

NICKEL: Well, first, I suppose, we have to find out what its form is.

PENNY: Good.   Then what?

NICKEL: Then we have to find out if its form is invalid.

PENNY: How do we do that?

NICKEL: I do know that if it is invalid, any conclusion we might put into the form isn't necessarily true even though the premises we put in are true, but I don't know how to show that.

PENNY: You say the conclusion isn't necessarily true.   It shouldn't be hard to show that.   All you need to do is find a proposition which could go into the form which is——

NICKEL: ——false?

PENNY: Exactly.   "Necessarily" excludes the possibility of an exception.   If you find a false conclusion to fit into the conclusion form, you've found an exception, and "necessarily" doesn't apply.

NICKEL: The Hatter's statements constitute a refutation of Alice's argument because they have the same form as Alice's argument and because his premiss statement is true while his conclusion statement is false.

I (see) what I /eat/

———————————————

I /eat/ what I (see)

I'm much clearer now about those concepts we use to think about arguments and validity; as a result, I think I see how to show a person that he has an invalid argument, even if he doesn't know what I know about logic in the narrow sense.   All I have to do is think of an argument with a similar form having premises he readily admits are true and a conclusion he admits is false.

PENNY: It's a good thing you were curious.   You pushed us to your discovery.   Let's call that method of finding invalidity the Same-form Method.

NICKEL: I'm proud of my aggressive curiosity, but I'd feel a lot better if I felt competent to use the Same-form Method. What chiefly bothers me, apart from not knowing very well how to tell when a combination of sentences is an argument and when it isn't an argument, is not knowing what part of an argument is the form and what part isn't the form.

PENNY: Those are important concerns which we ought to discuss before I turn you loose on the exercises I have in mind. But I'd rather discuss the way to identify arguments first, if you don't mind.

NICKEL: There's no point in worrying about the form of arguments until I can find arguments.

PENNY: Often, when people speak, they utter several consecutive sentences; but, as you're aware, not every group of sentences constitutes an argument. For example, the following group isn't intended to be an argument.

> The statement of source and application of funds is prepared from the data of two comparative balance sheets. The individual values of one balance sheet are compared with those of an earlier balance sheet. Differences between these individual values are shown in the "increase-decrease" column of the comparative balance sheets.

NICKEL: "Isn't intended to be an argument"? Can't a group of sentences be an argument even if no one intends it to be?

PENNY: No, although it might be that in a group of sentences not intended as an argument the truth of one of the sentences necessarily follows from the truth of others. Or, to state the same thing conversely: some sentences might entail another sentence regardless of intention.

NICKEL: Isn't that the same as being an argument? For if a sentence is entailed by others, it must be the conclusion of an argument, and the others must be its premisses.

PENNY: It isn't the same as being an argument. A group *could* be an argument, and a valid one, provided someone made it an argument and correctly identified the premisses and conclusion. Arguments are products of human intentions. Language makes arguments possible; but humans make them actual.

If you think back to the Italian consulate incident, you'll recall a distinction parallel to the one I'm now making.

NICKEL: That was the incident when, although a sentence was uttered, no message was intended.

PENNY: Sure. One can utter a combination of sentences that could be used to state an argument without intending it as an argument.

NICKEL: Would it be a good idea to have a pair of terms parallel to "sentence" and "message" to mark the distinction we've just made?

PENNY: That's an excellent suggestion. Let's use the term "entailment" to parallel "sentence," and the term "argument" to parallel "message." An entailment will be our name for a group of sentences in which one of them necessarily follows from another or others whether or not intended.

NICKEL: Entailments and arguments being different, we can't use the same criterion to identify them, can we?

PENNY: That's a good hunch we can support with an argument, Nickel.

Under the usual meaning of "argument," we can say of some arguments that they are valid and of others that they are invalid, can't we?

NICKEL: Yes, we can.

PENNY: But if the criterion for identifying entailments were also used to identify arguments, there wouldn't be such a thing as an invalid argument.

NICKEL: Do you mean the criterion according to which a group of sentences is an entailment if one of the sentences necessarily follows from others in the group?

PENNY: I do. Nothing would be an argument, according to that criterion, that wasn't valid; there could be no invalid arguments.

It would be impossible for there to be invalid arguments. For a combination of sentences to be an argument, according to your criterion, one of the sentences would necessarily have to follow, while for that combination to be invalid that same sentence couldn't follow. To have a sentence do both is self-contradictory. Hence, the valid-invalid distinction would no longer be applicable to arguments.

NICKEL: The moral to be drawn is that my earlier criterion is fine for identifying entailments, but, if we are to keep the usual meaning of "argument," we shall have to provide it with a different criterion, one containing intention as an ingredient.

PENNY: And why is intention important to the notion of argument?

NICKEL: Because intentions can fail, I guess.

PENNY: That sounds very keen. Do you know what you're saying?

NICKEL: I think so. We can define an argument as a combination of sentences intended to be an entailment. If our intentions fail, so that we fail to construct an entailment, we simply have an invalid argument rather than no argument at all. Intention commits a combination to be judged as an argument; and it remains an argument, whether we succeed or fail. Thus, intention is what makes the valid-invalid distinction possible, and preserves the usual meaning of "argument."

Now that I understand that intention is a necessary ingredient of the argument criterion, I'd like to understand also how I am to recognize such an intention.

PENNY: The first word in the next-to-last statement you made was a signal to me that you intended an argument.

NICKEL: What word was that? "Thus"?

PENNY: Of course. To show that a sentence is intended as a conclusion you can use "thus" or any of its synonyms in front of it.

NICKEL: Synonyms such as "therefore," "hence," "so," and "consequently"?

PENNY: They're enough, for where a conclusion is intended can an argument be far behind?

NICKEL: It would be fast upon us.

PENNY: Sometimes instead of indicating conclusions, we indicate premises. To do this we use different words from those we used to precede conclusions. Four tries for a nickel, Nickel.

NICKEL: "Since," "for," "but," and "because." I'm ready to turn to my question about which part of an argument is the form now.

PENNY: A last reminder before we turn: A combination of sentences isn't an argument just because it has conclusion or premiss indicators in it; the sentences have to be propositions as well.

At this time I'm interested only in getting across an intuition of form through a consideration of examples. In these examples I'll use a line to separate the premises from the conclusion; the line plays the same role as the words we use to indicate that we intend an argument.

Some astro-physicists are not blond.
All heroes are blond.
_____

No heroes are astro-physicists.

This argument doesn't convict itself of invalidity.

NICKEL: Because the second premiss is false.

PENNY: Right. Can you see what three subject matters are referred to in that argument?

NICKEL: Astro-physicists, blonds, and heroes.

PENNY: Form is usually contrasted with subject matter; so, by that distinction, what remains after you eliminate the subject matter is the form. However, not all features of subject matter may be eliminated. We have to retain as much as will show us the relative positions occupied by the subject matter terms, though we must eliminate any features that give us a clue to the specific subject matter.

NICKEL: That sounds impossible. Can we do both?

PENNY: We can, thanks to the most important of all human inventions, the variable. To find the form of an argument, we'll replace similar subject matter terms with similar variables and different subject matter terms with different variables; by doing that we preserve the relative locations of the subject matter terms. At the same time, since the variables' shapes are empty, there is no specific content in them.

NICKEL: Variables' shapes are important then, aren't they?

PENNY: Yes, though what particular shapes they have is arbitrary. /⎯⎯⎯/, (⎯⎯⎯), and)⎯⎯⎯(will serve very nicely as variables. They're diverse enough to preserve the relative locations of subject matter terms, yet empty enough to give us no clue to any specific subject matter.

NICKEL: It seems to me that variables are nothing but place-markers; they mark places into which we may put specific but varying subject matter, somewhat the way gravestones without names carved on them might mark places into which any bodies can be placed.

PENNY: That's a gruesome but fitting image.

NICKEL: May I try to find the form of that argument about astro-physicists?

PENNY: You may. I suggest you place the variables around the subject matter terms as a preliminary step to exhibiting the bare form.

NICKEL:

Some /astro-physicists/ are not (blond).

All)heroes(are (blond).

⎯⎯⎯⎯⎯

No)heroes(are /astro-physicists/.

If I drop out the subject matter terms I get this form:

Some /⎯⎯⎯⎯⎯⎯⎯/ are not (⎯⎯⎯)

All)⎯⎯⎯(are (⎯⎯⎯)

⎯⎯⎯⎯⎯

No)⎯⎯⎯(are /⎯⎯⎯⎯⎯⎯⎯/

PENNY: Perfect.

NICKEL: The words "some," "all," "no," "are," and "not" are part of the form then.

PENNY: Yes, though it may not seem intuitively obvious to you that they should be.

NICKEL: I'll have to think about that awhile.

PENNY: The next step in making you competent to use the Same-form Method of showing invalidity is to show you how to make a set of true premises and a false conclusion by fitting subject matter terms into the form you've just exhibited.

NICKEL: I'm not sure what you mean by "fitting."

PENNY: I mean simply placing a subject matter term in a particular variable shape; naturally, you have to place that same term in that particular variable wherever the shape appears in the form. By placing subject matter terms in all the variables you will produce sentences, and, of course, an argument.

Here is such a placement made by Sally Jamison.

Some /musical instruments/ are not (keyboard instruments).

All)pianos(are (keyboard instruments).

No)pianos(are /musical instruments/.

NICKEL: Pretty neat! Sally is down our alley. You can't deny the truth of the premises or the falsity of the conclusion.

I've got the idea now, but that raises another question. You suggested the Same-form Method for showing a person without training in logic the invalidity of his arguments. It seems so good to me that I can't see why we need to spend time learning logic. We can even use it on our own arguments to instruct ourselves, can't we?

PENNY: You certainly can.

NICKEL: At least, it seems to me we don't need to learn anything else but the Same-form Method insofar as logic is a civic virtue. I wouldn't argue that the Same-form Method is a substitute for the science of logic. But it does seem sufficient for practical purposes.

PENNY: If it were sufficient for practical purposes, it should enable us to find, without remainder of doubt, all invalid arguments.

NICKEL: Can't we do that with the Same-form Method?

PENNY: Decide for yourself after considering this. Suppose I gave you an argument into whose form you were unable to fit the proper combination of true premises and false conclusion. Could you conclude that the argument was invalid?

NICKEL: I think—see if I'm on the track—I'm faced with the same kind of question I was when we discussed the failure to find a cipher. And I guess I should face the same kind of doubt I did then. Just because a person can't find a cipher for a set of characters doesn't mean the set doesn't contain a message; likewise, just because you can't find a combination of true premises and false conclusion to fit into a form doesn't mean there isn't any such combination. You may not have been clever enough to find them.

PENNY: You're on the right track. And being so, what should you conclude about the practical sufficiency of the Same-form Method?

88   LOGIC: A DIALOGUE

NICKEL: That the Same-form Method does not enable me, without remainder of doubt, to find all invalid arguments. And so good-bye to my theory about the practical sufficiency of the Same-form Method.

PENNY: That isn't the only limitation of the Same-form Method. It isn't a test for validity except indirectly. We can say by the Same-form Method that an argument is valid if and only if it hasn't been shown to be invalid; but given our wise scepticism about our own cleverness, we can't be sure that our indirect proof of validity is complete.

Now, before you think of any more questions, I'm going to start giving you some exercises.

3.1: It's a good idea to have two sets of exercises on the same subject. Assign numeral strengths to the Polish and Principia expressions in exercise 2.5.

NICKEL: It seems that every day something happens that requires you to press scepticism on me again. You're going to make a sceptic out of me yet.

PENNY: If that's so, then you ought to think about the way to elude the favorite argument against scepticism. People frequently state the sceptic's position in such a way that it appears to be self-refuting. The position is often stated this way: No propositions are true.

NICKEL: I take it the argument that it is self-refuting goes something like this: If the sceptic is right in his claim, then his own proposition, the one stating his sceptical position, is false. Therefore, scepticism is false.

PENNY: You see the argument.

3.2: (a) Does the sceptic's proposition lead to paradox? (b) If it does, state the paradox. (c) What distinction that we introduced today allows us to re-state the sceptic's position in such a way as to elude the self-refuting argument? (d) Re-state the sceptic's position using that distinction. (e) Answer questions (a)–(d) with respect to another version of scepticism as expressed in this sentence: No proposition can be known to be true.

3.3: The following list contains sentences deliberately written without using quotation marks, some of them by Professor Arthur Burks. I want you to add the quotation marks that will make the sentences both true and unambiguous. Some of the sentences will have to be in the meta-meta-language in order to satisfy those two demands.

NICKEL: Meta-meta-language? We've never talked about that!

PENNY: True enough. I'll do so now. Just as we sometimes wish to mention expressions in the object-language, so sometimes we wish to mention expressions in the meta-language. In order to prevent the meta-language from mentioning its own expressions, we need to have another language; let that other language be the meta-meta-language.

Third conversation

NICKEL: We can have as many languages as we want very easily, then. All we need to do is keep adding to the quotation marks in order to produce a new vocabulary. Am I right?

PENNY: Yes, you are. Here's an example: In order to mention the meta-language word "'hug,'" we add another set of quotation marks to the meta-language word. Here are your sentences.

a. English is a word in English.
b. The name of the word English is English.
c. San Francisco consists of 12 letters; San Francisco consists of 12 letters and two quotation marks.
d. Long is a word that by becoming longer becomes longer.
e. Oakland has 7 letters is a false sentence.
f. Oakland has 7 letters is a true sentence.
g. San Francisco is a city, San Francisco is the name of San Francisco, San Francisco is the name of the name of San Francisco, while San Francisco is the name of the name of the name of San Francisco.
h. Tiny was called Tiny because of his size.
i. The meaning of Lincoln was assassinated is derived from the meanings of Lincoln, was, assassinated, and the ordinary rules of grammar.

We were quite cavalier about defining "proposition." It was taken for granted that it shouldn't be too hard to distinguish those sentences which are used assertively, that is, those sentences which are true or false, from those which are not.

NICKEL: You're implying that in practice it is sometimes hard to do?

PENNY: I am.

NICKEL: Because we don't always know whether or not a sentence is true?

PENNY: Not for that reason. One may be in doubt about the truth value of a sentence, for example, "I have exactly 23 cents in my pocket," without being in doubt about whether it is the kind of sentence which may be true or may be false. We do not have to know the truth value of a sentence in order to know it is a proposition.

The difficulty in identifying a sentence as a proposition comes when we are unable to tell whether it is the kind of sentence that may be either true or false. You'll see what I mean when you do this next exercise.

3.4: From among the following sentences taken from Boswell's *Life of Johnson*, I want you to separate those which are used as propositions from those which are not.

Johnson: [a] I could write a better book of cookery than has ever yet been written; [b] it should be a book upon philosophical principles. [c] Pharmacy is now made much more simple. [d] Cookery may be made so too. [e] A prescription which is now compounded of five ingredients formerly had fifty in it. [f] So in cookery, if the nature of the ingredients be well known, much fewer will do . . .

Dilly: [g] Mrs. Glasse's *Cookery*, which is the best, was written by Dr. Hill. [h] Half the *trade* know this.

Johnson: Well, sir, [i] This shows how much better the subject of cookery may be treated by a philosopher. [j] I doubt if the book be written by Dr. Hill; [k] for, in Mrs. Glasse's *Cookery* [1] which I have looked into, saltpetre and salprunella are spoken of as different substances, [m] whereas salprunella is only saltpetre burnt on charcoal; [n] and Hill could not be ignorant of this. [o] However, as the greatest part of such a book is made by transcription, this mistake may have been carelessly adapted. [p] But you shall see what a book of cookery I shall make! [q] I shall agree with Mr. Dilly for the copyright.*

NICKEL: Is there any subject about which Samuel Johnson did not have something to say?

PENNY: I think so. But what he didn't talk about was probably discussed by Lewis Carroll. I'll give you some samples of the range of his talk. The arguments that follow are taken from Lewis Carroll's book, *Symbolic Logic*. At least they have the appearance of being arguments.

NICKEL: Why do you doubt they really are?

PENNY: My friend, Prof. Francis Seaman, made me doubt when he asked about the arguments, "Did he [Lewis Carroll] really *intend* these or know someone who did?" Oh, well, maybe pretended arguments are just as useful to work with as intended arguments.

1. Some epicures are ungenerous;
   All my uncles are generous.
   _____
   My uncles are not epicures.

2. No fossil can be crossed in love;
   An oyster may be crossed in love.
   _____
   Oysters are not fossils.

3. No Professors are ignorant;
   All ignorant people are vain.
   _____
   No Professors are vain.

* *Everybody's Boswell*, ed. by Archibald Marshall, Dodd, Mead, New York, 1957, pp. 307–308.

4. No monkeys are soldiers;
   All monkeys are mischievous.

   Some mischievous creatures are not soldiers.

5. Some pillows are soft;
   No pokers are soft.

   Some pokers are not pillows.

6. Bores are dreaded;
   No bore is ever begged to prolong his visit.

   No one, who is dreaded, is ever begged to prolong his visit.

Without quibbling overmuch, I think the above arguments either have all premises true and a true conclusion, or some false premises and a true conclusion, or some false premises and a false conclusion. But I don't think there is any argument among them which has all premises true and a false conclusion. In case the latter were so, what would we know about its argument form?

NICKEL: We would know it is invalid.

PENNY: I'm going to give you some arguments now, each of which the author believed showed that one of Lewis Carroll's arguments is invalid.

3.5: I want you to tell me which of the following arguments show which of Carroll's arguments is invalid.

a. Some numbers are divisible by 2.
   No prime numbers are divisible by 2.

   Some prime numbers are not numbers.
                    —Carol Dalrymple

b. No Christians are Mohammedan.
   All Mohammedans are god-fearing.

   No Christians are god-fearing.
                    —Ira Lee

c. Flypaper is sticky.
   No flypaper is used to wrap presents.

   Nothing which is sticky is used to wrap presents.
                    —Carol Dalrymple

d. No musician can be allowed to speak in concert.
   A conductor may be allowed to speak in concert.

   Conductors are not musicians.
                    —Ira Lee

92

3.6: But enough of your depending on other people's cleverness! I want you to display your own wit. (a) I want you to exhibit the form of each of Carroll's arguments. (b) And I want you to find for each invalid argument form a set of true premises and a false conclusion that shows its invalidity.

NICKEL: In short, I am to test the validity of Carroll's arguments by the Same-form Method.

PENNY: That's right.

3.7: Suppose you had a card on one side of which nothing was written except this sentence: "The sentence on the other side of this card is true." What sentence should you write on the other side of the card in order to produce a paradox?

3.8: And one last, frivolous question. If you found an English-speaking dormouse who asked you to explain to him why the Dormouse's attempt to refute Alice's argument failed, what would you say to him?

NICKEL: Lewis Carroll, go home!

PENNY: I only said the question was frivolous; that doesn't mean the answer should be frivolous. I'm going to get even with you now. Here are your Review Questions.

Review Questions

1. How do you distinguish between logic in the narrow sense and logic in the wide sense?

2. What is the difference between using a word and mentioning it?

3. What may be the consequences of ignoring the use-mention distinction?

4. What device do we use in writing to observe the use-mention distinction? In speaking?

5. Is the fallacy of equivocation committed in this argument?

Typewriters are metallic.
Some typewriters are admitted to college.
_____
Some metallic things are admitted to college.

6. What is the importance of the object-language and meta-language distinction to the study of logic?

7. What is the connection between the use-mention distinction and the object-language-meta-language distinction?

8. Define "proposition" and distinguish it from "sentence."
   Define "argument" and distinguish it from "inference."
   Define "valid argument."

Third conversation

9. What useful purpose is served by valid arguments?

10. What concepts are needed to express succinctly the aim of logic in the narrow sense?

11. What are the aims of logic in the narrow sense?

12. Why does Penny call logic a civic virtue?

13. What is the Same-form method of showing invalidity?

14. Are all valid arguments also entailments? Are all entailments also valid arguments?

15. Why is intention an important ingredient of the criterion used for identifying arguments?

16. Why can't you use the Same-form Method to show validity?

NICKEL: It'll take me a while to do all these exercises, so we'd better not meet tomorrow. Is that all right with you, Mr. Penny?

PENNY: That's fine. That will give me time to think of form and non-form. Good-bye, Nickel.

NICKEL: Form and non-form . . .

Fourth conversation

RINGLING BROS., BARNUM AND BAILEY, AND VENN

Alle thynges undr ye Bigge Toppe ar wurth twyce if they amuz as well as ynstrukt.   Lett Ryng Majur crak hys wheip o'err annimuls and thawts of animuls.—Fanebius Perlyng

NICKEL: Form and non-form. . . .

PENNY: That's the last thing you said when we last parted, Nickel.

NICKEL: I've thought of hardly anything else since then.

PENNY: Have you come up with a theory about the difference between form and non-form?

NICKEL: I have, though it probably isn't worth much.

PENNY: Are you ready to place it in the public domain?

NICKEL: I guess so. Our talks have made it clear to me that both the science of logic, in its concern with entailments, and the practice of logic, in its concern with arguments, are concerned with form; subject matter can be eliminated and replaced by variables. Since "astro-physicists" and "blonds" and "soldiers" refer to subjects in the world, they are subject matter terms and can be eliminated. But we can't eliminate such words as "all," "is," "not," and "some," because in not referring to any subjects in the world they aren't subject matter terms. If they can't be eliminated, they must be form rather than non-form terms.

PENNY: That's an interesting view. Do you think every term that doesn't refer to a subject in the world is a form term?

NICKEL: I do. And if they don't refer to subjects they are not eliminable.

PENNY: Is this chart an accurate representation of your view?

Form Terms	*Subject Matter Terms*
non-subject matter	non-form
non-eliminable	eliminable
no subject reference	subject reference

NICKEL: Yes, it's accurate.

PENNY: Would your theory be defensible if we found a term that didn't refer to subjects in the world but was eliminable?

NICKEL: It looks to me as if that would ruin my theory. For then I'd have a term that would be both a form term and a subject matter term, a form term because of not referring and a subject matter term because eliminable. I would be logically stymied because I couldn't tell if such a term was a form term or not. But I have to be shown that there is such a term.

PENNY: Stout fellow! Take the following sentence: Five is greater than two. We could take a step toward exhibiting the form of that sentence by eliminating the terms "five" and "two," and replacing them with variables, as follows: /_____/ is greater than (_____).

NICKEL: That doesn't seem to ruin my theory, for aren't there numbers in the world?

PENNY: You won't get much of an argument about numerals. But it's different with numbers. Some people believe there are numbers and others believe there are not. The dispute about the existence of numbers is one of the oldest in philosophy; because it is so much in dispute, it doesn't seem good strategy to base your theory of form and non-form on it. It will inherit all the ancient divisive differences born of the disagreements about the existence of numbers. Those who believe there are numbers—these they call realists—may accept your distinction; while those who do not believe there are numbers—these they call nominalists—will not accept your theory.

NICKEL: Why do you say the realists "may" accept my theory? You seem to imply they might not.

PENNY: What is to prevent them from saying there are alls and nots and somes in the world if there are threes and fours?

NICKEL: Ooops! By that view, even form terms would be subject matter terms, since then they'd have referents.

PENNY: Exactly. So we'd better look for a different theory.

NICKEL: Wait a minute, Mr. Penny! I don't have to give up the ship yet. I can still challenge your statement that "five" and "two" are eliminable and replaceable with variables. If they aren't eliminable I can save my theory.

PENNY: It's not hard to prove they are eliminable. You know we've been holding that a combination of sentences is an entailment on the basis of form irrespective of the subject matter.

NICKEL: I realize that.

PENNY: Well, then, you'll see that "five" and "two" are eliminable, because, given the serial order of numbers, the following combination can be seen to be an entailment, and there are no specific numbers mentioned.

/‾‾‾‾/ is greater than (‾‾‾‾)

(‾‾‾‾) is greater than)‾‾‾‾(

‾‾‾‾‾‾

/‾‾‾‾/ is greater than)‾‾‾‾(

NICKEL: It is an entailment, I admit. And before you ask me, I'll admit that I could put "five" and "two" in the variables, but I don't have to in order to recognize the entailment; hence, "five" and "two" are eliminable.

PENNY: Bravely said, Nickel, I'm going to suggest a different theory. It's a very modest one. It really would not be worth our effort if it didn't have other advantages.

Last time we noted that the Same-form Method has two disadvantages.

NICKEL: It depends on cleverness of which we might not have enough; we might fail to find the set of true premises and false conclusion which show the invalidity of an argument.

PENNY: That was one disadvantage. Today I want to show you a method for deciding an argument's invalidity that doesn't depend on our cleverness.

NICKEL: The other disadvantage of the Same-form Method is that it doesn't directly show us when an argument is valid.

PENNY: Good. If the new method that frees us of the demands for cleverness also shows us validity, then we will have made an advance over the Same-form Method.

NICKEL: This new method that overcomes the two disadvantages of the Same-form Method will help us to distinguish form words from non-form words?

PENNY: I think so. Attend to the following words: all, no, some, not, and are. With these words, and allowing ourselves only two subject matter terms, we can construct the four following sentences. I'll put the letter names of the different kinds of sentences to their left.

> A – All tigers are cats.
> E – No tigers are cats.
> I – Some tigers are cats.
> O – Some tigers are not cats.

This new method I've referred to uses A, E, I, and O sentences for material, and we'll call it the Venn Method.

NICKEL: Out with the old—the Same-form Method. In with the new—the Venn Method.

PENNY: Use of the Venn Method requires translating. We'll be translating A, E, I, and O English sentences into the "Venn" language.

NICKEL: What we need then is a cipher.

PENNY: Let's consider the factors we have to deal with in making such a cipher. First, A, E, I, and O sentences all have a subject term, S, and a predicate term, P. Secondly, they all have a copula, or could have a copula, the link between the subject term and the predicate term, which in English is a form of the verb "to be," such as "is" and "are".

NICKEL: Would you explain "or could have a copula"?

PENNY: Sure. Take the sentence "All ships have barnacles." There is no copula in that sentence which is a form of the verb "to be," but we could insert one by making appropriate changes in the wording. That would give us the sentence "All ships are things which have barnacles."

Or take the sentence "No flea sucks water." It can be rendered as "No flea is a water sucker."

NICKEL: Could "Some spectators like to see acrobats fall" be changed to "Some spectators are people who like to see acrobats fall"?

PENNY: You've got the idea.

The third factor we have to deal with in translating English A, E, I, and O sentences into Venn are quantifiers and qualifiers. The quantifiers, "all," "some," and "no," indicate that the subject term refers to a class, and when combined with the qualifiers, "not" and the negative aspect of "no," tell us, if the class has members, how many members of the subject class are or are not members of the predicate class.

For example, "All tigers are cats" tells us we are talking about the beasts that are members of the class of tigers, and that if there are tiger beasts, all are going to be found in the predicate class, cats.

That exhausts all the kinds of words that can occur in A, E, I, and O sentences.

NICKEL: Terms, quantifiers, qualifiers, and the copula. If we put quantifiers and qualifiers together, which seems natural considering the double nature of "no," we need three divisions in our cipher rules for translating from English sentences to Venn sentences.

PENNY: Here they are.

Rule 1. (for S and P): In an A, E, I, or O sentence substitute a circle for the subject term and a circle for the predicate term, and place inside the circles some identifying mark, such as the first letter of the respective terms.

"All tigers are cats" becomes by Rule 1: "All (t) are (c)."

Rule 2. (for the copula): Delete the copula and arrange an overlap of the subject circle and the predicate circle.

"All (t) are (c)" becomes by Rule 2: "All (t)(c)."

Rule 3.A (for "All"): Delete "All" and shade that area of the subject circle which lies outside the predicate circle.

"All (t)(c)" becomes by Rule 3.A: " (t)(c)."

Rule 3.E (for "No"): Delete "No" and shade the overlap area of the subject circle and the predicate circle.

"No (t)(c)" becomes by Rule 3.E: " (t)(c)."

Rule 3.I (for "Some"): Delete "Some" and place an asterisk in the overlap area of the subject circle and the predicate circle.

"Some 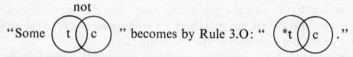 " becomes by Rule 3.I: "

Rule 3.O (for "Some . . . not"): Delete "Some" and "not" and place an asterisk in the area of the subject circle which lies outside the predicate circle.

NICKEL: Will that cipher work for sentences other than the four you just gave me about tigers and cats?

PENNY: Sure, providing you can see how to make a more general application of the rules.

NICKEL: Then you had better show me how the rule is to be applied more generally.

PENNY: It has to be done in the face of the fact that English sentences differ from one another. "All lions are tawny" differs from "All kudus are swift"; "Some acrobats are stiff" differs from "Some hartebeests are ill-tempered."

NICKEL: But they only differ with respect to the subject and predicate terms. The members of the first pair have the same quantifier and the same copula. Similarly for the members of the second pair.

Maybe I see how generality is obtained—by ignoring the differences in the sentences' subject and predicate terms. If we ignore them, "All lions are tawny" is an A sentence because it has the same quantifier and copula as "All tigers are cats"; and "Some acrobats are stiff" is an I sentence because it has the same quantifier and copula as "Some tigers are cats."

PENNY: Are you saying we can encipher, for example, any particular English A sentence into a Venn A sentence if we know what an English A sentence in general is and what a Venn A sentence in general is?

NICKEL: That is quite a leap. My thinking didn't exactly shape up that way, but it's not a bad hint, thank you.

PENNY: How do you get an A sentence in general?

NICKEL: I get an English A sentence in general by replacing the subject and predicate terms with circles in, for example, "All tigers are cats."

All 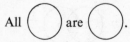 are .

I can also get general E, I, and O English sentences that way.

I can get a Venn A sentence in general by deleting the letters from the circles in Venn sentences:

Knowing both the English and Venn form of the general A sentence I can encipher a particular English A sentence into a Venn A sentence. All I have to do is substitute into the Venn A sentence in general: I substitute the English subject term's first letter into the left circle and the English predicate term's first letter into the right circle.

PENNY: Since the circles are things into which we substitute other things, I notice that in this respect they are like (   ), and /‾‾‾‾/, though, of course, they don't physically resemble them.

NICKEL: The circles are variables, then, aren't they? Just as (   ) is a variable.

PENNY: Yes, they are.

NICKEL: Does that give us a clue to the identification of form words?

PENNY: Good question, Nickel. It does give us a clue, for you'll recall from our previous conversation, I hope, that the presence of variables puts us on notice that we are dealing with linguistic form, in which, if in anything, we should find form terms.

A linguistic form is an expression of greater generality than the expression which results after substitution into the form. For example, the E sentence form,

,

is an expression of greater generality than the E sentences

and

,

for the latter two are substitution instances of the E sentence form.

A form is merely a spatial arrangement which reserves a place or places for particular substitutions.

NICKEL: In that case, if we take the initial letters, "t" and "c," out of all the circles of the Venn sentences you gave as examples in Rules 3.A,

3.E, 3.I, and 3.O, what we have left are forms. I realize these forms are general Venn sentences, but I don't see how that gives us a clue to the identification of form words.

PENNY: Is the Venn A form similar to the E form in any respect?

NICKEL: Yes. They both have two variables which overlap.

PENNY: Is the Venn A form dissimilar to the E form in any respect?

NICKEL: Yes. They are shaded in different areas.

PENNY: Those English words which are responsible for the different Venn shadings are the form words.

NICKEL: Then "all," "some," "no," and "not" are form words.

PENNY: They are. And we use two criteria to identify them. To be clear about the criteria we first have to understand clearly that A, E, I, and O sentence forms are linguistic expressions, though they are expressions of greater generality than A, E, I, and O sentences.

NICKEL: You said earlier that sentence forms are linguistic expressions, but I don't know why that is so.

PENNY: Do they not contain variables into which we may make substitutions and are the variables not arranged with respect to each other?

NICKEL: They are.

PENNY: Since sentence forms are governed by the two kinds of rules of regularity—substitution and arrangement—which establish linguistic systems, sentence forms must be linguistic expressions.

NICKEL: That makes sense. I think I'm clear enough about "form expressions" now to understand the two criteria for form terms.

PENNY: The first one is this: Form terms, because of the alteration they make in the spatial arrangement of variables, distinguish one kind of form expression from another.

NICKEL: Then form terms are arrangement rules rather than substitution rules.

PENNY: Yes, when considered in relation to form expressions. We can illustrate this in the following way. This diagram,

,

is as yet unaffected by form term arrangement rules.

Consider the following two arrangements of it.

NICKEL: A is arranged by "all" and E is arranged by "no." That's what I know I should say, but I don't see that there is any difference of arrangement in the variables.

PENNY: Perhaps you can after an explanation. Shading an area of a variable signifies that if the class we substitute into that variable has any members they will not be in the shaded area.

NICKEL: That sounds like negative information.

PENNY: It does, doesn't it? A and E sentences, being "shady" sentences, don't tell us whether a class has members, but they tell us where the members, if any, are not. But, of course, something positive does come of that, for by knowing where the members aren't we also come to know where they are—if there are any.

Shading clearly rearranges the variables. And I mean this literally; it makes spatial rearrangements. This can be seen more startlingly if we look at the effects of shading in another way, if we look at it as equivalent to erasing.

Instead of representing an A sentence form in this way,

we could represent it in this way:

This shows us that the effect of shading, or erasing, is to move the left variable into the area bounded by the right variable.

NICKEL: Under the erasure rule, an E sentence would look like this, wouldn't it?

PENNY: That's right. Shading, or erasing, moves any members they might have in common into their separate variables.

NICKEL: We can't equate the placement of an asterisk with erasure though, can we?

PENNY: No. Asterisks abhor a vacuum. Do you think the form terms "some" and "some . . . not . . . " show us anything spatially?

NICKEL: Sure. The location of the asterisk shows me spatially where a member of the left class is in relation to the right class.

PENNY: The other criterion for a form term is this: Form terms alter the variables in such a way that under some circumstances the alterations produce valid arguments.

NICKEL: That I don't get.

Fourth conversation   103

PENNY: I can show you this, Nickel, by considering sentence forms and syllogisms.

By using combinations of A, E, I, and O sentences which we can refer to as categorical sentences, we can construct syllogistic arguments. A categorical syllogistic argument is one which consists of two categorical sentences which are premisses and one categorical sentence which is a conclusion; those three sentences use three different subject-predicate terms, and each term is used twice and twice only.

NICKEL: By that definition, all the Lewis Carroll arguments were syllogisms.

PENNY: Correct. Do you recall that earlier we distinguished between arguments and entailments?

NICKEL: I do; we said that not every combination of sentences constitutes an entailment since the rules of regularity governing the construction of entailments might be violated.

PENNY: If I were to put three categorical sentences together, could you by merely looking at them—I mean literally looking at them—tell me if I had constructed an entailment?

NICKEL: I'm sure I couldn't. But it would be grand if I could.

PENNY: Then you have cause to be grateful to John Venn, for he designed the Venn language to give you that very power. Given some combination of A, E, I, or O Venn sentences, you can literally see if they constitute a valid argument.

NICKEL: The whole point of learning to encipher English sentences into Venn sentences is to take advantage of that marvelous property of Venn.

PENNY: Precisely.

NICKEL: If the English sentences are equivalent to the Venn sentences according to the cipher rules, then the English argument is equivalent to the Venn argument; and if we can see that the Venn argument is valid, we automatically know the English argument is valid.

That means our next step is to learn how to translate English arguments into Venn arguments.

PENNY: Not exactly. We want to see how to substitute English arguments into Venn argument forms. This is done stepwise, substituting one at a time the three English sentences composing the English argument into the three Venn sentence forms constituting the Venn argument form.

NICKEL: A Venn argument form is constructed from three Venn sentence forms?

PENNY: It is. How many variables do you think we need in order to do this?

NICKEL: You said that a syllogism uses three and only three terms, so I guess that we need three circles.

PENNY: Do you have any idea of their arrangement? Let me give you an example to think about.

All polar bears are fierce animals
Some fierce animals are white animals
———————————
All polar bears are white animals.

NICKEL: Let me number the terms in the order of their occurrence in the argument. "Polar bears" is 1, "fierce animals" is 2, and "white animals" is 3. Since every categorical sentence overlaps its two terms we have the following overlaps, by the number: 1 and 2; 2 and 3; 1 and 3. We can get those overlaps in this way:

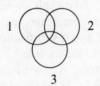

But that arrangement puzzles me.

PENNY: You've figured it out very well. I don't see why you're puzzled.

NICKEL: Variables 2 and 3 aren't horizontally arranged. Neither are 1 and 3. How do I substitute English sentences into them?

PENNY: The same way you did before. If their relative position bothers you, merely rotate the paper until they appear horizontal to you. Pretty soon you'll get used to using them at an angle; then you can save yourself the trouble of rotating the page.

NICKEL: But which way should I rotate the paper, clockwise or counterclockwise?

PENNY: Always take the shortest route, remembering that it makes no difference which circle is the subject in E and I sentences. They're symmetrical, since only the overlap area is involved.

NICKEL: That suggests "No dogs are birds" is logically similar to "No birds are dogs" and "Some animals are dogs" is similar to "Some dogs are animals."

PENNY: Quite right. To substitute A and O sentences, however, you have to rotate the paper in such a way that the subject circle is on the left, for it is the left circle which you alter.

NICKEL: And when I want to read a Venn sentence where an area other than an overlap is involved, I know that I have an A or an O sentence.

In that case I turn the diagram in such a way that the altered part is on the left.   For example, in this case,

the shortest route is counterclockwise until the shaded circle, 2, is on my left.   Then I can read it as "All 2 are 3."

PENNY: Good.   Let's see now how an English argument is to be substituted into a Venn argument form.

We're going to substitute English arguments into Venn argument forms by substituting English sentences into Venn sentence forms, arranged as you suggested.   To do this we need a standard procedure for matching English subjects and predicates with circle variables.

NICKEL: Why don't we give a substitution rule?

PENNY: Can you give me such a rule?

NICKEL: I'd be glad to try.   As I see it, we need a fourth rule to add to the other rules as modified.   How about this?

Rule 4.: When substituting an English argument into a Venn argument form, the first term that occurs in the premisses will be named "1," the second term that occurs will be named "2," and the third term that occurs will be named "3," where the order of occurrence is determined by reading the premisses in the English manner.   Term 1 will be substituted into circle variable 1, term 2 will be substituted into circle variable 2, and term 3 will be substituted into circle variable 3, where the circles are numbered as follows:

PENNY: That looks adequate to me.   We can encipher English arguments into Venn argument forms by enciphering English sentences into Venn sentence forms arranged in the three-circle overlap.

We now have two questions outstanding.   We have to answer both of them affirmatively if the machinery we've set up is to be better than the Same-form Method.

Do the English-Venn cipher rules free us from cleverness?   And do the English-Venn cipher rules show us the validity as well as the invalidity of arguments?

I'll make some remarks about the first question first. One short-coming of the Same-form Method is that we need to know that the premises are true. Here, we are freed from that burden, for in the universe of forms we are the complete master.

NICKEL: Can we be tyrannical?

PENNY: Just watch us order these forms about!

But first let's think of Venn sentences as pictures of reality. Take the sentence "All polar bears are fierce animals." The truth of that depends on the disposition of polar bears. We generally anticipate the displeasure of their temper. It's possible, though, that we might find some rehabili-tated polar bear, fit for society because he's not fierce. In that case, we shan't be able truthfully to shuffle all the polar bears in the left circle off into the area of overlap; so, instead of having this A picture of reality

,

we'll have this O picture,

.

NICKEL: Asterisk marks the spot of the rehabilitated polar bear. He sort of wrecks the A picture of reality by making an O picture.

PENNY: But he won't wreck the A Venn sentence form. When we move from English sentences, such as "All polar bears are fierce animals," in English arguments to Venn sentence forms in Venn argument forms, we don't care about the truth of the sentences; we only care about their form. And in the world of forms we have control of the asterisks and the shading. I am in control of the universe of forms existing on this sheet of paper. I write the form as if "All polar bears are fierce" is true.

NICKEL: That implies that the only thing relevant to the validity of arguments is the form of the sentences.

PENNY: Exactly! That's why we're freed from the limitation of the Same-form Method; testing for an argument's validity no longer depends on our knowing the truth of the sentences but on our knowing the form of the sentences.

We can proceed now to answer the other question, the one about whether we can show the validity as well as the invalidity of arguments by the Venn Method.

In terms of what we've said about the form of sentences in arguments, let me state our definition of validity in a different way than we did when we spoke about the truth of sentences in arguments. An argument is valid, that is, it is an entailment, when upon substituting the premises into the Venn sentence forms I necessarily substitute the conclusion into a Venn sentence form.

NICKEL: How do I know "I necessarily substitute the conclusion"?

PENNY: You know this by looking at the three overlapping circles after you've filled in the premiss forms. An example will show this very nicely.

1   2
All seals are animals.
    2   3
All animals are warm.
_____
1   3
All seals are warm.

I'll fill in the premiss forms, dropping a circle variable so you can best see what is going on.

1   2
All seals are animals.   1   2

2   3
All animals are warm.   2

       3

We now take those two Venn sentence forms and put them together so they have the overlapping necessary to represent a Venn argument form. When we do this, do you notice an additional Venn sentence form comes into being? Look at the form arrangement between variables 1 and 3.

   1   2

    3

NICKEL: I see an A form, I think, because the only unshaded portion of 1 lies within the area of 3. I see, to put it into English, that "All 1 are 3." Oh, oh, that's the form of our conclusion! By simply putting in the form of the two premisses alone, and that's all you did, you simultaneously put in the form of the conclusion. You couldn't have done otherwise. You *necessarily substituted the conclusion*," didn't you? Hooray for John Venn and his three-ring show! Jolly good show!

PENNY: Do you fully realize the enormous advantage of Venn?

NICKEL: I think so.

PENNY: When we write down two premisses in English, that's all we write down. At least that's all I see here.

All seals are animals.
All animals are warm.

But when we wrote down those same two premisses in Venn, we also wrote a third sentence, the conclusion. You saw that yourself.

NICKEL: I did.

PENNY: Did that take cleverness and does that show validity?

NICKEL: No, it didn't, and yes, it does. Everything in the world can take its turn in Venn's rings, being substituted for our instruction and our pleasure. I would that everyone had tickets to John Venn's three-ring circus!

But wait! What about invalidity? Does the Venn Method show invalidity?

PENNY: Try it yourself.

NICKEL: I'll take the third Carroll syllogism.

     1   2

No Professors are ignorant.   1 ◯◯ 2

     2   3

All ignorant people are vain.

PENNY: When you put them together, what additional Venn sentence form must you have if the combination is to be an entailment?

NICKEL: The overlap area between the first circle and the third circle must be shaded out, for the conclusion, "No Professors are vain," has an E form.

I *see* that the overlap of 1 and 3 isn't entirely shaded; hence, the argument is invalid. By substituting the premisses, I didn't simultaneously substitute the E conclusion.

PENNY: We should try some arguments with particular sentences in them now.

NICKEL: Let me try Carroll's fifth argument.

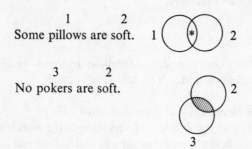

Some pillows are soft.

No pokers are soft.

Putting them together, I get,

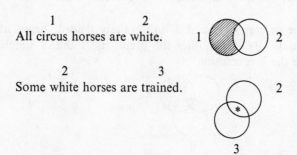

which isn't valid. Since the conclusion of that argument, "Some pokers are not pillows," has an O form, I should have an asterisk in the third circle outside the first and third circles' overlap, but I don't.

PENNY: So far, so good. Now test this argument's validity.

All circus horses are white.
Some white horses are trained.
_____
Some circus horses are trained.

NICKEL:

All circus horses are white.

Some white horses are trained.

Putting them together, I get

which is a valid argument.   I'm not surprised, for there are white, trained horses in a circus.

PENNY: You're not surprised because you've seen them in a circus. But if you knew only the premisses, could you infer there were?

NICKEL: I've just proved it by a Venn diagram.

PENNY: No, you haven't.   Because it can be shown by a Venn diagram to be invalid.   The matter turns upon the placing of the asterisk for the second premiss.   We have two places it can go.   To show this, we need to use all three circles.

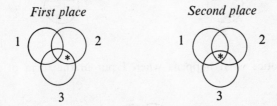

NICKEL: I chose the second place.   Should I have chosen the first place?   And how could I have known which one to choose?

PENNY: You should choose both places when it is possible.   If one of them shows the argument is invalid, it is invalid.   After all, either place is an I Venn sentence form, and if we can place the asterisk in such a way that the conclusion does not follow of necessity, then the argument is invalid.

NICKEL: That's true.   I could have substituted the premisses in this way:

But since such a substitution doesn't provide an asterisk in the first and third circles' overlap, the argument is invalid.   This has been most instructive.

Fourth conversation

111

PENNY: After such encouragement, I think I'll try to equal that piece of instruction with this one. Once more we're concerned with an argument containing a particular premiss that can be represented in two ways.

1   2

Some rhinos are near-sighted beasts.

2   3

All near-sighted beasts are shy.

1   3

Some rhinos are shy.

The form of the first premiss can be represented in two ways.

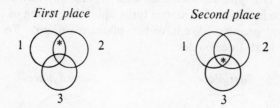

Now notice what happens when I put in the form of the second premiss.

NICKEL: The area where the top asterisk lies is shaded out. You said before that shading an area in effect moves the variable into the area of overlap, which, in this case, is the overlap of 2 and 3.

PENNY: What effect do you think this has on the top asterisk?

NICKEL: When I drew in the first premiss, we saw that some rhino could be in two possible places, but we didn't know which place. I think the second premiss shows us where he is. He's where the bottom asterisk is. I say that because in shading out the part of variable 2 lying outside variable 3, I showed that no near-sighted rhino beasts can be in that place because all near-sighted rhino beasts have been moved by the form term "all" into the overlap of 2 and 3.

I can state this another way by using the erasure rule, the rule that erasing part of a variable is equivalent to shading that part. Placing the second premiss in the argument form by erasing instead of shading, I would get this:

In erasing the area of variable 2 lying outside 3, I also erase the top asterisk. That shows me the only place for near-sighted rhino beasts is in the overlap of 2 and 3.

PENNY: What effect do you think this has on showing the validity of the argument?

NICKEL: It shows the argument is valid, for we see the only place where the near-sighted rhino beast can be found is where the bottom asterisk is—which is, of course, within the area of the third variable, just as the conclusion would have it.

I end up with a near-sighted, shy rhino beast, and I do find that instructive.

PENNY: After those experiments with asterisks that may be substituted into two (or more) places, do you have anything to tell the world about the validity of Venn forms from which we can read two conclusions?

NICKEL: Would you give me an example?

PENNY: Suppose we're given the following premiss forms:

Some 1 are not 2.
No 2 are 3.

Since a syllogism always states a relation between 1 and 2, 2 and 3, and 1 and 3, and since those two premiss forms already state a relation between 1 and 2, and 2 and 3, the conclusion will have to state a relation between 1 and 3.

Taking a look at the Venn form with those premisses

what relation can you read from it about 1 and 3?

NICKEL: Several.

Some 1 are not 3.

Some 1 are 3.

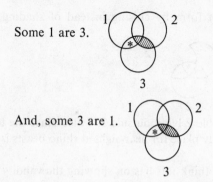

And, some 3 are 1.

The last two sentence forms are identical, I guess, for their Venn forms are identical, although they differ from the first form.

PENNY: Good. You can read two different conclusion forms from that Venn argument form, an O and an I. What does that indicate?

NICKEL: That the argument form is invalid, for it doesn't show me what relation holds between 1 and 3. It shows me that *either* some 1 are not 3 *or* that some 1 are 3; if the argument were valid, it would decide between them which relation holds. Generalization to the world: No Venn argument form is valid if we can read two or more different conclusions from it. Most instructive.

PENNY: Then it was worth it. But was it also amusing?

NICKEL: Somewhat. I recall smiling with pleasure a couple of times. And I've no bruises.

PENNY: Then it was more than worthwhile.

NICKEL: It was quite a circus. I guess the three-ring show takes care of logic in the narrow sense.

PENNY: I don't know if history repeats itself, but you've just shown me opinions do. Other people have expressed the same view: That the syllogism constituted the totality of logic in the narrow sense.

The syllogism does not in fact exhaust logic in the narrow sense. I'd rather wait until tomorrow to discuss that, however.

Today we've learned that we can utilize form better with the Venn Method than we did with the Same-form Method to test the validity of syllogistic arguments; it's easier to see if the regularity necessary for the construction of a syllogistic entailment has been followed.

We've also learned that in the womb of the form words lies the regularity from which entailments spring.

NICKEL: Born fully mature? Like Venus?

PENNY: They rescue man from the obscure silence of sea whispers and the dumb slosh of formless mire by casting him upon the shores of thought on the half-shell.

NICKEL: Why all these images?

PENNY: I'm trying to hedge the form words against common-placeness. In having no referents, they are too poor to nudge our imagination, and, so, they lapse like unloved ghosts. I want to ally them with the vital images of beginnings and fertility and potency.

NICKEL: I'm hooked.

PENNY: We can conclude for today, then.

4.1: I want you to show by the Venn Method the invalidity of Carroll's syllogisms 1, 2, 4, and 6 preceding exercise 3.5.

4.2: That's not enough syllogisms to show your mettle; here are a few more for you to master, Ring Major.

a. All Big Tops are exciting arenas.
   No exciting arenas fail to tempt adventurous youth.
   ———————
   No Big Tops fail to tempt adventurous youth.

b. Some bears are trained to ride bicycles.
   Some animals trained to ride bicycles can walk on their back legs.
   ———————
   Some bears can walk on their back legs.

c. All indigenous life is adapted to its environment.
   Some things adapted to their environment are performing dogs.
   ———————
   Some performing dogs are indigenous life.

d. No army ants live outside insect communities.
   No trained flea is an army ant.
   ———————
   All trained fleas live outside insect communities.

e. All lady trapeze artists have attractive figures.
   Some lady trapeze artists are without vanity.
   ———————
   Some people with attractive figures are without vanity.

f. Every circus performer is honest.
   Some circus performers are not guileless.
   ———————
   Some honest people aren't guileless.

NICKEL: With all these circus topics I feel a little adventurous, too.

PENNY: This next argument should raise you to fever pitch. It's somewhat more extended than a syllogism, but as you'll notice, apparently not completely unrelated. Just for the fun of it, you might shop around for a visual means of showing its validity or invalidity, whichever is the case.

4.3: You may use one or more sets of overlapping variables to determine the validity of this argument; let your fancy or your ability determine what you'll use.

Fourth conversation

All persons directing the action under the Big Top are Ring Masters.
All Ring Masters wear top hats.
All men who wear top hats are fops.
***
All persons directing the action under the Big Top are fops.

Arguments of this type—that is, those using A, E, I, and O sentences but containing more than two premisses—are called "sorites," pronounced, as one logic text has it, to rhyme with "nighties."

4.4: Make up two valid sorites, one of which must contain a negative premiss and one of which must contain a "some" premiss, and show their validity by the means you've designed to handle the sorites in 4.3.

NICKEL: I'm no longer rash enough to say that we have enough logic in the narrow sense to discern all entailments, but I should think we've got enough for practical purposes to cover all syllogistic arguments.

PENNY: There are a couple of obstacles I'd better mention, which will interfere with the practical application. They're of no great difficulty. To be aware of them is almost to master them.

The first obstacle is the enthymeme. An enthymeme is the name of an argument, not an entailment, in which one or more premisses and/or the conclusion is unstated but is understood to be intended.

NICKEL: Isn't it hard to decide sometimes whether they're intended?

PENNY: It is. Most enthymemes fail as entailments; thus, the number of argumentive successes the enthymemer has depends in great part upon our charitableness in crediting to his intention the absent sentences needed for an entailment.

Frequently, of course, the arguer doesn't realize he needs other sentences in order to have an entailment; if he knew what he'd left out, he would certainly have less faith in the truth of his conclusion. You'll notice this when you do the next exercise.

4.5: I want you to supply the premiss (or premisses) missing from each of the following enthymemes that will produce valid arguments.

a. Some people who lead exciting lives aren't interesting.
***
Some circus people aren't interesting.

b. All food sold at the circus is overpriced.
***
Nothing overpriced is bought in quantity.

c. Some barkers are persuasive.
***
Some barkers are fast talkers.

d. No tattooed lady is popular in polite society.
***
Some debutantes are not tattooed ladies.

The other obstacle to the practical application of what you've learned today is discernible in argument f of exercise 4.2.

NICKEL: The only thing out of the ordinary I see there is the "every."

PENNY: That's what I had in mind. In English, most form words have several synonyms.

4.6: I want you to list as many synonyms for the syllogistic form words as you can.

It's getting dark; we must have been here longer than it seemed.

NICKEL: I'd better beat it. The lights don't work on my old heap. Good night, Mr. Penny.

PENNY: Before "Good night" from me, I'll whip out Review Questions.

Review Questions

1. What was Nickel's theory of the difference between form and non-form words? What was Penny's?

2. Do you have the A, E, I, O sentence forms and their names memorized? (If not, you should review them until they are memorized.)

3. What advantage does the Venn way of writing syllogisms have over the English language way?

4. How is Penny's form-non-form theory related to the Venn Method of deciding validity?

5. What is a categorical syllogism?

6. Why isn't a Venn form from which we can read two or more conclusions valid?

7. Distinguish between a Venn sentence and a Venn sentence form.

Fifth conversation

"TRUE" AND "FALSE"
QUA BESTIAE

*Sende nun butt the most cunnyng, yntrepyd, and honeste huntr
mann ynto the jungel to caige eloosyve Tru and wilde Fals.*—
Fanebius Perlyng

PENNY: Good afternoon, Nickel.   What have you got in the package?

NICKEL: A small present I bought for you at the grocery store on my way over.   Open it.

PENNY: Animal crackers?

NICKEL: I don't like the taste of them either, but I had to have some revenge for the horrible nightmares I had last night, all as a result of our talk about animals and the circus yesterday, and from doing the three-ring exercises.

My mind was as full of beasts last night as an African game preserve.

PENNY: In that case, we'd better hunt for domestic varieties today.

I promised you yesterday that we'd discuss some arguments that showed the syllogism doesn't constitute the totality of logic in the narrow sense.   To that end, let me put the following to you.

You've studied algebra and geometry, each of which contains entailments.   Do you recall using the syllogistic entailments very often?

NICKEL: As a matter of fact, I don't.

PENNY: If there are entailments in mathematics, then there must be other forms of entailment than the syllogism.   After all, you don't find the whole world in a circus ring either.

NICKEL: I'd have known there were other argument forms if I had just remembered the argument form you used to show me that "five" and "two" were eliminable words.* It didn't use "all" or "some" or "no"; so, it couldn't have been a syllogism.

PENNY: Here is an entailment in which other than syllogistic form terms are used.

If some ink is black, then some ink can spot white shirts.
Some ink is black.
———————————
Some ink can spot white shirts.

NICKEL: I see a syllogistic form term there: some.

PENNY: Granted.   But as you'll notice, there are other terms there as well.   Here's the form of that argument; it's called *modus ponens*.

If /_____/ then (_____)

/_____/
———————————

(_____)

NICKEL: Do entire sentences go into the variables?   Rather than subject matter terms?

* Reader: See page 97.

PENNY: Yes, and, of course, that's why the syllogistic form term plays no entailment role in that argument other than contributing to the identification of repeated sentences.

NICKEL: You merely mean that if the second premiss had read "All ink is black," then "Some ink is black" wouldn't have been repeated.

PENNY: In which case it wouldn't have fitted into the *modus ponens* form. For similar sentences have to go into similar variables, just as similar subject matter terms had to go into similar variables.

NICKEL: The only words left in the *modus ponens* form are "if" and "then"; I guess they're form terms.

PENNY: We may say they're form terms, provided we find they alter the variables in an argument form in such a way as to help us decide on the validity of the argument form.

NICKEL: The phrase "alter the variables" reminds me of the criterion you used to distinguish the syllogistic form terms from non-form terms. You said then that the form terms are those for which you specified a change in the overlapping circles.

PENNY: Naturally; I want to be consistent. That accounts for the parallelism you just noticed between my criterion for syllogistic form terms and my criterion for deciding whether or not "if" and "then" were form terms.

NICKEL: But you indicated a minute ago that Venn's three-ring circus didn't contain the totality of entailments. Now you mention this parallelism of criteria. I don't know, I'm ——

PENNY: —— confused. You needn't be if you allow that the "variables" we "alter" may certainly be something other than overlapping circles. The lamb of form need not lie down with the lion of overlap.

NICKEL: If the variables are different, I guess we'll have to distinguish between different kinds of form terms.

PENNY: Not in so far as they are form terms. Generically, form terms are simply those for which we can specify alterations in the variables which lead us to detect validity and invalidity. But, as you suggest, we may have different specifications. We have already seen the specifications for the syllogistic form terms. Before I go into the specifications for the next kind, most often called "propositional" form terms, consisting of "if," "then," "and," "or," "if and only if," and the propositional "not," I think it would be the better part of decency not to abandon an old friend.

NICKEL: The Same-form Method?

PENNY: The very one. It is better to go to the ball at the King's palace in a pumpkin than not at all.

Here is an argument whose sentences I want you to eliminate in favor of variables.

If the whale is a mammal, then Pegasus is a mythical winged horse.
Pegasus is a mythical winged horse.
_____
The whale is a mammal.

NICKEL:

If ⟦_____⟧ then (_____)
(_____)
_____
⟦_____⟧

PENNY: You'll admit, won't you, that all the sentences you eliminated were true?

NICKEL: All the sentences that go into the variables are true. But is the whole first premiss a sentence?

PENNY: It is, but being composed of sentences itself it is what logicians call a compound sentence. Any sentence composed of two or more sentences they call a compound sentence.

NICKEL: In that case, not all the sentences in that argument are true, for the compound sentence isn't true. What has Pegasus to do with whales? Just because whales are mammals, it doesn't follow that Pegasus is a mythical winged horse.

PENNY: Of course it doesn't follow; but what clue do you have that would lead you to suppose I thought it did. Do you see any conclusion or premiss indicators in that sentence?

NICKEL: What about "if" and "then"?

PENNY: There's no doubt that they are sometimes used to indicate that the sentence or sentences following "if" are intended as premisses and that the sentences following "then" are intended as a conclusion; however, in the above argument, I had a different use in mind. There I was using "if . . . then . . . " as a means of forming a new sentence, not as a means of forming an argument. With that use I merely intend the sentence or sentences following "if" to be the antecedent of a compound sentence, and the sentence or sentences following "then" to be the consequent.

NICKEL: You don't intend there to be any kind of entailment relation between an antecedent and a consequent?

PENNY: I don't. Nor do I intend a causal relation, as I do in this sentence: If I increase my food consumption, then my weight will increase.

NICKEL: Why don't we call the "if . . . then . . . " use you had in mind in the whale-argument the "propositional use"? That fits in with the phrase "propositional form terms."

PENNY: That's a good name we'll hereby consider adopted. You'll need more than a name, though, to understand why that "if . . . then . . . " sentence is true.

NICKEL: I'd better understand it, for I won't be able to use the Same-form Method to decide on validity until I do. All I know so far is that the truth of the sentence doesn't depend on the presence of an entailment or causal relation between the antecedent and the consequent.

PENNY: Its truth depends on satisfying what I'll call the "hypothetical" relation.

NICKEL: How can I tell whether or not the hypothetical relation is satisfied?

PENNY: Perhaps the following Same-form argument of Sally Jamison's showing the invalidity of the whale-argument will prod discovery.

If /dogs are human beings/ , then (dogs have teeth)

(dogs have teeth)
_____

/dogs are human beings/

NICKEL: If that shows the invalidity of the form, then both premisses have to be true. As for the first premiss: The antecedent of the compound sentence is false and the consequent is true; and there is certainly no entailment or causal relation between them!

It seems most curious to me that the compound sentence is true despite the falsity of the antecedent. Let me think.

PENNY: Permit me to show you a true "if . . . then . . . " sentence that may seem even more curious. "If dogs are human beings, then no jugglers have teeth."

NICKEL: "Curiouser and curiouser," said Alice and Emory. So far an "if . . . then . . . " sentence is true if the antecedent and consequent are true, or if the antecedent is false and the consequent is true, or if both are false as in this last sentence.

That leaves, I believe, only one other case: The one where the antecedent is true and the consequent is false. Maybe if I made a table of those combinations and looked at it long enough . . .

Antecedent	Consequent	Compound	
true	true	true	(whales and Pegasus)
false	true	true	(human dogs and dogs with teeth)
true	false	?	
false	false	true	(human dogs and jugglers without teeth)

The compound conditional is probably not true under all circumstances; so, the "truth" table leads me to believe that when the antecedent is true and the consequent is false the compound is false.

You spoke of a hypothetical relation. There should be a clue in that. When we say something is hypothetical, we suppose or conjecture something.

PENNY: We state something conditionally, not categorically.

NICKEL: OK. Let me try it this way: If *this* is true, then *that* is true. I don't state the truth of "that" categorically, but conditionally upon "this."

PENNY: And remember it is the whole conditional for whose truth and falsity you're accounting.

NICKEL: The whole conditional will be true when my conjecture succeeds. Now if my hunch about the third line on the table is right, that's when the conditional fails and is false; for though I truly suppose "this," the conjectured "that" fails us, being false.

PENNY: Your hunch about the third line is right.

NICKEL: This may be shallow, but it's all I can think of. The hypothetical relation is not satisfied when the antecedent is true and the consequent is false, and it is present in all other cases.

All that comes to mind for justifying that statement is this rephrasing of a conditional: If this is true, then that is true.

PENNY: The third combination in your table, where the antecedent is true and the consequent is false, is a clear violation of your rephrasing, and accounts for the compound's falsity.

But what accounts for the truth of the compound when the antecedent is false as in the second and fourth lines? How do you use your rephrasing to account for the compounds' truth in those cases?

NICKEL: I warned you it may be shallow.

PENNY: So deepen it.

NICKEL: A hypothetical proposition, as with all propositions, is either true or false; the hypothetical relation is either satisfied or not satisfied. OK so far?

PENNY: Nothing is wrong so far.

NICKEL: If the hypothetical proposition isn't false, it must be true.

PENNY: How does that advance your explanation?

NICKEL: I'm trying to get clear about the conditions which must be present for the falsity of a hypothetical. When those conditions are absent, the hypothetical can't be false; and when it's not false, it's true.

Once more the shibboleth: A hypothetical says that *if* this is true, then that is true. I would say that the hypothetical states one of its own conditions for falsity!

124

PENNY: What is it?

NICKEL: The truth of the antecedent.   When the antecedent is false, the condition necessary for the hypothetical's falsity is absent; when the antecedent is false, the hypothetical can't be false; hence, it must be true.

PENNY: Good digging, Nickel.   Making the truth table was a good idea.   For your table, in exhibiting all possible true and false combinations of the antecedent and consequent, fully enumerated the cases where the hypothetical relation was satisfied, the first, second, and fourth cases, and the case where it wasn't, the third.

Do you think you could use the Same-form Method to show an argument containing a hypothetical sentence is invalid?

NICKEL: Try me.

PENNY:

If Vermeer was a French painter, then I smoke cigars.
Vermeer was not a French painter.
_____
I don't smoke cigars.

NICKEL: You slipped some "not's" in on me, but I'll handle them.

If /‾‾‾‾/, then (‾‾‾‾)

not /‾‾‾‾/
_____
not (‾‾‾‾)

Wait a minute!   I don't have to find sentences to show that argument's invalidity.   Your argument convicts itself.   It is false that Vermeer was a French painter and it's true that you do—cough—smoke cigars. That makes both premises true and the conclusion false.

PENNY: Heh, heh.   Quick thinking, Nickel.   Let's go on to the other propositional form terms.

The table was such a useful device that we may as well use it again. Let's start with "and."   In logic, compound sentences using "and," such as "Goethe married his cook and Jack cooked his Mary," are called conjunctions, and their two parts are called conjuncts.   I'll fill in the conjunct columns and you fill in the compound column.

Left conjunct	Right conjunct	Compound
true	true	true
false	true	false
true	false	false
false	false	false

NICKEL: I figure that when I say to a friend "I have $500 in my account and I'll lend you my whole account" and he says "You're not kidding me?" and I reply "No, I'm not," that he'll rely on both conjuncts being true. If one or both are false, I've jeopardized our friendship.

PENNY: All seems in order there. Compound sentences made from "if and only if" such as "An argument is valid if and only if the premises entail the conclusion" are usually called equivalence sentences.

NICKEL: That's the only hint I need. How about this table?

Left equivalent	Right equivalent	Compound
true	true	true
false	true	false
true	false	false
false	false	true

An equivalence compound, extrapolating from the way we used "equivalence" when talking about equivalence conversations, is true only when the equivalents have the same truth value.

PENNY: No cause for correction there. I'll do the table for the disjunctive relation. A disjunctive sentence is formed by using "or." There are two uses of "or," the inclusive use and the exclusive use.

NICKEL: What's the difference between those two uses?

PENNY: A father trying to persuade his youngster to go with him to a second-rate circus might do so by saying "The clowns will be funny or the acrobats will be breathtaking, maybe both." That's the inclusive use. But after they have been at the circus a while, and after the child has eaten excessively, the parent will probably reply to the youngster's request for more food by saying "You can have one more bag of popcorn or a cone of cotton candy, not both." That's the exclusive use.

This is the table for the inclusive use.

Left disjunct	Right disjunct	Compound
true	true	true
false	true	true
true	false	true
false	false	false

The only difference between the truth tables for inclusive disjunction and exclusive disjunction lies in the first line; the compound would be false in the exclusive table's first line; the second, third, and fourth lines are the same.

NICKEL: When I make the table for "not" I'm going to use only two lines.

Proposition	Negated
true	false
false	true

PENNY: That's all you need for negation.

NICKEL: I'm ready to use the Same-form Method now.

PENNY: Here's a form for you to try your skill on.

If /⁃⁃⁃⁃/, then (⁃⁃⁃⁃)

/⁃⁃⁃⁃/ or not (⁃⁃⁃⁃)
——————
(⁃⁃⁃⁃)

NICKEL: I'm surprised to see that form; I wasn't expecting two variables in the second premiss. But since it's formed with "or" and "not," I can think of no objection to it.

PENNY: This will make your job easier: Find a false sentence to place in the conclusion.

NICKEL: That also automatically takes care of the consequent in the first premiss and the right disjunct in the second premiss. Good idea! Then to construct true premisses all I have to worry about is finding a sentence with the proper truth values for the antecedent and left disjunct.

If /⁃⁃⁃⁃/, then (clowns aren't funny)

/⁃⁃⁃⁃/ or not (clowns aren't funny)
——————
(Clowns aren't funny)

To make the hypothetical form with a false consequent into a true sentence, I need to substitute a false antecedent; the fourth line in the hypothetical truth table shows me I have no choice about that.

This can be accomplished with "/bears are hairless/."

PENNY: Because the same sentence must be substituted into all occurrences of the same variable, you have to put "Bears are hairless" into the left disjunct of the second premiss as well. Does that affect the truth of your second premiss?

NICKEL: It won't make any difference to the truth of the second premiss, for that premiss is already true. The second line in the truth table for disjunction shows me that if the right disjunct is true, the compound is true. Clearly, the right disjunct is true, for "not (clowns aren't funny)" is true according to the second line in the truth table for negation.

PENNY: Give me the argument form completely filled in now.

If /bears are hairless/ then (clowns aren't funny)

/bears are hairless/ or not (clowns aren't funny)

————————

(clowns aren't funny)

PENNY: You're sure you haven't slipped up anywhere?

NICKEL: I can check it for you.

If /false/ then (false), which makes the compound premiss true;

/false/ or not (false), which makes the compound premiss true; and

(false), which makes the conclusion false.

PENNY: Clever fellow.

NICKEL: I knew it would check out.

PENNY: I wasn't referring to that. I was referring to the way you checked it. Do you know you could be even cleverer?

NICKEL: How?

PENNY: Your chance would be snatched away in my very telling.

NICKEL: I won't succeed at this rate, anyway.

PENNY: Nevertheless, here's your chance. A verse by Fanebius Perlyng poses the riddle appropriately enough.

> Mann taiks a road; and whenn hee getts,
>   Hee kens where—hee thynks.
> Refluction now!   Hys forhed fretts!
>   Hee wauks abak.   Hee wynks
> Soo slyly, I dyvyne a plan's in skull.
>   Hee kenneth how to chek.
> Mann taiks anoother way.   Soon's hull
>   Has shored, the watry trek
> Has provn hee'd kenne'd where hee'd got.
> Hee'd soon at furst hav rowed as not!

NICKEL: A riddle indeed. I don't think solving a riddle is quite identical to decoding, but it's not far away. Just as I talked about "checking" the first way I showed invalidity, so Fanebius's poem has the fellow "checking" where the first way got him. If the second way took him to the same place as the first and assured him where he'd been as well, he might just as well have gone that way in the first place.

Are you suggesting that I pass up the method of inserting sentences in the variables and insert "true" and "false" instead?

PENNY: Clever fellow! You've made us some new variables.

NICKEL: I thought I'd just filled in the old ones with "true" and "false."

PENNY: You're cleverer than you think. You've caught and domesticated the true and the false. You've made of them the beasts of burden that will bear us to the Byzantium of validity.

NICKEL: I have?

PENNY: Here is an old variable, "⎡＿＿＿＿⎤," and here are some new variables, "⎡true⎤" and "⎡false⎤." The new variables differ from the old in that they are more restrictive. I can place any proposition into the old one, but I place only a true proposition into the left new variable and only a false one into the right new variable.

These new variables lift the burden of finding actual true and false sentences from our shoulders, just as we were freed from that task when we found we needed to attend only to the form of the sentences when we used the Venn Method. The only feature of propositions that is relevant to showing the validity or invalidity of a propositional argument form is their truth value. Your new variables abstract that feature from propositions and let the rest of the proposition go hang. By doing this, we still maintain some generality, for no matter what other features propositions may have, if they are true, any one of them may be substituted into "(true)." The same holds for "(false)."

NICKEL: Can it be that these new variables lead us to identify the form terms in these propositional arguments? It was at about this same point that we were led to identify the form terms in syllogistic arguments. But I might be getting ahead of the game.

PENNY: You're synchronized, Nickel. Recall that we said form terms were those which altered the variables in such a way that under some circumstances the alterations produce valid arguments.

I gave you the Venn cipher yesterday which told you how to alter the circle variables for each form term. What have we done today for propositional form terms which is comparable to the Venn cipher?

NICKEL: My guess is that the truth tables are comparable, for they specify the conditions of change. For example, "If ⎡false⎤ then (true)" changes by the hypothetical truth table to "⟩true⟨," while "⎡false⎤ and (true)" changes by the conjunctive truth table to "⟩false⟨."

PENNY: Very good, Nickel. Have an animal cracker.

NICKEL: No thanks. But I'll get you another box if you'll answer this next question. Can I find out by this new variable method that arguments are valid as well as invalid? It should show that also, if this method is to have the same advantages over the Same-form Method for propositional arguments that the Venn Method had over it for syllogistic arguments.

PENNY: It should and can. Let's take the *modus ponens* form. You show its validity. (You should do it before reading on, Reader.— Emory Nickel)

NICKEL:

If /_____/ then (_____)

/_____/

_____

(_____)

First, I'll make the conclusion a variable into which I can substitute only false sentences. Must I do that first?

PENNY: Whether you start by making the premisses true or by making the conclusion false is arbitrary. It's just easier to start with the conclusion when it is a single variable; you have no choice except to make it a false variable.

NICKEL:

If /_____/ then (false)

/_____/

_____

(false)

I get this form because the consequent of the first premiss, by being a variable similar to the conclusion, must be changed concomitantly.

Next, in order to have all premisses true, I obviously have to make the second premiss a variable into which only a true proposition can go. That commits me to a similar operation on the antecedent of the first premiss.

If /true/ then (false)   —   )false(, according to the third line in the
                                            hypothetical truth table.
/true/   /true/

_____   _____

(false)   (false)

To show the invalidity of the *modus ponens* argument form, I have to show it is possible to make both premisses true and the conclusion false. But the specifications for variable changes given in the "if . . . then . . . " truth table force me to make the first premiss false; hence, I see it is impossible to show the invalidity of the argument form. And if it's impossible to show it is invalid, it must be valid.

Assuming that every argument is either valid or invalid, and not both, this method shows an argument form is valid by showing that invalidity is impossible.

PENNY: We can conclude for today, then.

NICKEL: I presume the exercises you're going to give me will be about arguments using propositional form words. Before you give them to me, I'd like you to check my efforts at changing the variables according to the truth table specifications.

(true) if and only if /false/ — }false{, according to the third line in the equivalence truth table.

)true(and /true/ — ⟦true⟧, according to the first line in the conjunction truth table.

not (true) — {false}, according to the first line in the negation truth table.

PENNY: You've got the idea. I'm going to be generous by giving you the following ten propositional argument forms.

1. /___/ if and only if (___)

   not (___)

   ___

   not /___/

2. (___) and /___/

   not /___/ or not (___)

   ___

   (___)

3. If /___/ then (___)

   /___/ and)___(

   ___

   (___)

4. If (___) then /___/

   /___/ and not (___)

   ___

   If)___(then /___/

5. (___) and /___/

   ___

   /___/ if and only if (___)

6. not (___)

   /___/ or (___)

   ___

   /___/

7. If ( ) then /⎡⎤/
   If /⎡⎤/ then) (
   ─────────
   If ( ) then) (

8. If ( ) then /⎡⎤/
   If /⎡⎤/ then) (
   ─────────
   If not)⎡⎤(then not ( )

9. not ( ) or /⎡⎤/
   not /⎡⎤/
   ─────────
   ( )

10. ( ) if and only if /⎡⎤/
    /⎡⎤/ or ( )
    not ( )
    ─────────
    not /⎡⎤/

5.1: I want you to use—What shall we call it, the Truth-table Method?—of showing the validity or invalidity of the ten argument forms.

NICKEL: By that method, I guess you mean me to place "true" and "false" into the variables and then alter them by the rules given in the truth tables until I have arrived at a decision about their validity.

PENNY: Yes, do the kind of thing you did with the *modus ponens* argument form I gave you just prior to the ten forms for 5.1.

5.2: The second argument form is an interesting one because the premisses are contradictory; that is, not both of them can be true and not both can be false. Use the Truth-table Method to show that the premisses in the second form are contradictory.

5.3: Here are three pairs of sentence forms. Using the Truth-table Method, show which pairs are contradictory and which are not.

1. (a) If /⎡⎤/ then ( )
   (b) not ( ) and /⎡⎤/

2. (a) /⎡⎤/ and not ( )
   (b) ( ) or not /⎡⎤/

3. (a) /⎡⎤/ if and only if ( )
   (b) /⎡⎤/ and not ( ), or ( ) and not /⎡⎤/

5.4: Consider each pair of contradictory sentence forms in 5.3 as the premisses of an argument form. For each such pair of premisses, write a conclusion sentence form that follows validly from the premisses.

5.5: Determine by the Truth-table Method which of the following arguments spun by Even and Odd are valid and which are invalid. You

132

realize, of course, that you'll have to determine the form of the sentences before you can use the Truth-table Method; that is, you'll have to replace the sentences related by the form terms with variables related by the form terms, and the same sentences have to be replaced by the same variables.

Here are a couple of examples.

A. (a) Knighthood is in flower if and only if a mace does not crush the flower's skull.

(b) ⟋_____⟋ if and only if not (_____)

B. (a) If Eve hadn't eaten the apple or God weren't omniscient, then we'd be living in Paradise.

(b) If not ⟋_____⟋ or not (_____), then ⟍_____⟍

1. *Even:* If you have no fame and need a memorial to remind people you once existed, then you'd better buy a long-lasting, granite headstone for your grave.
   Odd: I do need a memorial to remind people I once existed.
   Even: And you have no fame.
   Odd: I conclude that I'd better buy a long-lasting, granite headstone for my grave.

2. *Even:* A code correlates the rules of regularity of two languages or the application of the code to a language does not yield sensical expressions in the other language.
   Odd: The application of a code to a language yields sensical expressions in the other language if and only if the code enables us to translate poetry.
   Even: But we cannot translate poetry.
   Odd: That proves a code does not correlate the rules of regularity of two languages.

3. *Even:* My argument has two premises and the conclusion is self-contradictory.
   Odd: If the conclusion is self-contradictory, then the conclusion is necessarily false.
   Even: My argument form is valid.
   Odd: If your argument form is valid and the conclusion is necessarily false, then your premises are contradictory.
   Even: That shows my argument has two premises and my premises are contradictory.

4. *Even:* If there are innocent beings with souls on other planets, then to kill them is to commit murder.

Odd: If there are innocent beings with souls on other planets, then they do not look like humans.

Even: Hence, if we discover they do look like humans, then to kill them is not to commit murder.

5.6: Is every argument form with contradictory premiss forms valid? Give an argument for your answer and show that your argument is valid.

5.7: One more exercise before we quit: List as many synonyms for the form terms "if . . . then . . . ," "and," "or," "if and only if," and "not" as you can.

NICKEL: I'd better beat it. The lights on my old heap don't work. Remember? Good night, Mr. Penny.

PENNY: Before "Good night" from me, I'll whip out Review Questions.

Review Questions

1. What are the propositional form terms? Do you know the truth table of each? (If not, you should review them until they are memorized.)

2. Can capital letters, such as "A," "B," and "C," be variables as well as "_____," "(_____)," and ")_____("?

3. Why are the truth tables of the propositional form words important for the visual testing of arguments?

4. What is the logically important difference between these two variables?

/_____/   /false/

Sixth conversation

PHILOSOPHY AND LOGIC IN THE WIDE SENSE

Wurds, Wurds, Wurds!—Fanebius Perlyng.

NICKEL: Good day, sir. I hope you're feeling as refreshed as I am.

PENNY: I had thought the art of using more than one word in a greeting had passed. It unfortunately has come to be embarrassing to extend our greeting beyond "Hi" or "H'lo", unless we do so in jest. Is the loss of dignity worth the gain in humor?

NICKEL: I ——

PENNY: But then perhaps I simply lack Sir Tobey's vision-in-the-cups—Well, it's all one.

And good day to you, good Nickel. I am feeling fresh and perhaps more excited.

NICKEL: Why is that?

PENNY: Why, today we set out on an enterprise of high purpose. Today we shall set logic on its highroad to philosophy.

NICKEL: Logic in the narrow sense. Right?

PENNY: That's what I said the other day.

NICKEL: And what do you say today?

PENNY: I still say that I want to show how we can make a philosophic score with the ideal language of logic in the narrow sense as well as a civic-virtue and technical score, how studying it is for the good of your soul.

NICKEL: And why an introduction to logic is the best introduction to philosophy?

PENNY: It's all one. You should have some intimations of what's to come, now that you have some idea of logic in the narrow sense.

NICKEL: I think I understand the last three conversations. But I didn't notice any ideal language of logic in the narrow sense. Is that still to come, or are Polish and Principia such a language?

PENNY: Hush!

NICKEL: In the last three conversations we've related logic in the narrow sense to English. Why don't we do that for Polish and Principia? I've done Polish-Principia exercises, but I'm continually plagued by the fact that I don't know the meaning of their vocabularies; I don't know what the vocabularies are about. I know I've complained about this before.

PENNY: You complained about it the first day, in fact.

NICKEL: Yes, and I remember you assured me that my not knowing their meaning wouldn't prevent me from doing the exercises.

PENNY: I did. Apparently I have to say something else, for what I said then hasn't satisfied you.

Don't forget that the subject of logic is regularity. We are interested in the regularity of inscriptions and sounds, inscriptions made of ink or lead which you can see printed or written on paper, or voice sounds heard through the ear. We are not interested in studying anything other than their relative positions to one another. Our study of ciphers showed us there are only two kinds of rules of regularity—substitution and arrangement rules.

You do not have to know the "meaning" of the inscriptions and sounds in order to observe and catalogue their relative positions, do you? You saw that in our conversations about logic in the narrow sense. Validity was found by ignoring meaning, by replacing meaningful English expressions with variables; validity was a matter of form, of substitution and arrangement, alone. Don't worry about meaning; its irrelevant.

NICKEL: As I said, I realize that. I only bring it up again because I think I could do the exercises more easily if I knew the meaning or the use of the characters and their combinations.

PENNY: You still fail to take seriously a connection we have discussed at some length. We have talked considerably about the relation between meaning and regularity, about the dependence of meaning upon regularity. What if the dependence were extreme? What if the meaning of any character or combination of characters were fully known if we fully knew all the regularities governing it?

NICKEL: There would be no point in complaining about not knowing the meaning, as I just did. For in learning the regularities I am learning the meaning. But is that extreme dependence true of meaning?

PENNY: You admitted as much the other day when you agreed that another person means the same thing by a sentence as you do if his class of responses to it is the same as yours. In conversation every man checks another's sentences against the only regularity available to him, his own cornucopia. If you find matching regularities, you know the other person means the same thing by a sentence that you do.

NICKEL: But all this tells me is that a sentence has the same meaning for him as for me. I want to know what meaning it has for me.

PENNY: The same meaning it has for him.

NICKEL: You've led me in a merry circle, Mr. Penny. I'm serious.

PENNY: So am I. I'm not putting you off to needle you, Nickel. You should entertain the thought that you're asking for the impossible. You've got too much faith in nouns.

Because "meaning" is used as a noun, you think there are objects called "meanings." Further, I suspect, you think that, though they can be expressed in language, they aren't themselves verbal, that they exist independently of language. This leads you to conclude that though language is dependent on regularity, meanings, being non-verbal, aren't dependent on regularity. What about it, Nickel?

NICKEL: Well . . .

Sixth conversation

PENNY: Look here. When someone asks you for the meaning of something you said, what do you do?

NICKEL: I tell him what I meant.

PENNY: You *tell* him. And what do you use to tell him? Words! That's what. And how does he know what they mean? More words now? Sure. But there is nothing magical about the new words. They can't express or be *the* meaning any more than the ones the person didn't understand. They're just words, too. And can't somebody ask what they mean?

NICKEL: Wellll . . .

PENNY: If you say what they mean, you use more words. Where are you going to stop? Huh?

NICKEL: You've made your point, Mr. Penny.

PENNY: But let me try again. You think talking is like a baseball game. We advance, in your view, from one verbal base to another until we finally score at a non-verbal home plate. That's the wrong idea; there is no such home plate; communicating is simply going from one base to another, and this doesn't require objects called "meanings"; it only requires matching regularities.

When I don't know what somebody means, I can't match regularities, so he gives me another expression which he hopes is familiar enough to permit matching. That's all. I'm afraid the phrase "What I meant was. . . . " lures a lot of bad philosophy. That phrase is usually followed by words so familiar we forget they are words. Because we unconsciously convert mere familiarity into transparency, we believe we see through them to meaning itself.

NICKEL: I still can't help thinking regularity can't be the whole story. Your argument would be decisive except that you ignore something pretty important. You ignore the fact that sentences are made up of words which have meaning. When I understand the meaning of all the words in a sentence, I understand the meaning of the sentence.

It seems to me that sentences' meanings also depend on the meanings of words, not just their regular place in cornucopias.

PENNY: Then to make my point about the dependence of sentential meaning on regularity seem plausible to you, we'll have to show the dependence of words' meanings on *their* regularity.

NICKEL: That would be very convincing.

PENNY: It's also complicated; we can't finish the topic today or tomorrow, but we can bring out enough considerations today to lend the view plausibility. And it won't slow our effort to show how an introduction to logic in the narrow sense is related to philosophy. In fact it fits right in with the next step: Showing how logic in the wide sense is related to philosophy.

What kind of a book would you think that you had picked up if the index had word entries like the following: God, cause, mind, body, analogy, good, evil, self-contradictory, pleasure, existence, infinite, experience, reason, meaning, concept?

NICKEL: I would think it was a philosophy book.

PENNY: And what would you expect from the body of the work?

NICKEL: I would expect that the philosopher would be talking about God, cause, good, evil, existence, etc.

PENNY: That is, you would take the words in the index to be names.

NICKEL: Sure. They are names of the objects he is going to talk about.

PENNY: Then the body of the work will consist of propositions.

NICKEL: It will consist of propositions that the philosopher thinks are *true* propositions. And the true propositions will be about the objects named by those words which you listed.

PENNY: You seem to picture the philosopher as you would the scientist, as one who investigates the objects referred to by words and tries to find out and state the truth about the objects.

NICKEL: Yes, I guess so. Aren't philosophers like scientists?

PENNY: You realize that we are speaking loosely now, but I would say that philosophers are more like logicians in the wide sense than like scientists.

NICKEL: Logicians in the wide sense?

PENNY: We distinguished between logic in the wide sense and the narrow sense.

NICKEL: So we should distinguish between logicians in the wide and narrow sense?

PENNY: Why not?

NICKEL: I suppose you can compare philosophers to logicians in the wide sense because you think that philosophers study linguistic regularity.

PENNY: That's right. Son, in the mansion of logic (in the wide sense) are many chambers. One of these chambers, as you should recall, is logic in the narrow sense. Another chamber is＿＿＿.

NICKEL: Philosophy?

PENNY: You shall inherit the earth. You will remember we said that a language is a sum total of all its possible expressions.

NICKEL: Letter expressions, syllable expressions, word expressions, phrase expressions, sentence and proposition expressions, and inference and argument expressions.

PENNY: And what filled most of the space in the chamber of logic in the narrow sense?

NICKEL: Its primary interest is in entailments.

PENNY: And it aims to get knowledge of the way in which propositions have to be combined in order to yield entailments.

What mainly fills the chamber of philosophy is meaningfully formed sentences and propositions.

NICKEL: To keep the parallel going I would then have to say that philosophy aims to get knowledge of the way in which *words* have to be combined in order to yield meaningful sentences and propositions.

PENNY: Compare these two expressions:

> Example C: The heart is below the soul.
> Example D: The heart is below the lung.

In both cases we have familiar words combined to form a grammatically recognizable expression.

NICKEL: Yes, but Example C seems to me nonsensical, while Example D seems to yield sense.

PENNY: Why do you think that is the case?

NICKEL: Because "soul" isn't usually combined with "below."

PENNY: But we say, "His soul went up to heaven and her soul went below—to hell."

NICKEL: Well, we never combine it with "heart."

PENNY: But we say, "He threw his heart and soul into the affair, and lost them both, alas."

NICKEL: We don't combine "soul" with "heart" and "below." Try to find a sentence for them!

PENNY: "The heart is below the lung or the soul." What about that?

NICKEL: That's for philosophy to figure out. You just said that kind of thing was its business.

PENNY: Why don't you try whistling *Lillabullero*?

NICKEL: What good would that do?

PENNY: The same good it did Uncle Toby. Now you try to give me a sentence in which there is a violation of the rules governing the combination of words.

NICKEL: Monkey is telephone.

PENNY: How true.

NICKEL: What's true?

PENNY: That monkey is telephone.

NICKEL: Why do you kid around?

PENNY: Who's kidding around?

NICKEL: You are.

PENNY: How do you know I am?

NICKEL: Because "Monkey is telephone" doesn't make sense and you just acted as if it did.

PENNY: Code. Code. How do you know it is not a regular combination for me? Just because it is not a regular combination for you doesn't prove anything about my regularities.

NICKEL: I forgot so soon.

PENNY: But suppose you wanted to find out if I meant anything by "monkey" and "telephone," and if I did, what I meant. How would you go about finding out these two things?

NICKEL: I imagine I would have to get you to use those words some more, to put them in more sentences, that is, to combine them with other words whose regular rules of combination I know. Then I could form a hypothesis about their meaning, and thus, use the inductive method to see if you and I have a common meaning.

PENNY: Very good. Let me write down some such sentences now, and then you try to figure out what I meant by those words. "Everybody is monkeying so loud I can't hear what you're saying." "I monkeyed with my sister on the telephone the other night." "Animals can't monkey." "Children learn to monkey at the age of 1½ to 2 years." "I told her I was so mad at her that I wouldn't ever monkey to her again." "We had a very pleasant monkey the other day."

"She's nothing but a telephone little tart." "That's the telephonest place I know of around here." "How telephone can you get?" "This one is telephoner than that one, although it's of much better quality." "Don't be a telephone-skate."

NICKEL: In order to use the inductive method, I have to form a hypothesis which can be tested. Suppose I substitute "pounding" for "monkey."

PENNY: Do you think that has some plausibility?

NICKEL: I do, for that would give me "Everybody is pounding so loud I can't hear what you're saying." I can check this by the following hypothesis.

If Penny uses "monkey" as I use "pound,"
then in whatever sentence he uses "monkey" I can
substitute "pound" (adding similar endings),
thereby producing a meaningful sentence.

PENNY: And what happens to your hypothesis?

NICKEL: Whoops. I find it disconfirmed, for it's nonsensical to say "I pounded with my sister on the telephone the other night."

PENNY: That doesn't sound nonsensical.

NICKEL: I'm assuming telephone doesn't mean what it usually does.

PENNY: You can't be sure it doesn't.

NICKEL: That's right. At least it would be nonsensical to say "I told her I was so mad at her that I wouldn't ever pound to her again."

PENNY: So you had better try to substitute another word, try to frame another hypothesis.

NICKEL: "Shouting?" "Everybody is shouting so loud I can't hear what you're saying." That won't do either, because then I would have "Children learn to shout at the age of $1\frac{1}{2}$ to 2 years," and we know they learn before that.

PENNY: That last sentence is merely false, not nonsensical. It's a perfectly permissible combination, so it doesn't eliminate the possibility that "monkey" means "shout."

NICKEL: At least it's nonsensical to say "We had a very pleasant shout the other day."

PENNY: Maybe that's a matter of taste. Or maybe you've just never heard a pleasant shout, only unpleasant shouts.

NICKEL: It's impossible for a shout to be pleasant.

PENNY: Just because you never heard one that was——

NICKEL: Not that. I simply mean that I wouldn't call anything a shout if it was pleasant.

PENNY: That seems to me an interesting reply. You in effect are appealing to a rule of *non*-combination. So not only are there rules of combination, but there are also rules of non-combination; rules of sense and rules of *non*sense.

NICKEL: Isn't that reasonable enough? Isn't it as important to decide that a combination is nonsensical as to decide that it is sensical?

PENNY: Of course; I just never thought of it that way before. But now, let me ask you this. Is this rule of non-combination just your rule, or is it more general? If it is just yours, is it really a rule? If it is more general, how do you verify that it is?

NICKEL: Hmmm. Those are tough questions. But I can see that they are crucial to the whole logical enterprise, including both logic in the narrow sense and philosophy, for in order to get knowledge of regularity we have to know what is to be considered an instance of regularity.

PENNY: You see correctly. Let's hold those questions in abeyance for awhile; I only brought it up now because I thought you would appreciate their force best at this point.

NICKEL: Genetic order flourishes.

PENNY: Let's finish off the meaning of "monkey" and "telephone."

NICKEL: I think I see that "monkey" means "talk." If I substitute "talk" for "monkey" in every sentence, no sentence is nonsensical and all are sensical.

And "telephone" is easy now. It means cheap. The last sentence is a giveaway—"Don't be a cheap-skate." "Monkey is telephone" is the same as "Talk is cheap."

PENNY: You should have a good enough idea now of what I mean by "philosophy" to contrast the main business of the scientist and the philosopher.

NICKEL: I think so. Whereas a scientist's interest in word expressions is as expressions which refer to objects, a philosopher's interest in word expressions is in their *sensical combination*. And whereas a scientist is interested in asserting true propositions about the objects referred to by the words, the philosopher is interested in asserting true propositions about the words themselves, about the way in which words combine to yield sensical sentences.

PENNY: That's very good. I'm going to write down two sentences, one of them a philosophic sentence and the other a scientific sentence. Tell me which is which.

Proper nutrition for the body is required to prevent rickets.

"Body" is often used synonymously with "living physical object."

NICKEL: The first is scientific and the second philosophic.

PENNY: Yes, and do you notice a physical difference in the two sentences?

NICKEL: The second sentence contains quotation marks and the first does not.

PENNY: We can use the distinction between an object-language and a meta-language to state the difference between the scientists' and philosophers' enterprise. Anyway, "we can" if you can.

NICKEL: I think "we can." Philosophy is an enterprise which mentions the object-language or items in it, whereas the scientist uses the object-language. Thus, scientific discourse is in the object-language and philosophic discourse is in the meta-language.

PENNY: You're a regular rocket today, Nickel.

NICKEL: Far out, huh? But I'm not far enough out to see how your conception of philosophy is related to what I and, according to what you said earlier, many philosophers have thought philosophy was. Or maybe they're not related.

PENNY: If you picked up a book that contained the following word entries in the index, what kind of book would you think you had picked up: Accounts payable, annuities, cash, bonds, depletion, surplus, interest, sales, profit, installments?

NICKEL: An accounting or economics book.

PENNY: There are some words that are "philosophic" and others that are not. My notion of philosophy is allied to your conception by the fact that both are interested in "philosophic" words, not, for example, accounting words.

NICKEL: How can we tell which word expressions are philosophic and which are not?

PENNY: I don't know of an explicit criterion we apply.

NICKEL: Is it important to have one?

PENNY: I'm not sure we need any other than the historical distinctions. Even if it should turn out that part of the work in every field of study involves what philosophy does, our knowledge of tradition may be all we need to distinguish among, for example, philosophic, accounting, sociological, and mathematical words.

NICKEL: At any rate, the connection between your conception of philosophy and the more traditional one still seems tenuous. Talking about words seems a lot different from talking about objects, even if you talk about words that have traditionally been called philosophic words.

PENNY: Would you think it was so tenuous if I could show you that the traditional philosophers have always done what I think the "new" philosopher should do?

NICKEL: Do you mean to say they didn't know what they were doing?

PENNY: I don't mean to imply that. They might very well have known that they were doing one thing, but they might also have been doing something else they were not aware of doing, or that they didn't think was important. When a boy plays games, he knows that he's playing games and that he's trying to win; but he might also be learning about fair play and developing his body and not know that he is doing so.

NICKEL: How does this apply to philosophy?

PENNY: There might be *two* ways to look at a philosopher's sentences and you might be looking at them in only one way. Somebody might ask you what Spinoza's concept of God was; or he might ask you about Plato's concept of the Good; or you might be asked to write an examination question on Aristotle's concept of tragedy. Would such questions seem to fall outside the confines of traditional philosophy?

NICKEL: I don't think so.

PENNY: Suppose somebody did ask you those questions, how would you find out the answers to them?

NICKEL: In other words, how would I find out what their concepts about God, the Good, and tragedy were?

PENNY: Yes; what steps would you take?

NICKEL: I'd read what they had to say about them.

PENNY: How would you know that you were reading what they had to say about them?

NICKEL: Well, how do you usually know?

PENNY: Yes, how *do* you usually know?

NICKEL: I look for the sentences in which the key word, "God," or "the Good," or "tragedy," appears.

PENNY: How will looking at them help you to find out what their concepts were?

NICKEL: I distinctly feel a force pushing me.

PENNY: What do you mean?

NICKEL: Well, you're pushing logic and you wouldn't bring these questions up unless you wanted to force me into saying something about observing the way in which the philosophers regularly combine the key words with other words.

PENNY: Why are you reluctant to commit yourself to that?

NICKEL: Because I think the way to find out what their concepts of God, the Good, and tragedy are is by observing what they believe can be said *truly* about God, the Good, and tragedy. And that's not what you want me to think.

PENNY: It's not that I want to *force* you to a position.

NICKEL: What then?

PENNY: It's my argument which must force you. We are committed to dia-logic—not persuasion, friend. Now, what is it specifically that you think the argument will force you to think?

NICKEL: Well, I think you believe the argument will force me to say that finding out what Spinoza's, Plato's, or Aristotle's concept is is the same as finding out how they think the key words have to be combined in order to yield meaningful sentences.

PENNY: And you think that to find their concepts you must look for those sentences in which the key words appear, sentences which they believe can be asserted truly.

NICKEL: That's right; and "truly" and "meaningfully" aren't the same.

PENNY: Why do you say that?

NICKEL: If "truly" and "meaningfully" meant the same thing, then every time we used a word meaningfully we would automatically be using it truly. But a word can be used meaningfully in a false sentence.

PENNY: You're right, and my point depends upon their being distinguished.

NICKEL: What point?

PENNY: That a philosopher's sentences may be looked at in two ways.

NICKEL: You apparently tried to get at two ways of looking at philosophers' sentences when you asked me how I would find out what a philosopher's concept of anything was.

PENNY: And we have got at them.

NICKEL: We have?

PENNY: Yes, for it's clear you look at a philosopher's sentences as if they showed what he believes can be asserted truly. And I look at them as if they showed how he believes a word can be combined meaningfully.

Notice also that those two ways of looking at sentences produce two different interpretations of "concept of." I asked you how you would find out what a philosopher's concept of, say, tragedy was. In response to the question "What is X's concept of Y?" you reply by listing those propositions which X thinks can be asserted truly of Y.

In response to the question "What is X's concept of Y?" I would reply by listing the permissible ways X thinks the word Y may be combined.

NICKEL: I get it. We can look at a philosopher's sentences either as propositions revealing what he believes to be true, or we can look at them as sentences revealing what he believes to be permissible ways in which Y may be combined.

And you are advocating that we look at a philosopher's sentences in the second way, as yielding the second kind of concept.

If I have your notion of "concept" straight, you would identify the concept Y with all the permissible ways in which X thinks the word "Y" may be combined. And you would say, I think, that someone can be said to have the concept Y if he knows how to combine the expression Y with other expressions so that the new, bigger unit of expression yields sense.

PENNY: Let's call this the *combinatory* interpretation of "concept of," and we'll call yours the *propositional* interpretation.

NICKEL: Now if we are to see the connection between the "older" and the "new" philosophers who resemble logicians we are to——

PENNY: Simply read the older philosophers in my way, in addition to, or instead of, your way.

There's nothing recondite about this way of reading traditional philosophy. It's no different in nature than what you did in trying to figure out my concept of "monkey" and "telephone" in "Monkey is telephone."

NICKEL: So now, do you think I have been shown how the "new" philosophy is related to the more traditional philosophy?

PENNY: Haven't you?

NICKEL: I'm not sure.

PENNY: Look. Given that the "new" philosophy is concerned with combinatory concepts, we can relate traditional philosophy to the "new" philosophy if we read the traditional philosophers' sentences in such a way as to make them yield their combinatory concepts.

NICKEL: I get the connection all right. I think I'm reluctant about

146

the relation because I don't see how a person can have a combinatory concept of, for example, "tragedy," how a person can use it in a sentence without any consideration of what the word refers to. I think a person first has to know what "tragedy" is about; and if he knows what it's about, then he must know something true about it.

PENNY: In other words, you have doubts that there really are two ways to look at sentences?

NICKEL: I admit there might be two ways to look at them, but I'm not sure they're independent of one another. Earlier today we were talking about the total dependence of a word's meaning on its regular combinations with other words. After having talked about "telephone" and "monkey," you've certainly shown me that the view has some plausibility.

Still, I can't help thinking the meaning of a word does depend in part on what it's about and not totally on its combinatory regularities. I'm not sure we can read sentences in a purely combinatory way.

PENNY: As I said, this is a complicated topic. We won't finish analyzing the full meaning of "the meaning of a word" today, so I'm not surprised you're reluctant to admit it means the same as "combinatory concept."

But I do think we can satisfy ourselves on one point today: that combinatory concepts are independent of propositional concepts.

NICKEL: It's going to take a lot to satisfy me.

PENNY: Not if you realize how modest my distinction between combinatory and propositional concepts is.

NICKEL: Trying to lull me into a modest sense of loss, eh?

PENNY: Not at all. You yourself said a minute ago that "truly" and "meaningfully" don't mean the same, that a word can be used meaningfully in a false sentence. To be consistent, you have to admit combinatory concepts are independent of propositional concepts.

NICKEL: You'll have to explain why I'd be inconsistent if I didn't admit that.

PENNY: To honor your distinction between "truly" and "meaningfully," you have to admit that, though you know no true propositions about an object, you can still know the meaning of the false sentences containing the word which refers to the object. You couldn't know the meaning of the false sentences if you didn't know the meaning of the word.

NICKEL: I did say the meaning of a sentence depends in part on the meaning of all its words.

PENNY: But if you know no true propositions about the object, you don't have a propositional concept of it; in that case, the meaning of the word can't be dependent on a propositional concept. And what other kind of meaning is there left for the word to have than combinatory meaning?

NICKEL: How can I get out of this argument?

PENNY: One way is to allow yourself more kinds of meaning than combinatory and propositional meaning.

NICKEL: What do you suggest?

PENNY: How about acquaintance meaning? You might claim that though you know no true propositions about an object, acquaintance, that is, sensory observation of, the object to which the word refers is still possible, and that this acquaintance with the object, or the memory of it, gives meaning to the word and the false sentences.

NICKEL: That way I can save my "truly"-"meaningfully" distinction because meaning wouldn't be dependent on truth and propositional concepts; it would be dependent partly on acquaintance.

PENNY: At the same time, you don't have to admit that a word's meaning consists wholly of combinatory meaning.

I detect another way for you to get out of the argument. You can simply deny one can know the meaning of false sentences containing a certain word without having known at least one true sentence containing the word.

NICKEL: But wouldn't that make me inconsistent again?

PENNY: This tack is actually a retreat, a retreat to an amended, weakened version of your "truly"-"meaningfully" distinction. With this version you would hold that truth and meaning are distinct except when the word's meaning is first learned.

This can fit into what I take to be your view. I take it you think that part of a word's meaning is what a person has in mind when he uses it, and that what we usually have in mind is the object referred to by the word. To have the object in mind is to think about it; but one can't be thinking about it unless one thinks something true of it. What one thinks truly of it is expressible by a true proposition.

NICKEL: As usual, you know my view better than I do. It does seem obvious to me that a person can't be thinking about the object referred to if all his thoughts are false. In that case he has some other object in mind. So, for once in his life, as you say, when he learns the word's meaning, he must, to be able to think of the object at all rather than some other object, know something true of it.

What do you think of these two ways out of your argument?

PENNY: We don't need to assess them now. Even if they got you out of the difficulty, they wouldn't touch my point, which is a more modest one. I'm only arguing now that combinatory meaning is independent of propositional meaning, which is much more modest than saying that combinatory meaning is the only kind of meaning there is.

Do you remember how the issue you're arguing for arose in the first place?

NICKEL: It arose out of my complaint about doing Polish-Principia exercises without knowing the referents of the vocabulary.

PENNY: Just as some combinations of English words don't result in *bona fide* English sentences, so some Polish and Principia combinations don't result in *bona fide* Polish and Principia expressions.

What would be the consequence for the relation between combinatory and propositional meaning if you were able to decide which Polish and Principia combinations were *bona fide* Polish and Principia expressions without knowing the referents of their vocabularies?

NICKEL: The consequence of that would be to show me that the combinatory meaning of Polish and Principia expressions is independent of propositional meaning.

PENNY: To lead up to your first exercise, here are some Polish and Principia combinations. In the first and third columns are well-formed expressions, *wfe*, for short, and in the second and fourth columns are non-well-formed expressions, non-*wfe*. For the present I omit bars; they'll be easier to handle later.

1. $*pq$ $f\alpha\beta$	$*p$ $f\alpha$	1'. $(p{\supset}q)$ $m\alpha f\,\beta m$	$p{\supset}$ αf
2. p α	pq $\alpha\beta$	2'. p α	pq $\alpha\beta$
3. vpq $f\alpha\beta$	pqv $\alpha\beta f$	3'. $(p{v}q)$ $m\alpha f\beta m$	(pqv) $m\alpha\beta fm$
4. $v\cdot pqr$ $f\alpha\beta$ $f\ \ \alpha\ \ \beta$	$v\cdot pq$ $f\alpha\beta$ $f\ \ \alpha$	4'. $[\,(p.q)\,vr\,]$ $m\alpha f\beta m$ $m\ \ \alpha\ \ f\beta m$	$(p.q)v$ $m\alpha f\beta m$ $\alpha\ \ f$
5. $vp\cdot qr$ $f\alpha\beta$ $f\alpha\ \ \beta$	$vpqr$ $f\alpha\beta$ $\alpha\ \ \beta$	5'. $[\,p{v}(q.r)\,]$ $m\alpha f\beta m$ $m\alpha f\ \ \beta\ \ m$	$[\,(p{v}q)r\,]$ $m\alpha f\beta m$ $m\ \ \alpha\ \ \beta m$
6. $vr\cdot pq$ $f\alpha\beta$ $f\alpha\ \ \beta$	$v.*$ fff	6'. $[\,r{v}(p.q)\,]$ $m\alpha f\beta m$ $m\alpha f\ \ \beta\ \ m$	$v.{\supset}$ $ff\,f$

7. *. ※ *pqrp*

$f\ \alpha\beta$

$\underline{f\quad \alpha\ \beta}$

$f\quad \alpha\quad \beta$

7'. $\{\,[\,(p\equiv q)\cdot r\,]\supset p\}$

$m\alpha\,f\,\beta m$

$\underline{m\quad \alpha\quad f\beta m}$

$m\quad \alpha\quad f\,\beta m$

* ・*pqr p*

$f\alpha\beta$

$\underline{f\quad \alpha\ \beta}$

$\alpha\quad \beta$

$\{\,[\,(p\cdot q)\supset r\,]\,p\,\}$

$m\alpha f\beta m$

$\underline{m\quad \alpha\quad f\,\beta m}$

$m\quad \alpha\quad \beta m$

8. * ・※*pqr* ・ *prq*

$f\alpha\beta\qquad f\alpha\beta$

$\underline{f\ \alpha\ \beta}\ \underline{f\ \ \alpha\ \beta}$

$f\qquad \alpha\qquad \beta$

8'. $\{\,[\,(p\equiv q)\cdot r\,]\supset[\,(p\supset r)\cdot q\,]\,\}$

$m\alpha\,f\,\beta m\qquad m\alpha\,f\,\beta m$

$\underline{m\quad \alpha\quad f\beta m\ m\quad \alpha\quad f\beta m}$

$m\qquad \alpha\qquad f\qquad \beta\qquad m$

* ・※*pqr* *prq*

$f\alpha\beta\qquad f\alpha\beta$

$\underline{f\ \alpha\ \beta}\ \underline{f\ \ \alpha\ \beta}$

$\underline{f\quad \alpha\quad \beta}$

$\alpha\quad \beta$

$\{\,[\,(p\equiv q)\cdot r\,]\supset(p\supset r)q\,\}$

$m\alpha\,f\,\beta m\qquad m\alpha\,f\,\beta m$

$\underline{m\quad \alpha\quad f\beta m\quad \alpha\quad \beta}$

$m\qquad \alpha\qquad f\qquad m$

NICKEL: Man, there're a lot of symbols there.

PENNY: Don't panic. The exercises I have in mind won't be that hard. They're designed to supplement my argument about the independence of combinatory and propositional meaning. It's not enough to put you down with an argument; that may silence you, but it doesn't always convince you. But if you are able to distinguish *bona fide* Polish and Principia combinations, *wfe*, from those that aren't without knowing or being acquainted with any referents of the vocabulary items, then you'll have discovered for yourself that combinatory meaning is independent of referential meaning.

NICKEL: Before you go on, Mr. Penny, what do you mean by "referential" meaning?

PENNY: Any meaning that accrues to a term because of its referent; it could be, for example, acquaintance meaning, or the meaning that results from knowing a true proposition about the referent, or the referent itself if one exists.

NICKEL: You're broadening your claim, then, if I understand you. When you say that combinatory meaning is independent of referential meaning, you claim more than when you say it's independent of propositional meaning, for propositional meaning is only one part of referential meaning.

PENNY: A keen observation that seems perfectly accurate, Nickel.

Should you discover during the exercises that combinatory meaning is independent of referential meaning, what do you think of the prospects for finding combinatory concepts in traditional philosophy?

NICKEL: I'd say we could be sure that it's possible, and I'd be more confident of my own ability to find them than I am now.

PENNY: And what would you have learned about traditional philosophy?

NICKEL: That it can be related to logic in the wide sense.

PENNY: We'd better get on with the exercises, then; for if they do what I anticipate they will, we'll have accomplished today what we set out to do.

NICKEL: I'm not so sure that dia-logic is a means of freedom.

PENNY: I suppose you're joshing.

NICKEL: I don't know whether I am or not. Your argument has led me along a path and I don't feel I can get off it. My very complaint undid me. I objected to the Polish and Principia vocabularies' lack of referential meaning; all that came of my complaint was an argument proving I don't need it and exercises that keep referential meaning from me.

PENNY: Dia-logic gives us freedom from people persuaders, but it doesn't give us freedom from argument. We must choose some leader—people, our passions, or logic—and if we choose the latter, we are rational. For what makes us rational is that we commit ourselves to the direction in which valid arguments lead us.

NICKEL: But then we are in bondage to logic.

PENNY: Is this bad? What are its consequences? Rationality, freedom from people who may be no wiser than we, and freedom from passions which may commit us blindly. Would you be irrational? Is it rational to be irrational?

NICKEL: That sounds like a trick.

PENNY: It'd be better to talk about that later, preferably over honest beers. And now to get on with showing yourself that it can be "Wurds, Wurds, Wurds!" with traditional philosophers as well as with the "new" philosophers.

Take a look at the *wfe*s and non-*wfe*s I gave you before. In looking at the groups in the first column, one at a time, what do you notice about the *f*'s, alphas, and betas beneath the Polish expressions?

NICKEL: I notice that in each row they have the same order; from left to right it's always f, α, β.

PENNY: Is that true of them in the second column?

NICKEL: Nope. Either they have a different order, or one or more of them is missing. In the first group, for example, β is missing; and in the third group they have a different order.

PENNY: Surely we can learn something from that about distinguishing Polish *wfes* from Polish non-*wfes*.

NICKEL: If there is a regular way of placing f, α, and β beneath the expressions, we can use them to spot Polish *wfes*.

PENNY: Good. They help us to decide if the regularity required for *wfes* is present or absent. The same holds for Principia expressions. You should have no difficulty spotting the order there.

NICKEL: In *wfes* the order is always m, α, f, β, m.

PENNY: Except for the second case in the third column.

NICKEL: Just α beneath a letter! That's also true for the second case in the first column. Single letters must be *wfes*.

PENNY: At least p's can be.

NICKEL: I guess I did go beyond the evidence. Can't q and r be *wfes*?

PENNY: Sure they can.

NICKEL: I'd like to ask about the significance of the different layers of f's, alphas, and betas beneath the expressions.

PENNY: I'd like to tell you, but it would be more instructive if you found out for yourself. Once you do, then you'll know the regular way to assign f's, alphas, and betas, after which you're on the easy road to spotting *wfes*. I can give you a clue.

NICKEL: Fanebius?

PENNY: "Inne beegynngyng Godd dydna saye 'Nombrs go the way of horyzones.' I hav seen nombrs goe vertycal."

NICKEL: "Numbers"? Could that have something to do with expression strength?

PENNY: Fanebius hath spoken.

6.1: (a) I want you to assign f's, alphas, and betas in layers to the following expressions; (b) after you have done that I want you to distinguish the *wfes* from the non-*wfes*.

1. $p*q$
2. $.pq$
3. $v*pqp$
4. $*pvqr.p$
5. $vvpqr$
6. r
7. $**pq.qp$
8. $vq.r*pvpq$
9. $.v*pvqrv.*qr.qq.pr*pq$
10. $.prr.*rp..pq$

1'. $(\supset pq)$
2'. $(p.q)$
3'. $[(p \supset q)vr]$
4'. $[(p.q)vrq]$
5'. $[p \supset (\equiv p.q)]$
6'. $[(p.q) \equiv (rvsp)]$
7'. $\{[(p \supset q).(qr)] \supset (p \supset r)\}$
8'. $\{[(p \equiv r).r].[(p.r).q]\}$
9'. $\{p.[(p \supset r)v(p \equiv p)]\}$
10'. q

6.2: Up to now I have written all the Polish and Principia expressions. It's time you started using as well as observing the ideal languages. I want you to write six Polish-Principia equivalence conversations. Naturally, the expressions are to be well-formed. Two Polish and two Principia expressions are to be of expression strength three, two of each of them of strength four, and two of each of them of strength five.

6.3: (a) You are to state the rules of regularity for forming Polish *wfe*, (b) and to state the rules of regularity for forming Principia *wfe*. The answers to this exercise are Po-3 and Pr-3.

NICKEL: I draw a big blank on 6.3.

PENNY: Let's sow a few seeds, then. Have you seen any reason to suppose there are limits to the length of Polish and Principia expressions?

NICKEL: No.

PENNY: In that case it's impossible to enumerate the *wfe*s. Do you see why?

NICKEL: We could never finish the task, for there are an infinite number of possible *wfe*s.

PENNY: Right. Nor can we give a set of rules describing the different *wfe*s—for the same reason that it is impossible to enumerate them. Your problem is this: What must be the nature of our *wfe* rules if they are to be finite in number but adequate to help us decide whether or not any expression whatsoever is well-formed?

NICKEL: More big blank. Sorry.

PENNY: Can a square be divided into squares?

NICKEL: Sure.

PENNY: Could you decide that a figure was a square if you knew that *w* was a square, *x* was a square, *y* was a square, and *z* was a square, and you knew their size, and that they were arranged in a certain way?

NICKEL: Of course. And from this I am to infer that at least some *wfe*s are made up of other *wfe*s, as squares are made up of other, smaller squares; and that if I can decide that there are *wfe* parts arranged in a certain order, then I can decide that the whole is a *wfe*.

This means that the answer to my problem about the nature of the rules is repetition. By using the same rules over and over again on *wfe* parts, I eventually can canvass any whole *wfe*, no matter how long it is.

The only problem now is to decide what the parts are to be.

PENNY: Well done, Nickel. And parts are the next problem. Our rules will have to contain expressions representing parts; since the parts represented will be various, what do you suggest the representing expressions consist of?

NICKEL: Variables. Such as "/‾‾‾‾‾/," "(‾‾‾‾‾)"?

PENNY: Why don't we use f, α, and β? They are easier to write than the shapes.

NICKEL: Besides, we used them before to determine *wfes*. I get it now! Essentially our *wfe* rules will be descriptions of how to assign variables to the Polish and Principia vocabularies.

PENNY: Or, to put it another way, how to substitute the Polish and Principia vocabularies and expressions into the variables.

Look over the list I gave you, with four columns of expressions, and notice what variables get repeated. That will clue you to the parts that need repetition.

NICKEL: α, β, and f get repeated; and they also get repeated as a group, $f\alpha\beta$.

PENNY: We mustn't forget the bar. If we include it, then the following three variable expressions are all you need to state the Polish *wfe* rules: (a) α; (b) $f\alpha\beta$; and (c) $-\alpha$.

NICKEL: All I need to do is specify what may be substituted for the variables in order to complete the rules, of which there'll be three.

PENNY: That's right; in completing the rules you can make use of previous Po- and Pr- rules. For example, instead of enumerating the letters, you can refer to them by using the term "letters," for its use was established in Po-1; or instead of enumerating binary functors, you can refer to them by using the phrase "binary functor."

NICKEL: For its use was established in Po-1.

PENNY: You may want to make use of expression strength also. All you need to do is use the language or rules of Po-2.

NICKEL: Leave me now to 6.3.

PENNY: Once you have the Po-3 and Pr-3 rules, you can use them to do this next exercise.

6.4: (a) Formulate the cipher for translating from a Polish *wfe* to its equivalent Principia *wfe*. (b) Formulate the cipher for translating from a Principia *wfe* to its equivalent Polish *wfe*. The answers are Po-4 and Pr-4.

When we discussed ciphers in the first chapter, you'll recall that we spoke of substitution and/or transposition ciphers.

NICKEL: Thanks. Offhand, I'd say that I'll have both substitution and transposition rules in my ciphers. I know I have different functors in them; and I know that different positions will have to be given in order for the substituent's expression strength to stay the same. For example, I know that "*" will substitute for " $\supset$ "; and I have to rearrange their order in going from one ideal language to the other.

PENNY: I leave you now to 6.4 with the understanding that repetition is important to the ciphers as well.

Out of today's conversation we distilled the view that there are two ways of looking at sentences: (1) as revealing a propositional concept and (2) as revealing a combinatory concept.

When we express sentences, we have to allow that the person or persons addressed may look at our own sentences either way. Let's suppose I make a claim, that is, assert a sentence which I believe to be true, for example, "We had a very pleasant shout the other day." The person addressed may very well express his disagreement with our claim. Let's call his expressed disagreement a "counter-claim."

Here are some possible counter-claims to that sentence:

(a) It was an unpleasant shout.
(b) The last time we had a pleasant shout was two years ago.
(c) I wouldn't call anything a shout that was pleasant.
(d) You must be thinking of someone else, for we didn't have any shout together.
(e) It takes two to tango, but one to shout, so you can't have "we" as the subject of the sentence.

These counter-claims are of two kinds, either propositional counter-claims or combinatory counter-claims. The kind of counter-claim made reveals which way the person is looking at our sentence.

NICKEL: In case a person makes a propositional counter-claim, he is looking at your sentence as revealing a propositional concept; and if he makes a combinatory counter-claim, he is looking at your sentence as revealing a combinatory concept.

PENNY: You have it.

6.5: I want you to classify each of the counter-claims I wrote down.

NICKEL: Tell me, can every sentence be looked at in both the combinatory and propositional way?

PENNY: Why do you ask?

NICKEL: Because if every sentence can, then my next question would be: Which way of looking at a sentence is the philosophic way?

PENNY: Your question seems to imply that only one of the ways could be a philosophic way.

NICKEL: Then are both ways philosophic ways?

PENNY: I don't see what purpose would be served if I answered those questions.

NICKEL: I want to know how I should read a philosopher in order to get his philosophy. If I read his sentences in the propositional way, then as far as I am concerned his philosophy will consist of a collection of propositions for which he claims truth; on the other hand, if I read his sentences in the combinatory way, for me his philosophy will consist of a set of combinatory concepts. Now a collection of propositions is not identical to a set of combinatory concepts. Which is his philosophy?

Or maybe I should read him both ways, so that his philosophy consists of both propositions and combinatory concepts.

PENNY: I see no reason to rearrange the furniture in the philosophic chamber without regard for the other occupants. I don't wish to decide here which one way we should use the word "philosophy." All I wish to maintain now is that when we explore combinatory concepts we are doing philosophy. If you see this, then we have done what we set out to do today.

NICKEL: That is, we have seen that doing philosophy, in your sense of the term, is doing logic in the wide sense.

PENNY: That's right. I will make this remark, however. I think philosophers would look less inept and philosophy less a failure if we supposed that the aim of philosophy is the investigation of combinatory concepts.

NICKEL: And that philosophers shouldn't suppose their task is to arrive at the truth about the referents of philosophic words?

PENNY: Philosophers have been disagreeing for centuries over the same problems, never arriving at mutually satisfactory answers; consequently, philosophy seems a matter of opinion rather than a matter of knowledge. And only by judging philosophy according to the standards of science do we get this notion of philosophy. If we give up those standards——

NICKEL: We can restore philosophy its dignity?

PENNY: I make no reply other than to give you your Review Questions. You don't mind if I speak of us in the third person? OK.

Review Questions

1. What view of Nickel's about meaning does Penny think leads Nickel to doubt that sentence meaning depends solely on regularity?

2. After Penny has argued against Nickel's belief in the existence of non-verbal meanings, what reason does Nickel give for continuing to doubt that sentence meaning depends solely on regularity?

3. What has "Monkey is telephone" to do with (a) Nickel's belief that the meaning of sentences depends in part on the meanings of the words in the sentences, and (b) with Penny's comparison of philosophers to logicians in the wide sense?

4. What is the difference between Penny's view of the aim of philosophy and Nickel's view?

5. Why don't "truly" and "meaningfully" have the same meaning?

6. What two ways of looking at a sentence are there? To what two interpretations of "concept of" do they lead?

7. How does Penny think traditional philosophy can be fitted into his view of the aim of philosophy?

8. What is the argument Penny uses to show Nickel that combinatory meaning is independent of propositional meaning?

9. What is Nickel's idea of "propositional meaning"?

10. Why does Penny think making philosophy a branch of logic in the wide sense will help its reputation?

Seventh conversation

REFERENTS AND THE GLASS CAVE

*Som daye a mann wil ryse amung yu to talk of Wurds and
Objectes and hee will saye: "It is rather the object
designated by such a [singular] term that counts as a
value of the variable; and the objects stay on as values
of the variables though the singular terms be swept away."**
And hys naim shal bee Quine.—Fanebius Perlyng

---

* W. V. Quine, *Word and Object*, The MIT Press, Massachusetts Institute of
Technology, Cambridge, Mass., 1960, footnote p. 192.

NICKEL: Please forgive me, Mr. Penny, if I'm not as keen today as you'd like me to be. Those "honest beers" we drank yesterday while discussing the irrationality of irrationality have left me—shall I say? —slack.

PENNY: It's natural to relax among friends, Nickel.

NICKEL: The honesty effect of the beers has lasted longer than I expected. I feel weak enough to confess. No, that's not what I meant. I meant to say I don't feel strong enough to stifle a confession.

PENNY: Are you going to confess involuntarily?

NICKEL: If you mean against my will, no. The beers have anaesthetized my will. I'm neither for nor against the confession.

PENNY: In that case I don't think you meant to say you "don't feel strong enough to stifle a confession" any more than you meant to say "I feel weak enough to confess." The strength or weakness of your will isn't involved, for you're not exercising your will.

NICKEL: Maybe I shouldn't have said anything about a lack of strength, but I still could have meant to say it. After all, a person can mean to say something that's false.

PENNY: No doubt of that, for people often intend to lie, and in order to do so, mean to say something false. But if what they say turns out, to their surprise, to be true, do you think the sentence they uttered is what they meant to say?

NICKEL: They didn't mean to utter a true sentence, but, nevertheless, they could have meant to speak the particular sentence they in fact spoke; that sentence which was unexpectedly true could have been the one they had in mind.

PENNY: Then you're equating "the sentence I meant" with "the sentence I had in mind"?

NICKEL: I think so.

PENNY: Does saying a sentence you don't mean always happen because your voicing mechanism fails to produce the same words you have in mind, then? Because of a slip, so to speak?

NICKEL: Not always. There's another possibility. A person may have a sentence in mind, be interrupted, and forget he was going to say that sentence. He may say another sentence instead, then suddenly remember what he had in mind to say before the interruption, and correct himself by "I meant to say. . . ." This isn't a slip, just forgetfulness.

PENNY: How else do you account for a man saying what he doesn't mean to say?

NICKEL: It can happen when his words don't express his thought.

PENNY: If this explanation differs from the slip-explanation, the thought his words don't express must not be a sentence.

160

NICKEL: I agree. He's not thinking of a sentence; he just has a non-verbal thought. And when he utters a sentence that doesn't say what he means, it's because it doesn't express what he thought.

PENNY: There's that non-verbal thought again! I thought we'd finished it off yesterday. Oh, well. According to the explanation you've just given me, saying what you mean is picking sentences whose meaning expresses the thought you're thinking.

NICKEL: Right; and sometimes we make mistakes.

PENNY: Do you remember doing that?

NICKEL: Making mistakes?

PENNY: No, picking a sentence that expresses your thought. Do you remember ever actually matching sentences against a thought, debating which one expresses it and then deciding?

NICKEL: I can't remember for sure.

PENNY: I doubt if you ever matched sentences against a thought.

NICKEL: How do you know I've never done it?

PENNY: I don't think it's possible. Try doing it now.

NICKEL: I will. Hmmmm. Only sentences keep running through my head.

PENNY: I'm not surprised. You've got a theory that requires the use of non-verbal thoughts, but it doesn't seem to be supported by your experience. You think sentences are somehow superfluous to thought, that they are only needed for talk between two people, and that their main purpose is to mirror what goes on in our minds.

You imagine that, though the public dialogue has need of language, the private, interior dialogue can dispense with it. What makes you suppose that your private thinking has to be different in kind than what we do when we're talking? After I asked you to reflect upon matching sentences with thoughts, you discovered only sentences running through your mind. Likewise, only sentences run through our conversations.

NICKEL: Are you denying there are non-verbal thoughts?

PENNY: No. I'm just denying that you check your utterances against them to decide whether or not you've said what you meant.

NICKEL: If I can't check against my thoughts, what criterion can I use to decide my sentence didn't express what I meant? I'm not thinking of the slip- and forgetfulness-explanations, for they involve verbal thoughts.

PENNY: There are lots of criteria, depending on what you say. The criteria vary, depending on whether the sentence you utter is ill-formed, or confused, or vague, or false, or beside the point, or imprecise, or otherwise ill-conceived. A sentence can fail in many ways to do its job.

These criteria usually become operative only after we give voice, or shape, as when we write, to our running sentences. Hearing ourselves speak places us in a spectator's position. We suddenly hear our sentence as others do, and it occurs to us that it's imperfect.

Think back on the sentence that started this whole discussion, "I feel weak enough to confess." What criterion did you use to decide that wasn't what you meant?

NICKEL: I think I realized after I uttered the sentence that it could be taken as stating that my confessing depended upon weakness. That wasn't true.

PENNY: That shows truth was your criterion for deciding you didn't mean that sentence. Your sentence had this job: It was supposed to describe accurately what occasioned your confessing, and it didn't.

NICKEL: A sentence's "job" is important, isn't it?

PENNY: Let me explain why it is. You may have a goal in mind; the means you subsequently choose has the job of reaching the goal. We judge the success of the job done in terms of the goal, for the goal determines the criteria we use to judge the means. The goal of descriptive accuracy determined that truth was a criterion of the success of your "confession" sentence.

It's also important to realize a person can have in mind a goal without having in mind the exact means of reaching it; this sometimes accounts for "that's not what I meant."

For example, you may want to get a runner out at first base. You throw the ball; the throw has the job of getting the ball to the first baseman in time. It may be too short, or too high, or bouncing and not beat the runner. Now, you didn't have any particular throw in your mind all formed in detail. You only had the general means, throwing, in mind. That's why, after the bad throw, you can say, "I didn't mean to throw a high (or short, or bouncing) one."

Similarly, you don't always have in mind a sentence fully formed in detail; you sometimes have in mind only the general means, the saying of an undetermined sentence. That's why, after you've uttered a particular imperfect sentence, you can say, "I didn't mean to say a confused (or imprecise, or irrelevant, or vague, or false) sentence."

NICKEL: What you've said about the "job" theory of saying what we don't mean makes a lot of sense, but doesn't this sentence sound peculiar to you: "That wasn't what I meant to think"?

PENNY: It does.

NICKEL: It sounds peculiar to me just as Linus's first question in this *Peanuts** strip sounds peculiar. We don't have control over what we

* By permission *San Francisco Chronicle*, Copyright, 1961, by United Feature Syndicate, Inc.

think; maybe we decide what we're going to think about, but we don't decide to think such and such a thought. It just seems to happen.

PENNY: What has that to do with what we've been discussing?

NICKEL: If what we say is identical with what we think, that is, a verbal thought, as we've just supposed, then to say of what we said that it wasn't what we meant to say is also to say of our thought that it wasn't what we meant to think. Excuse the tortured sentence. I can't think of how else to say it.

PENNY: But a thought isn't identical with what we say, for thinking isn't saying. Saying involves the additional act of uttering; before we utter, we frequently consider whether or not we should utter, as a result of which we sometimes do not utter. You can see the difference if you insert "say" for "think" in Linus's first question.

NICKEL: You're right. "How can a person just *decide* what he's going to say?" doesn't sound odd. We do this all the time.

PENNY: I'm glad we accidentally got into this issue about not saying what we mean. It showed me another route psychology travels in its invasion of theory of meaning. It's tempting to account for our not saying what we mean by supposing there is a mismatch between what we utter and what we think. Then, Alice-in-Wonderland-like, how easy to suppose that what we think is a meaning our sentence didn't express. Given this identification of thought and meaning, and given that thought is a subject matter for psychology, psychological explanations appear relevant to theory of meaning.

However, I want to focus only on the logical requirements for communication, to which psychology is irrelevant. Psychology sneaks in because of a confusion between what a person means, that is, intends, and what a word, a phrase, or a sentence means. The latter sense of meaning, not the former, is our problem. That's why I've concentrated persistently on combinatory regularity, because I think it is a necessary condition of linguistic meaning.

NICKEL: That reminds me of what I was going to confess. It had to do with combinatory meaning. I was going over my notes and noticed the following two sentences of mine: "When I understand the meaning

Seventh conversation   163

of all the words in a sentence, I understand the meaning of the sentence," and "It seems to me that sentences' meanings also depend on the meanings of words, not just their regular place in cornucopias."* I was going to confess two things. Number one: I thought they expressed the same thing when I said them. Number two: After the "Monkey is telephone" example, I realized they didn't mean the same thing, but I didn't say so. The fact that I understood the meanings of "monkey," "is," and "telephone" but didn't understand the meaning of the sentence showed me my first sentence was false. That, however, didn't make my second sentence false, for though a sentence meaning may depend upon the meanings of its words, it may not depend on them alone.

PENNY: Logicians frequently use the terms "necessary" and "sufficient" to express the difference. You could say the meanings of the words in a sentence are a necessary but not a sufficient condition for understanding the meaning of the sentence.

NICKEL: My first sentence says that the meanings of the words are sufficient and my second sentence says only that they are necessary. Do I have that straight?

PENNY: You do.

NICKEL: To finish my confession, after I realized the difference between the two sentences, I should have said that I didn't mean the first sentence. I only—and this supports your "job" theory—wanted to state a view contrary to yours. To do this it would have been enough to say a sentence's meaning depends partly on the meanings of its words. My first sentence didn't have to walk the plank to state a contrary view.

PENNY: You mean my view that combinatory meaning is independent of referential meaning?

NICKEL: Yes. Of course, later, I did make the more modest claim.†

Speaking of modest claims, I hope you're not as reluctant as you were yesterday to venture beyond your "modest claim" that combinatory meaning is independent of referential meaning. That's really why I wanted to confess. I wanted to draw you into a discussion about how much of a term's meaning consists of referential meaning. Yesterday you didn't want to talk about a term's acquaintance nor propositional meaning. You remember they came up when you said I was caught in an inconsistency?

PENNY: I remember. I'm willing to discuss that a bit today if you want.

* Reader: See page 138.
† Reader: See page 147.

LOGIC: A DIALOGUE

If you can use cartoons to make a point, I can too. Take a look at this *Short Ribs** cartoon and tell me if you think it is instructive as well as amusing.

SHORT RIBS   By FRANK O'NEAL   (RELEASE IN P. M. PAPERS OF WEDNESDAY, APR. 19)

NICKEL: It's amusing, principally because it takes an unusual topic and shows how the teacher holds back progress. If you have something instructive in mind, it must have to do with the linguistic topic. I'll need some leading questions from you before I can extract the instruction, however.

PENNY: Plato's Allegory of the Cave should jog your creativity.

NICKEL: I don't know the Allegory.

PENNY: It's in *The Republic,* at the beginning of Book VII. I'll give you a short summary of it. Plato describes people who live all their lives in a cave, chained facing the wall in such a manner that they cannot move or turn their heads. All that they can see are shadows cast on the wall by the statues of men and animals, which are behind their backs, between them and a fire. If one of the chained people, having all his life seen only the shadows of statues, were released and shown the statues, he would be inclined to suppose the statues less real than the shadows. And if he were dragged out of the cave into the dazzling light of day, you can imagine how overwhelmed and puzzled he would be when shown the objects which the statues represented. Would he be able to accept the objects outside the cave as real objects?

NICKEL: Not all in a moment.

After looking at your cartoon again, I see that there is a cave. A lesson is being taught, but I don't know for sure who is teaching whom. I suppose I might speak of O'Neal's Allegory of the Cave if I knew he was the teacher.

PENNY: If it's an allegory, O'Neal is teaching us.

NICKEL: You want me to go on talking about the cartoon. I can tell by your pause.

---

* By permission, *San Francisco News-Call Bulletin*, Copyright, 1961, by Newspaper Enterprise Association

The cartoon shows a conflict between a man and a boy about two ways of writing; the boy writes the conventional way and the man writes the pictographic way.

PENNY: What if the boy had carved "or" on the wall?

NICKEL: The point of that question being to draw my attention to the fact that the cartoon is concerned with a word having reference, and that it is this which makes a pictograph possible; since we cannot see or's in the world, we can't draw pictures resembling them.

PENNY: You think both wall carvings are writing. Can you give me a reason why writing is useful?

NICKEL: One reason is that we sometimes want to communicate with people who can't hear us; sometimes we're too far away in distance. And sometimes we're too far away in time, as when we're dead. Also, it serves us as a memory device.

PENNY: We might take the cave in O'Neal's allegory, then, as symbolic of the time, distance, and memory to which we prisoners are confined, and from which written language frees us.

NICKEL: How about this? The pictographs on the wall are analogous to the shadows in Plato's cave; if we saw only them, we might think they were reality. That's why we have to get out of the cave to learn that they merely represent that to which they refer. But once we learn they have reference, then we are symbolically freed from the cave's symbolic confines.

PENNY: Why do you say this of the pictographs only?

NICKEL: I guess I could say it of the conventional writing as well. In fact, it seems to strengthen my hand about referential meaning, doesn't it? If we couldn't get out of the cave to see cats we wouldn't know the meaning of "cat"; we would think the shadow "cat" was the real object.

PENNY: "ℂ𝔸𝕋" looks real enough to me.

NICKEL: It is real and so is a shadow a real shadow, but what illusion if we think that that is all there is! I guess I fear we are subject to that illusion when we confine ourselves to combinatory meaning. Words with a reference have a significance that their nature as objects doesn't reveal.

PENNY: That's very well said, Emory. Does that suggest the pictographic method of writing is superior to the conventional way?

NICKEL: You mean because pictographs, when inspected as objects, reveal some knowledge of their referents?

PENNY: No, not when they're inspected as objects; in that role they don't have representative significance. I mean when we take them as expressions having reference. Don't you find pictographs as referential terms superior to conventional words when you consider acquaintance and propositional meaning?

NICKEL: Hey, there's something in that. If they do resemble their referents, I don't have to be acquainted with the referent in order to have acquaintance meaning.

PENNY: Providing they also sufficiently disresemble other possible referents. What about propositional meaning?

NICKEL: Well, if the pictograph resembles the referent in some respects, then I'll know at least one true proposition about the object referred to. For example, using O'Neal's pictograph, I'd know the true proposition, "A cat has a tail."

PENNY: So, where these aspects of referential meaning are concerned, pictographs are superior to conventional writing. However, they are on a par in that neither guarantees us of the existence of a referent, nor, consequently, of referential meaning in that sense. Why do people use conventional writing?

NICKEL: I thought we made that pretty clear the first day. It permits the use of a phonetic cipher. Besides it's easier and more economical of effort to write words than it is to draw pictures.

PENNY: The economy point has been used often. It has been hypothesized that conventional writing was suggested by the progressive dropping of pictorial details.

NICKEL: I also think the pictograph's advantage for referential meaning lessens when you realize that after we've learned a term's reference our own responses or reactions do as much for us as the picture. That being so, we lose no hold on referential meaning when we shift to conventional writing.

Well, Mr. Penny, it looks as if O'Neal's Allegory of the Cave has been instructive as well as amusing.

PENNY: What has it taught us?

NICKEL: That a term's meaning isn't wholly combinatory but partly referential, and that the teacher needn't be so angry at the boy.

PENNY: Explain that anger bit, will you?

NICKEL: The teacher is angry at the boy because the teacher doesn't think conventional words are as good as pictographs; but he needn't be angry since psychological responses can supply the referential meaning for conventional writing as well as resemblance can supply it for pictographic writing. Progress can go forward; it's possible for conventional writing to have referential meaning as well as combinatory meaning. Relax, Pop, youth may have its way without going straight to perdition.

PENNY: I'm not sure the youth in front of me should have his way, forgetful as he is. At least not before he explains this new twist he's slipped in here, this psychological key to the referential meaning of conventional writing.

You and I have been concerned all along about how we can tell if another person gives the same meaning to an expression as we do. We should have this concern about referential meaning as well. Can your psychological twist help us?

NICKEL: It's pretty obvious that if two people share a referential meaning, they must have a similar response to an expression.

PENNY: What do you count as a response? Mental images? Glandular and muscular changes? Neuro-physiological reactions? Activation of a disposition?

NICKEL: They're all responses, aren't they?

PENNY: Will any one of them do, then?

NICKEL: I don't see why not. They may all stem from acquaintance with a referent.

PENNY: Let's consider mental images first. Couldn't two people have the same image, say a green board, except that one of them has that imagistic response to "green" but not to "board" while the other has it to "board" but not to "green"?

NICKEL: Sure, that's possible. I get it; if the same image is the response to two different words, then the words should mean the same; but obviously "green" and "board" don't mean the same. Hence, responding with the same image can't be a criterion for having the same referential meaning.

PENNY: That's a good argument, but not the one I had in mind, which is this. It's necessary to conclude by your imagistic criterion that for our two people "green" and "board" have the same referential meaning. But similarity of images doesn't prove that, for images often are quite detailed and two people could pick out different details of the image as being the relevant part of the response. The first person could pick out the green aspect when he hears "green" while the second could pick out the board aspect when he hears "board."

NICKEL: In that case, though two words could cause similar images in two people, the words could still have different meanings.

My argument showed that two words with different meanings could cause similar imagistic responses while yours showed that even with similar imagistic responses the words could have different meanings.

Your argument is a good one, too, I think.

PENNY: But notice how speculative it is. Hasn't our discussion drifted a long way from actuality? Who matches their images against others' images to check for similarity of meaning? Is it common practice? Do you remember doing it?

NICKEL: I don't remember ever doing it in order to decide whether another person and myself give the same meaning to a term.

PENNY: This is a good place to ask the same question about glandular and muscular changes and neuro-physiological responses. Do you think we use them to decide whether——

NICKEL: ——or not two people give a term the same meaning? We sure don't in ordinary conversations; I'm afraid we don't usually carry around the kind of scientific equipment needed to detect those changes and responses.

PENNY: It doesn't look as if psychological responses stemming from acquaintance are a practical index to referential meaning, does it?

NICKEL: Before I leave that poor, little boy in the cave at the mercy of the bearded teacher, I have to fire my last psychology ammunition. Why can't we consider the learning of a term's referential meaning as the acquiring of a disposition?

PENNY: You're trying to put the bite before the food by putting psychology before logic.

NICKEL: Would you explain that, please?

PENNY: Have you acquired dispositions to walk? To knot your tie? To throw a ball?

NICKEL: Yes, all of them.

PENNY: How do you know that?

NICKEL: I know what walking is, what knotting my tie is, and what throwing a ball is.

PENNY: Have you acquired referential meaning dispositions?

NICKEL: Yes.

PENNY: How do you know you have?

NICKEL: Because I know what referential meaning is.

See how easily I slipped into that answer. I wish I could say that and believe it. At any rate, I think I finally get your point about logic before psychology. Until we know what we're doing when we refer, we have no standard for telling which of our dispositions are referring dispositions.

PENNY: Good. We've now discovered two ways in which psychology may slip into theory of meaning.

NICKEL: It may slip in due to a confusion between what a person means and what a linguistic item means. And it also may slip in because of the attempt to identify psychological response with meaning.

PENNY: I don't want to give you the impression that the psychological investigation of how we learn referential meaning, or any meaning for that matter, isn't interesting or important. It is; but first we have to locate the subject matter. The location of subject matter is a logical investigation and is prior to scientific investigation. Our job is the investigation of the logical portion of theory of meaning, not the psychological portion. My main concern is that we don't think we're doing the whole or the most basic part of theory of meaning when we're doing the psychological part.

Shall we get to it again?

NICKEL: What is referential meaning?

PENNY: Let's ask a more practical question, parallel to former questions of ours about meaning. Let's ask "How do you know that a term has the same referential meaning for you as it has for another person?"

NICKEL: We know that when we know they have the same referents in mind.

PENNY: But how do you know they have the same referents in mind?

NICKEL: I know they do if they pick up or point out the same object or objects when challenged to specify the referential meaning of a term.

PENNY: Let's be practical, Nickel. Read Boswell's record of the conversation between Samuel Johnson and Mr. Dilly in exercise 3.4.

NICKEL: I've read it.

PENNY: Do you think you understand the meaning of the sentences as Boswell, Johnson, and Dilly did?

NICKEL: Yes.

PENNY: Are there referential words in that conversation?

NICKEL: Yes; "book," "pharmacy," "prescription," "Dr. Hill."

PENNY: Aren't Boswell, Johnson, and Dilly dead?

NICKEL: They are.

PENNY: Pray, tell me. How are you going to find out if they would pick up or point out the same object or objects when challenged as you would?

NICKEL: You're trying to get me into a corner. Once there you think I'll have to say, "Because their combination of words are the same as mine. 'Write' is often placed in a sentence with 'book'; that takes care of Boswell's first sentence, etc." But I won't be trapped, because I know you wouldn't know what Johnson was talking *about* even if you knew the word combinations to a tee. And if you don't know what he's talking *about*, you don't know his referential meaning.

PENNY: Once again: How do you know you and they have the same referential meaning?

NICKEL: Although they can't point, their words point.

PENNY: And how do you know that words when uttered by them pointed to the same thing or things as they do when uttered by you?

NICKEL: Historical continuity accounts for knowing that. Some people who talked with them were younger than they. Younger people have children that learn to talk as they talked, and so forth.

PENNY: My kingdom for a glass cave!

NICKEL: A glass cave?

PENNY: I'm thinking symbolically of O'Neal's Cave again. If the walls of the cave were of a special glass, so we could hear, unconfined by space, time, or memory, any speech we wanted, we wouldn't have to write on the walls like bad boys. Historical continuity wouldn't be required if Johnson's and Dilly's words were always with us; nor would we need a written language.

NICKEL: But this wouldn't do away with the Boswell problem. Unless we also see somebody from Boswell's era pointing to a word's referent while pronouncing it, we wouldn't know for sure about the word's referential meaning for them. We always have to come down eventually to learning an association between a term and its referent.

PENNY: Uh uh, Nickel. No psychology. Remember, we're interested in the relation between a term and its referent, not in the process of learning it.

You seem to lay great store by pointing. First you tell me that words point and then you tell me that Boswell or his contemporaries point.

NICKEL: I call attention to Boswell's pointing because it shows us what the words point to.

PENNY: Some words have referents. That gives them referential meaning. The referential relation according to your mode of speech is "point to" or "refer to," for you say "The words point to so and so" or "The words refer to such and such." I don't understand this pointing relation. I always thought I pointed with my fingers not with my words.

NICKEL: I don't know how else to say it. I just am trying to hang on to my point that we've got to recognize there's referential meaning as well as combinatory meaning.

PENNY: You're a tenacious rascal, bless you.

NICKEL: My tenacity is strengthened by an argument I thought of last night. I think that "blue" may be combined in exactly the same way with other words as "red" may. Wherever the word "blue" appears, I can substitute the word "red." If "blue" and "red" have exactly the same combinatory possibilities, then their combinatory meaning is identical. But we know that "red" and "blue" don't have the same meaning; hence, they must have some other meaning than combinatory meaning if they differ in meaning.

PENNY: And this other meaning which accounts for the difference in their meaning is referential meaning.

NICKEL: That's just what I think. Unless someone is able to apply the word "red" correctly to things which are colored red, we doubt that he knows the meaning of "red." Furthermore, he'll never learn the correct application of "red" without knowing the referent for "red." Until he sees blue and knows "blue" refers to it, he won't know "blue" means something different from "red."

PENNY: What if the truth of the matter were, and I no longer made a secret of it, that referential meaning is a species of combinatory meaning?

NICKEL: I should be much surprised but not convinced. That sounds like trying to get the man who has the drop on you to turn around by saying, "Look out behind you, Nickel!"

PENNY: There isn't anything surprising in such a revelation. "Referential" meaning is a kind of meaning, after all; and we decided the first day that meaning depends on combinatory regularity.

There was nothing mysterious about this regularity: It was simply regular spatial placement of marks. That's all our Po- and Pr- rules are about. In spoken language, it's simply regular temporal order of sounds. This I can understand. But I'm always puzzled when people talk about words "referring" or "pointing." I want a description of this; I want to know what it is I see and/or hear when people teach me referential meaning.

NICKEL: I can see that referential meaning may depend upon regularity, but I can't see that we can explain it by combinatory meaning. Combinatory meaning is concerned with the regular placement of linguistic items. Referents aren't linguistic items.

How about this argument? I can admit there are combinatory rules for letter placement, spelling rules, that is. On that basis, letters have combinatory meaning. But that's a long way from the kind of meaning that referential words have. It's the fact that some words are related to non-linguistic objects that explains the difference between those words and letters.

PENNY: There is a difference between letters and words, all right. But I'm not willing to lay it to the same conditions you are. Your argument for the difference requires a distinction between linguistic and non-linguistic items.

NICKEL: I wouldn't think anybody would deny that distinction.

PENNY: It all depends on what the distinction comes to. You don't want to deny that linguistic items are things, do you?

NICKEL: No, for letters, words, phrases, and sentences are shapes or sounds or flashes of light or semaphore waves; however, we can still maintain the distinction, despite this, for something's being a thing doesn't prevent it from also being a linguistic item. At least it doesn't seem so to me.

PENNY: Nor to me. Since we're agreed that linguistic items are objects, and that objects can be linguistic items, we need to know what it is that transforms objects into linguistic items.

NICKEL: The letters of the alphabet are simply enumerated as such.

PENNY: What makes you think the alphabetical letters are linguistic items?

NICKEL: They approximate the sounds we use in talking.

PENNY: "The sounds we use in talking"—we make sounds that aren't talking sounds sometimes. How do we know which sounds are talk?

NICKEL: The first answer that occurs to me is that talk consists of uttering words and sentences, but then you'll ask me how I know those sounds are linguistic items.

PENNY: We don't have enough time to pursue this question about the transformation of objects into linguistic items satisfactorily. We have claimed, however, that whatever is considered a linguistic item has a place in a language structure and that this place is specified by the rules of regularity.

NICKEL: This would hold true even of the pictograph in O'Neal's Cave.

PENNY: True. I think we can build up to a description of what we learn when we learn referential meaning by considering the relation between spoken language and written language.

Written language consists of shapes structured in a spatial order. Words run from left to right in English and from top to bottom in Japanese. What allows us to read written English aloud?

NICKEL: The fact that we have a cipher and/or code for going from one to the other. In English for every word-shape we have a sound; we can pronounce the words.

PENNY: Do we have to preserve the structure or order?

NICKEL: Yes. We do this by pronouncing a word-shape that is to the left of another word-shape before the one to its right. To the spatial structure there corresponds a temporal structure.

PENNY: Does this cipher contain substitution rules?

NICKEL: Sure. When we read, we substitute a sound for a shape.

PENNY: Since, as we said before, linguistic items are objects, in order to read objects aloud, we have to learn how to pronounce objects. Take O'Neal's Cave. Would you say that the two objects, "cat" and the pictograph, receive the same pronunciation?

NICKEL: I'd say so.

PENNY: Is it possible, in your opinion, to have a sentence, a "mixed sentence" we might call it, some of whose words are audible entities and some of whose words are visible entities?

NICKEL: Would this be an example? [The underlined words in the following sentence were pronounced by me and the other words were written. I wrote the first word, spoke the second, and so alternated the sentence's words.—E. Nickel].   The pigeons fly low when the weather is windy.

PENNY: That's a good example.

NICKEL: I don't see why that's not a sentence.   People would know what I meant as well as if I'd written the whole thing or spoken the whole thing.   Besides, I could fit word-shapes into those places where sounds are, or *vice versa*.   By the principle of orderly substitution we talked about, we'd be saying the same thing.   There's no harm in mixing visible and audible entities.   Mixed sentences are sentences.

PENNY: I share your opinion and your reasons.   You understand the operation of reading and writing; it's a simple substitution procedure in which the order of things, sounds and shapes, is preserved.

Let us now imaginatively attend a remarkable event.

We're invisible occupants of O'Neal's Cave.   We've witnessed all the events except the one in the last frame.   As the teacher is pointing to the pictograph and saying "That way!" the cave gradually, but quickly, becomes flooded with light.   It becomes lighter for the incredible reason that the stone walls turn to glass.   We're literally in a glass cave. The writing on the wall disappears, and, as if heaven itself had ordered it, the teacher's finger is now pointing not at a cat pictograph but at a cat sitting on a rock outside the cave directly behind the former location of the pictograph.

Freeze that last frame.   Got the picture?

NICKEL: Yes, and I can also see the surprised look on the teacher's face.

PENNY: Take off the surprised look and put a self-satisfied one in its place.   Now have him uttering the word "cat."   Describe what is happening in that frame.

NICKEL: The teacher is teaching the boy the referent of the word "cat" by pointing to the cat and simultaneously uttering the sound "cat."

PENNY: Here's a slightly different frame I want you to describe for me.   We're back in the stone cave and the teacher is pointing to the cat pictograph and uttering the word "cat."

NICKEL: He's teaching the boy how to pronounce the pictograph word.

PENNY: You've given me two apparently different descriptions of the same act.

NICKEL: I should hope so, for they're not the same act.   The pictograph isn't the referent of the sound "cat"; it's the sound's written substitution.

PENNY: I agree.

NICKEL: You don't mean to tell me the cat isn't the sound's referent!

PENNY: No, I don't.

NICKEL: In that case, the acts in the two frames must be different.

PENNY: Not if the relation between a sound and its referent is similar to the relation between a sound and its written substitution; not if the referential relation is similar to the pronunciation relation.

NICKEL: Well, are they?

PENNY: Look, we have been trying to see in what respect referential meaning is a species of meaning, haven't we?

NICKEL: That's so.

PENNY: So far we've spoken of meaning in terms of regularity, combinations, ciphers, structure, marks and sounds and their spatial and temporal relations, and substitutions. In order to understand "refers" and "points to," terms which introduce, after all, simply a special case of meaning, we need to understand them in the terms we've used so far to talk about meaning.

I believe we can say that the teacher in our imagined frame, when he is uttering the sound "cat" and pointing to the cat, is pronouncing the object cat as well as we can say he is referring to the cat, because, I believe, the referring relation is like the pronouncing relation, pronunciation being, as we just saw, a substitution rule.

NICKEL: That sounds weird! That makes objects such as cats words!

PENNY: You find it hard to believe cats are words. There's an obvious sense, of course, in which they aren't words: They aren't made up of alphabetical letters or phonemes. But there's a sense in which they are: They do, after all, take places in the language structure. We frequently express mixed sentences, sentences in which some of the objects are audible and others are visible, such as cats.

NICKEL: I don't think I've ever done so.

PENNY: You have if you've ever expressed this kind of sentence: "That is a so and so."

NICKEL: I've done that, but I don't see that it's a mixed sentence.

PENNY: Simply uttering "that" in such a sentence isn't sufficient to pick out the subject. It has to be accompanied with some gesture locating the subject. Without the gesture we might as well say, "Blank is a so and so." Or if we wrote it, "_____ is a so and so."

NICKEL: Isn't "that" the subject of the sentence?

PENNY: No.

NICKEL: But it's in the subject place according to grammatical rules.

PENNY: Instead of saying it's in the subject place, and, consequently, the grammatical subject of the sentence, we should say it marks the grammatical place.

NICKEL: If it's a place marker, then it's a variable!

PENNY: Exactly. Why did you think I equated "That is a so and so" with "—————— is a so and so"? "That" simply shows a place where a subject may go, just as "——————" does. Without some additional act, such as my pointing, you won't know what I'm substituting into the subject place.

Suppose our sentence is "That is a Manx." To what would you point?

NICKEL: To a Manx cat, if the sentence is to be true.

PENNY: Since the Manx cat is the subject, and a visible entity, and since the rest of the sentence, "is a Manx," consists of audible entities, we've got ourselves a mixed sentence. And in the words of that great student of logic, Emory Nickel, "A mixed sentence is a sentence."

NICKEL: Wellll . . .

PENNY: Objects, such as cats, can also take their place in written sentences. How could you indicate the subject if you wrote the sentence, instead of speaking it, remembering that "That" in the written sentence without some gesture is of no more use in specifying the subject of the sentence than "_____"?

NICKEL: While writing "That" I could point to the cat.

PENNY: How could you do it in case the sentence was already written?

NICKEL: I could pronounce "That" while pointing.

PENNY: What could you do if you were mute?

NICKEL: I could pick the cat up and simultaneously point to "That."

PENNY: What if you had only one arm?

NICKEL: I could first point to the cat and then point to "is," "a," and "Manx."

PENNY: Why "first" point to the cat?

NICKEL: To indicate it's the subject.

PENNY: There! You have finally acknowledged a sentence made up of words and an object, with the object as the subject.

NICKEL: The object being the cat, of course.

PENNY: Of course. Suppose we made the blank in "_____ is a Manx" as long as the cat. Couldn't we pick the cat up and place it above the "_____"? And wouldn't you then be looking at a sentence, with the cat as subject?

NICKEL: It looks like "Yes" to both questions. Putting a cat in the subject place in a sentence doesn't seem any more unorthodox than putting a picture of a cat there as they frequently do in children's books.

I do feel a little uneasy, however.

PENNY: I'd like to hear why.

NICKEL: We distinguished between using and mentioning an expression. Normally, I'd say, when we have a sentence, such as "The cat is a Manx," the subject of the sentence, "cat," is being used to refer to a cat, while the cat itself is being mentioned.

PENNY: Why should that make you feel uneasy?

NICKEL: Your suggestion that the cat itself may be the subject of a sentence shows that you're confusing use and mention. The physical cat is that which is mentioned; the word "cat" is used. When you substitute the physical cat for the word "cat," you're substituting that which is mentioned for that which is used.

PENNY: Can't something be used on one occasion and mentioned on another?

NICKEL: Yes. A word such as "cat" is used sometimes and mentioned sometimes.

PENNY: Why can't a cat be used as well as mentioned, then? What makes you think it isn't being used when I place it in the "————" in this string, "———— is a Manx"?

NICKEL: A cat could be used, I admit, but I don't think it is being used in that string. I guess I don't think it is being used because when we use the subject of a sentence, we usually intend to refer to something. I intend to refer to you with "Penny" when I say "Penny is in the gazebo." But when we put the physical cat in that string, we don't intend to refer to anything with it, so it isn't being used.

Since the cat isn't being used, it's not a linguistic item. And if it's not a linguistic item, then that string of entities can't be a linguistic sentence for an essential part of it, namely, the subject, isn't a linguistic part.

PENNY: Let me assure you, I'm not confusing use and mention because the cat is being used in that string. Although the cat was mentioned by "cat" in "The cat is a Manx," when the cat itself appears in the string, it is no longer being mentioned, but is being used. The cat outside a string is a horse of a different color than when it's inside a string. Hence, substituting the cat for "cat" isn't substituting that which is mentioned for that which is used, for the moment the cat enters the string, it is no longer being mentioned, but is being used.

However, I am not under the impression that the cat is being used as "cat" is being used; the cat is not being used to refer to something else.

But just because the cat doesn't have referential meaning doesn't mean it isn't being used as a linguistic item.

NICKEL: I fail to see how it is being used as a linguistic item.

PENNY: Surely you don't want to hold that an entity isn't a linguistic item if it doesn't refer to anything!

NICKEL: I guess not.

Seventh conversation   I77

PENNY: You shouldn't be so uncertain. There are a lot of entities that you consider meaningful English words which do not refer to anything. "All," "and," and "unicorn" are some examples; you see them written here on this sheet of paper. Though they are ink marks to your eyes, they are words to you; they are words to you even though they don't refer to anything.

Why are those ink marks meaningful words to you?

NICKEL: Because they are governed by rules of regularity, and I know the rules.

PENNY: Sure; they take known places in a linguistic structure. That's exactly what the cat is doing. It's taking a known place in a linguistic structure, in a sentence. That's what makes the cat a linguistic item.

Seeing the cat in the subject place of a sentence is quite different from seeing it stalking a bird in the grass. Though normally no one would see the cat functioning linguistically in the grass, they certainly could when they see it in the subject place of a sentence.

NICKEL: What linguistic function is the cat performing if it's not referring?

PENNY: Is not the sentence "That cat is a Manx" about something? And is it not ascribing Manxhood to that which it is about?

NICKEL: Yes, to both questions.

PENNY: Is there only one way to indicate what a sentence is about?

NICKEL: I don't know.

PENNY: It seems to me there is more than one way.

In "The cat is Manx," we *say* what the sentence is about. When we place the physical cat in the subject place we *show*, or exhibit, what the sentence is about. Thus, the cat is performing the linguistic function of indicating what the sentence is about and what it is to which we are ascribing Manxhood.

After all, is picking the cat up and placing it above the blank in the written sentence at all different from the linguistic function of pointing to the cat while uttering "that" in speaking the sentence?

NICKEL: I guess not. They both pick out the subject.

PENNY: Turning again to the topic of referring, here's another way of referring to the cat: You can read the sentence with the cat above the "———" as: The cat is a Manx. What have you done when you've read the sentence?

NICKEL: Pronounced the cat.

I get the point. When we read we pronounce a physical mark. Pronouncing the mark is one way of referring to the mark. The pronunciation refers to the mark because the mark may be substituted for it. The same thing holds when I pronounce the cat. The sound "cat" referred to the actual cat because the cat may be substituted for it; hence, my ability to refer to the cat is based on a substitution rule.

I learn the pronunciation substitution rule, I guess, from mixed sentences, as when I point to a cat and say "That is a cat."

PENNY: You've got the hang of it, Emory Nickel.

NICKEL: You sound surprised.

PENNY: I am surprised. We've covered a great deal of unfamiliar and unconventional territory today. Now that we've reached a peak in your understanding, let's use the vantage point to survey the territory we passed through.

First, we descended into the dark valley of your doubt. You doubted that combinatory meaning was all. You couldn't shake your belief that we had to acknowledge that there is referential meaning as well.

Second, you bifurcated the universe.

Here I must mythologize a little in order to summon up a vision of a bifurcated universe that would account for the persistence of your belief in the existence of referential meaning devoid of combinatory regularity.

On the one hand there is the world as a collection of referents; on the other hand there is language as an orderly array of linguistic items. But as with Plato's universe in the *Timaeus*, where chaos and the Forms stand helplessly apart, so here referents and language stand apart. A God is all that will bridge the unbridgeable. Behold Man holding the orb of the world in one hand and the pen of language in the other! The two aspects of nature meet at the midpoint—the mind of Man.

How easy to suppose that the study of referential meaning is a study of the midpoint, through which language comes to inform the world and through which the world comes to give substance to language. The twentieth century's preoccupation with a cure for madness reinforces our hope that psychology will explain how through the mind of Man we can come to an understanding of referential meaning, that bridge between the lifeless bifurcates.

Third, I bade you to abandon the division between the world and language; it is this division which leads you to think referential meaning, conceived as a link between linguistic items and the world, is a thing apart from combinatory meaning, conceived as a link between linguistic items alone. By abandoning the bifurcation, we can lay aside the study of psychological relations and attend to our proper business, the study of logical relations.

I need hardly remind you what this involves.

NICKEL: The study of substitution regularities and arrangement regularities. They are the two kinds of logical relations. We learned that the first day when we studied ciphers and codes.

PENNY: Fourth, and this is the positive side of the third point, I suggested that instead of considering referential meaning as a thing apart from combinatory meaning you consider it as a species of combinatory meaning. The relations between linguistic items and referents is no different in kind from the relations between linguistic items and other linguistic items. They are all of one piece: Logical relations, relations of substitution, and arrangement. Come with me to a peak in Darien and see the world and language as one. Only if we take the machinery of nature apart do we need to call upon the gods to put it back together again, for not all the King's horses nor all the King's men can do it.

NICKEL: Before you go on with the summary, Mr. Penny, I'd like to interpose a question. It's about some terminology I learned in a speech class. In that class we were introduced to three terms, "pragmatics," "syntactics," and "semantics." I was told that pragmatics is the study of the effect of words on persons, which is a sociological, biological, and psychological study; and that syntactics is the study of the relations of words to each other, a study of the syntax or grammar of a language; and that semantics is the study of the relations between referents and words.

PENNY: That is a pretty standard terminology usually credited to Charles W. Morris.*

NICKEL: If I understood those terms, and if I'm applying them correctly to our discussion, you've said that pragmatics, the psychological study, is irrelevant to our concerns here.

PENNY: That's right. We're not studying the "mid-point," we're not engaged in an empirical study of the "mind."

NICKEL: And you're also suggesting that semantics is a species of syntactics when you say that "the relations between linguistic items and referents is no different in kind from the relations between linguistic items and other linguistic items."

PENNY: Very good, Nickel. We have to be careful about the term "semantics," though. The term is often used to cover not only the topic of referential meaning but also the topic of truth. We've said nothing about truth, so we have to confine our present remarks about semantics to meaning. The concept of "meaning" doesn't break down into "semantic meaning," or what you've called "referential meaning," and "syntactic meaning," or what I've called "combinatory meaning," but is seen in a unified way when referents are seen as linguistic items. For then we see all meaning as combinatory or syntactic meaning; knowledge of meaning becomes knowledge of the arrangement of visible and/or audible entities.

* Charles W. Morris, *Foundations of the Theory of Signs*, University of Chicago Press, Chicago, 1936.

Fifth, all of this began to come clear while we watched with fascination the stone cave turning to glass and the pictograph becoming a real cat. This led us to advance the view that the referring relation is the logical relation of substitution. Recall here that reading, pronouncing the mark on a page, was an example of referring *via* substitution of sounds for marks.

Sixth, the pronunciation example gave us an additional foothold for our ascent to the peak, for from it we saw the possibility of mixed sentences.

We said "mixed sentences" because in sentences we may have two different kinds of linguistic items, spoken sounds and written spatial marks. Through a correlation of temporal and spatial order, we can place the diverse kinds in a sentential arrangement.

Mixed sentences are important because they enable us to interpret such spoken sentences as "You are dirty," where a mistress is pointing, accusingly, at her cat. Such sentences show us that an actual cat can take a place not only in a sentence consisting solely of spatial items as in "———— are dirty," but also in a sentence composed of the spatial cat and the spoken sounds "are dirty." We use this kind of sentence all the time. Now we see through the medium of mixed sentences that such objects as cats are functioning linguistically because the spatial cat is the subject of the sentence.

NICKEL: The cat's being a physical object doesn't prevent it from functioning linguistically, for if it did, that would mean this spatial object, namely "cat," couldn't function linguistically.

PENNY: Right. I'd like to coin a neologism for objects that function linguistically but which are not constructed by using letters of the alphabet or phonemes; let the neologism be "lobject," which is short for "linguistic object."

NICKEL: Why do you use that part about "not constructed by using letters of the alphabet or phonemes"?

PENNY: I'm simply trying to overcome a common prejudice. People generally identify as linguistic items those physical entities that are composed of familiar shapes, letters. For example, "Fiddle" is recognized as a linguistic item because it is constructed of "F," "i," "d," etc., whereas the cat is not constructed of letters, but flesh, bones, and hair.

NICKEL: I get it. You want a functional criterion for an entity being a linguistic item, not a physical criterion.

PENNY: That's right. Objects become lobjects when they function linguistically; that is, when they are governed by rules of regularity as vocables and inscriptions are.

NICKEL: I can draw two consequences from this.

First, the substitution instances of variables are referents. I say this because you claim that an expression, E, refers to an object, O, because O may be substituted into the place occupied by E. Sometimes there are several objects I can substitute for an expression. For example, in "The cat is hungry," I can substitute for "cat" either my Aunt Nettie's cat or our neighbor's cat. Similarly, into f in $f\alpha\beta$, I can substitute ∨ or .; that makes ∨ and . referents of f, just as the two cats are referents of "cat."

This leads me to my second conclusion: All words with more than one referent are variables. "Cat" is a variable as is f in $f\alpha\beta$, since several objects may be substituted into it.

PENNY: Those are clever conclusions, though I am inclined only toward the second. However, to reject the first, I see I shall have to place a restriction upon my substitution theory of reference.

NICKEL: Why do you say that?

PENNY: Because not every substitution instance of an expression is a referent. Take this sentence: A part of the pie is mine. We can substitute "portion" for "part" and have a meaningful sentence: A portion of the pie is mine. But——

NICKEL: We know that everything that can be substituted into the place occupied by "portion" can be substituted into the place occupied by "part." That is, they have the same referent.

PENNY: You miss the point of my example. What I substituted for "part" is the physical mark, the inscription "portion." That inscription is not the referent of "part" even though it may be substituted for it. That shows not all entities which can be substituted for an expression are referents of that expression. "Portion" is not a referent of "part," but a synonymous expression.

NICKEL: I get you. Of all the entities that can be substituted for another expression, some of them are referents and others are not. Sometimes an entity that is substituted for an expression is simply another linguistic expression, as "portion" was. At other times such a substituted entity is not a linguistic expression, as the cat was not.

PENNY: No, no. The latter I deny. Don't you recall that the cat functioned linguistically, that it was a lobject? Any time an entity is substituted for an expression it is a linguistic expression, for it is governed by a substitution rule and an arrangement rule, both being rules of regularity. But sometimes an entity is a particular kind of linguistic expression; namely, a referent.

NICKEL: OK, then the problem is to distinguish between linguistic expressions which are referents and those which are not.

PENNY: You've got it this time.

I think we can identify linguistic expressions which are referents with this criterion: An entity functions as a referent on a given occasion if and only if it is substitutable into an expression but is not itself an expression into which I can substitute something else.

Here is an example: My cigar is a referent when I say "This (pointing at the cigar) has gone out." My cigar is substitutable for "This" but on this occasion I cannot substitute anything for the cigar.

I'm going to call this special kind of substituting "emplacing," mainly on the analogy of a gun being put into a place prepared for it. The cigar had a subject place prepared for it by the variable "This" in "This has gone out."

NICKEL: You stressed "on a given occasion." Why did you do that?

PENNY: Because on some other occasion that entity may not be a referent; on some other occasion the restriction that nothing can be substituted for it may not hold. For example, take this word: prig. On one occasion, below, it is a referent and on another occasion it isn't.

Suppose we have the following expression: (_____) is a four-letter word. Suppose further that I substitute into the expression as in (a):

(a) (prig) is a four letter word.
(b) The prig is coming to harass us.

On which occasion is "prig" a referent and on which occasion isn't it?

NICKEL: It's a referent in (a), but not in (b). My friend, Dime, is sometimes a prig; I could substitute him into the second sentence but not into the first. And from this I draw a conclusion. A linguistic expression is a referent when it is mentioned; it is not a referent when it is used. It seems to me that's what your criterion for identifying referents comes to.

PENNY: That's an excellent remark, Emory.

NICKEL: If you approve of that, maybe you'll think as highly of this remark: Now that we are allowed to emplace, we can do away with the meta-language.

PENNY: That sounds interesting, but before I laud you, I'd like to know if you have good reasons for believing that.

NICKEL: We wanted to avoid self-reference in order to avoid special kinds of ambiguity and equivocation. (See *Third conversation—* E. Nickel). For this purpose we decided it would be useful to invent a language of a higher level, the meta-language; it enabled us to refer to expressions in the object language. That's how we came to use quotation marks. Placing quotation marks around an inscription showed that we were referring to an expression in the object language rather than using it. It seems to me that we could do away with quotation marks and the meta-language if we actually emplaced the expression in an object language sentence, for emplacing shows the entity about which we are saying something and inhibits it from being used to refer to anything else.

PENNY: That was an excellent remark, Nickel. I think, however, that we'll be forced to come up with some device for indicating that we're emplacing an inscription and not using it.

When you emplace a cat in a written sentence, no one is likely to think you are using it to refer to something, for we don't normally do so.

NICKEL: That was before today. Now I'm not sure what is and what isn't normal.

PENNY: You have a point there. And that reminds me of a cartoon I saw, which, had you seen it before today, would have made you suspicious of what is and what isn't normal even earlier. Consider Beetle Bailey's comrade-in-arms.*

BEETLE BAILEY   by Mort Walker

Do you realize what it is about pointing that confused Zero?

NICKEL: I think so. Normally in pointing we are emplacing that at which we point. The poor soldier thinks Sarge is emplacing the map, because he is pointing at it, whereas Sarge is using the map.

I don't much like your bringing this cartoon to my attention, though.

PENNY: Why not?

NICKEL: I don't like to see myself compared to such a fellow.

PENNY: Why, Nickel, you are much better than he. You'd never get caught emplacing a map when it's not to be emplaced. At least we've learned from the cartoon that even the worst of us can make mistakes about emplacement, and that since objects constructed from letters are more often used than emplaced, to prevent a reverse Beetle Bailey error, we should warn our readers who are given to expecting the normal when an inscription is being emplaced rather than used.

NICKEL: For normally inscriptions are used and not emplaced.

PENNY: More often, at least.

* By permission, King Features Syndicate.

NICKEL: How about warning them by putting parentheses around emplaced inscriptions?

PENNY: Seems fine to me. How would our equivocation example* look if we employed parentheses to indicate that an inscription is emplaced and not used?

NICKEL: The second (brave) would be enclosed in parentheses.

I've got a lot of wild conjectures running through my head today, but this one is so wild I'm afraid to mention it.

PENNY: It's no fun hunting cows in the barnyard. Go ahead.

NICKEL: Since we can pronounce objects, we can read the world. Here I am looking into the sky at the clouds and their whiteness, and since I can pronounce the clouds and their whiteness and since I know the simple structure of a subject-predicate sentence, I can read off the world by saying "That cloud is white." Now here comes the wild part: This explains how children come to utter some sentences they never heard before. Once they learn to pronounce objects and to master sentence structure, they simply read the world.

PENNY: You've brought a fine snark to earth, Nickel. We ought, however, to keep in mind the distinction between reading and talking.

Reading, that is, pronouncing the written words on a page, is a way of referring to them. Being asked to read a part of the world is being asked to say what objects, for example, are in our field of vision. In that way we refer to the objects and qualities in our field of vision. Now, we aren't always able to read every part of the world; some of it lies beyond that hill yonder and is not in our visual field. In that case, we aren't pronouncing, that is, reading, the world, for we're not seeing it. We're merely talking about the world.

NICKEL: From that I conclude "referring" doesn't mean exactly the same thing as "pronouncing." For "talking about" is referring though it isn't pronouncing.

PENNY: I agree with your conclusion. "Referring" is a wider term than "pronouncing." However, if we magicize our glass cave once more, so that all objects that have ever been, are, and will be in the world become visible to us, referring could be identical to pronouncing. All uttering could be reading; there wouldn't have to be any talking.

NICKEL: In that case, the glass cave would no longer be a cave, it would be the world itself.

PENNY: Then we would be as gods. How do you like the taste of the glass apple?

NICKEL: I feel like a glass Adam, and it tastes sweet. Nevertheless,

* Reader: See page 66.

having tasted the glass apple, I see how ungodlike, how human I am. I realize that we can't see, hence, can't pronounce everything. So doesn't that limitation wreck your view that referential meaning is a species of combinatory meaning, since referring isn't always a case of pronouncing?

PENNY: I don't think so. Showing that referring is sometimes similar to pronouncing proved that referring can be explained as a combinatory substitution rule. The fact that referring is a wider notion than pronunciation doesn't counter that explanation, for those cases of referring that aren't pronunciation can be explained this way. When I talk about, that is, refer to, the cat I can't see, the cat is the referent of a term only because it can be substituted for the term. There's no essential difference between that and reading. Both are governed by a substitution rule.

NICKEL: Since a written word is the referent of a pronunciation only because it can be substituted for the sound?

PENNY: That's right. There isn't anything more radical about this than the following: Two people give the same referential meaning to a term if they would make the same emplacements.

NICKEL: What we've done has helped wear some of the weirdness off, but I must confess it is still with me. It's more a feeling than a conviction, however.

PENNY: Let's try another abrasive, then.

This should slim down your reluctance. Let's see if the walls of the ideal language are glass. By shifting to Polish and Principia, languages which are relatively unfamiliar to you, we can avoid the preconceptions foisted onto you by your picture of your native tongue.

In using the ideal language for this purpose, I can also give you a bonus; I can satisfy your persistent desire for learning the referential meaning of Polish and Principia expressions.

Imagine a Polish cave of language.

NICKEL: A cave containing all Polish *wfes*?

PENNY:

p, q, r
v, *, ., *
—
.*pq* *rp, . . . *wfe*

1, 0

NICKEL: With the Polish vocabulary and *wfes* in the cave, I take it the numerals 1 and 0 are referents because they're outside the cave.

PENNY: That's right. Every Polish and Principia *wfe* has for its referent either the numeral 1 or the numeral 0.

NICKEL: I don't get the significance of 1 and 0.

PENNY: Aren't you ever satisfied? You've been asking me for a long time about the referential meaning of Polish and Principia expressions, and when I finally tell you, you ask me about them in turn. Just let them be the shapes they are.

NICKEL: Sorry. Do the letters refer to 1 and 0 also?

PENNY: They do. I'm going to use matrices, that is, emplacement charts, to exhibit the referents of Polish expressions. I'll do it for letters first.

$$\frac{p \quad q \quad r}{1 \quad 1 \quad 1} : \text{We could have done it this way: } \frac{\alpha}{1}$$
$$0 \quad 0 \quad 0 \qquad\qquad\qquad\qquad\qquad\qquad 0$$

That would have been shorter. Each row in the matrix column shows a possible emplacement for the expression, α, above the line.

NICKEL: The alpha is operating as a variable here as it did in the first *wfe* rule, the first rule in the Po-3 entry.

PENNY: Exactly. We'll need matrices also for the variable expressions in the second and third *wfe* rules. I'll give the simplest, the third one, first.

$$\frac{- \quad \alpha}{0 \quad 1}$$
$$1 \quad 0$$

When we consider the variable expression in the second *wfe* rule, $f\alpha\beta$, we have to take into account that both alpha and beta can have expressions substituted into them that can mean either 1 or 0. That gives us four possible combinations. Each row shows us a different combination or order of referents.

$$\frac{f\alpha\beta}{11}$$
$$01$$
$$10$$
$$00$$

NICKEL: The whole $f\alpha\beta$ expression still doesn't have a referent though, does it, even if alpha and beta do?

PENNY: That's right. We have to remember that since we have four different binary functors to substitute into f, we can make four different expressions: $.\alpha\beta$, $\vee\alpha\beta$, $*\alpha\beta$, and $\ddagger\alpha\beta$. What do you think? Should we make them differ in their referential meanings?

NICKEL: I don't understand the question.

PENNY: If a dot expression, $.\alpha\beta$, differs from a vee, $v\alpha\beta$, ast, $*\alpha\beta$, and double ast, $\underset{*}{*}\alpha\beta$, expression, then its referential meaning will be different from that of the other expressions. Here, let me give samples:

$.\ \alpha\beta$	$v\ \alpha\beta$	$*\ \alpha\beta$	$\underset{*}{*}\ \alpha\beta$
1 11	1 11	1 11	1 11
0 01	1 01	1 01	0 01
0 10	1 10	0 10	0 10
0 00	0 00	1 00	1 00

The combinations for alpha and beta are identical in all four cases, but the columns under the functors are all different. The meaning of an $f\alpha\beta$ expression is determined differently for each functor by at least one combination for alpha and beta. For example, the combination in the fourth row of α as zero and β as zero determines that a $.\alpha\beta$ expression will mean zero while that combination determines that a $\underset{*}{*}\alpha\beta$ expression will mean one.

NICKEL: I understand your question now. To make it interesting, let's have the different $f\alpha\beta$ expressions differ in their referential meaning. That means we've now introduced a difference between the binary functors, functors that up to now have been treated alike.

It wasn't so hard to give referential meaning to Polish expressions, was it?

PENNY: What does $*rq$ mean?

NICKEL: It could mean the numeral 1 or the numeral 0. The * column of the matrix contains each of them.

PENNY: What if someone pointed out that this shows Polish expressions are ambiguous?

NICKEL: He would be right. But I don't see this as a criticism of Polish and Principia. English expressions also often have more than one possible meaning.

PENNY: You're right. Many English words are multi-vocal. Still, how would you communicate unambiguously to someone what you meant by $*rq$?

NICKEL: $*rq$ is ambiguous because its constitutents r and q are ambiguous. If a person knew the matrix for ast expressions and knew the meaning of r and q, he would know the meaning of $*rq$. Suppose you meant by r, 1, and by q, 0; then $*rq$, according to the third row in the ast matrix, would mean 0.

PENNY: But how would the other person know what you meant by r and q?

NICKEL: You'd have to say what you meant.

PENNY: How would you do it?

NICKEL: I don't see any problem; you'd simply say ast one zero.

PENNY: How bright it's become in our Polish cave! And no wonder; the walls are glass.

Suddenly the numerals 1 and 0 are part of Polish and Principia. They have entered into an expression, for you've pronounced 1 and 0. We can emplace them as well: *10.

NICKEL: How quickly you slipped that in. But then, it seems to me, we have to say that there is an increase in the number of Polish expressions.

PENNY: I don't mind saying that. I'm perfectly willing to allow that every time we introduce a new referential meaning we fall heir to additional combinations of entities. That's what referential meaning is all about.

Let's call an expression such as *10 a *wfe*10. A *wfe*10 can be written in a more complete fashion also. We could write 0*10. In the complete writing the expressions wear their meaning on their sleeve.

NICKEL: This slick maneuver you just pulled has sandpapered my feeling of weirdness about your emplacement theory of referential meaning pretty thin.

PENNY: What a splendid time to throw a clincher.

"*E* (an expression) refers to *O* (an object)" is interpreted as "*O* is emplaceable into *E*." This gives us:

"*p* refers to 1" means "1 is emplaceable into *p*."

p is a Polish expression (*wfe*); so, 1 (by being emplaceable into *p*) is a Polish expression (*wfe*10).

"'Square' refers to □" means "□ is emplaceable into 'square'."

"The square is black" is an English sentence; so, "The □ is black" is an English sentence.

Perhaps any lingering doubts can be dispelled by the familiarity which comes from working with the referential meanings of Polish expressions—from working exercises.

7.1: This exercise will provide Po-5 and Pr-5 for our rules. Write the simplest and least number of rules you can (a) for the referential meanings of all Polish letters; (b) for the referential meanings of ast, vee, dot, and double ast expressions; and (c) for the referential meanings of expressions with a bar to the extreme left. (d) Do the same for Principia.

Ast, vee, dot, and double ast expressions are *wfe*s whose strongest binary functor is, respectively, an ast, vee, dot, and double ast. To find their rules you must refer to the four-row matrices that showed the differences between the binary functors.

What kind of *wfe* is this one: v.*pqr*?

NICKEL: That's a vee expression.

PENNY: Do you know how to exhibit all the possible *wfe*10s that fall under it?

NICKEL: If that question is the same as "Do you know how to construct its matrix?" the answer is "No."

PENNY: The questions are the same, and here are some simple rules which will give you directions for constructing the matrix for any *wfe*.

We have to consider three things: First, the number of rows in the matrix; secondly, the character of the columns under the letters; and, third, the character of the columns under the functors.

First, the number of rows in any matrix is computed by using the formula, 2^n, where n is the number of different letters contained in the *wfe*. How many rows would there be in the matrix of v.*pqr*?

NICKEL: There are three different letters. That would give me 2^3. $2^3 = 8$. I would have eight rows.

PENNY: Good. Now about the character of the letter columns. In this case we have to observe three rules. (a) We start with the letter farthest left in the *wfe* and place beneath it a column with 2^n rows composed of 1's and 0's alternating with each other.

NICKEL: Like this?

v.*pqr*
1
0
1
0
1
0
1
0

PENNY: Yes. (b) Proceeding to the right, each different letter that has not yet been assigned a column will alternate *groups* of 1's and 0's for 2^n rows, with its groups containing twice as many 1's and 0's as the groups in the last different column to its left did.

NICKEL: Are these columns for *q* and *r* correct?

v.*pqr*	v.*pqr*	Here is the matrix	v.*pqr*
1	1	with all letter columns	111
1	1	filled in.	011
0	1		101
0	1		001
1	0		110
1	0		010
0	0		100
0	0		000

PENNY: You're right on both counts. (c) When a letter recurs in a *wfe*, its column is the same as the column under its first occurrence. That should give you no difficulty.

Now for the character of the functor columns. You remember we found that one way of stating the rule for finding the expression strength of binary Polish functors was this: A binary functor has a strength one greater than that of the strongest of the two expressions immediately to its right that have not previously been used to determine a functor's strength.

NICKEL: I remember, and I take it that rule will help me to assign the binary functor columns their proper 1's and 0's.

PENNY: It will. It works as follows: Using the appropriate rule you gave in answer to exercise 7.1 (b), and applying it to each row in the two columns under the expressions that were used to determine the binary functor's strength, you can place a 1 or 0 in each row under the functor until the column has 2^n rows. I'll write down what is relevant in the matrix for determining the vee and dot columns for v.*pqr*.

v.*pqr*	v.*pqr*	
111	11	1
001	10	1
010	10	1
000	10	1
111	11	0
001	00	0
010	00	0
000	00	0

In determining the dot column, I apply the dot rule from 7.1 (b) to the columns under *p* and *q* since I use *p* and *q* to determine the dot's expression strength; in determining the v column I apply the v rule from 7.1 (b) to the dot column and the *r* column since the dot and *r* are what I use to determine the v's expression strength.

If we put all the columns together now, we will have the matrix for the *wfe*, v.*pqr*.

I prefer to put them together in the following way. I prefer this way because it incorporates 1's and 0's into Polish very neatly; and it provides us with new well-formed expressions—*wfe*10's.

v .*pqr*
1v1.111
1v0.011
1v0.101
1v0.001
1v1.110
0v0.010
0v0.100
0v0.000

NICKEL: Is each row of that matrix a *wfe*10?

PENNY: It is, and now each belongs to the Polish language.

There is only one other factor we have to take into account in constructing emplacement charts.

NICKEL: The bar is the only thing we haven't treated. I don't think that's much of a problem, at least not if my next remark is right. We produce matrix columns in the order of their expression strength, starting with the weakest expressions. Thus, since a bar always has the same expression strength as the vocabulary item to its immediate right, if a vocabulary item has strength *N*, before I can go on to construct columns for any expressions of strength $N+1$, I have to see if there are any bars of strength *N* for which I must construct columns.

PENNY: Very good. Notice that in the example below, *p–q, that the *q* column is not used to determine the ast column. The bar column is used instead. *q* is of expression strength 0, so before I construct a column for ast, which is of expression strength $0+1$, I have to construct a column for the bar, which is of expression strength 0.

*p–q	*p –q	*p –q	*p –q
1 1	0–1	0*10	0*10–1
0 1	0–1	1*00	1*00–1
1 0	1–0	1*11	1*11–0
0 0	1–0	1*01	1*01–0

−*q·qp	−*q ·qp	− *q ·qp	− *q ·qp
1 11	1.11	1*11	0–1*11.11
0 01	0.01	1*00	0–1*00.01
1 10	0.10	0*10	1–0*10.10
0 00	0.00	1*00	0–1*00.00

The order of producing columns for a Principia *wfe* is exactly the same; consequently, we don't need to spend any time showing you how to produce matrices for them.

7.2: Produce the matrices for the Polish and Principia expressions in exercise 1.9. For the Principia expressions you only need produce the matrices; you do not need to write down *wfe*10; that is, simply put columns under the constituent expressions.

7.3: If referents like 1's and 0's can enter into language, we increase the number of expressions in that language, as you observed. Naturally, if referents are to be linguistic entities in spite of themselves, poor Robin, we must observe rules of regularity governing them, so that the expressions of which they are constituents are well-formed. I want you to express the rules for Polish *wfe*10. They will be Po-6.

Perhaps the following will be of help in answering 7.3. Once again I ignore the bar, for you can state a rule for it quite simply as we did before.

$$
\begin{array}{cccccc}
1v01 & 0v0.010 & 1*0.10 & 1v01 & 1*11v0.01 & 1\overset{*}{*}00 \\
\gamma f \alpha \beta & \gamma f \alpha \beta & \gamma f \alpha \beta & \gamma f \alpha \beta & \gamma f \alpha \beta & \gamma f \alpha \beta \\
 & \overline{\gamma f \ \ \alpha \ \ \beta} & \overline{\gamma f \ \ \alpha \ \ \beta} & \overline{\gamma f \ \ \alpha \ \ \beta} & \\
 & & & \overline{\gamma f \alpha \ \ \ \ \ \beta} & \\
\end{array}
$$

NICKEL: You seem to have sundered the Siamese twins. You haven't shown me a Principia *wfe*10.

PENNY: You're right, and we don't want the twins to die of a parted heart. Let that be your next exercise, you old Sentimentalist.

7.4: (a) Work out suitable Principia *wfe*10s; (b) state the rules for them and let them be Pr-6.

NICKEL: It does me no good to do good.

PENNY: You must think of others, Nickel! Just as I'm thinking of you right now, thinking of what other exercises I can generously give you. Oh, take not this dagger of kindness from me.

NICKEL: I grow faint. Faith, I am quit.

PENNY: Ready for scene 7.5. You've had a lot of opportunities to note that a binary functor in a *wfe* is always associated with two other expressions.

NICKEL: The expressions that go in the alpha and beta place?

PENNY: Yes. Now, if a matrix is to contain all possible combinations of what the expressions in the alpha and beta places can mean, it has to contain four rows. Because four rows exhaust all possible combinations and orders of 1's and 0's.

Let's consider this expression the general form of a Polish *wfe* containing a binary functor: $f\alpha\beta$. Since the column under the f can contain only 1's and 0's, and since there are only four rows, how many different kinds of columns can there be under f?

NICKEL: Let me see; I think we can have sixteen different kinds of columns.

PENNY: Since f can have sixteen different columns and since we defined the differences between the binary functors, ast, dot, vee, and double ast, with respect to the difference in their columns, what do we know about the number of binary functors in our Polish language so far?

NICKEL: We know it can contain only sixteen binary functors.

PENNY: Suppose each column I'm going to write down were a binary functor column.

1	2	3	4	5	6	7	8	9	10	11	12	13	14	15	16
1	0	1	1	1	0	1	1	1	0	0	0	0	0	1	0
1	1	0	1	1	0	0	1	0	1	1	0	0	1	0	0
1	1	1	0	1	1	0	0	1	0	1	0	1	0	0	0
1	1	1	1	0	1	1	0	0	1	0	1	0	0	0	0

You'll undoubtedly recognize some familiar columns among the sixteen.

NICKEL: I do. Column 4 is the same column that you gave for ast; column 5 is the same column you gave for vee; 15 is the dot column; and 7 is the double ast column. We could make up some more functor marks now if we wanted to. We already have four, so we only need to make up twelve more.

PENNY: You don't have to make up that many distinct marks if we make use of the functors we already have. For example, we don't need an additional mark for column 13.

NICKEL: But it's a distinct column; no other column is like it, so it must have a distinct functor.

PENNY: Yes, it's different, but maybe we can provide for that column without having to introduce a new functor. Watch this.

4			13		
*	*rq*		–	*	*rq*
1	11		0	1	11
1	01		0	1	01
0	10		1	0	10
1	00		0	1	00

NICKEL: Why, by simply putting the monary functor bar to the left of ast, we can produce column 13! You're right we don't need a distinct functor mark for 13 when a combination of bar and ast will do. That means we can reduce the number of distinct marks needed to eight.

1	16		15	2		3	14		4	13
#	–# (pound)		.	–.		$	–$		*	–*

5	12		6	8		7	11		9	10
v	–v		%	–%		*	–*		&	–& (amper-sand)

There. Now we have only eight functors: #, ., $, *, v, %, *, and &.

PENNY: That's good. Now suppose we reduce the number

even more. I suggest that we get rid of, for example, the dot. Watch this.

$$
\begin{array}{ll}
\cdot\ qp & -\ \vee\ -\ q\ -\ p \\
1\ 11 & 1\ 0\ 0\ 1\ 0\ 1 \\
0\ 01 & 0\ 1\ 1\ 0\ 0\ 1 \\
0\ 10 & 0\ 1\ 0\ 1\ 1\ 0 \\
0\ 00 & 0\ 1\ 1\ 0\ 1\ 0
\end{array}
$$

NICKEL: Both *wfe*s have the same far left column. Does that mean $\cdot qp$ and $-\vee-q-p$ have the same meaning?

PENNY: Yes, it does. Whenever, for example, q means 1, and p means 0, as in the third row, each *wfe* will mean 0. This sameness of meaning holds for all combinations of the meaning of q and p.

We know that if we replace an expression by another having the same meaning we won't change the meaning of the larger expression containing it. Thus, the following two expressions have the same meaning, even though I replace $\cdot qp$ by $-\vee-q-p$.

$$*r \cdot qp$$
$$*r-\vee-q-p$$

You can see the expressive power of Polish wouldn't lessen if we left the dot out of its vocabulary. For we could always replace it with an expression using only bar and vee as its functors.

NICKEL: That's economy, man. How many functors do we actually need in Polish?

PENNY: Why that is the very thing of which exercises are made.

NICKEL: I keep telling myself: "Logic should be my discovery. Logic should be my discovery."

PENNY: Before I drop the bricks, notice that we have now shown equivalence conversations are possible within Polish itself, and, of course, within Principia itself also.

NICKEL: Sure, since "$\cdot pq$" and "$-\vee-q-p$" have the same meaning. Also, translation occurs within a single language as well as between two languages.

PENNY: This next exercise is about Polish equivalence conversations.

7.5: You showed we could reduce the number of Polish functors to eight. I showed you how we could reduce them to seven when I showed that an expression containing only the bar and vee as functors could be formed which says the same thing as a dot expression. Thus, we can rid ourselves of the dot functor. You are to find for each of the following expressions an equivalent expression containing only vees and bars as functors:

(a) $\#pp$, $-\#pp$; (b) $\cdot rq$, $-\cdot rq$; (c) $\$rq$, $-\$rq$; (d) $*pq$, $-*pq$; (e) $\%qr$, $-\%qr$; (f) $\ast\!pq$, $-\!\ast\!pq$; (g) $\&rp$, $-\&rp$.

(For help with (f), I suggest that you take a look at expression 21 below.)

NICKEL: In other words, I am to find the other half of the equivalence conversations for each of those expressions? And, I take it, I am to do it the same way you did it for the dot expression?

PENNY: Twice right. In order to find the other half of an equivalence conversation beginning with #*pp*, for example, you have to find an expression which contains the same letters, used as often in the expression as you like, whose only functors are bars and vees and whose matrix has a far left column composed only of 1's.

NICKEL: You know, it's a relief to have some expression which means 1 no matter what its constituent expressions mean. Likewise for 0. No hedging about with that kind of expression.

PENNY: They're univocal expressions.

NICKEL: Univocal?

PENNY: A univocal expression is one with a single meaning. In case the univocal expressions become important later, I think we ought to give them names. So, let's add "tautology" and "contradiction" to our meta-language vocabulary. All Polish *wfe*s whose far left matrix column contains only ones we'll call tautologies; all Polish *wfe*s whose far left matrix column contains only zeros we'll call contradictions. Multi-vocal expressions also should have a name; we'll call all Polish *wfe*s whose far left matrix column contains both ones and zeros indeterminates.

You can see that tautologicalness, contradictoriness, and indeterminacy are properties of a *wfe*'s matrix. They are not properties of *wfe*10s.

7.6: Classify the following expressions, indicating which are tautological *wfe*s, which are contradictory *wfe*s, and which are indeterminate *wfe*s.

1. *vpq–·–p–q
2. *·*pqpq
3. –*vpqvqp
4. *pvpq
5. *·pq·qp
6. *·pq·pq
7. *vpvqrvvpqr
8. –*·p·qr··pqr
9. *·*pq–q–p
10. *pvpp
11. *·*pqqp
12. –*p·pp
13. *·*pq–p–q

14. **·pqr*p*qr
15. *·*pq*qr*pr
16. *p––p
17. –**pqv–pq
18. –*·vpq–pq
19. *·pvqrv·pq·pr
20. *vp·qr·vpqvpr
21. **pq·*pq*qp
22. **pqv·pq·–p–q
23. *·pqp
24. **pq*–q–p
25. –*–·pqv–p–q
26. *··*pq*–prv–pvqr

NICKEL: That's quite a few ducks to knock over isn't it?

PENNY: But the prize is of great value. And, you can choose your weapons.

You grasped the point of the "Monkey is telephone" quite well. This next exercise involves something analogous in Polish.

7.7: You'll notice that there are five groups of expressions below, and that each expression contains at least one question mark. The question marks are in positions that would ordinarily be occupied by a functor. All the question marks in each group may have one and only one functor substituted into them if each expression is to be a *wfe*10. Identify which functor may be substituted into all the question marks in group (a) if each expression is to be a *wfe*10; do the same for group (b), (c), (d), and (e).

NICKEL: So, you're testing me on my combinatory knowledge? That is, you're testing to see if I have a combinatory concept of the functors?

PENNY: That's exactly right.

(a) 1?01
    1.1v01?111
    1?0.010
    0.0?101

(b) 0.1?000v00
    0?1v010.00
    0.0.1v1101?11
    0?0v0.0?0*101101

(c) 1*1v0?0111
    0?1v0.0010*10
    1?11*00
    0.0?000

(d) 1?1?0?0011?10

(e) 1v1?0*1.110v001
    0.1*0?110v00

NICKEL: The binary number system was never like this!

PENNY: The Review Questions will rescue you for a moment from numerals.

Review Questions

1. Give an account of the three explanations, the slip-, forgetfulness-, and job-explanations, for our not saying what we mean.

2. How do the above explanations differ from Nickel's explanation? And how does Nickel's explanation of what a person means lead to psychology's invasion of theory of meaning?

3. Why does Penny think psychology is irrelevant to his and Nickel's conversation?

4. Why is writing useful?

5. What view of his does Nickel think is supported by comparing the writing on the stone cave's wall to the shadows in Plato's Cave?

6. How is the superiority of pictographs over conventional writing supported by the notions of acquaintance and propositional meaning?

7. Why does Nickel think the man in O'Neal's cartoon needn't be so angry at the boy? And why does Nickel's account displease Penny?

8. Why does Penny think imagistic responses, glandular and muscular changes, and neuro-physiological reactions are not useful for accounting for communication?

9. Why does Penny think an attempt to give a dispositional account of referential meaning is putting the bite before the food?

10. Why won't a glass cave solve the Boswell problem, where the glass cave allows us to hear any speech sound ever uttered?

11. What is Penny's view of the relation between referential and combinatory meaning?

12. Do you understand the relations among the following sentences?

    (a) Mixed sentences are sentences.
    (b) Pronouncing utilizes a substitution code.
    (c) As the walls in O'Neal's Cave turn to glass we see the teacher pronouncing the cat.
    (d) Objects, when emplaced, become lobjects.
    (e) Placing a cat above the blank in "＿＿＿＿＿ is a Manx" is linguistically equivalent to pointing to the cat.
    (f) Referring, either when pronouncing or talking, requires a substitution code.

13. Why does emplacement allow us to dispense with quotation marks?

NICKEL: I thought you'd never end.

PENNY: It's a difficult subject we've discussed and I wanted to make sure you had all the intricacies laid out before you so you could reflect upon them.

NICKEL: I'll do that. And don't look for me again until I find a glass apple for the teacher.

PENNY: Good-bye, Nickel.

Eighth conversation

A SEQUENCE
OF KINGS: *M, N*

Bye their argyment shal ye ken them, for Phylosofers ar a most disputatious lott.—Fanebius Perlyng

NICKEL: I have a friend, Dime, who has taken a logic course. He has been reading my notes and disagrees quite definitely with some of the things we have been saying. And he brought up an argument against your view that the traditional philosophers have always done what you think the "new" philosophers do.

PENNY: Your friend Dime rates as an expert, having taken a course in logic.

NICKEL: He also reads a lot.

PENNY: Oh. Before I hear this argument, which I can see you are eager to press on me——

NICKEL: Yes, for I do not know what to make of it.

PENNY: ——let's see if you grasped the moves we made in our sixth conversation. Perhaps you'll see Dime's argument in a clearer light when you review our conversation.

NICKEL: That's a good idea. Your ultimate aim, you said, is to give another justification for learning the ideal languages of logic in the narrow sense; you want to show that learning Polish and Principia will be of value even if we forget them.

PENNY: Yes; despite your forgetting them, you will get something from Polish and Principia that is good for your soul.

NICKEL: I guess you don't mean anything technical by "good for your soul."

PENNY: No. I only mean that anyone concerned about the good of his soul has the kind of concern that would send him to philosophy rather than to accounting or chemistry or psychology.

NICKEL: So, if you could show that learning logic in the narrow sense yields philosophic profit, you would have made your point about its being good for our souls.

PENNY: Exactly.

NICKEL: But you said that before you could show philosophic profit can be made from a study of logic in the narrow sense, you had to show that philosophy is part of logic in the wide sense.

PENNY: Right, and we found that combinatory philosophy is part of logic in the wide sense, since it is concerned with investigating linguistic regularity. The expressions whose regularity it investigates are philosophic words.

NICKEL: Then, as far as you're concerned, philosophic profit consists of philosophic combinatory concepts.

PENNY: On the nose, Nickel.

NICKEL: On the other hand, I had a traditional notion of philosophic profit. I thought it consisted of propositional concepts, for I thought philosophy aimed at finding out the truth about the referents of philosophic words rather than finding out the truth about the words themselves.

However, I don't recall your saying this traditional notion of philosophy is a mistaken idea.

PENNY: I didn't and wouldn't say that. All that historically goes under the name of philosophy doesn't purport to have the same aim; and I'm loathe to say that only one of the aims is genuinely philosophic and the remainder spurious. We should love philosophy enough to tolerate all its many moods.

NICKEL: But you did maintain that traditional philosophers' works could also yield combinatory-concept profit.

PENNY: Ah, so. They are twice blessed, because they are twice philosophers.

NICKEL: By the way, there aren't many people who think of philosophy as you do, are there?

PENNY: Are you afraid that this is Yeats' rough beast, its hour come round at last, that slouches towards Bethlehem to be born?

NICKEL: Well, I would like to know just how widespread the combinatory conception of philosophy is.

PENNY: Look! Look! The star has stopped. Madam, just a little peek into the crib? Ah, a darlin' child. And who is its father? John Wisdom? For was it not he who said . . . Excuse me, I have to look it up again. Nickel, would you hand me that book at the end of the shelf, *Philosophy and Psychoanalysis*? Let's see; here we are, page 168 . . . John Wisdom said, "A philosopher is an animal in which the scientist vanishes into the logician—not to mention here the poet and psychoanalyst."*

Ah, no. It is not Wisdom, for a few sentences later, he says, "For the metaphysical and Copernican discovery of how nearly philosophy is really logic [G. E.] Moore did as much as, and perhaps more than any other man."

It is not as important to worry about how many "new" philosophers there are as to recall my argument for traditional philosophers being twice philosophers.

NICKEL: I believe you argued that anybody who believed that the traditional philosophers yield a propositional-concept profit would have to concede that they also yield a combinatory-concept profit because it is necessary for sentences to have meaning before they can have truth. Nonsensical sentences are neither true nor false.

* John Wisdom, *Philosophy and Psychoanalysis*, Basil Blackwell, Oxford, 1953, p. 168.

You also pointed out that we could decide whether or not a Principia expression is well-formed without knowing whether it is true.

PENNY: Good. Don't you think that should settle the matter?

NICKEL: That brings me to Dime's argument, for he doesn't think so. He pointed out that we made a distinction between using a word and mentioning it, and that we said any sentences in which a word is mentioned belongs to the meta-language.

PENNY: Yes, we said that.

NICKEL: Dime then pointed out to me that if philosophy is a study of the regularity of philosophic words, the sentences expressing the results of the study are in the meta-language. Is this correct so far?

PENNY: Go on.

NICKEL: Wait and watch, eh? Dime then took me over to his bookshelves and invited me to look in any of the traditional philosophers' books I pleased. "Open them," he said, "and see if you can find any meta-language sentences there. See if you can find reports on how philosophic words are used." I did look, and couldn't find any.

PENNY: What did you say this was supposed to prove?

NICKEL: That the traditional philosophers did not do combinatory philosophy.

PENNY: You might have pointed out to Dime that failure to find meta-language reports in a philosopher's work doesn't prove he didn't do combinatory philosophy nor that he didn't arrive at any results. He might have done both, but simply not have reported his results.

NICKEL: But why would a man do combinatory philosophy and not report it?

PENNY: That's an easy one. He might do it in order to avoid uttering and writing nonsensical expressions. Can't that be as important an aim as writing meta-language reports?

NICKEL: I guess so.

PENNY: Let's fly into the teeth of Dime's argument. He thinks we can't classify a man as a combinatory philosopher unless we catch him making meta-language reports. Well, I say we can.

NICKEL: Grabbing another forelock, eh?

PENNY: Hang on; here we go. Don't you think that if a man has done combinatory philosophy, the least we can expect from him are answers to combinatory questions?

NICKEL: Combinatory questions?

PENNY: Like this: "Mr. Philosopher, with what other words do we combine word W to produce a meaningful expression?" That's the general form of a combinatory question. You can substitute "tragedy," "good," or "God" for W if you want to.

NICKEL: In that case, yes, we should expect an answer from Mr. Combinatory Philosopher.

PENNY: What's wanted next is an explanation of how Mr. Philosopher can answer such a question without giving us a meta-language report.

And now, good Nickel——

NICKEL: Yes, sir.

PENNY: Attend well.

NICKEL: My mind is keening t'a dagger's point. But before you go on I must ask this question: Are you trying to prove that traditional philosophers *are* combinatory philosophers?

PENNY: No. I'm only interested in showing that they can be *interpreted* that way; I'm not interested in showing what they "really" did or what they "really" intended to do. Remember the boys playing their games, happily, though unknowingly, building their character.

Soft now. Music, Maestro. For a story is upon me.

Once upon a time there were two men, *M* and *N*. They lived in different countries. *M* never was heard to speak a word, while *N* talked incessantly.

M was at the head of the troops when they went into battle; *M* led the dancing at all the state balls; *M* stood more erect and moved more gracefully than any other man in the country; *M* accepted praise with such modesty and poise that he was the envy of the whole court; *M*'s grave deliberations and firm nod made his judgment the most respected at the diplomatic table; when *M* walked through a crowd, the people opened a path for him like the waters of the Red Sea parting for the Israelites at the bidding of Moses, and when they closed behind him he left a wake of dumb, bobbing faces struck with respect, wonder, and awe.

And *N*. *N* was none of these things; yet *N* never for a moment let you forget that he was the king. For he kept saying, "Look here, I shall be first into battle for I am the king," or "I shall be the first to dance, and with whom I choose, for I am the king," or "I should think you would do me honor for——

NICKEL: I am the king."

PENNY: And what strikes you here?

NICKEL: *M exhibits* kingliness while *N tells* us he is the king.

PENNY: Like King *M*, a traditional philosopher may by his acts exhibit his combinatory concepts, and thus answer combinatory questions.

NICKEL: What acts?

PENNY: The acts of writing or uttering his sentences. But not meta-language sentences. For that would make him like King *N*.

NICKEL: And King *N* philosophers proclaim rather than exhibit their combinatory concepts. I have an image of the contrast now, but I still have no notion of how one can exhibit combinatory concepts.

PENNY: "A philosopher exhibits his combinatory concepts." That is the same as saying, "A philosopher's use of a word exhibits regularity."

NICKEL: Then the other method of finding a philosopher's answer to a combinatory question is to observe the regularity of his use?

PENNY: Of course. What we need now is an analogy to illuminate the path leading to the two ways in which a philosopher may answer a combinatory question.

Do you know what a sequence is?

NICKEL: If I recall my mathematics correctly, a sequence is a set of numbers arranged in a definite order.

PENNY: Can you give me an example of one?

NICKEL: 2,4,6,8, etc.

PENNY: Suppose we observe a stranger to have written on a piece of paper the following: 1,3, ... You say to yourself, "I wonder if he has a sequence in mind? Well, I'll just ask him." "Sir, do you have a sequence, a regular combination of numbers, in mind?"

The man can give an affirmative answer in two ways: I'll call them Way M and Way N: and I'll give two examples of each.

Way M_1: 1,3,5,7,9, ...   Way N_1: $2n-1$
Way M_2: 1,3,7,15,31, ...   Way N_2: 2^n-1

Either way gives you an indication of what sequence the man has in mind. Way M does it by exhibiting the sequence he has in mind; Way N does it by giving you a combinatory rule which, if followed, will produce the sequence he has in mind.

NICKEL: $2n-1$ and 2^n-1 are combinatory rules?

PENNY: Yes; we can consider a sequence as an expression composed of numbers. Every different combination of numbers constitutes a different expression. Thus "1,3,5,7,9, ..." and "1,3,7,15,31, ..." are different expressions. The rules $2n-1$ and 2^n-1 tell us how to combine which natural numbers to form those expressions.

NICKEL: I think you'd better review those rules for me.

PENNY: Notice that the rules contain a variable, n; if you substitute a number for that variable, then by using the arithmetical operations, you will be able to produce another number. For example, suppose I substitute 1 for n in $2n-1$; I get this: $(2 \times 1) - 1 = 1$. If I substitute 2, I get this: $(2 \times 2) - 1 = 3$.

If I specify a sequence of substitutions for n, then we can produce a sequential expression, for we can use the rule to produce the numbers we are to combine. These diagrams will show you that if I substitute the natural numbers for *n* in their sequential order, each rule will give us a different combination of numbers, that is, will produce a different expression.

$n=$	1	2	3	4	5	6 ...
$2n-1=$	1	3	5	7	9	11 ...

$n=$	1	2	3	4	5	6 ...
$2^n-1=$	1	3	7	15	31	63 ...

NICKEL: But in order to combine the numbers in the new expression in the right order, I must substitute the natural numbers into the rule in their order.

PENNY: That's right.

NICKEL: You know, $2n-1$ and 2^n-1 strike me as being cipher rules.

PENNY: Why do you say that?

NICKEL: Ciphers are rules holding between a familiar and an unfamiliar regularity. Suppose we consider the natural number sequence, N, as the familiar regularity, and consider some other sequence, X, for example, "1,3,5,7,9, . . . ," as the unfamiliar regularity.

$2n-1$ is a rule that helps me translate from the familiar expression N to the unfamiliar expression X. I can disguise N as X.

PENNY: Do you have two expressions, N and X, with a common meaning?

NICKEL: Gee, I don't know.

PENNY: I don't know of any situation in which we claim that "1, 2, 3, 4, 5, . . ." and "1, 3, 5, 7, 9 . . ." have a common meaning, do you?

NICKEL: No, I don't.

PENNY: I grant that we perhaps could make up such a situation, but I suggest we stick closer to actual situations in order to classify $2n-1$ more realistically.

Instead of likening $2n-1$ to a cipher rule, I think we should liken it to a *wfe* rule. Given the natural numbers as a base, it tells us how to form another sequence. And a *wfe* rule is after all a combinatory rule.

NICKEL: Besides, that's the kind of rule we were looking for when we wanted a King N answer.

PENNY: Sure. We wanted the combinatory philosopher to tell us how he combined a word with other words. "$2n-1$" is analogous to one of the ways, because it gives us a rule for combining the numerals the stranger wrote down, "1, 3, . . .", with other numerals, and without exhibiting the other numerals with which it is combined.

Okay, now we're straight about Way N of answering combinatory questions. I want to see if you can apply this to language, if you can give me a King N answer to a combinatory question about language. I suggest you do it in terms of our "Monkey is telephone" example from the other day. The combinatory question is: How do you combine the word "monkey" with other words?

NICKEL: This would be a King N answer: "Monkey" is combined with other words as "talk" is.

PENNY: Right, and that answer is a combinatory, *wfe* rule as "$2n-1$" is, "monkey" being analogous to "1, 3, ..." In the "monkey" case we need a rule telling us how to combine that word with other words, and in the "1, 3, ..." case we need a rule telling us how to combine those numerals with other numerals.

NICKEL: And now we have to explore the King M type answer to combinatory questions. I'd like to ask the first question about Way M.

PENNY: You're most welcome to the court, Sir Emory. Tilt away.

NICKEL: I don't see how a person can answer a combinatory question the King M way.

PENNY: That doesn't seem mysterious. A stranger writes down "1, 3, ..." and you want to know how he combines it with other numerals, so he gives you other numerals and shows you how.

NICKEL: But even if he says, "1, 3, 5, 7, 9, ...", he hasn't fully answered me. In fact, he can't fully answer me that way because he can't exhibit the total combination; the numbers in the sequence are infinite.

PENNY: That's a good observation, but there does come a point at which you begin to grasp the sequence he has in mind, for if he stopped at 9, couldn't you go on?

NICKEL: I suppose so.

PENNY: How would you go on?

NICKEL: "... 11, 13, 15, 17 ..."

PENNY: Then you know how to combine them as well as he does now. And so you share his combinatory concept.

NICKEL: But I don't know that he won't go "21, 25, 29, 33, ..." when he gets to 21. That's why the rule, "$2n-1$," is better. With the rule he has to go "21, 23, 25, ...".

PENNY: But that's no objection to answering combinatory questions by exhibition. If a man fully answers a combinatory question, he must fully exhibit his regularity. That is, he must give enough exhibitions to enable you to find the *wfe* rule.

If a person intends the sequence, "1, 3, 5, 7, 9, 11, 13, 15, 17, 19, 21, 25, 29, 33, ..." and only gives you "1, 3, 5, 7, 9, ...", then he hasn't given you an adequate combinatory answer, for he hasn't given you enough exhibitions to enable you to find the correct *wfe* rule. He hasn't given you enough for you to go on as he would. After all, there are such things as wrong combinatory answers by exhibition too.

NICKEL: That seems reasonable enough.

PENNY: That will seem even more evident, perhaps, when we consider exhibitory answers to combinatory questions about language.

NICKEL: You want me to apply Way M to language now, I know. How's this? I'll use the "Monkey is telephone" example again. A person can give a Way M answer to the combinatory question about "monkey" by exhibiting several sentences in which the word "monkey" is correctly used.

All those sentences in which you used "monkey" the other day, would be an exhibitory answer to a combinatory question about your use of "monkey"; and I grasped that you were using it like I use "talk."

PENNY: Good, but instead of giving me a combinatory rule to show me you grasped my combinatory concept of "monkey," can you give me exhibitory proof that you grasped it?

NICKEL: I don't see what you're asking for.

PENNY: Can you "go on" linguistically? Can you combine "monkey" correctly?

NICKEL: I get it. Sure. "Al Jolson appeared in the first monkey ever made," and "People from the deep south monkey with a drawl," and "People who suffer strokes often lose their ability to monkey."

PENNY: Good going on. Now I'd like to clinch that point about complete exhibitions. A child could never learn his native tongue if his parents kept changing their exhibitions, if they never, for example, used "monkey" twice in the same way. No more than you could learn what sequence a man had in mind if he kept altering it, so that he never, in effect, let his exhibitions be complete, as you suggested might be done in skipping from "21" to "25" and from "25" to "29." You can't keep pulling the rug out from beneath a person and also expect him to walk.

NICKEL: You've clinched it. I give.

PENNY: Speaking of children, we're in a position to see how important exhibitions, Way M answers, are to combinatory questions. When a child is learning his native tongue, he is continually searching for combinatory knowledge. He acquires practically all of it from observing exhibitions; teaching him the language by combinatory rules comes relatively late. Further, his suppositions about combinations are verified and dis-verified by the encouragement and discouragement he receives when he attempts to "go on," when he attempts new sentences.

NICKEL: That makes good sense, but I can't help believing that rules are more basic than exhibitions at least for adults.

PENNY: On the contrary, the opposite is true; exhibitions are more basic than rules.

NICKEL: I don't see why you say that.

PENNY: Let's use our sequence analogy once more. Suppose two persons, A and B, are talking about sequences, and A says, "I have a sequence in mind," to which B replies, "So do I, $2n-1$." A is surprised and exclaims, "Why that is the very one I had in mind!"

They both appear satisfied and walk away, smiling. But I think we should call them back and say to them, "Don't be so sure, A and B, that you agree in sequence."

NICKEL: But couldn't they reply, "Of course we do, for we agree in rule."

PENNY: Here's my point. How do they know they agree in rule? Just because their rules sound alike when they speak them, or look alike when they write them, doesn't mean they have the same sequence in mind. How do they know they give a common meaning to "$2n-1$?"

Suppose you are given the task of teaching someone, let's say C, how to use the rule "$2n-1$." You admit that someone has to be taught this sort of thing, don't you?

NICKEL: I'd better, for just a little while ago, you had to teach me how to use it again.

PENNY: Suppose you say to C, "Come here to the blackboard. I am going to teach you the use of the rule $2n-1$." He replies testily, "Who sent you this time? I wish they would stop bothering me, for I already know that rule."

NICKEL: Someone apparently, or maybe several people tried to teach him the rule before.

PENNY: Clearly. Now, do you think you should bore him anymore? Wouldn't it be better to do him a favor and teach him a new rule?

NICKEL: I don't think so; not until I find out whether he really knows the "$2n-1$" rule.

PENNY: Now apply this to A and B. Should A and B part so quickly? Shouldn't each find out whether the other knows the rule before they part in agreement?

You won't take C's word for it that he knows the "$2n-1$" rule; the evidence which A has that he agrees with B is no better than the evidence you have that C knows the rule.

NICKEL: I think you're right there. What should I do?

PENNY: I think you had better "eat a peach——"

NICKEL: 'Eat a peach'?

PENNY: Wear white flannel trousers and devise a test for C, just as A had better devise a test for himself and B.

NICKEL: How would A and I go about this?

PENNY: The same way your teacher went about it when he wanted to find out if you knew any algebra. You have to ask C a question about "$2n-1$" to which you know the answer. What kind of a question? What is "$2n-1$" a rule for?

NICKEL: It's a rule for producing a sequence. Oh! So, to test C, I have to ask him if he can produce a sequence from the rule.

PENNY: Good. Now suppose C answers as follows: Sure, 1, -3, 3, -5, 5, -7, ... ? What do you conclude?

NICKEL: That C does not know the use of the rule, and that it is a good thing they again sent someone to teach him the use of it.

PENNY: I think you will see what comment to make on your answer if we apply this to the A and B situation.

I call A and B back and say to them, "Each of you thinks he has the same rule in mind. What does it mean here to say that you have the same rule in mind?" What do you think their answer should be, Nickel?

NICKEL: Since the rule is used to produce a sequence, I think they had better answer, "To say one cites the same rule as someone else is to say that by following the rule you both would produce the same sequence."

PENNY: And now let's press A and B some more. "Well, then, A and B, to see if you actually did have the same rule in mind, I suggest you both follow the rule and produce a sequence." Isn't that a fair request, Nickel?

NICKEL: Yes, it seems so to me.

PENNY: Notice that we have shifted the focus from the rule to the sequence. Now let us imagine some possible answers to our request.

A: 1, 3, 5, 7, 9, 11, ...
B: 1, -3, 3, -5, 5, -7, ...

What do you think would be their reactions if they gave those answers?

NICKEL: They would probably be much surprised, but I doubt if they would have the same reaction. A would probably say, "$2n-1$ doesn't produce that sequence, B."

PENNY: Was that what was in question? Whether they could use it correctly? Or was it whether they had the same sequence in mind?

NICKEL: Whether they had the same sequence in mind.

PENNY: And you can't doubt that B has a sequence in mind, can you? Can't you go on?

NICKEL: Yes. 7, -9, 9, -11, 11 ...

PENNY: You perceived a sequence, the number combinations that are wanted. A's reaction should be, "We didn't have the same sequence in mind after all. You must use the rule differently than I. Please show me how you use the rule $2n-1$." And B's reaction should be the same.

Here is a diagram B can use to show A how he used the rule.

$n=$	1	-1	2	-2	3	-3 ...
$2n-1=$	1	-3	3	-5	5	-7 ...

Can you apply this to C?

NICKEL: B's answer is the same as C's. So I should not have said that C didn't know the use of the rule; I should have said instead that C used a different rule.

PENNY: No, I don't think you should have said quite that. You should have said that C used the rule expression differently.

Our conceptual experiment shows we can't talk simply about "rules"; we need to distinguish between a *rule expression* and the *use* of that rule expression. Both A and B, and both you and C, have the same rule expression in mind; but whether you have the same sequence in mind depends on whether you *use* that rule expression in the same way.

NICKEL: And clearly, a rule expression can be used in several ways. Your diagrams show two ways "$2n-1$" can be used.

PENNY: Yes. The important thing here is that having a similar rule expression in mind does not guarantee having either the same sequence in mind or the same combinatory concept in mind.

NICKEL: I can see now that what was in doubt in both the A and B case and the C case was the way in which each person *used* the rule expression "$2n-1$." To resolve the doubt we had to get them to actually use it. And since a rule expression like "$2n-1$" is used to produce a sequence, that meant we had to get them to actually produce a sequence.

That doesn't seem like much of a mystery. To find out how a person uses a rule expression, you have to observe him using it.

PENNY: Yes, that's clear enough, isn't it? But we need to say something else to account for your reaction to C's reply when you tested him. When you asked him to prove that he knew how to use "$2n-1$," and he replied, "1, -3, 3, -5, . . . ," your reaction was that C didn't know how to use the rule. Similarly, you thought A ought to say to B when B produced the sequence "1, -3, 3, -5, . . .", "'$2n-1$' doesn't produce that sequence, B."

NICKEL: I thought they gave incorrect answers.

PENNY: Which is the concern anyone feels who gives tests. Now, suppose we have an algebra teacher who asked his pupils to show what sequence is produced by following the "$2n-1$" rule. If he got a reply such as "1, -3, 3, . . ." and if he marked it incorrect, shouldn't he be prepared to give the pupil a reason why he marked it incorrect?

NICKEL: Especially if the student is a testy one, like C was.

PENNY: Yes, you always have to figure that some students will have cheek.

If we said no more about rules than we have to this point, the student might argue with the teacher as follows: "Professor, what does a student have to do to get a grade in this course? Read your mind? Just because I don't use the '$2n-1$' rule expression the way you do doesn't mean I can't use it. I simply use it in another way. What are you testing me on? My ability to use the rule expression or my ability to read your mind?"

NICKEL: That guy wouldn't last long.

PENNY: That's the special significance of using "F" for a failing grade, you know. Notice how shaped like a gallows that capital "F" is?

NICKEL: Yeh, and your student just kicked his own trap door.

PENNY: But we can suppose that at least some professors are rational and that this one would want to be not a hangman but an answerer. What would the rational professor have to say in defense of his grade?

I think it should go something like this. "I taught one particular use of the rule expression; and I didn't willy-nilly select that particular use out of the many possible ones I could have taught you. I taught you a *standard* use. A standard use is the one which a mathematician would use to produce a sequence from, e.g., $2n-1$, unless he were given instructions to the contrary. And when I give you an examination, unless I instruct otherwise, I expect you to produce an answer according to the standard use."

NICKEL: Mightn't the student be all the more puzzled? He might say, "Now I have to read not only your mind, but *all* the mathematicians' minds."

PENNY: That simply is not so. He does not have to read minds; he simply has to act sequentially as a mathematician does when told to show the standard use of "$2n-1$." And he has been *shown* in class how to act in a sequentially standard way; the test requires only that he make those standard sequential acts.

Look, we can put the issue in a familiar way. "$2n-1$" is a linguistic expression; so is "$f\alpha\beta$." Linguistic rules are linguistic expressions, so we can raise our familiar question about them: How do we know that another person and I mean the same thing by the rule expression?

NICKEL: You're now posing the question about the common "use" of a rule expression in terms of the common "meaning" of a rule expression.

PENNY: Yes. A standard use of a rule to produce a standard sequence doesn't require reading minds; it requires a grasp of a common rule of regularity, the same kind of regularity you had to learn in order to use the $f\alpha\beta$ rule in a standard way.

NICKEL: A rule of substitution?

PENNY: At least. Testing someone in algebra or logic is testing to see whether or not they have the grasp of the relevant rules of regularity. The mathematician requires that the student has grasped a rule of substitution into n in "$2n-1$"; the student must know he is to substitute the natural number sequence.

NICKEL: And I had to learn to substitute binary functors for f and letters and other *wfe*s for alpha and beta.

PENNY: Notice now that such a test requires the student to exhibit expressions in Way *M* in order to show that he understands the Way *N* rule. Ultimately the test for all common meaning lies, not in citing similar sounding rules, but in producing similar exhibitions; similar exhibitions show similar rules of regularity.

It would be nice to know if you see how this is related to our discussion about referential meaning last time.

NICKEL: It would be nice for me, too.

Well, if an expression has referential meaning, we want to know if two people give the same referential meaning to it. My guess is, since you bring it up at this point, that we give an expression the same referential meaning if we share a rule of substitution or emplacement. And the only way I can find this out is to observe your emplacements.

PENNY: Do you see any relation between *n* in "$2n-1$" and "pencil" in "Every pencil is short"?

NICKEL: Sure. I have to know among other things how to substitute into both of them before I know the meanings of the expressions in which they occur.

PENNY: Is there any way of showing someone you know the meanings of the expressions in which they occur except by exhibiting some substitution instances of *n* and "pencil"?

NICKEL: No, I don't think so, for *n* and "pencil" are both variables, the kind of thing which functions as that into which we may substitute. The only way we can know we use variables the same way is to find out whether we substitute similar things into them.

I think I know now how our discussion today is related to our discussion about referential meaning. Words with referential meaning are variables, and sentences containing them give combinatory order to the world of referents, just as mathematical expressions containing variables, for example, order numerals into sequences.

PENNY: That was more than I was hoping for.

NICKEL: It's not wrong, is it?

PENNY: The linguistic order of the world! It was such an ambitious remark.

NICKEL: Well, you said that the wall between language and the world must be swept away when we see that referents enter into language as lobjects. Once the world is in the language it has the order of that language.

PENNY: Though that may not be the only order it has. For example, it has a temporal order; one thing happens before another.

NICKEL: I understand that, but at least it has a linguistic order as well. The world is the cave of the man who knows a language. And if two people don't understand the expressions of a language in the same way, they occupy different caves.

PENNY: Do you see now why exhibitions are more basic than rules?

NICKEL: I do. We don't know whether we mean the same thing by a rule expression or an expression with referential meaning until we exhibit the expressions that result from substitutions.

PENNY: And do you see now how we can consider traditional philosophers as combinatory philosophers?

NICKEL: I think so. If we find a philosophical treatise on good, we can consider that all the sentences in which the word "good" occurs are that philosopher's exhibitory answer to our combinatory question, "How do you combine the word 'good'?" Whether he wrote them with that question in mind is beside the point, isn't it?

PENNY: Yes, it is.

NICKEL: I've had something nagging at the back of my mind for quite a while now, and I have to ask it. Is the rule "$2n-1$" to a sequence like a definition is to the regular use of a word? What I'm getting at is this. We've talked about meta-language reports on the regular combination of a word. Isn't that what we usually speak of as a definition?

PENNY: I would like to be able to discuss combinatory philosophy without reference to that old chestnut, but I guess it can't be avoided. Yes, meta-language reports are related to definitions.

NICKEL: Well, then, how does a combinatory philosopher differ from a, a . . . What do you call those people who compile dictionaries?

PENNY: Lexicographers.

NICKEL: Yes, how does a combinatory philosopher differ from a lexicographer?

PENNY: Do you find arguments in dictionaries?

NICKEL: No.

PENNY: Do you find arguments in combinatory philosophers' works?

NICKEL: I remember some in the books Dime showed me.

PENNY: There's the difference. You can tell a philosopher by his arguments.

NICKEL: I'm not sure I get the significance of that. I know that logic in the narrow sense is concerned with arguments. You're suggesting now that in so far as philosophy is logic in the wide sense, it too is concerned with arguments. Consequently, you must be hinting that arguments form a bridge between logic in the narrow sense and logic in the wide sense.

PENNY: I am indeed. Logic in the wide sense, including philosophy, has an aspect that can't be developed without logic in the narrow sense.

That's one of the reasons why I've maintained that a study of logic in the narrow sense will yield philosophic profit; why it will be for the good of your soul.

What step have we made toward explaining such philosophic profit today?

NICKEL: I guess the step of showing how we can look at traditional philosophy as combinatory philosophy.

PENNY: Sure. We had to do that to approach an understanding of the role of argument in traditional philosophy. Traditional philosophy proceeds by argument; argument after argument occurs in its pages. What are they doing there? What's the point of using these arguments? If we can see traditional philosophy as combinatory logic in the wide sense and if we can understand the dependence of combinatory logic in the wide sense upon logic in the narrow sense, then we will come to see how logic in the narrow sense, the logic of argument, is important to philosophy and yields philosophic profit.

NICKEL: Then our next step is to understand the dependence of logic in the wide sense upon logic in the narrow sense.

PENNY: That's so, but first I would like to consolidate our gains on the distinction between exhibiting a combinatory concept and giving rules for it. And, naturally, I think it is best done in relation to——

NICKEL: Principia and Polish.

PENNY: You're so right. There is an important similarity between combinatory rules for sequences and the combinatory rules of the ideal languages. In both cases the rules contain at least one variable and specify what may be substituted into the variable.

NICKEL: I know that n in $2n-1$ is a variable, and I know we specified that numerals could be substituted into it, but I didn't know that we used variables in the Polish and Principia rules.

PENNY: You knew we used variables; you've just forgotten. What were the variables in the Po- and Pr- rules about *wfes*?

NICKEL: Oh, yes. I remember now: f, α, and β.

PENNY: In order to observe best the genesis of a Polish rule utilizing such variables, let's go through the following six fertility rites, wherein a new Polish combinatory concept is exhibited.

1. $$\frac{/pq}{\text{v}-p-q}$$ 2. $$\frac{\text{v}-p-q}{/pq}$$ 3. $$\frac{/p-q}{\text{v}-p--q}$$ 4. $$\frac{\text{v}-r-\cdot pr}{/r\cdot pr}$$

5. $$\frac{/*rq-\cdot pr}{\text{v}-*rq--\cdot pr}$$ 6. $$\frac{\text{v}-\cdot*\text{v}\,rppq\ -*{}^*_*pr.qp}{/\cdot*\text{v}\,rppq\ *{}^*_*pr.qp}$$

NICKEL: I've never seen anything like those expressions before. So far as I can see, you've introduced not one but two new Polish combinatory concepts, the double line "=======", and the stroke "/".

PENNY: Only the stroke functor belongs to Polish; the double line is a meta-linguistic term that allows us to make a statement about Polish and Principia expressions. Whenever we write a double line with expressions above and below, we can read that as "The expression above the double line is equivalent to the expression below the double line."

NICKEL: In that case, it says two expressions constitute an equivalence conversation.

PENNY: Good, Nickel. We will also speak of the double line as the transformation line; we can use the expressions "double line" and "transformation line" interchangeably.

NICKEL: Why speak of it as a transformation line?

PENNY: We'll come to that in a bit. For now, sharpen the pencil of your attention and complete the following statement for me.

7. $\dfrac{/.rqp}{}$ Can you complete it?

NICKEL: I think so.

$$\dfrac{}{v{-}.rq{-}p}$$

PENNY: You can go on; you grasped the regularity very quickly.

NICKEL: It makes no difference whether the stroke expression is above or below the line, does it?

PENNY: None whatsoever.

NICKEL: But how do I know that the seven statements are true? How do I know each is an equivalence conversation? I don't as yet know the meaning of the stroke.

PENNY: You must know some of its combinatory meaning or you couldn't have completed 7. What stumps you is your inability to *say* what it means.

NICKEL: Its meaning will be the same as ... as ... I don't know how to say it. I guess you're right.

PENNY: What's wanted here is a rule, a rule defining stroke. What did we just get through saying about combinatory rules?

NICKEL: Combinatory rules use variables and specify the kinds of substitutions that can be made into them.

PENNY: That should help you to state the meaning of stroke.

NICKEL: How's this? $\dfrac{v{-}\alpha{-}\beta}{/\alpha\beta}$

PENNY: We should write "definition" (*df*) beside that rule to indicate that we have introduced a new vocabulary item into Polish and that it doesn't allow us to say anything new, but that it says the same thing that another combination of vocabulary items already allows us to say.   The full rule looks like this:

$$\frac{\text{v}-\alpha-\beta}{/\alpha\beta}\ df,$$ where any *wfe* can be substituted for alpha and any *wfe* can be substituted for beta.

Let's refer to such a combinatory rule as a schema; and let's call this particular schema, the Stroke schema.   Now ask yourself the question, "But how do I know that the seven statements are true?" and give your own answer.

NICKEL: Each of them is true by definition, for each of them can be substituted into the Stroke schema.   For example, I can substitute "*r*" for alpha and ".*pq*" for beta and get the fourth fertility rite*; or I can substitute "**rq*" for alpha and "–.*pr*" for beta and get the fifth fertility rite.

PENNY: That's very good.   A rule governs instances.   Which instances?

NICKEL: Substitution instances of the rule's variables.

PENNY: How crucial the variable, and how powerful!   The number of substitution instances of the Stroke schema rule are infinite, and it governs them all.

Above all, variables are great place holders.

NICKEL: You couldn't have prickled my ears faster.

PENNY: Regardez.

NICKEL: Our old friends, the shapes from the Same-form Method.   I see roundends has replaced alpha and parallelogram has replaced beta, and I take it that we could put *wfes* into those shapes.

PENNY: You can indeed.   What conclusions do you draw from this?

NICKEL: Your question suggests I must draw at least two.   Thanks. How's this for one?   Roundends and parallelograms and alphas and betas perform the same function: They indicate relative places for *wfes* within another *wfe*.

PENNY: That's a good one.   And I prefer alphas and betas to roundends and parallelograms simply because alphas and betas are easier to write.   Do you?

NICKEL: Oh, yes.   Here's another conclusion.   The top and bottom part of a schema show the form of an expression, in fact of an infinite number of expressions.

PENNY: Excellent.   Logic is concerned with the regularity of shapes or sounds.   Polish and Principia consist of shapes and sounds we call their

* Page 214.

vocabularies, *wfe*s and *wfe*10s. When we wish to express a rule of regularity, we should do it in the clearest and most succinct way. Schemas afford us a clear way, for they show everything and hide nothing. And what could be more succinct?

NICKEL: Is this a good time to explain why you called the double line the transformation line?

PENNY: Why not? You must observe the word "transformation." Notice that it contains the word "form," which you just now pointed out is what the top and bottom part of a schema show us; and it contains the prefix "trans-." The double line is to logic what the witch's wand is to fairy tales; it has magical power. The magical power of the double line consists of this: When I transport an expression across the double line, either from top to bottom or bottom to top, the double line transforms the expression. Voila! Across the line, and a new form.

This happens not only to *wfe*s, but also to *wfe*10s.

$$\frac{1\mathrm{v}11}{1\text{--}0.0\text{--}10\text{--}1} \qquad \frac{1\mathrm{v}01}{1\text{--}0.1\text{--}00\text{--}1} \qquad \frac{1\mathrm{v}10}{1\text{--}0.0\text{--}11\text{--}0} \qquad \frac{0\mathrm{v}00}{0\text{--}1.1\text{--}01\text{--}0}$$

NICKEL: That must be quite a pair of lines, for there is certainly plenty of transformation there.

PENNY: I want you to write the schema of which these *wfe*10s are substitution instances.

NICKEL: I didn't realize *wfe*10s could be substituted into a schema.

PENNY: You shouldn't be surprised; that's what we did when we made the matrices.

NICKEL: Right. Is this the schema? $\dfrac{\mathrm{v}\alpha\beta}{-.-\alpha-\beta}$

PENNY: It is.

NICKEL: The full expression of the schema would require writing "definition" beside it and specifying what may be substituted for alpha and beta, in this case one and zero.

PENNY: You're half right. We do have to specify the substitutions, but we don't have to write "definition," because we aren't introducing a new vocabulary item. In this case the schema is not a new rule to follow; it is a report on observed exhibitions.

The schema being a report, it must be a true or false report. How would you determine its truth or falsity?

NICKEL: Well, when we assert a schema we claim that the uniform substitution of *wfe*s into the variables above and below the double line will result in a pair of equivalent *wfe*s.

PENNY: Is there any limit to the number of *wfe*s that might be substituted into the variables?

NICKEL: No.

Eighth conversation

PENNY: Then there must be an infinite number of pairs of *wfes* which are equivalent.

NICKEL: That seems true.

PENNY: Doesn't it follow, then, that the schema isn't true unless all those many pairs are equivalent?

NICKEL: I guess so.

PENNY: But how can you check on the equivalence of an infinite number of pairs?

NICKEL: Obviously, I can't.

PENNY: Then how do you know the schema report is true?

NICKEL: Don't search me.

PENNY: I must. What does it mean to say two *wfes* are equivalent?

NICKEL: Two *wfes* are equivalent if they both mean 1 or they both mean 0.

PENNY: How do you find out they both mean the same?

NICKEL: By substituting 1's and 0's uniformly into the Polish letters and using the functor rules.

PENNY: Sometimes two *wfes* are equivalent under all possible substitutions of 1 and 0.

NICKEL: Like the α and β parts of a tautological double ast expression?

PENNY: Right. They can be members of an equivalence conversation; some people speak of such pairs as logically equivalent. We'll just call them equivalent for short, because for now that's the only kind of equivalence we have in mind.

How do we know that all of the infinite pairs are equivalent?

NICKEL: I'm stumped.

PENNY: Do all *wfes* mean either 1 or 0?

NICKEL: That's what we said.

PENNY: Then, so far as their referential meaning is concerned, none of the infinite *wfes* we substitute into the variables differ; they will all mean either 1 or 0.

NICKEL: No difference.

PENNY: Don't these four *wfe*10 equivalences show the meanings of all possible *wfe* substitutions into α and β in $\dfrac{\vee\alpha\beta}{-.-\alpha-\beta}$, then?

$$\frac{1\vee11}{1-0.0-10-1} \qquad \frac{1\vee01}{1-0.1-00-1} \qquad \frac{1\vee10}{1-0.0-11-0} \qquad \frac{0\vee00}{0-1.1-01-0}$$

NICKEL: That's right, isn't it? We don't need to write a matrix for each of the infinite number of pairs of *wfes* that substitute into that schema; for since all the *wfes* can only mean 1 or 0, and because all possible combinations of 1 and 0 are given in those four pairs of *wfe*10s, that one set of

2I8

four equivalent *wfe*10s will serve to give the meaning of all of the infinite pairs equally.   Neat-o.

PENNY: I'm going to use "$*Twfe$" to refer to all double ast *wfe*s that are tautological; "$*Cwfe$" for all double ast *wfe*s that are contradictory; and——

NICKEL: "$*Iwfe$" for all double ast *wfe*s that are indeterminate.

PENNY: All $*Twfe$s can be converted into true meta-linguistic statements about the equivalence of two *wfe*s.

NICKEL: Which *wfe*s?

PENNY: You know that the general form of a double ast expression is $*\alpha\beta$. The *wfe* which substitutes into alpha is equivalent to the *wfe* which substitutes into beta.

Take 5 in exercise 7.6, $*.pq.qp$.   We can convert it into a true meta-linguistic statement about the equivalence of *.pq* and *.qp*.

NICKEL: Is the meta-linguistic statement this: *.pq* is equivalent to *.qp*?

PENNY: It is.   I prefer to write equivalence statements in this more elegant way: $\dfrac{.pq}{.qp}$.

The double line can replace "is equivalent to," since both are meta-linguistic terms.   But the double ast cannot replace "is equivalent to," because the double ast is not a meta-linguistic term.

8.1: Give as succinct an informal proof of this generalization as you can; namely, "All $*Twfe$s can be converted into true meta-linguistic statements about the equivalence of two *wfe*s."

It seems you now understand that transformation schemas are general statements. $\dfrac{.pq}{.qp}$ is a particular statement and a substitution instance of this general statement: $\dfrac{.\alpha\beta}{.\beta\alpha}$.

Give me two more substitution instances of that schema, one of strength two, the other of strength three.

NICKEL: Would you explain that, please?

PENNY: You have to substitute *wfe*s into α and β in such a way that the strength of dot in $.\alpha\beta$ or $.\beta\alpha$ is of strength two in the first case and of strength three in the other case.   Obviously, before the dot can be of strength two, one of the *wfe*s you substitute into α or β must be of strength one.

NICKEL: I think I get it.   How about these?

21 1		32 1	
$\dfrac{.\text{v}qr*pp}{.*pp\text{v}qr}$	where $\alpha = \text{v}qr$ and $\beta = *pp$	$\dfrac{.*\text{v}rqp.pr}{..pr*\text{v}rqp}$	where $\alpha = *\text{v}rqp$ and $\beta = .pr$
21 1		31 2	

PENNY: Perfect. Do you still see why transformation schemas are general equivalence statements?

NICKEL: Because they state that *any* two *wfe*s which are substitution instances of the top and bottom part of a schema are equivalent?

PENNY: Correct. Now consider $*Cwfe$s, for example, 3 in exercise 7.6, $-*vpqvqp$. What's the easiest way to change that $*Cwfe$ into a $*Twfe$?

NICKEL: The easiest way is to drop the bar to the left of the double ast.

PENNY: Once you do that, the resulting $*Twfe$ can be converted into an equivalence statement. Into what schema could that equivalence statement be substituted?

NICKEL: Since the equivalence statement would be $\dfrac{vpq}{vqp}$, I would say the schema would be $\dfrac{v\alpha\beta}{v\beta\alpha}$.

PENNY: You deserve the following splendid list of transformation schemas.

TRANSFORMATION SCHEMAS

$\dfrac{\alpha}{--\alpha}$ Double Bar (DB)

$\dfrac{v\alpha\beta}{v\beta\alpha}$ Vee Commutation (V Com)

$\dfrac{.\alpha\beta}{.\beta\alpha}$ Dot Commutation (D Com)

$\dfrac{v\alpha v\beta\gamma}{vv\alpha\beta\gamma}$ Vee Association (V Assoc)

$\dfrac{.\alpha.\beta\gamma}{..\alpha\beta\gamma}$ Dot Association (D Assoc)

$\dfrac{.\alpha v\beta\gamma}{v.\alpha\beta.\alpha\gamma}$ Distribution (Dist)

$\dfrac{v\alpha.\beta\gamma}{.v\alpha\beta v\alpha\gamma}$ Distribution (Dist)

$\dfrac{*\alpha\beta}{.*\alpha\beta*\beta\alpha}$ Double Ast (D Ast)

$\dfrac{*\alpha\beta}{v.\alpha\beta.-\alpha-\beta}$ Double Ast (D Ast)

$\dfrac{*\alpha*\beta\gamma}{*.\alpha\beta\gamma}$ Exportation (Exp)

$\dfrac{\alpha}{v\alpha\alpha} \quad \dfrac{\alpha}{.\alpha\alpha}$ Tautology (Taut)

$\dfrac{B.B\alpha B\beta}{Bv B\alpha B\beta}$ DeMorgan (DeM)

$\dfrac{*B\alpha\beta}{v B\alpha\beta}$ Ast

$\dfrac{*B\alpha B\beta}{*B\beta B\alpha}$ Transposition (Trans)

$\dfrac{v B\alpha B\beta}{|B\alpha B\beta}$ Stroke (St)

$\dfrac{-\alpha}{|\alpha\alpha}$ Nobarsatall (Nob)

$\dfrac{v\alpha\beta}{||\alpha\alpha|\beta\beta}$ Handy

220

8.2: For each transformation schema in the left-hand column and the first two in the right-hand column, find the $\ast Twfe$s and/or $\ast Cwfe$s in 7.6 which when converted into equivalence statements are substitutable into it.

8.3: For each transformation schema in the left-hand column and the first two in the right-hand column, write a substitution instance such that the top or bottom *wfe* (or both) is of strength 3. Specify your *wfe* substitutions into alpha and beta, and gamma where there is one.

While we're on this generalizing kick, let's consider the general form of the Vee and Dot Commutation schemas: $\dfrac{f\alpha\beta}{f\beta\alpha}$. The general form for the Vee and Dot Association schemas is: $\dfrac{f\alpha f\beta\gamma}{ff\alpha\beta\gamma}$.

8.4: (a) Will the resulting schema statement be true if we substitute $\ast$ for f in the general form of Commutation schemas? Give a reason for your answer. (b) Will the resulting schema statement be true if we substitute $\ast$ for f in the general form of Association schemas? Give a reason for your answer. (c) Answer the same two questions, supposing we substitute $\ast$ into f in the general form of Commutation and Association schemas.

I invite you now to look at some of the schemas in the right-hand column of our list of transformation schemas and note the presence of a new symbol.

NICKEL: B?

PENNY: B, capital bee, is a variable into which we may substitute the bar. Consider these four expressions.

1. $\dfrac{\ast pq}{\text{v}\!-\!pq}$ 2. $\dfrac{\ast\!-\!pq}{\text{v}pq}$ 3. $\dfrac{\ast\!-\!p\!-\!q}{\text{v}p\!-\!q}$ 4. $\dfrac{\ast p\!-\!q}{\text{v}\!-\!p\!-\!q}$

In describing these transformations, we can say two things about them. One, going from top to bottom, the v replaces the ast, and, going from bottom to top, the ast replaces the v. Two, in all four cases the first letter to the right of the binary functor has a bar either in the top *wfe* or in the bottom *wfe*, but not in both.

We can handle the regularity about the bar with either of two different Ast schemas. The first schema is this: $\dfrac{\ast\alpha\beta}{\text{v}\!-\!\alpha\beta}$.

Suppose I wish to transform this ast expression, $\ast\!-\!p\!-\!q$, into a v expression. How should my expression look?

NICKEL: According to your exhibition, 3 above, and description, it should be v$p\!-\!q$.

PENNY: If we are to substitute $*-p-q$ into our schema, we have to substitute $-p$ into alpha and $-q$ into beta. We'll write it like this:

$$\frac{*\alpha\beta}{\text{v}-\alpha\beta} \qquad \alpha=-p \qquad \frac{*-p-q}{\text{v}--p-q}$$

NICKEL: But you don't have below what you're supposed to have. The p isn't supposed to have two bars in front of it according to our earlier exhibition and description.

PENNY: You're right, but we can get rid of the two bars if we permit ourselves the luxury of a replacement rule. And I don't see why we don't vote ourselves that luxury; it gives us another reason to use transformation schemas.

Whenever we have two *wfe*s, one of which is a substitution instance of the top part of a transformation schema and the other of which is a substitution instance of the bottom part, we know they are equivalent. A replacement rule simply allows us to replace any *wfe* within a larger *wfe* with its equivalent. Such replacement doesn't change the meaning of the larger *wfe*.

NICKEL: Replacement is always concerned with part of a *wfe* then, is that right?

PENNY: It is. And that part must always be a *wfe*.

NICKEL: How can I tell which part is being replaced?

PENNY: The double lines will always fall under only the part which is being replaced. You should be able to tell which *wfe*s are being replaced in these examples:

$$\frac{*q \cdot \text{v}rpq}{*q \cdot \text{v}prq} \qquad \frac{\text{v}*rp \cdot qp}{\text{v}*rp-\text{v}-q-p} \qquad \frac{\cdot *rp\text{v}rq}{\cdot *-p-r\text{v}rq}$$

NICKEL: In the first one vrp is being replaced; in the second $\cdot qp$; and in the third $*rp$. And I guess the rest of the larger *wfe* is brought down unchanged.

PENNY: Unscathed by human transformation schemas.

Let's apply this to our problem of eliminating the two bars we acquired when we transformed $*-p-q$ to $\text{v}--p-q$.

In our present instance, we can get rid of the two bars by replacing $--p$ in $\text{v}--p-q$ with its equivalent, p. This utilizes the Double Bar schema in Step 2 below.

Step 1. $\dfrac{*\alpha\beta}{\text{v}-\alpha\beta}$ $\alpha=-p$ $\dfrac{*-p-q}{\text{v}--p-q}$ $p=\alpha$ $\dfrac{--\alpha}{\alpha}$ Step 2.

$$\frac{}{\text{v}\ \ p\ -q}$$

NICKEL: That gives us what we want, all right. But isn't the DB schema upside down in Step 2 above?

PENNY: You can write transformation schemas either way, whichever

222

suits your purpose, since equivalence holds in both directions. In this case our purpose was to get rid of the two bars, so we put them on top.

The other way of writing the Ast schema was the way I wrote it in the list of transformation schemas I gave you. That way of writing it saves us the Double Bar step in going from $*-p-q$ to $\vee p-q$. But it does involve the new variable, B.

We'll use a B in all those schemas which require a bar, or bars, in it to obtain equivalent *wfe*s. You'll notice that includes DeMorgan, Ast, Transposition, and Stroke schemas.

NICKEL: I could use some enlightenment on the use of B.

PENNY: First of all, every schema will have an even number of B's in it. Secondly, the B's divide up into pairs. Third, you can identify the pairs by the kind of expression immediately to their right. If a B has an alpha immediately to its right, the other member of the pair will be the B with the alpha immediately to its right. If the B has the main binary functor immediately to its right, the other member of the pair will be the B with the main binary functor immediately to its right.

I'll number the B's in the schemas and I want you to tell me which B's are pairs.

$$
\begin{array}{ccc}
1\ 2\ 3 & 1\ 2 & 1\ 2 \\
\overline{\overline{B.B\alpha B\beta}} & \overline{\overline{\vee B\alpha B\beta}} & *B\alpha B\beta \\
B\vee B\alpha B\beta & \overline{|B\alpha B\beta|} & *B\beta B\alpha \\
4\ 5\ 6 & 3\ 4 & 3\ 4
\end{array}
$$

NICKEL: In the DeMorgan schema 1 and 4, 2 and 5, 3 and 6 are pairs; in the Stroke schema 1 and 3, and 2 and 4 are pairs; and in the Transposition schema 1 and 4, and 2 and 3 are pairs.

PENNY: Try to draw out the rule for substitution into the B variable by contemplating these substitution instances of the DeM schema.

$$
\begin{array}{cccc}
1\ 2\ 3 & 1\ 2\ 3 & 1\ 2\ 3 & 1\ 2\ 3 \\
B\ B\ B & B\ B\ B & B\ B\ B & B\ B\ B \\
\overline{\overline{-.\ p-q}} & \overline{\overline{\vee -p\ q}} & \overline{\overline{-\vee\ p\ q}} & \overline{\overline{.\ p-q}} \\
\vee -p\ q & -.\ p-q & .-p-q & -\vee -p\ q \\
B\ B\ B & B\ B\ B & B\ B\ B & B\ B\ B \\
4\ 5\ 6 & 4\ 5\ 6 & 4\ 5\ 6 & 4\ 5\ 6
\end{array}
$$

To draw out the rule, note the six places where the pairs of B's would fit into those expressions.

NICKEL: In all four exhibitions, I see that of the 1 and 4 pair one of the members has a bar in it, but only one of them; similarly for the 2 and 5 pair, and the 3 and 6 pair.

How's this for a substitution rule for B? Into one of a pair of B's we must substitute a bar, but into no more than one of them.

PENNY: You should have no trouble with this exercise.

8.5: (a) Do for the DeMorgan, Ast, and Trans schemas what you did for the transformation schemas in 8.2. (b) Do for the DeM, Ast, and Trans schemas what you did with the transformation schemas in 8.3.

8.6: I want you to write a description of five transformation schemas. Here's an example of such a description. It's a description of the V Com schema: When a v *wfe* crosses the double line, the alpha and beta expressions change places.

NICKEL: I'm curious about the schemas we haven't talked about as yet, the Nobarsatall and Handy schemas.

PENNY: We'll have to make you worthy of them before we discuss them. We can induce the proper worth in you only by working up to and doing some exercises involving transformation schemas.

Think about transforming $-.rp$ into an expression having as its only functor the stroke functor.

NICKEL: We can't do that. We don't have a transformation schema that goes from a dot expression to a stroke expression.

PENNY: We don't need one if we take advantage of the schemas already in our armory. I'll show you.

$$
\begin{array}{lll}
\alpha = r & B.\,B\alpha B\beta & -.rp \\
\beta = p & \overline{\overline{}} & \overline{\overline{}} \\
\text{dot's } B = - & B\lor B\alpha B\beta & \lor\!-\!r\!-\!p \quad \lor B\alpha B\beta \quad \alpha = r \\
& & \overline{\overline{}} \quad \overline{\overline{}} \quad \beta = p \\
& /rp & /B\alpha B\beta \quad \text{the top } \alpha\text{'s and } \beta\text{'s } B = -
\end{array}
$$

NICKEL: It looks as if I can use any of the schemas I need to get the desired *wfe*.

PENNY: That's right. It's like trying to get from one city to another; sometimes you have to go through other cities to get there.

Notice that if we start with an expression, such as $-.rp$, and use a transformation schema on it to get, as in this case, $\lor\!-\!r\!-\!p$, and use another transformation on it to get $/rp$, that we have produced a new equivalence statement.

NICKEL: $\dfrac{-.rp}{/rp}$?

PENNY: And by replacing the letters with variables, $\dfrac{-.\alpha\beta}{/\alpha\beta}$, we can bring forth a new schema.

NICKEL: By using the new schema, we could save a step in going from a $-.$ expression to a $/$ expression.

PENNY: We could. It's worth noting that this "collapsing" procedure by which we get a new equivalence statement, and, eventually, a new schema, can be done at any level in a chain. Whenever we have a chain of expressions produced by the use of transformation schemas or by the use of transformation schemas and replacement, we can always collapse the chain. Here's an example of a transformation chain.

1. $\underline{\underline{.vqrp}}$ D Com

2. $.p\underline{\underline{vqr}}$ V Com

3. $\underline{\underline{.pvrq}}$ Dist

4. $\underline{\underline{v.pr.pq}}$ Ast

5. $\overset{*}{\underline{\underline{-.pr.pq}}}$ DeM

$*v-p-r.pq$

In Step 1 we move from the top *wfe* to the next *wfe* by the use of the D Com schema; in Step 2 we move from *.pvqr* to *.pvrq* by the use of the V Com schema and the replacement rule. Step 5 also uses the replacement rule, v–p–r replacing its equivalent, –.pr. You can tell the replacement rule has been used when you see the double lines lying under only a part of a *wfe*.

By placing the top *wfe* in a chain above a double line and the bottom *wfe* in a chain below the double line, we can produce a true equivalence statement. In this case the collapse gives us: $\dfrac{.vqrp}{*v-p-r.pq}$.

NICKEL: Can we collapse a chain because every *wfe* in the chain is equivalent to every other *wfe*?

PENNY: Yes.

NICKEL: In that case, there are several ways to collapse a chain.

PENNY: Here's a chance to back up that observation. Write all the possible equivalence statements you can get by collapsing the above chain, using the top *wfe* in every collapse.

NICKEL: $\dfrac{.vqrp}{.pvrq}$ $\dfrac{.vqrp}{v.pr.pq}$ $\dfrac{.vqrp}{*-.pr.pq}$ $\dfrac{.vqrp}{*v-p-r.pq}$.

Man, we sure could work up a lot of schemas, couldn't we? If we replaced all letters in all those new equivalence statements with variables, we'd get a passel of schemas.

PENNY: We would, but if we get too many, you won't be able to remember all of them. The trick is to get few enough to remember and use easily, but enough to do transformation with economy.

I'd like to introduce a shorter way of showing transformation steps. Instead of writing the schema every time, we'll write the name of the schema; but we'll retain the substitution specifications. Thus, our DeMorgan and Stroke transformations would look like this.

$$\dfrac{-.rp}{v-r-p} \text{ DeM, } \alpha=r,\ \beta=p,\ \text{dot's } B=-$$

$$\dfrac{v-r-p}{/rp} \text{ St, } \alpha=r,\ \beta=p,\ \text{the top } \alpha\text{'s and } \beta\text{'s } B=-$$

We'll call any series of such transformations a transformation proof, or transformation chain.

NICKEL: What do they prove?

PENNY: The one above proves that $-.rp$ is equivalent to $/rp$. And we have done it without recourse to matrices. We have, in effect, a new way of gaining meta-language knowledge of our two ideal languages, of gaining knowledge of their regularities.

NICKEL: That seems impressive to me.

PENNY: I'm glad you appreciate the accomplishment; we owe a great deal to logicians like Boole, DeMorgan, Frege, Russell, and Whitehead.

8.7: In this exercise you are to name the schemas used in the transformation proofs and to specify the substitution instances.

	a.		b.		c.		d.
1.	$\underline{\underline{^*pq}}$	1.	$\underline{\underline{\text{-----}.rq}}$	1.	$\underline{\underline{q}}$	1.	$\underline{\underline{\overset{*}{\underset{*}{}}.rq.pr}}$
2.	$\underline{\underline{\vee-pq}}$	2.	$\underline{\underline{\text{--}.rq}}$	2.	$\underline{\underline{\vee qq}}$	2.	$\underline{\underline{.^*.rq.pr}}$ $\underline{\underline{^*.pr.rq}}$
3.	$\underline{\underline{-.p-q}}$		$.rq$	3.	$\underline{\underline{\vee qq\vee qq}}$	3.	$.\vee-.rq.pr$ $\underline{\underline{^*.pr.rq}}$
4.	$\underline{\underline{-.-qp}}$			4.	$\underline{\underline{\vee qq}}$	4.	$.\vee-.rq.pr$ $\vee-.pr.rq$
5.	$\underline{\underline{\vee q-p}}$				q		$.\vee-.pr.rq$ $\vee-.rq.pr$
6.	$\dfrac{^*-q-p}{^*pq}$						

	e.		f.		g.
1.	$\underline{\underline{\vee p\vee rq}}$	1.	$\underline{\underline{^*r^*qp}}$	1.	$\underline{\underline{^*pq}}$
2.	$\underline{\underline{\vee\vee prq}}$	2.	$\underline{\underline{^*.rqp}}$	2.	$.^*pq^*qp$
3.	$\underline{\underline{\vee\vee rpq}}$	3.	$\underline{\underline{\vee-.rqp}}$	3.	$.\vee-pq^*qp$
4.	$\underline{\underline{\vee q\vee rp}}$	4.	$\underline{\underline{\vee\vee-r-qp}}$	4.	$.\vee-pq\vee-qp$
5.	$\underline{\underline{\vee\vee qrp}}$	5.	$\underline{\underline{\vee-r\vee-qp}}$	5.	$\vee.\vee-pq-q$ $.\vee-pqp$
6.	$\underline{\underline{\vee^*-qrp}}$	6.	$\dfrac{\vee-r^*qp}{^*r^*qp}$	6.	$\vee.-q\vee-pq$ $.\vee-pqp$
7.	$\underline{\underline{\vee^*-rqp}}$			7.	$\vee\vee.-q-p.-qq$ $.\vee-pqp$
8.	$\dfrac{^*-^*-rqp}{^*-p^*-rq}$			8.	$\vee\vee.-q-p.-qq$ $.p\vee-pq$
				9.	$\vee.-q\vee-pq$ $.p\vee-pq$
				10.	$\vee.\vee-pq-q$ $\underline{\underline{.p\vee-pq}}$
				11.	$\vee.\vee-pq-q$ $\underline{\underline{.\vee-pqp}}$
				12.	$\underline{\underline{.\vee-pq}}$ $\vee-qp$
				13.	$.^*pq$ $\underline{\underline{\vee-qp}}$
				14.	$\dfrac{.^*pq \;\; ^*qp}{^*pq}$

NICKEL: That looks like rugged exercise.

PENNY: I'm just getting you in condition for the next exercise. Actually, 8.7 is not as rugged as it appears. You can get hints at which schema was used by taking note of the main functors above and below the transformation line. For example, if you see a dot above and below, you reduce the possibilities to two schemas, the D Com and D Assoc, for they are the only schemas whose main functors are dots above and below.

8.8: Two of the following transformation chains show that the Commutation schema holds for the stroke functor. Which two?

a.	b.	c.	d.
/p/qr	//qrp	/r/pq	//rpq
v–p–/qr	v–/qr –p	v–r–/pq	v–/rp–q
v–p–v–q–r	v–v–q–r–p	v–r–v–p–q	v–v–r–p–q
v–p.qr	v.qr –p	v–r.pq	v.rp –q

8.9: (a) Cite the schemas used in the following transformation proofs and specify for each step the substitution instances.

(b) Step 6 in f and Step 3 in g use schemas that can be found by collapsing two of the chains below. Identify the chains which when collapsed yield the equivalence statements from which we can get the schemas. Those collapsed chains are substitution instances of two transformation schemas in the list I gave you.

a.
1. *q–r
2. v–q–r / /qr

b.
1. –p
2. v–p–p / /pp

c.
1. .qp
2. –v–q–p
3. –/qp
4. v–/qp–/qp / //qp/qp

d.
1. *pq
2. v–pq
3. /p–q
4. /pv–q–q / /p/qq

e.
1. vrp
2. /–r–p
3. /v–r–r–p
4. //rr –p
5. //rrv–p–p / //rr/pp

f.
1. *·pq
2. v·pq ·–p–q
3. v–v–p–q·–p–q
4. v–v–p–q–vpq
5. / v–p–q vpq
6. / /pq vpq / //pq //pp/qq

g.
1. ·–qp
2. –vq–p
3. –/–qp
4. –//qqp
5. v–//qqp –//qqp / ///qqp //qqp

8.10: Use transformation chains to determine which of the following pairs of *wfe*s are contradictory.

(a) $.p-q$ $\vee q-p$ (b) $*r\vee pq$ $.-\vee pqr$

(c) $-\overset{*}{*}pq$ $-\vee .p-q-*qp$ (d) $.\vee qr*pr$ $*-r.q-p$

This exercise calls for a decision on your part, in fact, several decisions. You have to decide which schemas to use. Your decisions will be guided by the end in view. In this case the end in view is so to apply transformation schemas to one member of the pair that at the end of the chain it looks just like the other member, except, where the two are contradictory, that one of them has a bar to its extreme left. Here's an example of how to do this exercise: $*pq$ $\dfrac{.p-q}{}$ DeM

$\dfrac{-\vee-pq}{-*pq}$ Ast

$-*pq$ which is clearly contradictory to the other member of the pair, $*pq$.

8.11: Does a Tautology schema hold for the Stroke functor? Submit a transformation proof for your answer.

When you did 7.5 you reduced all binary functors to a combination of $\vee$ and bar. 8.9 shows that you can reduce all binary functors to stroke because all binary functors can be reduced to a combination of $\vee$ and bar, which in turn are reducible to stroke. That pares Polish and Principia to a rather spare vocabulary.

NICKEL: Is there any advantage in trying to get along with a single functor?

PENNY: Yes. For one thing we come to see that a language's expressive power need not be lost when we reduce its vocabulary. It is always interesting to see what a language's minimum vocabulary consists of. In the process of reduction one also discovers the internal relations of that language; in addition, and this may be the most important aspect of all, in discovering the internal relations we also discover a way of constructing proofs or deductions.

NICKEL: Our transformation proofs are deductions?

PENNY: They are that. By using schemas to state discovered internal relations, for example, relations between *wfe*s within Polish, we forged an instrument enabling us to move from one *wfe* to another; we forged an instrument of transformation. And a series of transformations is a proof; we proved in 8.7, e, for example, that $\vee p\vee rq$ is equivalent to $*-p*-rq$; the proof carries conviction because each step utilizes a verified statement of an internal relation.

NICKEL: That is, it utilizes a schema.

PENNY: Exactly, and we say of the last *wfe* in a series of transformations that it is deduced from the first *wfe* in the series.

NICKEL: Then proof or deduction is simply moving about in a language.

PENNY: Through the tunnels of schemas. If we constantly use an ideal language as a model, as I think we should, then questions we raise about it should suggest similar questions about natural languages.

NICKEL: Then after trying to get along with a single functor in Polish and Principia, we should ask what the minimum vocabulary of a natural language is.

PENNY: A good idea. In teaching someone a language, it might prove useful; in case speed is of the essence, we would want to teach someone the least he has to know, but without sacrificing expressive power.

Then, too, as a result of introducing a single functor we had an opportunity to distinguish between defined schemas and reported schemas, and got a clean slice of definitional life. But quickly now, in order to give you a chance to state what you've learned, I give you the following exercises.

8.12: This exercise is to be added to the Po-7 and Pr-7 entries in your notebook. You are to state the rules for anything being a transformation schema.

8.13: (a) State the rules for anything being a transformation step in a transformation proof. (b) State the rules for anything being a transformation proof or chain. Make your answers to (a) and (b) the Po-8 and Pr-8 rules.

8.14: I want you to write transformation proofs with the following expressions as the first *wfe*, the last *wfe* in the proof being a *wfe* containing the stroke as its only functor. Of course, you are to name the schemas used and specify the substitutions. You can develop other schemas involving stroke than those we have worked out if you find it advantageous. I only require that you write out and name the new schemas so I know what's going on.

(a) $\lor{-}qp$

(b) $.{-}p{-}q$

(c) $\lor.{-}p{-}qr$

(d) $*{-}.pq.qr$

(e) $[(p\supset q)\lor r]$

(f) ${-}(q\supset r)$

(g) $\overset{*}{*}{-}pp$

(h) $.{-}pp$

(i) $({-}p\lor p)$

(j) $*{-}.\lor pqr \ \lor.q{-}rp$

NICKEL: It appears to me I'm on my way to understanding how logic in the wide sense depends on logic in the narrow sense, for today I've gotten a glimpse of the bridge between regularities and proofs.

PENNY: And what does it look like?

NICKEL: A Golden Gate schema.

PENNY: Bon voyage.

NICKEL: Help! I feel my ship sinking in the west!

PENNY: In that event, you'll want to have your life suddenly flash before your eyes. The least I can do is give you some Review Questions to nudge memories of today's conversation.

Review Questions

1. Why would it be wrong to infer that a philosopher did not do combinatory philosophy from the fact that you do not find meta-linguistic sentences (or emplacements) in his work?

2. Why is a traditional philosopher like King M? And a new philosopher like King N?

3. Linguistically, which is more basic, combinatory rules or combinatory exhibitions? Why?

4. Relate Way M manner of communicating the numerical sequence you have in mind and the way Nickel discovered the meaning of "Monkey is telephone" to Penny's belief that we can find answers to combinatory questions in traditional philosophy.

5. May one give an incorrect exhibitory answer to a combinatory question? How?

6. Why is the distinction between a rule expression and the use of the rule expression important?

7. What is that of which both combinatory rules for sequences and the ideal languages make use?

8. Is a schema a report or a rule?

NICKEL: I go in peace now to meet my Unmaker. Good-bye, Mr. Penny.

PENNY: Good-bye, Nickel.

Ninth conversation

THE LEXICOGRAPHER
AND THE CONSTANT
NYMPH

*Cartunes have lately cum amungst uss; moste respekfully I
sugeste that theyr essence is ye puttyng of sygns inn the playce
of expreshun.   Hear is a modest suggestshun for cartunists:
Drawe a starr withe rayes shynnyng owtwords abov a hed to
sygnify the occurance of an ydea.*—Fanebius Perlyng

N ICKEL: Good afternoon; and I'm surprised I can say so.

PENNY: Why is that?

NICKEL: I've been at Dime's apartment all morning, and naturally he wanted to hear what you thought of his argument about traditional philosophers not being combinatory philosophers. Well, when I showed him the notes I had typed up, and he saw how the argument fared, he wasn't too pleased. Dime has a temper; so, we really went around.

PENNY: How did you make out with him?

NICKEL: I don't seem to have your ability to make the reasonable look reasonable.

PENNY: Perhaps he doesn't have the ability to see the reasonable as reasonable. Or perhaps he has the ability to make the reasonable seem unreasonable. In which case he may be more interested in pride than truth.

NICKEL: It's true that Dime doesn't like to admit error, at least not when he's being confronted with it by someone else; but he's not a bad guy, he usually comes around later—after convincing himself.

PENNY: At least the internal dialogue is usually carried on with love.

NICKEL: Speaking of internal dialogue, I've been thinking about a question I asked you yesterday, the one about how lexicographers differ from combinatory philosophers, and I think, even if I say so myself, that it is a pretty good question.

PENNY: It's a very good question. Better perhaps than you realize. And don't worry about "saying so yourself," for vanity is tolerable when self-praise is deserved.

By the way, what led you to ask the question?

NICKEL: A couple of things. One thing I still had in mind was the idea that sentence meanings depend in part on the meanings of the words in the sentences. We discussed that a few days ago.* At the time you said that we'd have to discuss more fully the dependence of word meanings on their regularity. I thought my question might prompt the promised discussion. It seemed a natural one, since lexicographers work on word meanings and combinatory philosophers work on regularity.

PENNY: It certainly will prompt the discussion, I promise. In fact, most of our discussion from now on will be concerned with the regularity and meaning of words. Don't forget, however, that we've already discussed the topic to some extent. We did so in connection with a word's referential meaning.

NICKEL: I never made that connection; but you're right, because a rule of emplacement is a substitution rule of regularity for words. That

* Reader: See page 138.

reminds me, we also discussed word meaning when we talked about "Monkey is telephone."

The other thing that led to my asking the question was a prior question, the one about the comparison between meta-language reports and definitions.

We had talked about the study of combination regularities and about combinatory philosophers and meta-language reports. It was clear that such reports give us information about the word. Suddenly I thought of those times when in reading I don't know the meaning of some word, and it occurred to me yesterday that what I don't know is the author's combinatory concept.

Now when I don't know the meaning of a word, I usually look its definition up in the dictionary, which, if you are right, is the same as looking up the combinatory concept. And since the information about a combinatory concept can be given in a meta-language report, the definition must be such a report.

PENNY: You're suggesting then that dictionary entries give us information because they are reports of how words have been combined.

NICKEL: That's right.

PENNY: I agree with that, but if dictionary entries are to give us the information we want, must they not be more than reports?

NICKEL: I can't see what you're driving at.

PENNY: Dictionaries have dates; they are compiled at a certain time. It's possible that the dictionary which you use was compiled before the sentence in which that word expression occurs was written. The entry which you read in that dictionary can't possibly be a report of that occasion of use.

NICKEL: That's true.

PENNY: Well, then, you can't get the information you want from that dictionary unless its entry is a correct prediction of how the author would combine that word expression, can you?

NICKEL: That sounds very strange.

PENNY: Yes, it does. But, on the other hand, if the lexicographer *didn't* know when he wrote the dictionary how the author was going to combine that word expression, what good would it do for you to go to the dictionary for information about it?

NICKEL: None, it would seem.

PENNY: Then the entry must be a prediction. Yet, consider this. Isn't a sentence expressing a prediction in the future tense?

NICKEL: Sure.

PENNY: But a dictionary entry has no future tense. So how can it be a prediction?

NICKEL: This is very puzzling. It is a prediction and yet it isn't a prediction.

PENNY: The Paradox of the Dictionary Entry. It seems to me there is another and stronger reason for not considering a dictionary entry a prediction.

NICKEL: Other than the tense reason?

PENNY: Yes. If I make a prediction about some event, the event confirms or disconfirms the prediction. For example, the color of the paper which I have immersed in a solution confirms or disconfirms my prediction that it would turn red when immersed. But in this case——

NICKEL: The occurrence of the word expression in the sentence can't be used to confirm or disconfirm the dictionary entry prediction.

PENNY: How do you mean it "can't"?

NICKEL: Well, we started with the hypothesis that I didn't know the meaning of the word; so, when I come to the word expression in the sentence, since I don't know its meaning, I can't tell whether or not it confirms the dictionary prediction. And, of course, it won't do to look up its meaning to see if it confirms the prediction, for that would be looking up the prediction to confirm the prediction. That's absurd enough to show we really do have paradox here.

PENNY: That is circular enough to be absurd, but it is a different conclusion from the one we started to develop. The one we started to develop was that a dictionary entry is and is not a prediction. I had convinced you that it is, and you were trying to prove the other half, that it also isn't.

NICKEL: Haven't I shown that?

PENNY: No. You've actually been arguing for something quite different. You've been trying—unwittingly—to show that a dictionary entry is an odd kind of prediction, one that can't be confirmed or disconfirmed without using that prediction itself. But even this can't be concluded unless you assume that all persons are like yourself, ignorant of the word's meaning.

Suppose, due to color-blindness, you couldn't see the color of the paper in the solution. That wouldn't imply, would it, that the prediction about its color couldn't be tested?

NICKEL: I guess not, because somebody who wasn't color-blind could see it, and they could confirm or disconfirm the prediction.

PENNY: And can't we with equal reason suppose there is someone with sufficient knowledge of a language to enable him to test the dictionary entry's prediction?

NICKEL: Yes, we can.

PENNY: And, consequently, we can't conclude, can we, that a dictionary entry is necessarily an odd, paradoxical type of prediction?

NICKEL: No, we can't.

PENNY: Said with generous spirit, Nickel! I must say, you're a rare one, capable of learning without rancor. I mention it because I am appalled at the number of students who have no conception of the Morality of Learning. Most confuse learning with being put down.

NICKEL: Maybe this is another result of the lecture method of learning; their joints squeak from disuse of response and venture.

PENNY: Quite possibly, Nickel. Now that we've established the possibility of confirming dictionary predictions, I'd like to explore your conception of what's involved in such confirmation.

I think we are both agreed that whenever humans carry out confirming activities, they must observe some relevant event, such as the color of the paper turning red. Wouldn't you agree also that a well-informed lexicographer who wished to test a dictionary entry's predictive success would have to observe something?

NICKEL: Yes, I would agree to that.

PENNY: And what is it you think a well-informed lexicographer could and would have to observe in order to test a dictionary entry prediction?

NICKEL: I think he would have to observe the word's meaning.

PENNY: Meaning!

NICKEL: You make "meaning" sound like an indictment.

PENNY: Don't you feel guilty?

NICKEL: I didn't up till now. Just a second, I'll pull the corners of my conscience down.

PENNY: Let me state my point about this assumption more clearly, or, rather, more elaborately.

If we are to treat a dictionary entry as a report and/or as a confirmable prediction, there must be something the lexicographer observes.

NICKEL: That's what I think, too. And if he is to report the *meaning* of the word, mustn't he be able to observe the meaning of the word? How do you fancy that self-indictment?

PENNY: With all the disappointment of a Torquemada. At least it's what I want to get clear about. Remember the situation from which you started? You were reading along and came upon a word whose meaning you didn't know, so you looked it up in the dictionary.

NICKEL: Right.

PENNY: You saw one occurrence of that word expression, and only one. Now there's no question about your *seeing* the expression, is there?

NICKEL: No.

PENNY: I gather from the way you talk that in addition to observing some patches of ink constituting the seen word expression you expect that there is something else to be observed, viz., the *meaning* of the patches of ink. And that wherever those patches of ink, or their sound when read, goes, there the meaning goes. Kind of like a traveling companion; or perhaps more like a boon governess; or maybe even a booner mistress or lover?

NICKEL: That sounds pretty silly.

PENNY: All right. Let's just call it the Constant Nymph. I suppose it's the Constant Nymph that the lexicographer must observe, and which you sometimes aren't able to observe.

Do you suppose you aren't able to observe the Constant Nymph because you have the disease of meaning-blindness? Have you been affected?

NICKEL: I never heard of *that* disease!

PENNY: Umm, yes; very rare. Now, I don't want to alarm you, Mr. Nickel, but we should have the facts, so we can see if the disease is progressing or not. Have you noticed lately that you've been using the dictionary more than usual?

NICKEL: I don't want to appear rude or dull, but don't you think argument would be more in place than jokes?

PENNY: A joke can be a very good argument, though, of course, a very good argument is no joke. I suppose it is obvious, isn't it, that one can't see the Constant Nymph like one can see the patches of ink? So much for that; yet, we have to have some means of observing the Constant Nymph. For by your hypothesis the lexicographer observes it.

Tell me what you think of this, Nickel. Imagine a progressive lexicographer pondering in his bath one day. Suddenly he leaps from his bath and dashes naked into the street, shouting, "Lexicon! Lexicon!"

NICKEL: He'd made a discovery?

PENNY: Sort of. It had just occurred to him how we might be able to dispense with dictionaries. He reasoned as follows: Since each occurrence of a word, spoken or written, is accompanied by the Constant Nymph, instead of sending people to a dictionary (that's where they put Nymphs on report) every time they don't know the meaning of a word, why not simply give them directions for observing the Constant Nymph for themselves?

Isn't that a good idea? Doesn't that deserve "Lexicon! Lexicon!"?

NICKEL: If I say "Yes," you'll ask me what directions we should give people to help them observe the Constant Nymph.

PENNY: I will. And yet you can't deny that it would be a great improvement.

NICKEL: Maybe we can't give general directions for observing the Constant Nymphs. Maybe each, or at least a lot of them, require individual directions.

PENNY: I only want from you directions for observing the Constant Nymph of *one* word.

NICKEL: Maybe the lexicographer can give them.

PENNY: You have to. If you can't, I doubt that you know what you're talking about when you talk about observing the "meaning" of a word.

NICKEL: Let me start over. Everything that we call a word has a meaning; that meaning is given in a dictionary entry. The lexicographer, or any person for that matter, to confirm a dictionary entry's prediction or to gather information for an entry, has to be able to observe the "meaning" of the word, observe that which constantly accompanies the word. You're asking me to identify this Constant Nymph, to say what it is that the lexicographer must observe.

PENNY: That's right. Is the Constant Nymph a thought, a psychological response, such as an image, or a non-physical, abstract entity, or what?

NICKEL: We've already determined it can't be a thought.* And it can't be a psychological response.† We can't observe thoughts or responses. Besides, if we could observe them, there would be no need for talking or writing.

PENNY: There wouldn't?

NICKEL: People often think of language as a means of conveying thoughts from one person to another. If meaning were a thought and could be observed directly, we could dispense with the linguistic means; for the "speaker" could present his thoughts directly to the "hearer."

PENNY: Since you won't identify "meaning" with a thought or psychological response, would you identify it with a non-physical, abstract entity?

NICKEL: No, I wouldn't.

PENNY: That was quick.

NICKEL: Well, gosh, I don't have the slightest idea of how to put anyone in touch with such a thing. I don't know how to give directions for putting people in touch with non-physical things. Normally, when I give directions, I have to mention physical things. I say, for example, to go to a certain corner, or to turn left at the bowling alley, or to go up the hill, or something similar.

PENNY: That's so sensible, Nickel, that I can't believe you should forget so quickly what we have learned. We learned about the relation between the meaning and regularity of shapes and sounds. And we learned something about linguistic rules or directions; and now you fail to apply what we learned there to dictionary definitions. Think, Nickel!

*Reader: See pages 44 and 161.
† See pages 168–169.

What must you observe to grasp the meaning of a word? What must a lexicographer observe in order to gather the information for his report or to confirm an entry's prediction?

NICKEL: The only thing he can observe. A sound or shape, the sound or shape we identify as the word whose meaning we're trying to grasp.

PENNY: Do we observe only that one word?

NICKEL: No. We have to observe the other words with which it is combined. We can see that with "part." It has more than one meaning and I can often tell which meaning it has in a particular case when I see with what other words it is combined. In "I like this picture so much I hate to part with it" it means something different than in "You may have the largest part of the pie."

PENNY: Do you still think the Constant Nymph is any kind of entity?

NICKEL: No, I don't, although I don't know how else to identify it. In fact, I guess we shouldn't even speak of a Constant Nymph. We should banish the Constant Nymph. There isn't anything called "meaning" we are supposed to get in touch with. Learning the meaning of a word isn't learning about a something, it is learning how to do something; it is learning how to combine one shape correctly with other shapes; it is being able to "go on."

I sound like a loyal subject of King *M*.

PENNY: Hail, Caesar! But mustn't you render unto King *N* also the things that are his? What about dictionary entries?

NICKEL: Right enough. A dictionary entry mustn't be thought to put us in touch with a Constant Nymph; it must be thought of as giving us directions for doing something.

PENNY: As giving directions for living happily ever after in Lingoland?

NICKEL: It will be a happy land as long as we don't enfranchise the Constant Nymphs.

PENNY: You've become such a convinced convert and things are going so smoothly that I hate to remind you of what I'm nevertheless going to remind you of.

I think we're pretty well agreed that to speak of the meaning of a linguistic item is to speak of the combinatory possibilities allowed by its rule of regularity; and that to learn its meaning is to learn its combinatory regularity; and that meaning is predicated of shapes and sounds because they are what we actually combine in regular ways; and that some dictionary entries give us the meaning of a shape because they give us combinatory directions.

NICKEL: "Some" dictionary entries?

PENNY: Yes, for example, "lam," according to one dictionary, means "to thrash; whack." You can see this gives you combinatory directions;

you are to combine "lam" as you combine "thrash" or "whack"; that is, you can substitute "lam" for "thrash."

NICKEL: But why do you say "some" dictionary entries? What do the "other" dictionary entries do if they don't give us combinatory rules?

PENNY: They refer us to entities; sometimes they even show us pictures of them. Take a Hottentot word, "kudu," and notice that in this dictionary they refer us to "a large grayish-brown African antelope," and give us a picture of one.

NICKEL: Are you suggesting that because some definitions refer us to entities, we have the Constant Nymph with us again?

PENNY: Do you think it is?

NICKEL: The Constant Nymph was your name for the fanciful entity, meaning, supposedly accompanying a shape or sound. I doubt that kudus accompany "kudu."

PENNY: What about images of kudus?

NICKEL: You knocked the imagistic stuffing out of me for good the other day.

PENNY: Are we to deny, then, that words with referential meaning have Constant Nymphs?

NICKEL: I think so. Apart from the fact that kudus don't accompany "kudu," it seems to me we can give a combinatory account of "kudu" just as well and in the same manner that we did for "lam." After all, I can substitute "large grayish-brown African antelope" for "kudu" in such sentences as "Look at that kudu run!"

PENNY: But what if someone insists that the descriptive phrase in turn has its Constant Nymph? And, further, insists that the Constant Nymph, without which neither the phrase nor "kudu" can be understood, is the animal entity?

NICKEL: I think our long conversation about reference and emplacement showed why we can banish the Constant Nymph and why lexicographers need rely only on observations of combinatory regularity, even when a referential word is involved. The lexicographer need only note that kudus may be emplaced in sentences where "kudu" occurs. This is a rule of combinatory regularity because it is a substitution rule.

Do you know something, Mr. Penny?

PENNY: Yes, though I don't know whether I know what you're thinking of.

NICKEL: You've rather a literal streak today. Here's what I was thinking: I'm not likely to forget that linguistic meaning depends on combinatory regularity and that combinatory regularity involves substitution and arrangement. I do believe my previous habits have been seriously unhinged—which, by the way, takes the shackles off my imagination.

PENNY: The prisoner has escaped the cave?

NICKEL: I think so. I've just thought of another way of writing a dictionary. Do you have time to hear of it?

PENNY: It is cool and leafy and unhurried here in the gazebo. And logic does not know the clock.

NICKEL: Here it is, then. Imagine a dictionary with one page, albeit a very large page. All English words appear on this one page. And it's arranged something like this.

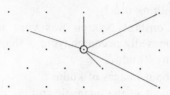

PENNY: A Star of Meaning! But would you tell me what it shows? Does it represent the occurrence of an idea much in the manner of cartoonists' drawings?

NICKEL: That's a pretty close guess. The Star is meant to represent an idea, a combinatory concept. It is meant to represent combinatory meaning. Let me explain this.

My dictionary is really a word map. Points represent words and when there is a line between points we know those two words can be combined into a sentence. Thus, when I want to know the combinatory meaning of a word I look on the dictionary and follow the various lines to other words. There are as many lines as combinatory possibilities. What do you think of it?

PENNY: It's not a bad idea. You've given us a spatial analogue for the idea of combinatory meaning. That is sometimes useful. I do have some questions about it, however.

How do you distinguish between two meanings of a word?

NICKEL: I could do it this way. For every different meaning of a word I could have a different inscription entered on the page. Take the word "part"; one use of it might be entered as "part$_1$" and another use might be entered as "part$_2$." They will occupy different points and, naturally, have different lines.

PENNY: What do you do for two different words that have the same meaning?

NICKEL: I enter them at the same point, for to say they have the same meaning is to say they have the same combinatory possibilities. Another thing about same meaning: If two people give the same meaning to an expression, their Stars of Meaning are isomorphic.

PENNY: Aren't you going to have a lot of lines going to words such as "the," "a," "is," "all," "not," and "have"?

NICKEL: I suppose so, for I can combine "the" as in "the dog," "the cloud," "the memory," etc. Suppose I make a distinction between the subject and predicate of a sentence and the other words that appear in a sentence such as those you mention. Let me call all the latter words "auxiliary" words.

PENNY: What does isolating syncategorematic words, for that is what your auxiliary words have often been called, do for you?

NICKEL: I'll exclude from my word map all auxiliary words. We can give separate rules for them later. My lines will then connect subjects and predicates that may go together.

PENNY: How are you going to handle referential meaning?

NICKEL: Hmm. That piece of paper is going to be awfully large; in fact, it's going to be as large as the universe, for certainly any dog may be emplaced in "dog" in "The dog is brown." That means I need a line between some dogs and "brown." The same thing certainly holds for all other entities that may be emplaced. They may be the subjects of sentences as well as dogs may.

Speaking of "subjects" of sentences, I see I should add another factor to my map. My connecting lines should have arrows indicating direction from the subject to the predicate. At least I need some device doing what the arrows do, for I have to indicate somehow the grammar of the language. I need something equivalent to the *n* for "noun" and the *v* for "verb" that we find in ordinary dictionaries.

PENNY: Is a map useful if it's as large as what it represents?

NICKEL: It is if it contains something which isn't contained in the thing mapped. In this case the map contains connecting lines and the universe doesn't, so we could learn something by looking at the map that we couldn't learn by looking at the universe.

PENNY: Are you, Lexicographer, going to draw lines representing only combinations that you have observed in the past or are you going to draw lines representing combinations which no one has yet made but which they might make in the future?

NICKEL: If I make it a historical document, my dictionary won't be as useful as I'd like it to be; so, it appears I must make some provision for the future.

PENNY: I think you are ready for the argument showing that a dictionary entry is not a prediction.

NICKEL: I am ready to receive paradox?

PENNY: It is my belief that you are. Consider the possibility of misuse. We sometimes say that someone misused a word expression, and proceed to correct him. We do this frequently with children and foreigners.

NICKEL: Can you give me some examples?

PENNY: I think I can remember some my son, Benny, uttered. "What does 'beer' spell?" "I can run faster than me." "Daddy, I was learning how to stand on my head. If I did it once, was that a long time?"

NICKEL: Misuses or miscombinations, all right.

PENNY: I think so; I felt called upon to correct him. But there is no question, is there, that we do have *a* combination here?

NICKEL: One can't deny that "beer" is in fact combined with other words, if that's what you mean.

PENNY: That's what I mean. Imagine now that Benny challenged my correction, as he often does, with "How do *you* know?" Could I use the dictionary as a ground for saying that his combination is incorrect if we consider its entries as predictions?

NICKEL: I don't think so. If a dictionary entry is a prediction about future combinations, we have to allow that *any* future combination will be a test of the prediction. But in the case of a questionable combination, it is just the opposite; it is the combination itself which is being tested by the dictionary entry.

PENNY: You see the point perfectly. If a dictionary entry were only a prediction, we could not use it to determine that any actual combination is correct or incorrect. The entry must be the standard for the correctness of the combination and not vice versa. Otherwise, there would be nothing to appeal to in order to settle a dispute about misuse.

You must realize, of course, that I am referring to the "perfect" dictionary, one that contains a report on all the shared regularities.

NICKEL: Well, at last! It looks as if a dictionary entry is not a prediction, and that we have rid ourselves of paradox.

PENNY: On the contrary, Sir, we have just now acquired paradox. A dictionary entry is paradoxical if it is both a prediction and not a prediction. While we had shown before that it must be a prediction, we have just now shown that it also cannot be a prediction. Now—are you ready to accept paradox?

NICKEL: I see it, but I don't believe it. It can't be both. It's either a prediction or not, so one of the arguments must be wrong.

PENNY: Which one is in disfavor? The last one?

NICKEL: Nope. I can see that a dictionary entry can't be a prediction, for rather than say the dictionary entry is disconfirmed, we say a person,

Benny, for example, has misused the term. I don't see how we can deny that.

PENNY: You want to cling to the notion that a dictionary entry is a standard then?

NICKEL: That's right.

PENNY: Then the first one must be in disfavor.

NICKEL: It has to be, although it certainly seems reasonable. For if dictionaries don't account for future uses, they will be of no use to us tomorrow.

PENNY: I do think we have to acknowledge that dictionaries have a temporal existence. Since words come to be used in new ways, dictionaries become dated and lose some of their usefulness. And certainly the temporal facts about the changes in permissible combinations of word expressions are repeatedly acknowledged by the *Oxford English Dictionary* (OED). In the Preface the Editors refer to the "history" of words; and in the entries, when they exhibit, King *M*-like, the use of a word, they frequently give dates for that use.*

NICKEL: And many of the entries in dictionaries are preceded by "archaic," while others are preceded by "obsolete."

PENNY: Other acknowledgments of their historical nature.

I think we may, however, assent to these temporal facts without assenting to the view that they entail a dictionary entry's being a prediction.

NICKEL: You think we can get out of the paradox then?

PENNY: Yes, I do. That a 1959 use of a word expression accords with a 1940 dictionary entry can be accounted for in a more natural way than supposing that the lexicographer was prescient. And so can the fact that it doesn't accord.

Instead of considering a reader's ignorance of a word's meaning as the occasion requiring the use of a dictionary, let's consider a writer's or speaker's doubt about a word's meaning as the occasion. Suppose it is you who are writing, and the word "prescient" comes to mind as the one you wish to use, but you are in doubt about its being a correct use. What do you think you would do?

NICKEL: Probably I would look it up in the dictionary, if I had one handy, and felt strongly about using that word rather than another.

---

* At the end of our conversation for this day, I went to the library to secure a quotation of the reference Mr. Penny made to the Preface of the OED. It follows: "The aim of this Dictionary is to furnish an adequate account of the meaning, origin and history of English words ... to illustrate these facts by a series of quotations ranging from the first known occurrence of the word to the latest, or down to the present day; the word being thus made to exhibit its own history and meaning." (*Oxford English Dictionary*, Oxford University Press, New York, 1888.)

PENNY: Now imagine that your guess about its use was incorrect, and that you use that word in accordance with the definition. Later a callow youth reads your sentence and, not knowing the meaning of "prescient," looks it up in the dictionary. Upon reading the dictionary entry, an appreciative smile crosses his face, followed by a head-shake signifying respect.

NICKEL: He liked my sentence?

PENNY: No; he silently praised the lexicographer who so cleverly predicted that use. Our youth checks the date of the dictionary and exclaims, "Compiled nineteen years before this sentence was written, and he hit it right on the nose! Fantastic! You've sure got to hand it to those lexicographers."

NICKEL: And all the while my use accords with the dictionary definition only because I was a good boy, not because of the lexicographer's predictive skill. This does seem to be a more natural way of explaining that "miraculous" accord between my use and the dictionary entry.

Since that gets rid of the paradox, we don't have to consider a dictionary entry as a prediction in order to account for its usefulness in the future. It continues to be useful because people continue to use the entry as a rule.

PENNY: You're getting good, Nickel. And in case they do not continue to use the entry as a rule?

NICKEL: But continue to use the word expression?

PENNY: Yes.

NICKEL: Then that dictionary entry loses some of its usefulness; it requires replacement or addition with the new rule that is being followed. And it's this, isn't it, which gives word expressions their history?

PENNY: That's right. It is this which also accounts for the dating of dictionaries. The "perfect" dictionary requires constant addition and revision.

NICKEL: It feels good to be rid of paradox. Don't you think so?

PENNY: It seems to me we have got out of one only to get into another, so I'm not sure what it feels like.

NICKEL: Another paradox?

PENNY: If a dictionary is to be kept perfect, we have to keep adding and revising. Why?

NICKEL: Because people start using the words in new ways.

PENNY: Sure, and the dictionary, to remain current, has to report these, doesn't it?

NICKEL: Obviously.

PENNY: Then, you've reaffirmed our previous statement that a dictionary entry is a report; but only a moment ago you said it was a rule. How can something be both a rule and a report? A dictionary entry as a report simply tells how *in fact* people use a word; a dictionary entry as a rule is used to show us how we *ought* to use a word if we are to be understood by others. A dictionary entry as a rule serves as a guide for communal meaning. As it did for you in the example about "prescient." Consequently,——

NICKEL: A dictionary entry is a report and it isn't a report. Or, it is a rule and it isn't a rule.

PENNY: Give my regards to Paradox. Say "Hello" to Report Square.

NICKEL: I'm not worried. You got us out of the last paradox, and I'll bet you can get us out of this one.

PENNY: I appreciate your confidence, but I think it would be better if you tried to get us out of this one yourself.

NICKEL: I haven't the slightest idea how to begin.

PENNY: Clue: A dictionary entry can be both a report and a rule.

NICKEL: Some clue! That's exactly what bugs me, that it seems to be both.

PENNY: Look on a dictionary entry as only an expression and distinguish it from its uses as we did the other day.* We allowed that a rule expression can be used in several ways. Why can't we extend this insight and say that an expression including dictionary entries may have two kinds of uses?

An expression may have a reportorial use with respect to exhibited expressions and a rule use with respect to new expressions. For example, the Commutation schema is a report on the commutability of ∨ expressions; given the matrix exhibitions showing us how to assign 1 and 0 to the ∨ functor, we can, by means of the Commutation schema, report that the relative positions of the alpha and beta constituents in a ∨ expression do not affect the meaning of the ∨ expression.

Now, give me an example of a schema that was used as a rule.

NICKEL: It would have to have been one which covered expressions that had not been exhibited. Was it the Stroke schema? That schema governed stroke expressions, a kind that had not been exhibited until you introduced the stroke functor.

PENNY: That's an example. The Stroke schema was a definition giving us directions for transforming a ∨ expression into a stroke expression.

* Reader: See page 210.

You learned to follow those directions in doing exercises in the last chapter.

NICKEL: I see that two different schemas can be used in two different ways. But that's different from saying the same schema can be used in two different ways.

PENNY: A relevant observation. Ah, help is coming. Here come Even and Odd. An expression is to be distinguished from its use; we agreed on that. Isn't it possible for an expression to be used by Even in one way and by Odd in another way?

Suppose Even is a Principia lexicographer who has observed all Principia *wfe*s and *wfe*10s expressed to date. He writes up a report, among which is the De Morgan schema, the De Morgan schema thus being a report with respect to Even. But Odd, who is just learning the language, hasn't seen all the Principia exhibitions. He has seen and knows how to use only the v and bar functors. Suddenly he comes across an expression containing a vocabulary item he has never seen.

NICKEL: The dot?

PENNY: He decides he wants to use the dot in an expression just as you, in our earlier supposition, wanted to use "prescient." But he isn't sure how to use dot, so upon hearing of Even's lexicographical reports, he hies himself to it, and looks full on the open, honest face of the De Morgan schema.

NICKEL: I see. The De Morgan schema is used by Odd as a rule, in fact, as a definition; that is, it gives him directions for assigning meaning to the dot.

PENNY: Precisely. This shows us that one and the same physical expression can be used in two ways. Apply this to ordinary dictionary entries.

NICKEL: I guess, so far as the lexicographer is concerned, he is interested in looking at the past uses; so that, for him, a dictionary entry would be a report on them.

PENNY: As it is for us, too.

NICKEL: Whereas, for anyone interested in communicating with others in the future, or now, but ignorant of a word's meaning, they will use the dictionary entry as a rule or guide.

PENNY: Exactly. In order to communicate, that is, formulate sensical combinations, he must respect the regularity of use; and since a dictionary entry reports past regularity, it serves him as a guide to the conditions upon which his communicative success depends.

NICKEL: All hail, Dictionaries! Keepers of regularity!

PENNY: I wouldn't be quite so lavish in praise of them.

NICKEL: Why not?

PENNY: They won't lead us out of Egypt and to the promised land. Suppose my daughter, Megan, said "I felt a funeral in my brain."

NICKEL: Clearly, she was misusing "funeral."

PENNY: And I could appeal to the dictionary as our standard to show her that.

NICKEL: Of course.

PENNY: And thereby keep her in Egypt!

NICKEL: How so?

PENNY: Don't you remember? That's the first line of Emily Dickinson's poem; the one we used on the first day.

NICKEL: Oh, yes. I'd forgotten.

PENNY: So, is the line an instance of a misuse or is it a metaphor?

NICKEL: Maybe a metaphor *is* a misuse?

PENNY: Or maybe it will part the Red Sea?

NICKEL: This seems like a really interesting issue.

PENNY: An issue that we can't take time to pursue at present. Nor can I promise that we'll return to the issue of metaphors. Though if we can use what we're going to talk about in our course in logic to enlighten the concept of metaphor, that will be the crowning glory of our conversations.

NICKEL: Another delay?

PENNY: Have I delayed so much that you should dare to remark about it?

NICKEL: You delayed the question about how we decide whether a rule of combination is only my rule or a more general rule. That came up when we were discussing pleasant shouts.*

PENNY: Any other delays?

NICKEL: Le Grand Delay: How logic in the narrow sense yields philosophic profit. And we've left quite a few other carcasses along the way. You mentioned the methodology of the new philosophy. I'm sure its bones are bleached a pretty white by now. Yesterday, after I asked you for the difference between a lexicographer and a combinatory philosopher, you said they were different because philosophy contained arguments. I expected that today we would explore that answer and find out more exactly what you meant.

PENNY: But, we didn't.

NICKEL: No, and that's another delay.

PENNY: The thread of anxiety, unfulfilled tendencies, threats, and promises; that's the thread of drama, friend.

NICKEL: It's also the thread of melodrama.

* Reader: See page 142.

PENNY: You're improving in these skirmishes. Here's an attack on your left flank! At least you have to allow that it wasn't a total washout. We've learned that the results of a study of regularity can be either exhibited or meta-linguistically reported;

NICKEL: King M or King N.

PENNY: ——that such reports can also serve as rules;

NICKEL: Look, C, here's the way to use $2n-1$.

PENNY: ——that rule expressions can be used in diverse ways;

NICKEL: OK, C, I grant that you *do* have another way of producing a sequence with $2n-1$, but try using it our way.

PENNY: —— that the verification of similar, and standard, uses of rule expressions ultimately depends on exhibition;

NICKEL: Here is your examination, C; you have five minutes in which to produce the standard sequence from $2n-1$.

PENNY: —— that the dependence of "meaning" on regularity of use hadn't thoroughly penetrated nor replaced your former beliefs, for you still flirted with the Constant Nymph, which prompted the Star of Meaning to rise in the east;

NICKEL: Guilty!

PENNY: —— that dictionary entries are reports *and* rules, and aren't predictions;

NICKEL: And as the Paradox of the Dictionary Entry sinks in the west, we bid farewell to ——

PENNY: And say hello to misuse and metaphor, which when contrasted, give us pause about excessively praising standard uses and dictionaries.

NICKEL: Take us to your poet, Megan.

PENNY: And now the frontal attack! It could be that all of these points had to be covered before we could show how logic in the narrow sense yields philosophic profit; how combinatory philosophers differ from lexicographers, and what role arguments play in that difference; and what the methodology of combinatory philosophy is. Perhaps in one fell blow we shall inherit the world's philosophic salt. Perhaps.

Now that you've put on the pressure, I'd like to launch into the pivotal area—arguments. Hewing to the line of our own advice, let's start working with Polish and Principia, our ideal languages.

NICKEL: I don't see how we can do that. Arguments are cast with the use of propositions, and you said propositions are sentences that are true or false. Principia and Polish don't contain true or false sentences; at least I don't recall our using "true" or "false" or "sentence" in any Po- or Pr- rules. So we can't cast arguments in Polish and Principia.

PENNY: An excellent observation, Nickel. That being so, we have no choice except to define "Polish proposition" and "Principia proposition."

df $\dfrac{\text{Polish proposition}}{\text{Polish expression meaning 1 or 0}}$

NICKEL: By this definition, is every Polish *wfe* and *wfe*10 a proposition?

PENNY: A *wfe*10 can't mean 1 or 0; a *wfe*10 *is* 1 or 0. Only a Polish *wfe* may mean referentially 1 or 0 because it's the kind of thing into which its referent, the numeral 1 or the numeral 0, may be substituted. *Wfes* by the Po-5 rules are such things.

NICKEL: Then only *wfes* are suitable for forming argument expressions in Polish?

PENNY: They aren't suitable in that sense, for there are no argument expressions in Polish.

NICKEL: Why is that?

PENNY: Do you remember that we spoke of premiss and conclusion indicators earlier?

NICKEL: I do.* They were such words as "because," "since," and "hence." With them we indicate our intention to express an argument.

PENNY: Do you find any such expressions in the Polish vocabulary?

NICKEL: No, I don't.

PENNY: Then how do you expect someone to express an argument in Polish?

NICKEL: Maybe we'll have to expand the Polish vocabulary, add premiss and conclusion indicators to our Po-1 rules.

PENNY: Instead of doing that, let's add a Po-10 and Pr-10 rule.

NICKEL: Haven't we skipped a rule? What happened to Po-9 and Pr-9?

PENNY: I gave Po-9 but forgot to say it was Po-9. Po-9 was the definition of "Polish proposition." "Polish proposition" is a meta-linguistic term we have added and defined for purposes of talking about Polish, just as "letter," "functor," "functor strength," "*wfe*," "*wfe*10," "transformation schema," and "transformation proof" are meta-linguistic terms given and defined by a Po- rule.

NICKEL: And now you're proposing a Po-10 rule for the term "Polish argument," aren't you?

PENNY: I am.

Po-10: $\dfrac{\text{Polish argument}}{}$ df

A meta-linguistic claim about a collection of Polish propositions that if all propositions designated as premisses mean 1, then the Polish proposition designated as the conclusion necessarily means 1.

* Reader: See page 86.

NICKEL: Premiss and conclusion indicators will have to be meta-linguistic terms if "Polish argument" is a meta-linguistic term.

PENNY: That's right. Let me introduce now the meta-Polish mark we'll use to indicate that we intend an argument: _____. We can pronounce it as the single line or the argument line or the therefore line. The premisses are above the single line and the conclusion is below it.

Here is an instance of a Polish argument: $\dfrac{*pq \quad p}{q}$.

NICKEL: Is that a valid Polish argument?

PENNY: How can we answer if we don't have a Po- rule defining "valid Polish argument"?

NICKEL: Bingo. But that shouldn't be hard to do. How's this? It's done by simply adding "true" to Po-10.

Po-11: $\dfrac{\text{Valid Polish argument}}{\text{A true meta-linguistic claim about} \underline{\quad\quad}}$ df

PENNY: That will do very nicely. Now, is that argument, $\dfrac{*pq \quad p}{q}$, valid?

NICKEL: There's only one way to find out. I'll have to substitute 1's and 0's into the Polish letters in the premisses *pq and p and see if, when the premisses mean 1, I necessarily have to substitute a 1 into the conclusion.

The most systematic way to substitute is to make matrices for my premisses and the conclusion.

(a)	1*11	1
(b)	1*01	0
(c)	0*10	1
(d)	1*00	0
	*pq	p

I get these matrices if I substitute uniformly, as it seems I must if I am not to equivocate. Each row is the result of a different combination of uniform substitutions.

$$\frac{}{q}$$

(a)	1
(b)	1
(c)	0
(d)	0

The argument is valid. Row (a) shows me this, for it is only in this row that both premisses mean 1 and that row in the conclusion means 1. That row in the conclusion must mean 1 if I substitute uniformly.

PENNY: Rows (c) and (d) where the conclusion means 0 don't bother you?

NICKEL: Not at all.   Neither shows the invalidity of the argument.
We are unable to show invalidity, or validity, until we satisfy the condition
"if all those propositions designated as premisses mean 1"; the definition
of "valid" in Po-11 requires this.   Now, neither row (c) nor row (d)
satisfy that condition, for in (c) the first premiss, $*pq$, is 0 and in (d) the
second premiss, p, is 0.

For the same reason row (b) doesn't help establish the validity of the
argument even though in that row q, the conclusion, means 1.

PENNY: Once you satisfy the condition that in some row all premisses
mean 1, what have you found out about an argument when you find that
in the same row the conclusion means 0?

NICKEL: That the argument is invalid.

PENNY: Which row shows the following argument is invalid?*

$$
\begin{array}{lll}
\text{(a)} & 1*11 & 1 \\
\text{(b)} & 1*01 & 1 \\
\text{(c)} & 0*10 & 0 \\
\text{(d)} & 1*00 & 0 \\
\hline
& *pq & q \\
\end{array}
$$

$$
\begin{array}{ll}
& p \\
\text{(a)} & 1 \\
\text{(b)} & 0 \\
\text{(c)} & 1 \\
\text{(d)} & 0 \\
\end{array}
$$

NICKEL: Row (b), for in that row both premisses mean 1 while the
conclusion means 0.   That makes any meta-Polish claim for the validity
of this argument false.   Since by Po-11 the claim for validity must be
true, we have to conclude that this argument is invalid.

I see something now.   The introduction into Polish of referential
meaning, 1 and 0, is what makes arguments in Polish possible.   That
explains why you've had me working on matrices and wfe10s.   The
matrix of every wfe is made up of 2^n wfe10s and only by looking at the
matrices of the wfes in an argument are we able to decide on the argument's
validity.   The introduction of wfe10s was no small matter.   I'm feeling
pretty good right now about my insistence on referential meaning, for
without it we couldn't have arguments.

PENNY: Congratulations.   Is this argument valid?

$$
\frac{*.rqp \quad .rq}{p}
$$

*Try to answer the question before you read my answer.—E. Nickel.

NICKEL: I'll have to construct matrices again to find out.

(a)	1*1.111	1.11	
(b)	1*0.011	0.01	To tell you the truth, I'm
(c)	1*0.101	0.10	surprised. Not that the ar-
(d)	1*0.001	0.00	gument's being valid sur-
(e)	0*1.110	1.11	prises me, but that I can tell
(f)	1*0.010	0.01	it's valid from row (a) alone.
(g)	1*0.100	0.10	That's the only row in which
(h)	1*0.000	0.00	both premisses are 1.

$$\frac{*\quad .rqp \qquad .rq}{p}$$

(a)	1
(b)	1
(c)	1
(d)	1
(e)	0
(f)	0
(g)	0
(h)	0

PENNY: You could have found the validity of the argument by a much shorter means, which I'll call the Shorter Matrix Method. You only need look for a single row to find out if an argument is valid.

NICKEL: A row such as (a)?

PENNY: No. One such row doesn't guarantee validity unless it's the only such row, as in this argument; but this doesn't happen all the time. The kind of row I have in mind is one in which all the premisses are 1 and the conclusion is 0. If such a row exists in the argument's matrix, you know the argument is invalid. If it doesn't exist, what do you know?

NICKEL: That it is not invalid, which is the same as knowing it is valid. But how do I look for this row without writing down all the rows?

PENNY: Easy enough. We can proceed in either of two ways.

Suppose we take as our argument $\dfrac{*.rqp \quad .rq}{p}$.

The first way is to find a premiss, such as a dot expression or a single letter, which by appropriate substitution can be made to mean 1 in only one way.

$$\frac{1.11}{p} \quad *.rqp \quad .rq$$

Once you substitute for the letters in that premiss, you have to substitute uniformly for those letters wherever they occur in the argument.

$$\frac{1.11 \quad 1.11}{p} \quad * \quad .rqp \quad .rq$$

252

Knowing your wish to make all the premisses mean 1, you may have to substitute in a single way for the other letters in the premisses as well, just as you are forced to substitute 1 into *p* in this case. Continue this process until you find out whether all premisses can be made to mean 1 and the conclusion can be made to mean 0.

$$\frac{1*1.111 \quad 1.11}{\begin{array}{c} *\ .rpq \quad .rq \\ \hline p \\ 1 \end{array}}$$

NICKEL: The conclusion must mean 1 under the uniform substitution rule.

PENNY: So, we know that we can't make all the premisses mean 1 and the conclusion 0; no such row exists, for there is no other way to make all the premisses mean 1, and under that duress the conclusion also means 1.

NICKEL: That way won't work, will it, unless the argument has a premiss that can be made to mean 1 in only one way?

PENNY: That's right. If there are two or more ways of making the premisses mean 1, it might turn out that under one set of substitutions the conclusion means 1 and under the other set it may mean 0. If you were to use only the first substitution set, you wouldn't realize there is another set which shows the argument is invalid. Here's an example of that:

$$\frac{*pq \quad *qr \quad \lor pr}{q}$$

Under the first substitution set of *p*=0, *q*=1, and *r*=1, the premisses all mean 1 and the conclusion means 1.

$$\frac{1*01 \quad 1*11 \quad 1\lor01}{1}$$

Under the second substitution set of *p*=0, *q*=0, and *r*=1, the premisses mean 1 and the conclusion means 0.

$$\frac{1*00 \quad 1*01 \quad 1\lor01}{0}$$

NICKEL: I see your point, but now I'm puzzled how we can use the Shorter Matrix Method on this last argument, for none of the premisses can be made to mean 1 in only one way.

PENNY: That brings up the second way of proceeding. Instead of first substituting for a premiss, we can first substitute for the conclusion. If the conclusion can be made to mean 0 in a single way, and we can make the premisses mean 1, as in the above argument, then we will have selected immediately the second substitution set, the one which shows the argument's invalidity. Let me take you through this procedure one step at a time, using $\frac{*.rqp \quad .rq}{p}$ again.

We first substitute in such a way that the conclusion means 0, and substitute uniformly for the letter or letters throughout the argument.

$$\frac{\overset{\displaystyle 0}{*.rqp\ .rq}}{\underset{\displaystyle 0}{p}}$$

Then we make the first premiss mean 1 by appropriate substitution.

$$\frac{\overset{\displaystyle 1*0.100}{*\ .rqp\ .rq}}{\underset{\displaystyle 0}{p}}$$

When we continue substituting uniformly throughout the argument, we notice that our second premiss necessarily means 0; I have no way of making the first premiss mean 1 that doesn't make the second premiss mean 0.

$$\frac{\overset{\displaystyle 1*0.100\ \ 0.10}{*\ .rqp\ .rq}}{\underset{\displaystyle 0}{p}}$$

Once again we see that no row exists in that argument's matrix in which all the premisses mean 1 and the conclusion means 0. We have found out, in short, that the argument is valid.

NICKEL: Suppose that I have an argument with three premisses; if I find that by substitution I get $\frac{1\ 1\ 1}{0}$, then I know the argument is invalid. Right?

PENNY: Right.

NICKEL: That's nice and short. I like that method.

PENNY: Yes, the Shorter Matrix Method is nice and short.

NICKEL: Do you know that at this moment I have a slight tingling around my ears? I detect a parallel between the Shorter Matrix Method and the Truth-table Method we used on propositional arguments. Substituting 1 in letter variables seems similar to substituting "true" in parallelograms and roundends, and substituting 0 seems similar to substituting "false."

Might there be a cipher between Polish arguments and English propositional arguments, just as there was a cipher between Venn arguments and English syllogistic arguments?

PENNY: There might be. Wouldn't that be interesting for you to think about between today and the next time we meet?

You said you liked the Shorter Matrix Method because it was nice and short. There was an even shorter way to have known that this last argument, $\frac{*.rqp\ .rq}{p}$, is valid.

NICKEL: There was?

PENNY: You should have noticed that its form was similar to that of the first argument, $\dfrac{*pq\ p}{q}$, which we had already proved was valid.

NICKEL: You've reminded me of something I shouldn't have forgotten: That the validity of arguments depends upon their form. Then is it the arrangement of the Polish expressions which determines whether their *wfe*10 matrices yield a row in which all the premisses mean 1 and the conclusion means 0?

PENNY: You can see that for yourself if you consider this argument, $\dfrac{*pq\ q}{p}$, which is similar to $\dfrac{*pq\ p}{q}$ except in its arrangement.

NICKEL: Let me try my hand at determining its validity by the Shorter Matrix Method.

$$\frac{*pq\ q}{p} \quad \frac{*pq\ q}{0} \quad \frac{*0q\ q}{0} \quad \frac{*0q\ 1}{0} \quad \frac{1*01\ 1}{0}$$

It's invalid, since I can make all the premisses mean 1 and the conclusion mean 0.

I'm aware of form once more, thank you. Let me try my hand at picturing, exhibiting, the form of $\dfrac{*pq\ p}{q}$ and $\dfrac{*.rqp\ .rq}{p}$. I take my hint from the transformation schemas. How's this? $\dfrac{*\alpha\beta\ \alpha}{\beta}$.

PENNY: Can you justify the claim that that argument schema is the right picture of the form?

NICKEL: Both arguments are substitution instances of the schema. By appropriate substitution into its variables I can construct each argument. If I substitute p for α and q for β, I get $\dfrac{*pq\ p}{q}$; and if I substitute $.rq$ for α and p for β, I get $\dfrac{*.rqp\ .rq}{p}$. Isn't it true to say that if I can construct both arguments by appropriate substitution into the same schema, that the arguments have the same form?

PENNY: It seems so to me, Nickel.

NICKEL: I also see some sense in schemas now. They save work.

PENNY: Why do you say that?

NICKEL: A schema is a picture of a valid form. Whenever we see an argument with the form pictured by the schema, that is, an argument which is a substitution instance of that schema, we know that the argument is valid. That saves us the work of making a matrix for the argument or of using the Shorter Matrix Method. Substitution into a valid schema is a great idea.

PENNY: It's so great that we ought to christen it.

NICKEL: I hereby christen thee Substitution Method. May you have a long and useful life.

PENNY: It will, as you'll soon see. But, do you know that schemas may be put to other, cunning uses?

NICKEL: What do you have in mind?

PENNY: Suppose you believed that the enemy had cracked your code and was able to intercept your messages; wouldn't it be helpful if you didn't have to write the whole message?

NICKEL: I'm not sure of that. How would the person for whom the message is intended know what I didn't write?

PENNY: He could derive it from what you did write by the cunning use of your argument schema. The argument schema could be used to augment the message. For example, if you sent the Polish expressions *vqp.rq* and *vqp*, the person for whom the message is intended could use your argument schema, which I'll call Modus ponens from now on, to derive the rest of the message.

NICKEL: How is that possible?

PENNY: Suppose Modus ponens constitutes part of the code. He has it in front of him. Upon receiving your message he notes that he can substitute your two expressions into the premisses, for he can substitute *vqp* for α and *.rq* for β. That gives him

$$
\frac{
\begin{array}{ccc}
*vqp & .rq & vqp \\
* \alpha & \beta & \alpha
\end{array}
}{\beta}
$$

Obviously, your Modus ponens code allows him to substitute for β beneath the single line once he has substituted for β above the line—and he knows what he can substitute.

NICKEL: *.rq*?

PENNY: Sure. And isn't that a distinct Polish expression that didn't occur in the message you sent your comrade?

NICKEL: It augments my message, all right. Pretty neat. Will this always work?

PENNY: Over and over again. Whenever you have Polish expressions that substitute into the premiss variables above the single line of the Modus ponens schema, you can always augment them with the expression that substitutes uniformly into the variable below the single line.

NICKEL: A person must frequently send a longer message than he's aware of if there are many such schemas lying about. For I imagine that by the use of schemas it is frequently possible to augment.

PENNY: That's why a criminal has to be careful of what he says.

256

Suppose detectives have determined that anyone who knows p is guilty, and that a person they're questioning looks like a suspect because he utters $*q*rp$, q and r; he refuses to say any more.

NICKEL: Why do you say he looks suspect on that evidence?

PENNY: Because from what he's said, the detectives can derive p. Since the suspect has enough information to derive p, he might know p and, thus, be the guilty party.

NICKEL: But how can the detectives derive p?

PENNY: With two applications of the Modus ponens schema.

$$(1) \ \underline{*q*rp \quad (2) \ q} \quad (3) \ r$$
$$\underline{(4) \quad *rp \quad\quad\quad\quad}$$
$$(5) \ p$$

(1) and (2) are the premisses for the first argument; from it we generate (4), which, in turn, can be used as one of the premisses of the second argument along with (3) whose conclusion, (5), is the "guilty" information.

NICKEL: Schemas are useful, all right.

PENNY: Yes, they enable us to do something with Polish and Principia. English serves our purposes; we can do things with it. We can give directions, get a loan, prove we're right ——

NICKEL: And now we can catch criminals in Polish as well. I never realized as fully as I do now how much of our life's fabric is woven from the thread of language. I guess this is what has made Polish and Principia seem artificial to me, that I didn't see how I could use them, how they would serve any of my purposes. You've given me some hint now by analogy. If people spoke Polish or Principia, we could still detect criminals or send secret messages.

PENNY: Do you realize that you could use transformation schemas to make your messages even more secret?

NICKEL: How can I do that?

PENNY: First, imagine that you want to send the message p. But instead of sending p you send some other expressions, some premisses, from which p could be derived.

NICKEL: By the way, how can I figure out which premisses I should use?

PENNY: Turn the Modus ponens schema upside down. We can write the conclusion above the single line and the premisses below. Let's place a colon at the right end of the single line to indicate that we've inverted a schema and an argument:_____:. We'll call this inverted figure a "justification" because it's giving premisses or reasons for our conclusions after first stating our conclusion.

How would the Modus ponens schema look as a justification schema?

NICKEL: $\dfrac{\beta}{*\alpha\beta \quad \alpha}$: β is the conclusion and $*\alpha\beta$ and α are the premises.

PENNY: Now, substitute p for β throughout.

NICKEL: $\dfrac{p}{*\alpha p \quad \alpha}$:

PENNY: What have you got left to do in order to have a justification for p?

NICKEL: Find a Polish expression to substitute for α. Will any expression do?

PENNY: I see nothing here that restricts your choice.

NICKEL: If I substitute r for α, that would give me $*rp$ and r as premises from which to derive p. $\dfrac{p}{*rp \quad r}$:

PENNY: Sure. You can always find premises from which to derive an expression by using a justification schema.

But it would be pretty easy for the enemy to derive p from those expressions. Make it harder for him. Add another justification.

NICKEL: How will adding another justification make it harder?

PENNY: Watch. He needs $*rp$ as a premiss in order to derive p. We'll make it harder by not sending $*rp$. Instead we'll force him to derive $*rp$. We can do this by having $*rp$ as the conclusion of another justification.

NICKEL: Then we'll need to find more premises to send, premises from which to derive $*rp$.

PENNY: That's right, but at least we won't need to send $*rp$, for that can be derived from the new premises. Give me a justification for $*rp$ by standing Modus ponens on its head.

NICKEL: $\dfrac{*rp}{*\alpha*rp \quad \alpha}$: $\dfrac{*rp}{*q*rp \quad q}$:

PENNY: Good. Now put the two justifications together and tell me what you're going to send as the purported message.

NICKEL: $\dfrac{p}{\dfrac{*rp}{*q*rp \quad q} \quad r}$:

I'm going to send $*q*rp$, q, and r for those expressions are not the conclusions of a justification.

PENNY: Compare those justifications with the detectives' derivation.

NICKEL: Why, they are the inversion of each other! How could that have happened?

PENNY: You're very suggestible, perhaps.

NICKEL: Not as suggestible as I'd like to be. Nothing has come

258

through the mist to suggest how transformation schemas can be fitted into all this increase of secrecy.

PENNY: If you see the two expressions $*q*rp$ and q, you see pretty quickly that you could derive $*rp$ by Modus ponens. And that occurs to you because you see an ast expression, "$*q*rp$," and the α of that ast expression, q. You wouldn't have seen it so quickly if I had transformed the ast expression into another kind of expression, say a v expression. All I need do is add an Ast transformation to the justification in order to hide the ast expression under the cloak of a v.

$$\frac{\dfrac{\dfrac{*q*rp \quad q}{*rp} \;:}{v-q*rp}}{} \frac{\dfrac{p}{*rp}\;:}{r}$$

Now you would send $v-q*rp$ as a premiss rather than $*q*rp$.

NICKEL: Yes, and we could have made it still tougher to derive the message if we had added more transformations, such as:

$$\frac{\dfrac{\dfrac{\dfrac{v-q*rp}{v-qv-rp}}{-.q-v-rp}}{-.q\;.r-p}}{}$$

Then, $-.q.r-p$, q, and r would be the purported message. And to get to p from them, you'd have to go through four transformation steps and two Modus ponens argument steps.

PENNY: Providing there weren't any other argument schemas you could use on some expression you transformed, allowing you to by-pass some of the transformations.

NICKEL: Now that you mention it, there isn't any reason why we couldn't have more argument schemas, is there?

PENNY: There are as many argument schemas as there are tautological ast expressions, $*Twfes$.

NICKEL: Does that mean we can get argument schemas from $*Twfes$ just as we got transformation schemas from $*\!_*Twfes$?

PENNY: In exercise 7.6 we find the $*Twfe$ from which the Modus ponens schema can be gotten. It is 2, $*.*pqpq$. We can get the schema by the following steps:

(1) $\dfrac{.*pqp}{q}$ Write the α part of the ast expression above the single line and the β part below it.

(2) $\dfrac{*pq \;\; p}{q}$ Remove the dot from the expression above the line, thus giving us two premiss expressions.

(3) $\dfrac{*\alpha\beta \quad \alpha}{\beta}$ Generalize over the argument by uniformly replacing the Polish letters with variables.

NICKEL: Why is it that in argument schemas we have a single line while in transformation schemas we have a double line?

PENNY: Transformation schemas are gotten from double ast expressions, and double ast expressions are commutative. The double line reflects this commutativity. Argument schemas, on the other hand, are gotten from ast expressions, which are not commutative. And the single line reflects this non-commutativity.

NICKEL: The double line shows me I can infer in either direction, while the single line shows I can infer in only one direction.

PENNY: Are you sure you know what you mean by "infer in either direction"?

NICKEL: I think so. Whenever I have a *wfe* that is a substitution instance of the top part of a transformation schema, I can, by uniform substitution into the schema's variables, write a *wfe* that is a substitution instance of the bottom part of the schema; I can infer the two *wfe*s will mean the same. I can reverse the order of substitution without loss of information. That is, I can have a *wfe* that is a substitution instance of the bottom part of a transformation ——

PENNY: OK, OK. But you can't do this with argument schemas.

NICKEL: Before you ask me if I know what I mean by "go in that direction," that is, from above to below, let me volunteer my interpretation.

Whenever I have some *wfe*s that are substitution instances of the top part of an argument schema, I can, by uniform substitution into the variables below the line, write a *wfe* that is a substitution instance of the bottom part of the schema, and I am guaranteed that if the *wfe*s above mean 1, the *wfe* below will mean 1 also. However, I cannot reverse the process. A *wfe* substitution instance of the bottom part that means 1 guarantees me nothing about the meaning of the *wfe* substitution instances above the line.

PENNY: I'll go that route.

NICKEL: Doesn't it follow that justifications also allow us to infer in a single direction only, in their case from below to above; that only when the expressions below the single line with the colon at its right end mean 1, can I infer the expression above the line means 1?

PENNY: It follows.

The single line lying between expressions in arguments indicates *derived* or *deduced* from the expressions above the line; or that the expressions above the line *prove* the expression below it. All these are English expressions we can use when we have a Polish argument.

NICKEL: I'd like to have an explanation of the relation between Polish arguments and those English expressions, but it can wait until tomorrow.

PENNY: I suspect that if you find a cipher between Polish and Principia arguments and English propositional arguments, you'll be able to explain the relation yourself.

NICKEL: A hush has fallen upon this solitary space of air.

PENNY: It's the lull before the crash of exercises.

9.1: Below is a list of valid argument schemas. Find the tautologies in 7.6* from which they can be gotten. One of them, Vee Syllogism, can be gotten from a contradiction in 7.6 if you drop the left-most bar from the expression.

You'll notice that some of the schemas contain *B*. It's used the same way in argument schemas that it was used in the transformation schemas.†

We'll let this list of schemas be the Po-12 rules, and with the appropriate changes, the Pr-12 rules.

ARGUMENT SCHEMAS

		Abbreviation
$\dfrac{*\alpha\beta \quad \alpha}{\beta}$	Modus ponens	Mp
$\dfrac{*B\alpha B\beta \quad B\beta}{B\alpha}$	Modus tollens	Mt
$\dfrac{*\alpha\beta \quad *\beta\gamma}{*\alpha\gamma}$	Hypothetical Syllogism	HS
$\dfrac{vB\alpha\beta \quad B\alpha}{\beta}$	Vee Syllogism	VS
$\dfrac{\cdot\alpha\beta}{\alpha}$ and $\dfrac{\cdot\alpha\beta}{\beta}$	Simplification	Simp
$\dfrac{\alpha \quad \beta}{\cdot\alpha\beta}$	Conjunction	Conj
$\dfrac{\alpha}{v\alpha\beta}$	Addition	Add

9.2: Take each of the argument schemas and substitute Polish expressions into the variables until you have a Polish argument which is a substitution instance of that schema. Do this three times for each schema. The first time, the weakest expression in the argument should have

*Page 196.
†See pages 223–224.

a strength of 2; the second time, the weakest expression should have a strength of 3; and ——

NICKEL: —— the third time, the weakest expression should have a strength of 4.

PENNY: When we considered the detectives deriving the expression from the suspect's remarks, we saw that arguments can be linked together to form a chain. Here is another chain, together with the names of schemas. Tell me what the schema names are doing there.

$$
\begin{array}{ll}
\text{Simp} & \dfrac{(1)\ \cdot\!-\!^*qpp \quad (2)\ ^*q^*qp \quad (3)\ \underline{\ q\ \ } \quad \text{Add}}{}\\
\text{Mt} & \dfrac{(4)\ -^*qp \qquad\qquad\qquad\quad (5)\ vqr}{}\\
& \dfrac{(6)\ -q}{\qquad\qquad (7)\ r}\quad \text{VS}
\end{array}
$$

NICKEL: There being four single lines, I take it there are four arguments in the chain. The way I see it, the Polish expressions immediately above a single line are the premises of an argument, and the expression immediately below a single line is the conclusion of an argument. There are as many single lines as schema names, and the schema names are placed to the right or left of the lines. I'd say the schema names indicate into which schema an argument may be substituted; thus, (1) and (4) can be substituted into the Simplification schema; (3) and (5) can be substituted into the Addition schema; (4), (2), and (6) into the Modus tollens schema; and (6), (5), and (7) into the Vee Syllogism schema.

PENNY: Excellent. Which expressions are the ones given originally, as in a purported message or a suspect's testimony, and by which are they augmented?

NICKEL: All underived expressions, (1), (2), and (3), belong to the original class; they are augmented by (4), (5), (6), and (7), expressions derived from the originals.

PENNY: Why do you say "derived"?

NICKEL: Because they are proved?

PENNY: Why do you say they are "proved"?

NICKEL: Because each of them is the conclusion of a valid argument.

PENNY: How do you know the arguments are valid?

NICKEL: They are substitution instances of the schemas you gave me.

PENNY: How do you know the schemas are valid? And don't answer by "Because you gave them to me," for I might have made a mistake or I might not know if they're valid. Answer in a way that shows me you know how to check their validity.

NICKEL: Why can't we use the Shorter Matrix Method to test the validity of a schema? Since Polish expressions may be substituted for the variables in the schema, and since we may substitute either 1 or 0 into the Polish expressions, why not simply substitute 1 or 0 directly into the variables?

PENNY: Why not, indeed.

Let me ask you about your reasons for another, allied remark. You said that (4), (5), (6), and (7) were "derived from the originals." Why did you say that?

NICKEL: Because they all lie beneath single lines in the same chain.

PENNY: "The same chain"—you think you have one chain then. This means you must know when you have one chain rather than several. How do you know my example is a single chain rather than, say, two?

NICKEL: Well, all the expressions are linked together.

PENNY: Are all the following expressions linked together? Do we have one chain?

$$\text{Simp} \quad \frac{(1)\ \cdot\!-\!\overset{*}{*}qpp \quad (2)\ {}^{*}q\overset{*}{*}qp \quad (3)\ \dfrac{q}{(5)\ \mathrm{v}qr}\,\text{Add}}{\underset{(6)\ -q}{\underline{(4)-\overset{*}{*}qp}}}$$
$$\text{Mt}$$

NICKEL: I don't think so. There are two chains; the Addition argument is one chain and the Simplification and Modus tollens arguments are another chain.

PENNY: What would you have to do to make one chain out of them?

NICKEL: Link them together. I could do that just as you did before, by making (5) and (6) the premises of another argument. That would give me a single conclusion instead of two conclusions.

PENNY: I infer from your remark about the single conclusion that you think identifying a chain depends upon identifying a conclusion.

NICKEL: I didn't consciously think so before, but I do now. Sure, a chain of arguments can be identified by starting with a single conclusion and working upward in the justification direction, from conclusions to premises. Everything that is used to justify the conclusion is a link in the chain. An argument chain is a justification chain inverted.

PENNY: That's a good remark to make, but it won't tell anyone else how to identify an argument chain by telling them it's an inverted justification chain. What's wanted here for purposes of defining an argument chain is a rule about an arrangement of arguments, a rule of regularity, or a rule about an arrangement of justifications.

Do you think, for example, that a single argument will constitute a chain?

NICKEL: No. That would just be an argument, not a chain of arguments. A chain must contain at least two arguments.

PENNY: Then you'd better take back what you said a moment ago when you said Addition, (3) and (5), was a chain.

NICKEL: Why not? Sound retreat, Bugler!

PENNY: Here's new quarry for you to get the upper hand of, Emory.

9.3: Fill in the blanks in such a way that we have a correct definition of "chain of arguments."

Chain of Arguments

Po-13 and Pr-13: (a) _____ or more (b) _____ so arranged that the (c) _____ or its equivalent of all except (d) _____ of them is a (e) _____ of at least (f) _____ other arguments, and the (g) _____ of the argument excepted above is the (h) _____ of the chain.

You can use the expression "argument" in this Po- rule because it was the subject of a previous Po- rule, Po-10.

9.4: When the blanks in the following expression are appropriately filled in, and when the expression is inserted immediately after the (b) blank in Po- and Pr-13, you will have Po- and Pr-14, the rule for "valid chain of arguments": each of which is a (a)_____(b)_____of a valid (c) _____(d) _____.

NICKEL: Now can I say what a justification chain is?

PENNY: Right now.

NICKEL: An inverted argument chain.

PENNY: With colons. And thanks for the suggestion for 9.5.

9.5: I gave you seven argument schemas. From them you can make seven justification schemas. I want you to make up seven justification chains, each containing four justifications. Each justification in a justification chain will utilize the same justification schema, but each of the seven justification chains will use a different justification schema.

Using the underived expressions as originals, you can practice your proof technique, your inchoate ability to make argument chains, by attempting to derive the conclusion of your justification. Don't peek at your justifications until you get stuck and don't know what to do.

NICKEL: That shouldn't be too hard, especially since the same schema is used throughout.

PENNY: That's right.

Do you think the following is an argument chain?

$$\begin{array}{ll} (1) \ *pq & \\ (2) \ \dfrac{-vqr}{} & \text{DeMorgan} \\ (3) \ \dfrac{\cdot -q-r}{} & \text{Simp} \\ (4) \ \dfrac{-q}{} & \text{Mt} \\ \overline{(5) \ -p} & \end{array}$$

NICKEL: I don't, because it's got a transformation in it and I don't think Po-13 says such a thing is permitted.

PENNY: A sharp observation, Nickel.

9.6: Supplement Po- and Pr-13 in such a way that the presence of a transformation in an arrangement won't prevent it from being a valid argument chain.

NICKEL: Why do you want transformations in argument chains?

PENNY: We need them in order to conceal our message from the enemy, or to prevent the detectives from holding us for bail. Remember?

Actually, there's another reason. Suppose I want to know whether or not this argument is valid: $\dfrac{v \cdot qrp \quad -\cdot qr}{p}$ How can I find out?

NICKEL: You could use the Shorter Matrix Method or the Substitution Method. I can see it is valid because it is a substitution instance of a Vee Syllogism schema.

PENNY: Can you tell by the Substitution Method that this argument is valid? $\dfrac{-\cdot-\cdot qr - p \quad -\cdot qr}{p}$

NICKEL: No, I can't, because we haven't got an argument schema in our list of which it is a substitution instance.

PENNY: That's where the usefulness of transformation schemas is shown. Suppose we could alter an expression (or expressions) in the argument without changing its (or their) meaning in such a way that after alteration the argument is a substitution instance of an argument schema. What then?

NICKEL: Then we'd know that the argument is valid.

PENNY: We can do that.

$$\text{DeM} \dfrac{\dfrac{-\cdot-\cdot qr - p \quad -\cdot qr}{v \cdot qrp}}{p} \quad \text{Vee Syllogism}$$

Can you tell whether the argument is valid now?

NICKEL: Sure. I can see after application of a transformation schema that the altered argument is a substitution instance of a valid argument schema, the Vee Syllogism.

PENNY: That shows you why I want to permit transformations in an argument chain. They enable us to make greater use of the Substitution Method of determining validity. The use of transformation schemas in constructing an argument chain is as important to us as is the use of a saw to the carpenter in constructing a house. Just as the carpenter has to saw the wood to suit the plan, so the logician has to transform the expressions to fit the schemas. Schemas govern our arrangements just as architects' plans do, and we sometimes need to alter the material that is to be substituted into the places shown in the plans and in the schemas.

Here we meet again our twins of regularity, substitution and arrangement.

But I should acknowledge this: We could do without the transformation schemas if we're willing to pay a price. We could have a valid schema into which that last argument could be substituted.

NICKEL: That would be: $\dfrac{-.\alpha B\beta \quad \alpha}{B\beta}$.

PENNY: In fact, it's logically possible to have a valid schema for every valid argument, isn't it?

NICKEL: It's logically possible, but practically impossible. After all, there are an infinite number of possible valid Polish arguments, and we can't write that many schemas.

PENNY: Suppose we cultivated practically feasible ambitions; suppose we wrote only fifty volumes of schemas down.

NICKEL: I don't think it would be worth it. We'd spend too much time searching through the volumes to see if they contain a schema into which we could substitute the argument.

PENNY: That's the price you'd pay if you wanted to do without the transformation schemas. They afford us the economy of seven argument schemas, which is quite a reduction from the fifty volumes.

NICKEL: I like transformation schemas now, just as much as the carpenter likes his saw. It reduces the lumber inventory.

PENNY: The fifty-volume ambition, besides being uneconomical, is subject to an even more shattering objection.

We might come across an argument for which there could be a valid schema, but whose schema simply is not in the fifty volume collection, though it might have been if we had fifty-one volumes.

NICKEL: And no matter how many volumes we had, we'd never elude this difficulty, would we? We could always construct another argument whose schema is not in the collection.

PENNY: Without transformation schemas, the Substitution Method is fatally handicapped. That raises an interesting question.

9.7: Will the seven argument schemas along with the transformation schemas we have be enough to construct a chain showing the validity of every valid Polish argument?

NICKEL: If they're not enough, the Substitution Method is still fatally handicapped.

PENNY: That shows how important an answer to 9.7 is.

9.8: Here are some argument chains. I want you to identify which transformation and argument schemas are used. You can simply write down the number of each expression below the double or single lines and say which schema was used to derive it. Don't be alarmed when you find "*o*," "*s*," "*t*," and "*u*" in them; we can merely change our Po-1 and Pr-1 vocabulary rule and add them to the list of letters.

1.   (1) **pq* (2) $\underline{\underline{-vqr}}$

         (3) $\underline{\underline{.-q-r}}$

         (4) $\underline{-q}$

         (5) *–p*

2.   (1) *v.pq.rs* (2) $\underline{\underline{*p-p}}$

         (3) $\underline{\underline{v-p-p}}$

         (4) $\underline{-p}$

         (5) $\underline{\underline{v-p-q}}$

         (6) $\underline{\underline{-.pq}}$

  (7) $\underline{\underline{.rs}}$

  (8) $\overline{r}$

3.   (1) $\underline{\underline{-s}}$ (2) $\underline{\underline{vs*pr}}$ (3) $\underline{\underline{v.p-r.pq}}$

    (4) $\overline{*pr}$ (5) $\underline{\underline{.pv-rq}}$

           (6) $\underline{\underline{v-rq}}$

           (7) $\underline{\underline{*rq}}$

    (8) $\underline{*pq}$

4.   (1) **p*qr* (2) $\underline{\underline{*.rtu}}$ (3) $\underline{\underline{*-o.t-u}}$

    (4) $\underline{\underline{*.pqr}}$ (5) $\underline{\underline{*r*tu}}$ (6) $\underline{\underline{*-.t-uo}}$

    (9) $\underline{*.pq*tu}$ (7) $\underline{\underline{*v-tuo}}$

            (8) $\underline{\underline{**tuo}}$

    (10) $\underline{\underline{*.pqo}}$

    (11) $\underline{*p*qo}$

5.   (1) *.*pq*rs* (2) $\underline{\underline{vpr}}$

    (3) $\overline{*rs}$ (4) $\underline{\underline{*-pr}}$ (3) **rs*

          (5) $\underline{\underline{*-ps}}$

          (6) $\underline{\underline{*-sp}}$ (1) *.*pq*rs*

            (7) $\underline{*pq}$

         (8) $\underline{\underline{*-sq}}$

         (9) $\underline{\underline{vsq}}$

       (10) $\underline{\underline{vqs}}$

(In writing proofs we can use a premiss or a derived expression as often as we wish. Here, for example, (1) is used twice.)

6.   (1) *.*pq*rq* (2) **svpr* (3) *s*

               (4) $\underline{vpr}$

    (5) $\underline{\underline{vqq}}$

    (6) $\underline{\overline{q}}$

I want you to notice something special about chain 6. Step (5) was derived from (1) and (4), but does our argument schema list contain a schema into which (1), (4), and (5) would substitute?

NICKEL: No, it doesn't. Is it a valid step?

PENNY: We've just proved it is with chain 5. Do you remember how we got the Nobarsatall schema?

NICKEL: We took the original expression at the top of a transformation proof and the last expression in such a proof, dropped all the other steps, separated the original and last expressions with a double line, substituted variables for the *wfes*, and had a new schema. In short, we collapsed chain b. in 8.9, according to my exercise sheet here.

PENNY: We can do a parallel thing with argument chains. We can take the original expressions used in a chain and the last expression, drop all other steps in the chain, place a single line between those original expressions and the last one, generalize over them with variables, and we then have a new argument schema. In 5, (1) and (2) were the original expressions; (10) was the last expression. If we assume that the originals mean 1 and if we use only valid schemas to derive further expressions, what must be the meaning of the last expression in the chain?

NICKEL: 1.

PENNY: We know the new argument schema that would result from applying the steps I just outlined to chain 5 is valid. If the premises, the originals, mean 1, the conclusion, the last expression must mean 1.

Here's the argument we get by dropping all steps in chain 5 except the originals and the last expression:

$$\frac{.^*pq^*rs \quad \lor pr}{\lor qs}$$

And here's the schema we get from it when we substitute different variables for each different letter:

$$\frac{.^*\alpha\beta^*\gamma\delta \quad \lor\alpha\gamma}{\lor\beta\delta} \quad \text{Constructive Dilemma (CD)}$$

NICKEL: With the Constructive Dilemma schema I can get (5) from (1) and (4) in chain 6.

PENNY: This next chain, 7, will provide us with a Destructive Dilemma (DD) schema.

7. (1) $.^*pq\ ^*rs$ (2) $\lor{-}q{-}s$
    (3) $\dfrac{^*pq}{}$ (4) $\dfrac{^*q{-}s}{}$
        (5) $^*p{-}s$ (1) $.^*pq^*rs$
                           (6) $\dfrac{^*rs}{}$
                           (7) $^*{-}s{-}r$
        ———————————————————————
        (8) $\dfrac{^*p{-}r}{}$
        (9) $\lor{-}p{-}r$

NICKEL: Is this the schema I get from (1), (2), and (9) in chain 7?

$$\frac{.*\alpha\beta*\gamma\delta \qquad v{-}\beta{-}\delta}{v{-}\alpha{-}\gamma}$$

PENNY: You really should use the B variable to make it more general. Try it again.

NICKEL: $\dfrac{.*B\alpha B\beta*B\gamma B\delta \quad vB\beta B\delta}{vB\alpha B\gamma}$ Destructive Dilemma (DD)

PENNY: That's better. You'll find occasion to use DD in chain 8.

8. (1) .*pq*ro (2) .*qt*ou (3) $\overline{*t{-}u}$ (4) $\overline{*pr}$
        (5) $\overline{v{-}t{-}u}$ (6) $\overline{*{-}r{-}p}$
          (7) $\overline{v{-}q{-}o}$
            (8) $v{-}p{-}r$
            (9) $\overline{*p{-}r}$
              (10) $\overline{*p{-}p}$
              (11) $v{-}p{-}p$
              (12) $-p$

9. (1) *-q*pt (2) *-pr (3) $\overline{*{-}p{-}r}$ (4) *s-t (5) .so
            (8) $\overline{*rp}$ (6) $\overline{s}$
            (9) *-pp   (7) $-t$
            (10) $\overline{vpp}$
            (11) p
              (12) $\overline{.p{-}t}$
              (13) $-v{-}pt$
              (14) $-*pt$
          (15) q
          (16) $\overline{vqr}$

10. (1) *rs (2) *sp (3) *qu (4) *up (5) *pt (6) $-t$
      (7) $\overline{*rp}$ (8) $\overline{*qp}$ (9) $\overline{-p}$
        (10) .*rp*qp   (11) $v{-}p{-}p$
          (12) $v{-}r{-}q$

11. (1) *ur (2) u (3) *rp (4) $-p$
      (5) $\overline{r}$ (6) $-r$
      (7) $\overline{vrq}$
          (8) q

Chain 11 is marvelously different, for from those originals I can derive any Polish expression I wish; instead of having q for the conclusion, we could have any conclusion you might want.

NICKEL: I know one we couldn't have: $.q-q$.

PENNY: Why don't you think we could have that conclusion?

NICKEL: $.q-q$ is a contradiction; it always means 0. Chain 11 contains only valid arguments, so I couldn't derive an expression which means 0.

PENNY: You couldn't if all the premises mean 1. But maybe they don't all mean 1. In fact, can't you infer they don't all mean 1? In order to know that a conclusion means 1, two conditions must be satisfied: First, the premises must mean 1, and secondly, the argument must be valid. Now in this case we know the arguments are valid and we know it is impossible for the conclusion $.q-q$ to be 1; hence, ——

NICKEL: The premises can't all be 1.

PENNY: That's not too hard to see. Notice (5) and (6) in chain 11.

NICKEL: If (5) is r and (6) is $-r$, they can't both be 1; one of them must be 0. Does that mean that one of the originals must mean 0? That two expressions are contradictory?

PENNY: It does. You can test that for yourself by the Shorter Matrix Method. You won't be able by substitution to make all the originals mean 1.

Let me explain why I can derive any other Polish expression I want from two contradictory Polish expressions, α and $-\alpha$. I can always add any expression β to α by Addition, as I did to get (7) in chain 11; and since I have $-\alpha$, step (6), I can derive my added expression by the Vee Syllogism as I derived (8).

$$\frac{\alpha \quad -\alpha}{\frac{\vee\alpha\beta}{\beta}}$$

where β could be $.q-q$ if I wanted it to be.

NICKEL: I guess it's not too good to have contradictory premises.

PENNY: It won't help the man derive the hidden message you're sending him, for since he can derive every expression from what you've sent, he won't be able to select from the totality of Polish expressions those you intended to send.

However, there is one time when having contradictory premises is advantageous to us; we may sometimes deliberately try to introduce a contradiction into premises. We do this to derive an expression by the *reductio ad absurdum* Method, or the Reductio Method in short. But I'd rather not take that up until tomorrow. Let me give you one more exercise before we fold our tent.

9.9: Test the validity of the following arguments by the Shorter Matrix Method. Remember, it's generally good practice to start by making the conclusion mean 0, providing that it can be made to mean 0 in a single way.

1. $\dfrac{(1)\ (q \supset p)\quad (2)\ (-p.t)}{(-q \lor s)}$

2. $\dfrac{(1)\ *_*q.rp\quad (2)\ -v qs\quad (3)\ *-qr}{*p-r}$

3. $\dfrac{(1)\ v.qr*pr\quad (2)\ -r\quad (3)\ *ps}{q}$

4. $\dfrac{(1)\ .v-qrvp-r\quad (2)\ .q-p}{vr-r}$

5. $\dfrac{(1)\ (q \equiv p)\quad (2)\ (p \lor q)\quad (3)\ -q}{(-p.p)}$

6. $\dfrac{(1)\ *.pqr\quad (2)\ -r}{/pq}$

7. $\dfrac{(1)\ *qs\quad (2)\ (p \supset r)\quad (3)\ *rq}{(s \supset p)}$

8. $\dfrac{(1)\ *qvrp\quad (2)\ -p\quad (3)\ *qr\quad (4)\ vsp}{.-sr}$

NICKEL: Well, I hope all this commerce with arguments will soon yield the philosophic profit you've promised me.

PENNY: One more day's investment is all we'll need, Nickel. Are you willing to invest it?

NICKEL: Sure. Although I may sound impatient, it's not because I don't like what we're doing. In fact, I rather enjoy the suspense as well as the unexpected elaborations of Polish and Principia.

PENNY: The next time we meet we'll finish our discussions about Polish and Principia arguments. Just to whet your appetite, I'll give you a preview of what's coming next to your neighborhood gazebo. We'll find a connection between Polish and Principia arguments and the propositional arguments we studied in our fifth conversation.

NICKEL: That connection can be expressed with a cipher.

PENNY: Yes, it can.

NICKEL: Was I anywhere near the truth when I saw the similarity between the Truth-table Method of showing the validity and invalidity of English propositional arguments and the Shorter Matrix Method of showing the validity and invalidity of Polish and Principia arguments?

PENNY: You were. Why don't you try to work out the cipher by the next time we meet? To give you plenty of time, we'll not meet until the day after tomorrow.

Review Questions

1. How did Nickel first answer the question about what a person has to observe in order to confirm or disconfirm a dictionary entry's "prediction"?

2. Why was Nickel's first answer unsatisfactory?

3. What was Nickel's second answer to the question?

4. How is Nickel's Star of Meaning related to his agreement that the Constant Nymph should be banished?

5. How does Nickel's one-page dictionary map provide for:
   (a) An inscription with two meanings?
   (b) Two inscriptions with the same meaning?
   (c) Referential meaning?
   (d) Auxiliary expressions?

6. If a dictionary entry were a prediction, what function would it fail to perform?

7. How is it possible that a dictionary entry is both a report and a rule?

8. What is the definition of a valid Polish and Principia argument?

9. Why is the Shorter Matrix Method adequate for evaluating the validity of Polish and Principia arguments?

10. What is the difference between an argument schema and a justification schema?

11. Why are transformation schemas important to the Substitution Method of proving the validity of Polish and Principia arguments?

12. How can you produce new argument schemas from valid argument chains?

13. What English expressions can you use when you see "————" lying between Polish expressions? And between Principia expressions?

14. What is the difference between "————" and "======"?

Tenth conversation

REDUCTIO AND ALL THAT

I was amuz'd to reed a Dyry of my yuth.
Lyfe wus difrent in those Dayes.

> '*Vyctym: Helpp!*
> *Knyght: Whence cam the caul?*
> *Fanebius: Frum this cav mauth.*
> *Vyctym: The draigoon keepes mee!*
> *Knyght: Shall I sav himm, Fanebius?*
> *Fanebius: Nott weithout donnyng armour forme.*'
> —Fanebius Perlyng

PENNY: You look rather . . . er . . . indeterminate today, Nickel.

NICKEL: We're juggling so many issues at once that I don't know which to catch first.

The most I know is which one to catch last.

PENNY: How logic in the narrow sense yields philosophic profit?

NICKEL: Yes. This chart I've drawn, if accurate, shows it is the final goal of our conversations.

LANGUAGE: An ordered collection of expressions.

LOGIC IN THE WIDE SENSE: A study of the regularity governing the order of the combination of expressions.

EXPRESSIONS

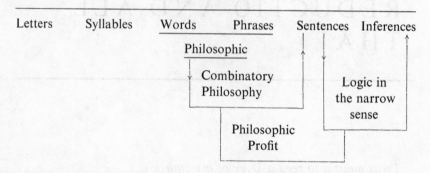

You said that when we come to understand the dependence of combinatory philosophy upon logic in the narrow sense we would reap our philosophic profit.

I think I've got a pretty good idea of combinatory philosophy now because I have a pretty good idea of the combinatory theory of meaning, especially after having had the Constant Nymph exorcised. And I think I've got a pretty good idea of logic in the narrow sense, providing you confirm my cipher between Polish and Principia and English sentences. But I don't yet see how combinatory philosophy depends on logic in the narrow sense. It seems one thing to find valid relations between sentences but another and different thing to find the proper combinatory relations between words in sentences.

PENNY: They are quite different.

NICKEL: I have a theory as to why they're different. But maybe you'd better check my cipher between Polish and English first.

PENNY: Let me hear the theory first if you can state it briefly.

NICKEL: So far, our study of logic in the narrow sense has been confined to arguments, to the valid relations between propositions—relations which exist between propositions in virtue of their truth value. We've been studying a truth logic; this holds for both syllogisms and propositional arguments. If my cipher is correct, the transformation and argument schemas are truth schemas.

Philosophic words and phrases, not being sentences, aren't true or false. So, obviously, the relations between them can't be based on their truth value. From this I conclude that a truth logic is not adequate to combinatory philosophy. We're going to need schemas which aren't truth schemas; in short, we need a different logic.

What this different logic is like, I don't know, but until I do know, I suspect very strongly that I won't understand the dependence of combinatory philosophy upon logic in the narrow sense, nor consequently, how a study of logic in the narrow sense yields philosophic profit. And I suspect, further, that I won't understand the dependence until I understand how the philosopher's use of inference in studying linguistic regularity distinguishes him from the lexicographer.

PENNY: Say, that sounds like a good topic to talk about today.

NICKEL: Very funny! But, ironically enough, it's my turn to delay. I'd like you to go over my cipher first.

PENNY: I think I can hold my patience in check. Go ahead.

NICKEL: First I'll give the substitution rules.

1. Polish (and Principia) letters are variables into which we may substitute English propositions. This is so because Polish and Principia letters play the same role that the variables such as parallelograms and roundends did.

2. 1 is a variable into which we may substitute true English sentences, and 0 is a variable into which we may substitute false English sentences. This is so because 1 plays the same role that a restricted variable such as /true/ did, and 0 plays a role similar to /false/.

3. a. For dot substitute "and."
   b. For vee substitute "or."
   c. For ast substitute "if ... then...."
   d. For double ast substitute "if and only if."
   e. For stroke substitute "not both."
   f. For bar substitute "not."

Since those English words have synonyms, their respective synonyms are covered by the respective rules.

It looks to me as if we'll need arrangement rules only for Polish. The relation of Principia letters to their functors is similar to the relation of English sentences to their functors. Thus, in "I am tall and you are short" the functor "and" falls between the two sentences just as dot falls between variables. But in Polish we have to place the functor to the left of the variables.

4. The Polish functor that substitutes for the English functor is placed to the left of the *wfe*s into which the two English sentences related by the functor are substituted. The order of the English sentences and the *wfe*s into which they are substituted is the same, the left sentence being substituted into the left *wfe* and the right sentence into the right *wfe*.

PENNY: You have to watch out for variations in the order of the English functor "if . . . then . . .". Sometimes the "if" follows the "then," as in "I will be rich if I inherit my Aunt's estate," in which case it's the right sentence, "I inherit my Aunt's estate," which is substituted into the left Polish *wfe*.

You will also come across ". . . only if . . . " as in "The train is late only if the flag is up." When placed into the "if . . . then . . ." form the order of the individual sentences remains unchanged, that is, "If the train is late, the flag is up."

"If . . . then . . ." has another variation in "unless" as in "The chicken is first unless the egg is first." "Unless" plays a dual role; it acts as both an "if" and a "not." The sentence when placed in the "if . . . then . . ." form becomes: "If the egg is not first, then the chicken is first."

NICKEL: You haven't said my cipher was wrong; so, I guess I can assume it's correct?

PENNY: I think you've done an accurate job.

NICKEL: Thanks. Of course, the truth tables can be translated into matrices simply by substituting "true" for 1 and "false" for 0. In fact, it was the parallelism of the truth tables and the matrices that convinced me my cipher was correct.

Your prediction that I would understand how we could apply the English expressions "derived," "deduced," "follows," and "prove" to Polish arguments came true after I had figured out the relation between Polish and Principia arguments and English propositional arguments.

PENNY: What do you think the relation is?

NICKEL: It's a substitution relation. English arguments are substitution instances of Polish arguments. That's what my cipher says.

PENNY: Do you realize how the little myth of the clean and dirty window panes that we spoke of the first day has fared?

NICKEL: I'd forgotten about that. As I recall, I asked about the superior transparency of an ideal language.

PENNY: You did.* Reflecting on all you now know about the regularity of Polish and Principia, and on the fact that a portion of English, your native tongue, may be substituted into Polish and Principia, what do you think about the relative transparency of the ideal languages?

NICKEL: I like the clean window pane. All the knowledge I have of the regularity of Polish and Principia automatically transfers to that part of English which may be substituted into the ideal languages. I say, let's keep the image of the panes.

PENNY: What logicians have really done, Nickel, is to invent new languages, Polish and Principia and Venn, in order to give us a clearer view of our native language.

NICKEL: It sounds marvelously, wildly unlikely that anyone should think of inventing a new language in order to study another language. I've got to admit that logicians, despite their reputation for dryness, do have imagination—and cleverness.

PENNY: Cleverness can be acquired, you know.

NICKEL: I'm not sure that's true. I think it's more of a gift.

PENNY: Why don't we experiment to find out which of us is right?

NICKEL: Good idea. But how?

PENNY: I'll give you some exercises which will force you to develop your cleverness because to do them you'll have to construct argument chains.

NICKEL: If I can acquire cleverness, I must be able to learn how to construct argument chains. Do you agree?

PENNY: I do.

NICKEL: Do you also agree that if it's something I can learn, it must be something you can teach me?

PENNY: To a certain extent.

NICKEL: You're hedging. Is it because you suspect there may be something of a gift to it after all?

PENNY: Can I teach you how to ride a bicycle? Maybe learning to construct proofs is comparable to learning how to ride a bicycle; there may be a limit to what you can be taught. As I said, let's experiment.

NICKEL: I'd like to improve the experimental conditions. Why don't you construct the proof for an argument and tell me why you took each step. Maybe you can teach me how to construct chains and acquire cleverness if you show me how to do it.

PENNY: That's a good idea, Nickel. Here's an argument for us.

$$\frac{(1)\ -vb{-}r \quad (2)\ {*}rt \quad (3)\ {*}m{-}t}{-m}$$

* Reader: See pages 16 and 17.

I frequently start with the conclusion and try to find premisses from which it might be derived.

NICKEL: You use justification schemas, then.

PENNY: I do. I suggest you have your justification schemas in front of you while we experiment. You wrote them in doing exercise 9.5.

NICKEL: How do you know which schemas to use?

PENNY: That is the burning question. I see which schema has a conclusion that looks most like the conclusion of the argument I'm working on. This isn't a foolproof method, you understand. Sometimes I have to transform a conclusion to make it look like the conclusion of some schema or other.

NICKEL: As I look over the schemas, I'd say that the conclusion of our argument, $-m$, looks most like the conclusion of the Modus tollens schema. That's the only one which explicitly suggests a letter with a bar on it.

PENNY: Very good. So we write down $\dfrac{}{-m}$ and set off in search of its premisses.

I know that the *wfe*s in the conclusion of every schema (except one) are contained in at least one premiss of that schema. Look at Modus ponens; the β *wfe* conclusion is contained in the first premiss; in Modus tollens the α *wfe* conclusion is contained in the first premiss; in the Hypothetical Syllogism the α *wfe* part of the conclusion is contained in the first premiss, and the β *wfe* part of the conclusion is contained in the second premiss; and so forth.

NICKEL: The one exception is Addition, I guess. The β *wfe* part of the conclusion isn't contained in the premiss.

PENNY: Though the α part is contained in the premiss.

NICKEL: How does this help me to find premisses for $\dfrac{}{-m}$?

PENNY: Easy. You know you have to have a premiss which contains m. So you look amongst your premisses to see if you have such a premiss. Do you?

NICKEL: Yes. (3) contains m.

PENNY: Then make (3) a premiss and see what you have.

NICKEL $\dfrac{-m}{(1)\ *m{-}t}$: is what I have. But that doesn't fit into any justification schema.

PENNY: What would you have to add to make it a substitution instance of a schema? Now, you do have something to go on. You hypothesized that we should use the Modus tollens schema because $-m$ looked most like that schema's conclusion. Has our recent addition, (3), $*m{-}t$, done anything to confirm your hypothesis?

NICKEL: Yes, it has, for we need an ast premiss for a Modus tollens schema and that's what we got with $*m{-}t$, the *wfe* with an m in it.

PENNY: Well, then, since m is the substitution instance of α and $-t$ is the substitution instance of $B\beta$ in $*B\alpha B\beta$ in the Modus tollens schema, giving us

$$\frac{\begin{array}{c} -m \\ B\alpha \\ \hline *B\alpha B\beta \quad B\beta \end{array}}{*\quad m-t}:,$$

and since you need another premiss, $B\beta$, for that schema, you know what your other premiss must be.

NICKEL: The substitution instance of $B\beta$, which is $-t$.

PENNY: No, t. You've already used the bar in $B\beta$ in $*B\alpha B\beta$; you can't place a bar in both members of a pair of B's.

NICKEL: Right you are. Now I can complete the first step. We have $\dfrac{-m}{(3)\ *m-t\ \ t}$:, a substitution instance of $\dfrac{B\alpha}{*B\alpha B\beta\ \ B\beta}$:, the Mt justification schema.

But that doesn't get me very far, for I don't have a t among my original premisses.

PENNY: Nothing left then but to find premisses from which to derive t, proceeding in exactly the same way we did to find premisses from which to derive $-m$. We first make t the conclusion of some justification, picking that justification on the basis of t's resemblance to the conclusion of a schema.

NICKEL: I'm in a quandary; t could fit equally well into the conclusions of Mp, VS, and Simp. How do I pick from among the three?

PENNY: We know we need a premiss which contains t.

NICKEL: It's contained in (2), $*rt$.

PENNY: That gives you $\dfrac{t}{(2)\ *rt}$: Doesn't that extricate you from your quandary?

NICKEL: Very nicely. My justification schema has to be Mp, for it's the only one of the three schemas (Mp, VS, and Simp) which contains an ast wfe such as (2).

PENNY: From here it's no trick to find the other premiss.

NICKEL: I can see from

$$\frac{\begin{array}{c} t \\ \beta \\ \hline *\alpha\beta \quad \alpha \end{array}}{*rt}:$$

that it has to be the substitution instance of α, the other premiss of the Mp schema. Since r in $*rt$ is the substitution for α in $*\alpha\beta$, my other premiss is r. That gives me $\dfrac{t}{(2)\ *rt\quad r}$:, which is clearly a substitution instance of $\dfrac{\beta}{*\alpha\beta\quad\alpha}$:, the Mp justification schema.

But now I need to derive r since it's not given as a premiss. Back to the old justification grind, I see. (1), $-vb-r$, is the only premiss that contains r, but r looks deeply buried. I don't see how it can be dug out in time to prevent suffocation.

PENNY: Why do you say that?

NICKEL: In the first place, I don't have a justification schema with a $-v$ premiss, and in the second place what I need is an r not a $-r$ as it is in (1).

PENNY: My friend, you're forgetting Santa's little helpers, the transformation schemas. Perhaps in one fell swoop you can get rid of the $-v$ and the bar in front of r.

NICKEL: The DeMorgan schema?

PENNY: Take heart, r, help is on the way.

NICKEL: DeMorgan would change $-vb-r$ to $.-br$ and then I would have $\dfrac{r}{.-br}$:, a substitution instance of Simp, $\dfrac{\beta}{.\alpha\beta}$:.
What's next, or am I finished?

PENNY: You're finished. You know you're finished because you've moved from the conclusion via justification schemas to the original premisses. There's nothing else to derive; all else is given.

Assemble all the justifications into a single chain.

NICKEL:

$$\dfrac{\dfrac{\dfrac{\dfrac{-m}{(3)\ *m-t\quad t}: \text{Mt}}{(2)\ *rt\qquad r}: \text{Mp}}{.-br}: \text{Simp}}{(1)\ -vb-r}\ \text{DeM}$$

PENNY: How would you make an argument chain out of that?

NICKEL: Turn it upside down.

$$\begin{array}{l}
\quad\ (1)\ -vb-r\quad (2)\ *rt\quad (3)\ *m-t\\
\text{DeM}\ \overline{\overline{}}\\
\text{Simp}\ \dfrac{.-br}{r}\\
\text{Mp}\ \overline{}\\
\qquad\text{Mt}\ \dfrac{t}{-m}
\end{array}$$

PENNY: You're ready for 10.1, after acquiring cleverness.

NICKEL: What I've acquired is some knowledge, not cleverness.

PENNY: How will the uninformed tell the difference when they see you whiz through 10.1?

10.1: Take the following arguments and prove their validity by the Substitution Method. None of them as they stand are direct substitution instances of any schema; so, you'll have to construct argument chains to derive the conclusions of the arguments. Once again we'll supplement our Po-1 and Pr-1 vocabulary rule for letters by expanding the list. We'll let any English letter except v be a Polish and Principia letter.

1. (1) ***fmr*pj (2) ***jpl**fmr (3) **pjd (4) **jpl
    _____
    d

    (Hint: Use Modus ponens several times.)

2. (1) .*rmd (2) ..*jg.mf* (Hint: Use Simp and Conj.)
    _____
    .*md*

3. (1) .*s–l* (2) *–*pvlt* (3) .*s–t*
    _____
    v*pvvrsm*

    (Hint: Use Simp, Conj, Mt and Add; or: Simp and Add several times.)

4. (1) *v*abm* (2) .*bj* (Hint: Use Simp, Add, and Mp.)
    _____
    m

5. (1) *v*lt–m* (2) *–*m**f*rg (3) **f*rgvrs (4) –*vrs*
    _____
    –*t*

    (Hint: Use Mt several times.)

6. (1) .*pr . .*mnj* (Hint: Use Simp, Add several times, and Conj.)
    .v*j**lmvmp

7. (1) –.*p–m* (2) *rs (3) v–*q–s* (4) *–*q–m*
    _____
    –.*pr*

    (Hint: Use HS several times.)

8. (1) ⚡*rt* (2) *t*
    _____
    r

I know how well you'll like constructing argument chains—so well that you'll ask for more to do. Just to assure you that I am not unprepared to satisfy your desire, I give you 10.2 and 10.3.

10.2: Prove the validity of the following arguments by the Substitution Method.

1. (1) *–*tr* (2) **d–r* (3) –*r* (4) v*rd*
    _____
    –v*r–t*

2. (1) .*ab*bc (2) vd–c (3) –*–ab
    _____
                v–ad

3. (1) *.pq.rs (2) –*qr
    _____
                –p

4. (1) vcr (2) –.sc
    _____
           *–r–s

5. (1) vab (2) –.ca
    _____
           *–b–c

6. (1) *si (2) *ui (3) *cvsu (4) c
    _____
                     i

7. (1) v.vntr.vnts (2) –.n–h
    _____
              –.–t–h

8. (1) *d*st (2) *dq (3) v.dm.dr
    _____
                v–st

9. (1) .*sbw (2) *as (3) –w
    _____
              v–.sb–a

10.3: Prove the validity of all the valid arguments in 9.9 by the
Substitution Method.

NICKEL: Are there any tricky arguments in 10.2?

PENNY: Tricky arguments?

NICKEL: Yes, arguments like chain 11 in 9.8, the one which contained
contradictory premisses from which we could derive any expression, even
a contradiction.

PENNY: As a matter of fact, one.

NICKEL: I knew there would be one. That's the kind of argument
whose conclusion can be proven true by *reductio ad absurdum*, isn't it?

PENNY: No. In fact, that's the one argument whose conclusion can't
be proven to be true, or 1, by the Reductio Method.

Let me explain the Reductio Method to you. It's a variation of the
Substitution Method of proof. The Substitution Method is a set of
tunnel-schemas leading us to the dark within the cave of a premiss or set
of premisses; if we are clever enough, we carry out a prize, namely, the
conclusion or conclusions contained in the cave.

NICKEL: It sounds dangerous.

PENNY: It's only a more dramatic way of saying that with the use of
argument and transformation schemas we can augment a class of expressions.

Suppose we know that *pq and p constitute a class of expressions
each of which means 1; the Modus ponens schema shows we can augment

that class with the expression q, for we know that q, too, means 1. We shouldn't be surprised that q also means 1, for q was contained, though covertly until we discovered it, in the premises.

We can relate this notion of augmentation to the reason we gave for the importance of studying "reliable" arguments now that we have found the relation between Polish arguments and English arguments.

NICKEL: When did we give the reason?

PENNY: On the third day.*

NICKEL: Oh, yes, I see it. "Reliable," that is, valid arguments, enable us to increase our knowledge, for if we have a set of propositions we know to be true, we can discover other propositions that are true. Valid arguments are the means we have of augmenting a class of propositions already known to be true.

PENNY: Sometimes within the dark chambers of a class of expressions there covertly reside other expressions. All the expressions derived from one, several, or all of the members of the class, such as the many derived conclusions we get in the process of constructing a chain, were residing in the dark chambers. It is the purpose of an argument chain to bring them to light.

NICKEL: They were hiding behind the dirty pane, so to speak.

PENNY: Logicians love form, but these creatures of the dark hate form. Form is their undoing. It is an unceasing contest, this bloodless struggle, between logicians and the furtive slinkers loathe to leave their caverns.

Part of the difficulty in hunting conclusions is the intense darkness of the cavern; it's difficult to tell whether the conclusion lies within. The Reductio Method is a way of inducing conclusions to betray their presence. Suppose we have a class of premises $P_1 \ldots P_n$; we suspect, but do not know that conclusion C is contained in them.

NICKEL: We want to know if $\dfrac{P_1 \ldots P_n}{C}$ is valid.

PENNY: That's right. If it is valid, then we know that C is contained in the premises, though covertly. That is, we know that this situation obtains: $\dfrac{P_1 \ldots (C) \ldots P_n}{C}$.

NICKEL: Does the pair of parentheses around the C in the premises indicate covert residence in the cavern?

PENNY: It does. The first step toward self-betrayal is the use of an anti-C. We add to the premises the negation of the conclusion; we introduce $-C$. $\dfrac{P_1 \ldots P_n \; -C}{C}$

* Reader: See page 75.

Recall, now, chain 11 in 9.8, the argument with contradictory premisses. From such an argument we can validly derive any proposition, including, absurdly enough, contradictions, propositions which necessarily are false, necessarily 0.

NICKEL: I have that in mind.

PENNY: Suppose now that you know the set $P_1 \ldots P_n$ is consistent, that is, it does not contain a contradiction.

NICKEL: It's possible for all the premisses to mean 1, for all to be true.

PENNY: And suppose after adding $-C$ to the premisses that you are able to derive a contradiction?

NICKEL: Using only valid schemas?

PENNY: Yes.

NICKEL: When $-C$ is added to the premisses, a contradiction is created among them.

PENNY: How do you know that?

NICKEL: You supposed a contradiction was derived by the use of valid schemas. Well, whenever I have a valid argument and the conclusion is 0, as a contradictory conclusion must be, we can't suppose all the premisses are 1; for if they were, the conclusion would be 1.

PENNY: Good. Since the premisses $P_1 \ldots P_n$ are consistent, since we can suppose they all mean 1, what can we conclude from the fact that the addition of $-C$ to them creates a contradiction?

NICKEL: I don't know.

PENNY: Maybe this question is a better one. How many expressions do we need in order to have a contradiction?

NICKEL: At least two, α and $-\alpha$.

PENNY: If the addition of $-C$ to the premisses created a contradiction, and if it takes two expressions of the form α and $-\alpha$ to have a contradiction, what must already have been contained in the premisses?

NICKEL: I get it! C must be contained in $P_1 \ldots P_n$ only, of course, not covertly anymore.

PENNY: You have got it. Deriving a contradiction betrays the presence of C among the premisses. The fact that we are able to validly derive a contradictory *wfe* shows a contradiction exists among the premisses; and it can exist there only if C is actually contained there. C is now overt, as you say.

NICKEL: Would this be a good symbolization of the struggle in the cavern? We go from $\dfrac{P_1 \ldots ?(C)? \ldots P_n}{?C?}$ to $\dfrac{P_1 \ldots C \ldots P_n}{C}$.

PENNY: Here's a better way of symbolizing it: $\dfrac{\begin{array}{c} P_1 \ldots (C) \ldots P_n \ -C \\ .\alpha - \alpha \end{array}}{C}$

Once we get $.\alpha{-}\alpha$ we can always get C. We explained that when we discussed chain 11 in 9.8, $\dfrac{\overset{\alpha}{}\overset{-\alpha}{}}{\vphantom{|}\mathrm{v}\alpha C} \bigg/ C$.

NICKEL: I wish you would do a proof by the Reductio Method.

PENNY: I'll do even more than that. I'll give you what I'll call the Reductio argument in English, and then give the Polish argument of which it is a substitution instance; I'll use the Reductio Method on the Polish argument.

I'm going to italicize all the English functors in this argument, for that's always a good way to begin finding the Polish form into which the English argument may be substituted. That way you know right off which Polish functors are needed.

To have a uniform way of producing the Polish argument forms, we'll always replace the first English sentence with the letter p, the second with the letter q, and so forth in the order of the alphabet, skipping v, of course. Whenever a sentence recurs, we'll replace it with the same letter we used the first time it occurred.

(1) *If* a contradiction can be derived from premisses $P_1 \ldots P_n$ and $-C$ (p), *then either* $P_1 \ldots P_n$ are in*con*-sistent (q) *or* $P_1 \ldots P_n$ and $-C$ are *in*consistent (r). (1) $*pv{-}q{-}r$

(2) A contradiction can be derived from premisses $P_1 \ldots P_n$ and $-C$ (p). (2) p

(3) *If* $P_1 \ldots P_n$ are consistent (q) *and* $P_1 \ldots P_n$ and $-C$ are *in*consistent (r), *then* C is contained in $P_1 \ldots P_n$ (s). (3) $*.q{-}rs$

(4) $P_1 \ldots P_n$ are consistent (q). (4) q

(5) *If* C is contained within $P_1 \ldots P_n$ (s), *then* C can be derived from $P_1 \ldots P_n$ (t). (5) $*st$

C can be derived from $P_1 \ldots P_n$ (t). t

Our argument is: (1) $*pv{-}q{-}r$ (2) p (3) $*.q{-}rs$ (4) q (5) $*st$ / t

Our first step is to add premiss (R), for Reductio, to the premisses, and then try to derive an expression α and an expression $-\alpha$.

(1) $*pv{-}q{-}r$ (2) p

$\dfrac{}{(10)\ v{-}q{-}r}$Mp

$\dfrac{}{(11)\ v{-}r{-}q}$VCom

(3) $\dfrac{*.q{-}rs}{*q*{-}rs}$Exp

$\dfrac{}{(8)\ *{-}rs}$Mp

(4) q (5) $\dfrac{*st\ (R)\ -t}{(6)\ -s}$Mt

$\dfrac{}{(9)\ r}$Mt

$\dfrac{}{(12)\ -q}$VS

(4) $\dfrac{q}{(13)\ .q{-}q}$Conj

(13) is of the form $.\alpha{-}\alpha$.

NICKEL: We've derived an absurdity when we derive an expression of the form $.\alpha-\alpha$.

PENNY: And what does this prove about our argument?

NICKEL: It proves just what the Reductio argument says; namely, that t, which is C, can be derived from $(1)\ldots(5)$, which are $P_1\ldots P_n$, when a contradiction can be derived from $(1)\ldots(5)$ and (R), where (R) is $-t$. In short, it proves the argument is valid.

PENNY: After going through the Reductio argument, perhaps you now understand why I said the conclusion of "tricky" arguments, arguments with contradictory premises, can't be proven to be true by the Reductio Method.

NICKEL: Is it because "tricky" arguments don't satisfy premiss (4), $P_1\ldots P_n$ is consistent?

PENNY: It is.

NICKEL: The Reductio argument is pretty complicated. Would you do a simpler Reductio proof to show me how to do them?

PENNY: I'll give you one so simple you'll be able to do it yourself.

But before I give it to you, let me give you a schema to add to your list of argument schemas. We'll call it the Reductio schema, R, for short.

$$\frac{\Pi}{\beta} \text{ is valid if } \frac{\Pi\ -\beta,}{.\alpha-\alpha} \text{ is valid,} \qquad \text{where we substitute for } \Pi \text{ one or more consistent premisses.}$$

NICKEL: In terms of our discussion, I guess "$P_1\ldots P_n$" is what we substitute into Π.

PENNY: That's right.

I have only one piece of advice for doing Reductio proofs that differs from the way you do any Substitution Method proof. To derive something of the form $.\alpha-\alpha$, you'll generally have to derive two conclusions, α and $-\alpha$. We said before that in looking for premisses from which to derive an expression, we should look for premisses which contain that expression. In Reductio proofs you——

NICKEL: —— should look for expressions which occur twice, each time in different premisses?

PENNY: Yes. Do you know why?

NICKEL: I have to derive α twice. Since one of the αs must have a bar on it, they can't be derived from the same premiss. This means I must have two different premisses, each of which contains α.

PENNY: This is the argument I think is so simple to prove valid by the Reductio Method that I think you can do it yourself:

$$\frac{(1)\ ^*pq\quad (2)\ p}{q}$$

What do you think you should try to derive?

286

NICKEL: $-p$, for p is the only expression which occurs twice in the premisses, and in different premisses. Here goes.

(1) *pq (2) p (R) $-q$

$$\frac{\dfrac{(1)\ *pq}{(3)\ -p}\ \text{Mt}}{(4)\ .p\text{-}p}\ \text{Conj}$$

That last proof is interesting because it suggests we don't need both the Modus ponens and the Modus tollens schemas. We proved the validity of a Modus ponens argument by using Modus tollens. Am I right?

PENNY: Watch this.

$$\text{I}\ \frac{*pq\ \ -q}{-p}\ \text{Mt} \qquad\qquad \text{Trans}\ \frac{\dfrac{*pq\ \ \ -q}{*-q\text{-}p}}{-p}\ \text{Mp}$$

NICKEL: II's proof shows that we can get the same conclusion from the same premisses with the use of Modus ponens that we can get with the use of Modus tollens, providing we use Transposition. That proves we don't need the Modus tollens schema, doesn't it?

PENNY: It does. We've shown that given the Modus ponens schema, we can generate the Modus tollens schema just as we generated the Constructive Dilemma schema in chain 5 in 9.8, and the Destructive Dilemma schema in chain 7 in 9.8. We need only drop out all steps between the original premisses and the conclusion in II, generalize over the letters with variables, and give the schema a name such as Modus tollens.

10.4: Show that we could dispense with Modus ponens and keep Modus tollens; or, in other words, show that given Modus tollens we could generate the Modus ponens schema.

You might also contemplate how many other argument schemas we could drop without losing any logical powers. See how this affects your answer to 9.7.

10.5: Prove the validity of all the arguments in 10.2 by the Reductio Method.

Now that you have discovered the cipher between Polish and Principia arguments and English arguments, it would be a good idea to give you some translation practice.

10.6: Write the Polish arguments into which the odd-numbered English arguments below may be substituted and the Principia arguments into which the even-numbered English arguments may be substituted.

1. Either response dictors apply to music or the use of linguistic terms to describe music is metaphorical. If the use of linguistic terms to

describe music is metaphorical, then a literal use of linguistic terms is not made in describing music. Either a literal use of linguistic terms is made in describing music, or we cannot say that music has meaning as a language has meaning. Therefore, if response dictors do not apply to music, we cannot say music has meaning as a language has meaning.

2. We know there is communication between two persons if and only if we know an expression or expressions have a common meaning for them. We don't know an expression or expressions have a common meaning for two persons unless we know the two persons' Stars of Meanings for the component words are isomorphic. If the only means of judging isomorphism occurs during a conversation, then we won't have conclusive evidence that the component words have isomorphic Stars of Meaning for them, and if we don't have this conclusive evidence, then we don't know that the Stars of Meanings for the component words are isomorphic for them. This forces us to conclude that either there isn't merely a conversational means of judging isomorphism or we don't know two persons are communicating.

3. If an expression does not contain a variable, it is not a rule expression. A rule expression is general and a rule expression contains a variable. A rule expression is not understood unless we know how to substitute into its variables. Hence, if an expression is a rule expression and it is understood, then we know how to substitute into its variables.

4. If it is possible that "I am tired" is true when I say it and false when you say it, and the same thing can't be both true and false, and "I am tired" as a sentence is one thing, then it is not sentences which are true or false. If it isn't sentences which are true or false and there is something which is true or false, then it is statements which are true or false. It is possible that "I am tired" is true when I say it and false when you say it and the same thing can't be both true and false. So, either "I am tired" as a sentence isn't one thing or if there is something which is true or false, then it is statements which are true or false.

5. Either "I am tired" as a sentence is not one thing or if there is something which is true or false, it is statements which are true or false. Since there is something which is true or false, I infer that either it is statements which are true or false or "I am tired" as a sentence is not one thing.

6. If what is ordinarily called a sentence contains such words as "I," "you," "here," and "now," then it contains variables and it is a sentential function, not a sentence. If what is ordinarily called a sentence, e.g., "I am tired," contains variables, then it is not true or false (any more than "X is tired" is true or false). An expression is a sentence if and only if it is an expression which results from emplacing referents in the variables

of a sentential function. If what is ordinarily called a sentence is not true or false, then it is not an expression which results from emplacing referents in the variables of a sentential function. If if what is ordinarily called a sentence contains variables then it is not true or false, then what is ordinarily called a sentence contains such words as "I," "you," "here," and "now." I conclude, and so will you if you have followed my argument, that what is ordinarily called a sentence, e.g., "You are tired," is a sentential function, not a sentence.

7. If one purpose of speaking is to communicate and we know that we have communicated, then we must have some empirical evidence showing we communicated successfully. If we are speaking to one another on the telephone, then we can decide we are successfully communicating only if we use each other's voice sounds as evidence. I take it you'll grant me that one purpose of speaking is to communicate. And I don't expect you to deny we're speaking—Hello, Hello. Still there? OK—to one another on the telephone. Now, either we know that we have communicated or we use each other's voice sounds as evidence of successful communication. Evidently, strangely enough, if we cannot decide we are successfully communicating, we must have some empirical evidence of successful communication.

8. We cannot learn to use correctly the phrase "physical object" if we are not shown an example of a physical object and do not observe the phrase "physical object" applied to that example. If physical objects did not exist, we couldn't be shown examples of physical objects nor could we observe the phrase "physical object" applied to a physical object. Since we have learned to use correctly "physical object," we can infer that physical objects exist.

9. Note the following diagram.

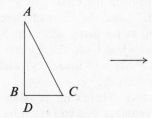

If man A and man B are on a train moving to the right and man A lights a match, then the light from man A to man B will travel along path AB for observer B; and for observer D, who is not on the train, the light from man A to man B will travel (because of B's moving to D's right while the light is traveling from man A to man B) along path AC. Now we suppose that man A and man B are on a train moving to the right and that man A lights a match.

If for observer D the light from man A to man B will travel along path AC, then path AC is longer than path AB. If light travels at the same speed for all observers, and path AC is longer than path AB, then time must seem to pass faster to man D than to man B.

Since light travels at the same speed for all observers, we have to conclude that time seems to pass faster to D than to B, and so time is not uniform for all observers.

10. If $a \neq 0$ and $b \neq 0$, then $a.b \neq 0$. Therefore, if $a.b = 0$, then either $a = 0$ or $b = 0$.

10.7: (a) Use the Shorter Matrix Method of deciding the validity of the arguments given in 10.6. (b) Prove the validity of all the valid arguments given in 10.6 by the Substitution Method, using, also, if you wish, the Reductio Method, because it's a variation of the Substitution Method. You may use either the Polish or Principia symbolism.

10.8: (a) Write the Polish arguments into which the arguments in 5.5 may be substituted. (b) Use the Shorter Matrix Method of deciding the validity of those arguments. (c) And prove the validity of the valid arguments by the Substitution Method.

NICKEL: 10.7 and 10.8 make me wonder about the need for the Substitution Method. It seems superfluous to me. If I can find the validity of Polish and Principia arguments by using the Shorter Matrix Method, I don't really need to go through all the torture of learning how to construct argument chains. The chains don't give me any additional information about arguments' validity even though they do give me extra work.

Besides, the Shorter Matrix Method is more conclusive; it doesn't depend upon my cleverness. Just because I am unable to produce a chain proving the validity of an argument doesn't mean the argument is invalid. I may be short of cleverness. In this respect the Substitution Method is no better than the Same-form Method. I'm never in this position when I use the Shorter Matrix Method. With it I can prove both validity and invalidity, while with the Substitution Method I can only prove validity.

PENNY: There's no question that the Shorter Matrix Method has all the advantages that you say it has over the Substitution Method. Those are good points, Nickel.

You mustn't despair, however; there are times when the Substitution Method is faster; you saw that the other day. And as you grow more skilled in discerning form, you will be able to increase the speed with which you spot validity.

Still, we have to admit that from the passive standpoint the advantage lies with the Matrix Method.

NICKEL: What's the passive standpoint?

PENNY: We assume the passive standpoint when we evaluate arguments that are presented to us already completed. Contrast this with the generative standpoint which represents the attempt to construct arguments and to draw conclusions. We do, after all, sometimes wish to generate arguments of our own in order to take an active part in a discussion or debate; we do want to augment the secret message sent to us by a comrade in arms, or try to find out if a person is a suspect in a crime.

When we assume the active standpoint, we want to augment a set of premises by deriving a conclusion; or if we have a conclusion to justify, we want to know what premises will justify it. Instead of proceeding to generate derivable conclusions or to generate justifying premises by guesswork or intuition or bad habit, we may wish to proceed by deliberate, conscious steps.

NICKEL: I take it that the deliberate way of generating arguments is to use argument schemas, and the deliberate way of generating justifications is to use justification schemas.

PENNY: So do I. They are the forms of our thought. Deliberate, conscious thinking is simply the utilization of the forms of valid thought. Your eyes, when trained to look at expressions through the lenses of argument and transformation schemas, will be capable of informed vision. They will be able to see conclusions hiding within the caverns of premises just as a trained paleontologist's informed vision enables him to distinguish periods in the history of life on earth when he observes fossils in geologic strata.

Here's a puzzle from *Telenews*, Northwestern Bell Telephone Company's communication to its subscribers. You aren't given any conclusions, so you have to take the active, not the passive attitude to the expressions.

> Mr. and Mrs. Green and their three children are home, and the TV set is on.
>
> (1) If Mr. Green is watching (p), so is his wife (q). (2) Either Ed (r) or Sue (s) or both are watching. (3) Either Mrs. Green or Don (t) but not both is watching. (4) Ed and Don are either both watching or both not watching. (5) If Sue is watching, then Mr. Green and Ed are watching. Who is watching TV?

I've added the numbers and letters, of course, for our own purpose. Notice that I'm symbolizing (2) as vrs; the "both are watching" part of (2) is taken care of by our inclusive disjunction v, an inclusive disjunction being true if both disjuncts are true. It might also be instructive to point out the difference in symbolism between "not both" in (3), $-.qt$, and "both not" in (4), $.-r-t$.

(1) *pq   (2) v̲r̲s̲   (3) .vqt-.qt   (4) v̲.̲r̲t̲.̲-̲r̲-̲t̲   (5) *s.pr

(6) *̲-̲r̲s̲   (12) -̲.̲q̲t̲   (13) v̲.̲-̲r̲-̲t̲ .rt   (6) *̲-̲r̲s̲

(21) v̲-̲q̲-̲t̲   (14) .v.-r-trv.-r-tt   (7) *̲-̲r̲.̲p̲r̲

(15) v̲.̲-̲r̲-̲t̲t̲   (8) v̲r̲.̲p̲r̲

(16) v̲t̲.̲-̲r̲-̲t̲   (9) .vrpvrr

(17) .vt-rvt-t   (10) v̲r̲r̲

(18) v̲t̲-̲r̲   (11) r̲ (Ed is

(19) v̲-̲r̲t̲   watch-

ing)

(20) t (Don is watching)

We know at this point that Don and Ed are watching. Is anyone else watching? Have we derived all the conclusions it is possible to derive from our premisses?

NICKEL: We still don't know whether Mr. Green, Mrs. Green, or Sue are watching. Is it possible to prove they aren't watching?

PENNY: Maybe. How could you prove they aren't watching?

NICKEL: We can prove they aren't if we can derive the negations of p, q, and s.

PENNY: Good. We can surely do that, can't we?

NICKEL: I see how to derive –q and –p.

(21) v̲-̲q̲-̲t̲   (2) t   (1) *̲p̲q̲   (23) –q

(24) –p (Mr. Green isn't

(22) v̲-̲t̲-̲q̲   watching).

(23) –q (Mrs. Green

isn't watching.)

I don't see how to derive –s though.

PENNY: You can use an addition that you probably thought was illogical; namely, the addition of –r to get (25).

(24) –p

(25) v̲-̲p̲-̲r̲

(26) –̲.̲p̲r̲   (5) *s.pr

(27) –s (Sue isn't watching.)

NICKEL: Well, our derivations from the premisses covered all the persons who could have been watching TV. We know now, for sure, that only Ed and Don were watching.

I see the advantage of the Substitution Method now. Its advantage is, as you say, a deliberate, careful way of finding the conclusions we can draw from some given information. It's a lot less confusing than trying

292

to think it through verbally, which also shows the advantage of using symbols.

PENNY: Mathematics, physics, astronomy, and many other sciences have done well by using symbols. No reason why that advantage shouldn't be extended to you and other students, Nickel. There's plenty for all in this wonderful land of opportunity.

I don't want to give you the mistaken impression, however, that the Polish and Principia symbolization we've used so far exhausts the logic you need for the sciences. That is far from the truth. For example, we haven't talked of the kind of symbolization adequate to showing the validity of the following argument.

> There is a mathematician who knows more physics than any astronomer.
> Every astronomer knows some physics.
> ———————————
> There is a mathematician who knows some physics.

I think you're ready to do some exercises which require you to look at arguments from the active standpoint.

10.9: From the sets of information given below, use the Substitution Method to determine the conclusion or conclusions which follow from that information.

1. If Tompkins was in the library, then Myers held Tompkins and Gould stabbed him. If Wineman didn't stab Tompkins, then Tompkins was in the library (studying). If Gould did stab Tompkins, then Fee was an accomplice. Fee was not an accomplice.

Who stabbed my friend Tompkins?

2. Mrs. Hurlbutt is trying to figure out if her husband came home late the night she had to stay at a sick friend's house. This is what she thought she had to go on.

"My husband didn't come home late or he was delayed at a committee meeting. If Professor Dewey knows what he's talking about, my husband was not delayed at a committee meeting, and if my neighbor was not telling the truth, then the house was dark until midnight. Either my neighbor is not telling the truth or she is trying to make trouble for our family. There is no evidence that my neighbor is trying to make trouble for our family. Neither do I want to mistrust my husband nor was the house dark until midnight."

3. Three construction companies are bidding for a contract: the Ricklin Co., the McNitt Co., and the Osterloh Co. The City Council must decide to whom they shall award the contract. It may be to more than one of them.

Councilman Ballard advises the Council as follows: If McNitt doesn't get the contract, we'll alienate him for future bids on construction in which he specializes. And we know the statement made by McNitt's attorney, namely, "If you don't alienate McNitt, he will give you the lowest bids on everything else you submit for contracts" is certainly false. Either McNitt will give us the lowest bids on all our other submissions or our recent bond issues won't be sufficient to pay for all the planned construction.

Councilman Stephens added some characteristically complicated remarks: If McNitt gets the contract and Osterloh doesn't get it, then our recent bond issues won't be sufficient to pay for all the planned construction. And if Ricklin doesn't get the contract or we alienate McNitt, then McNitt will give us the lowest bids on everything else we submit for contract, providing Ricklin gets the contract, for McNitt and Ricklin are good friends.

If the City Council thinks the problem through as well as you're going to, Nickel, to whom will they award the contract (in the absence of graft)?

4. The scene is the Command Headquarters of the Sallied Forces. A decisive action is in the offing. To insure that a decision in accord with reason is made, Field Marshal Dabek has a logician, Corporal Nickel, in attendance at all times. Corporal Nickel is under orders to evaluate all the arguments made by the Staff Officers. Each Staff Officer makes his arguments. Let us listen to what they're saying on Worldwide Intercom.

Admiral Feinberg: The enemy knows we have a 70-megaton nuclear bomb and they know we can deliver it to them f.o.b. in four minutes. If they know we have the bomb and can deliver it in four minutes, they will not use their nuclear bombs and will use their conventional weapons instead. We should use our 70-megaton bomb if and only if the enemy uses their nuclear bombs. Since, according to my reasoning, the enemy won't use their nuclear bombs, we shouldn't do so either.

General Brown: I have concluded we should use our 70-megaton nuclear bomb.

The enemy will use their nuclear bombs and will defeat us only if they can predict we will decide not to use ours. We are cautious, humanitarian people and the enemy knows we are cautious, humanitarian people. If we are, indeed, cautious, humanitarian people, we will not use our bomb and the enemy can predict we will decide not to use it. From these premises we can conclude that the enemy will drop their nuclear bombs and will defeat us.

You don't like that, do you, Gentlemen? We want to defeat the enemy. What follows from that desire and the following facts?

If we want to defeat the enemy, then we must surprise him; and if we must surprise him, then the enemy cannot predict that we will decide not to use our bomb. What follows is that the enemy cannot predict that we will decide not to use our bomb.

Now if the enemy cannot predict our decision not to use our bomb and we wish to defeat the enemy, then we must drop our bomb. That's why I've concluded we must use our 70-megaton bomb.

General Eddins: I agree with Admiral Feinberg, but for different reasons.

If we use the 70-megaton bomb and manage to over-kill the enemy, they will be able to retaliate sufficiently to destroy 70% of America. If only 30% of America survives and we over-kill the enemy, life as we have known it will be wiped out. Suppose we do what Brown recommends, that is, drop our big bomb. I leave you to draw the catastrophic conclusion.

Secondly, even if the enemy uses their nuclear bombs and defeats us, at least we won't have been the ones who destroyed civilization.

Besides, we, the armed forces, protect the American citizens. But we do not protect Americans if we use our nuclear bombs. Hence, we should not use our big bomb.

Field Marshal Dabek: I have an awful responsibility. I do not wish to err. The world's future depends on my decision. You, Gentlemen, may leave now. I want Colonel Gieschen and Corporal Nickel to stay.

Colonel Gieschen, as head of Intelligence, I want you to tell me if all the statements we heard today are true; if they are not, tell me which of them you think are not borne out by the facts.

Colonel Gieschen: Admiral Feinberg's first statement is false. General Brown's statement, that we are cautious, humanitarian people and that the enemy knows we are, is false. I am not certain enough about General Eddins' last premiss to affirm its truth, so I think we'd better consider it false.

Field Marshal Dabek: Thank you, Colonel Gieschen.

Corporal Nickel, I want from you (a) an evaluation of all the arguments given by the Staff Officers prior to Colonel Gieschen's report and (b) the conclusions to be derived from the total information we have left after and including Colonel Gieschen's report.

NICKEL: You've really put me in the middle of it, Mr. Penny.

PENNY: You can see how important it is sometimes to know that you know what you're doing. An instructor will not always be around to help. I hope you've learned your Substitution Method well. The symbols of the ideal language and their schemas should have given you a sufficiently informed vision to do your job well, Corporal Nickel.

Tenth conversation 295

NICKEL: Believe me, I hope so too.

PENNY: Here's one more exercise for you to do. It should relieve any feelings of incompleteness exercise 9.7 may have aroused in you.

10.10: Prove the validity of these arguments by the Reductio Method.

1. $\dfrac{p}{vq-q}$ 2. $\dfrac{*pq}{*p \cdot pq}$

NICKEL: Those are the arguments for which I couldn't find a proof. They're the same ones you gave me in the answer to 9.7.

PENNY: They are.

I hear the phone ringing. Excuse me.

It's your Aunt; she'd like to leave in about fifteen minutes and wants you to drive her.

NICKEL: I'd better beat it. Sorry.

PENNY: I have some Review Questions first. They will only take a couple of minutes.

Review Questions

1. Why does Nickel think that a truth logic will not be adequate for combinatory philosophy?

2. Why does the cipher from English to Polish require an arrangement rule while the cipher from English to Principia does not? (Be sure not to forget the ciphers. You'll need to know them.)

3. Why are English arguments substitution instances of Polish and Principia arguments?

4. Why are Polish and Principia like clean window panes?

5. Why can't we use the Reductio Method on an argument whose premisses are inconsistent?

6. How does a valid argument's conclusion being contained in its premisses make the Reductio Method possible?

7. What are the advantages of the Shorter Matrix Method over the Substitution Method? And *vice versa*?

Eleventh conversation

THE LEXICOGRAPHER, THE PHILOSOPHER, AND A PARROT

Devil: Dost hav a soule, Byrd?
Parrot: Polly wants a cracker.   Polly wants a cracker.
*   Polly wants a cracker.*
Devil: Here's wone fore tu styk inne thy crawe.
*   Dost have a soule, Fanebius?*
Fanebius: Aye.   Fore I hav witte for speache.
Devil: Will't hav an apel, Fanebius?
—Olde Playe

NICKEL: Sorry I had to leave so abruptly the other day, Mr. Penny.
PENNY: It's summer time, and the livin' is easy, so why should we fret?

Let's pick up the topic we delayed when we decided to practice your cipher between Polish and English. We had started to talk about how the philosopher's use of argument in studying linguistic regularity distinguishes him from the lexicographer.

NICKEL: Before we continue that, Mr. Penny, I'd like to take back my enthusiasm for the one page map-dictionary.

PENNY: Do you have some good reasons for doing that?

NICKEL: I have two reasons and they seem good enough to me. Essentially, they're both practical reasons.

The first reason cites the difficulty we would have in locating the words in a map-dictionary.

PENNY: That's not much of a problem. We could arrange the words alphabetically just as conventional dictionaries do.

We could start with "A" at the left of the top line and proceed alphabetically across and down on the paper.

A	A–1	aardvark	aardwolf	....
....	gobo	goby	gocart	....
....	raster	rasure	rat	....

NICKEL: I guess that would be all right. But what about all the objects in the world?

PENNY: You know how to pronounce them, so with the aid of a phonetic cipher, you can place them alphabetically on the page. It's a big moving job, I know, but at least the world would be ordered linguistically.

If it seems like too much of a job to move the world to your dictionary, maybe we should take the person to the world. After all, this is in fact how we often do it now. I take Megan to the mountains rather than bringing the mountains to Megan.

Travel, however, does get tiresome even for the curious. How much handier to have words we can easily utter or write whenever we want someone to know what we're thinking of. No need then to take them within pointing distance of the objects.

NICKEL: My second reason for losing enthusiasm for the map-dictionary is related to this transportation problem. Though language may be a surrogate for travel, still we do move about on the earth and when doing so we may have to take our dictionary with us in order to have a guide to our language. It's going to be quite a job to carry such a cumber-

298

some dictionary as I've proposed. The conventional dictionary does have the advantage of compactness.

PENNY: It does, but it gains that advantage at a price. It loses the very feature which has made me grow more enthusiastic about your map-dictionary. That feature is its King *M* nature; your dictionary exhibits combinations visually.

NICKEL: A conventional dictionary is a King *N* type. It states a rule.

PENNY: Right, and because it does, though this makes it compact, such a dictionary can be used only by someone who already knows a good deal of the language. I don't mean that he must know how to read; he could have someone read it to him. I mean that a verbal lexical definition won't help a person to learn how to sensically combine the word defined, unless he already knows the meaning of the words in the definition.

The lexicographer's main trade is substitution of one expression for another that is synonymous.

NICKEL: I'm not surprised at that; after all, that is one kind of rule of linguistic regularity.

PENNY: Quite true. However, in limiting himself to synonymity substitution, he necessarily limits what we can learn about a language from a dictionary.

NICKEL: Unlike the combinatory philosopher who makes use of inferences.

PENNY: Right, though there are some inferences in dictionaries. There is one in *Webster's New Collegiate Dictionary;* at least the word "hence" appears in the definition of "point." But we can learn a lesson from that entry about lexicographers' evaluation of inferences.

NICKEL: What is that?

PENNY: That they don't lay much stock by them. The next edition of that dictionary, *Webster's Seventh New Collegiate Dictionary*, has dropped the "hence."

NICKEL: Apparently "hences" are of little importance to lexicographers.

PENNY: Philosophy, on the other hand, can hardly be conceived without inferences; it is abloom with them.

NICKEL: Here we are again, on the threshold of the difference between lexicographers and combinatory philosophers, namely, that the latter do and the former do not use inferences.

PENNY: We want now to be more exact about the role inferences play in distinguishing them. First, let's remind ourselves of the kind of information we normally expect to get from each of them, of the kind of questions we are interested in having them answer.

NICKEL: What kind of questions are "we" interested in having them answer?

PENNY: Combinatory questions. That's what combinatory philosophers try to answer. And you know what we want of the lexicographer. We discussed that thoroughly enough when we gave the Constant Nymph the heave-ho.

NICKEL: Oh, yes. We go to dictionaries to get reports of the lexicographer's discoveries about past standard uses when we come across a word whose meaning we don't know. And we go to it for a guide or rule in our own use of a word.

PENNY: That information, as I said, is usually given to us in a dictionary by means of a rule of synonym substitution. We should note, though, that the dictionary does give us some rudimentary arrangement rules as well. Before the synonym rule, the parts of speech of the word are given by such abbreviations as "*v*" and "*n*."

NICKEL: I notice that different meanings attach to a word when it takes different places in a sentence. Here's an example from *Webster's Seventh:*

> ¹**pole** *n* **1 a:** a long slender usu. cylindrical substance (as wood).
> ²**pole** *vt* **2:** to impel or push with a pole.*

PENNY: What do you conclude from this about meaning?

NICKEL: That a word's meaning is affected by its arrangement rules.

PENNY: Our central concern now is with the substitution part of the dictionary entry.

Let me give you two examples. I think you'll see why they illustrate my point. The first one is from *Webster's Seventh.*

> ²**poke** *vt* **1 a** (1): PROD, JAB. (2) to urge or stir by prodding or jabbing.†

The second example is from an article entitled, "Portrait of the Beatnik."

> Beatific talk is the very soul of brevity, if not wit. It is deliberately functional, for the hipster rejects euphemism. He "sets a scene" when he tells, "wigs" when he's worried, "gigs" when he works, "bugs" when he's annoyed, "wails" when he functions, "floats" when he's drunk, "grazes" when he's content, "bends" when he's tired, "scenes" when he arrives, "splits" when he goes.‡

NICKEL: Yes, I think I see why they illustrate your point. Just as you said, verbal definitions presuppose previous knowledge of meanings.

---

* By permission. From *Webster's Seventh New Collegiate Dictionary*, Copyright 1963 by G. & C. Merriam Co., Publishers of the Merriam-Webster Dictionaries.
  † *Ibid.*
  ‡ Caroline Freud, "Portrait of the Beatnik," in *Encounter*, July, 1959, p. 42.

Freud is obviously relying on our previous knowledge of the meanings of "tells," "worried," etc. She locates the Star of Meaning of "wigs" in the array for us by identifying it with the Star of "worried."

I gave a combinatory rule in the same way before, when I said "talk" can be substituted for "monkey."

PENNY: And what do you think of "poke?"

NICKEL: Synonymous substitution there too; "jab" or "prod" for "poke." And the dictionary also gives a hint of the word's place in a sentence when it says "to urge or stir by prodding."

PENNY: The synonymity technique used here helps us locate a word's Star in the array by giving us a substitutable word or phrase whose Star's location is already known. Do you see any need for inferences with this verbal technique?

NICKEL: No, I don't here either. When Freud tells me "wigs" can be substituted for "worried" she has given me the information about the Beatniks' standard use of it that I need.

PENNY: I can imagine that at some time a person would like to know what members of that short-lived movement had to say. Freud's synonymity substitution rules would be of no use to them for the interpretation of, for example, "wigs" unless they knew the meaning of "worried." That's where your King M map-dictionary shows its advantage.

NICKEL: Someone looking up the meaning of "wigs" in my dictionary would not have to know the meaning of "worried" in order to learn its combinatory rules, right?

PENNY: Right. That should bring back some of your early enthusiasm for the map-dictionary.

NICKEL: That's why you implied that its advantage over the verbal dictionary is that a person wouldn't have to know the meaning of any words before he could use it. It exhibits before our eyes everything that anyone could know about combinatory meaning.

PENNY: It exhibits, true enough. But it doesn't exhibit everything. Other things we want to know about linguistic combinations come out of the philosopher's investigations, investigations which require the use of inference.

NICKEL: By the way, what are these things "we" want from the philosopher? I don't want to be left out of this covering "we."

PENNY: I'll get to philosophical questions in a minute. First I'd like to forestall some harassment from your literal friend Dime. Lexicographers do not always give us straight out-and-out substitution rules. Their definitions are sometimes more indirect. I think I ought to take some time on examples and explanation.

NICKEL: That would help.

PENNY: Take a look at the first definition of "pole" again.

¹**pole** *n* **1 a:** a long slender usu. cylindrical substance (as wood).

Here we have essentially a description. It's neither detailed nor very precise, but, for most purposes detailed and precise enough. It gives you a pretty good indication of the connections of "pole" with other terms in the array. What you said before about a long slender piece of wood, you now can say about a pole; for example, "Sometimes a long slender piece of wood is light" can be changed into "Sometimes a pole is light."

Here's an example of a definition which doesn't describe the appearance of something as "pole's" definition did, but describes the relations it has to other things.

> **pole plate** *n* **1:** a horizontal timber resting on the tie beams of a roof rather than on the wall and supporting the ends of the rafters—compare PLATE 5a (1); see ROOF illustration...*

If you knew enough architectural terms, you would know that you could say, "Pole plates run parallel to the wall." Or "The pole plate should be a 2×4." You would know you couldn't say "Pass me a pole plate for my soup."

NICKEL: I'm not sure I know enough architecture for that.

PENNY: The lexicographer responsible for that entry thought of your kind. That's why he refers you to an illustration exhibiting roof parts.

Other definitions describe neither appearances nor relations, but effects.

> ¹**poison** *n* **1 a:** a substance that through its chemical action usu. kills, injures, or impairs an organism.*

On the basis of the first part you could formulate a great many sentences.

NICKEL: Yeh. Such as, "Keep your poison to yourself, Lucretia, I wasn't going to usurp anyway."

PENNY: Adjectives are rather interesting. Take this one.

> ¹**Polish** *adj:* of, relating, or characteristic of Poland, the Poles, or Polish.*

Here is a case where we substitute a word for a prepositional phrase. Instead of saying, "This ham is of Poland," we simply say, "This is Polish ham." In place of, "He is an inhabitant of Poland," we say, "He is Polish."

I think you have the idea.

* By permission. From *Webster's Third New International Dictionary*, copyright 1961 by G. & C. Merriam Co., Publishers of the Merriam-Webster Dictionaries.

LOGIC: A DIALOGUE

NICKEL: I think so. And I guess the important point is that the entries give us a rough indication of those words' Stars of Meaning without the use of inferences.

PENNY: Sure. We have to decide next whether philosophical questions can be answered without the employment of inferences. I don't think they can, and if we can come to rational agreement about this, we will have found the difference between lexicographers and philosophers.

To begin with, let me contrast two parallels. The first parallel is between the lexicographer and the mathematics teacher who is trying to teach a student the standard use of "$2n-1$." Both of them presuppose previous knowledge.

NICKEL: I know what the lexicographer presupposes, but what about the math teacher?

PENNY: He, as the lexicographer, is concerned with substitution. To teach someone to produce a standard sequence with $2n-1$ involves teaching him to substitute the natural numbers into n.

NICKEL: Of course! He presupposes that the student has previous knowledge of the natural number system.

PENNY: The second parallel is between philosophers and people interested in the foundations of mathematics. A person intent on investigating the foundations of mathematics doesn't presuppose the natural number system, for it is one of the very things which he wants to account for. Likewise, the philosopher doesn't presuppose the language system, for it, or part of it, is the subject of his investigation.

NICKEL: I don't think I fully grasp the importance of the contrast. The lexicographer seems as much interested in the natural language system as the philosopher. Besides, the philosopher also has to presuppose some language in order to communicate his discoveries.

PENNY: You've made two points. Your first one shows why you don't appreciate the importance of the contrast. You don't realize what significant difference the introduction of the notion of a system will make in our inquiry. The lexicographer is interested in the natural language, but he's not interested in it as a system. The philosopher on the contrary puts an emphasis on system, and that is the wedge of contrast between him and the lexicographer.

All we ask of the lexicographer is to locate a word's star *in* a system. But the kind of questions we ask the philosopher to answer force him to utilize a language's system. This in turn necessitates the use of inferences.

NICKEL: What I'd like to do now is talk about the relations between the three things you just mentioned: philosophical questions, language systems, and inferences.

PENNY: I would too, but I think it would be better if I first cleared up your second point, the one about both the philosopher and the lexicographer needing to presuppose a language with which to communicate their information.

NICKEL: Again?

PENNY: Behold, our taxéd Job. Yes, again, indeed. Obviously I haven't made this business of presupposition totally clear, if a smart guy like yourself doesn't get the point. You must give me a chance to improve. Besides, I think it will lead us into what you want to talk about—providing you ask the right questions.

Do you agree that both the lexicographer and the philosopher could be interested in the same term "X" in the object language?

NICKEL: I agree.

And the lexicographer and the philosopher alike have to presuppose some language in which to communicate their discoveries about X. What they both presuppose for this purpose is a meta-language. Both their statements about X would be in the meta-language.

PENNY: Now, you don't mean to say a philosopher has to presuppose a meta-language. You can't have forgotten that it's possible to exhibit an answer to a combinatory question in the King M style. Only the King N style of answering requires a meta-language.

NICKEL: You're wrong, I did mean what I said and I did forget; however, you did right in reminding me that a philosopher doesn't have to presuppose a meta-language in order to communicate his linguistic studies.

PENNY: I'm trying to point out that the difference between the philosopher and the lexicographer lies in the fact that there is a kind of knowledge about the object-language which the lexicographer presupposes but which the philosopher does not presuppose. To prevent confusion, let's take it that for present purposes both the lexicographer and the philosopher will report their findings in the meta-language.

The general form of the lexicographer's meta-language reply to a question about X's Star is: X is synonymously substitutable for Y; for example, "'wigged' is synonymously substitutable for 'worried.'" Here the lexicographer is definitely relying on, that is, presupposing, your knowledge of a part of the *object*-language, Y's Star. The philosopher cannot similarly rely on this knowledge of the object-language; he can't rely on the lexicographer's synonymity method.

NICKEL: Because not everyone may know the meaning of Y.

PENNY: Nothing like that. The synonymity technique would be defective even if everyone knew the meaning of Y. It's because reference to Y's Star would beg the kind of question the philosopher is trying to answer.

Consider X and Y in "X is synonymously substitutable for Y."

Suppose there is agreement that Y has rays connecting it to words A, B, C, D, and E, and agreement that X has rays connecting it to A, B, C, and D.

NICKEL: What about E's connection with X?

PENNY: Ah, there is the crux! Doubt or disagreement with someone about a connection is what generates philosophical questions.

Now let me explain why philosophical questions, expressions of doubts or disagreements about E's connection with X, cannot be allayed or settled by the synonymity technique, why an answer based on that technique begs the philosophical question.

Clearly that technique involves appealing to our knowledge about Y's rays. This appeal to Y's rays, you realize, is relevant only if X and Y have isomorphic Stars. What do we have to know about X, however, before we can know that X and Y have isomorphic Stars?

NICKEL: We have to know that X, like Y, has a ray connecting it to E.

PENNY: Which is the very thing we were in doubt about. Consequently, any appeal to Y's Star to settle a dispute about X's Star would beg the question we're trying to answer.

NICKEL: I think now I get your point about the presupposition the lexicographer can make use of, but which the philosopher can't. The philosopher can't presuppose our knowledge of Y's Star to explain X's Star, because in effect, it's the isomorphism of the Stars itself which is in doubt.

Incidentally, is "begging the question" the same as "arguing in a circle"?

PENNY: The two phrases are often used interchangeably. Let me recast the argument so you can see the circularity; you'll see the argument moves in a circle, that it ends, 6, where it began, 2.

Odd and Even are talking.

Odd (1): Does X have a connection with E?

Even (2): Yes, it does.

Odd (3): How do you know?

Even (4): Because Y does, and X and Y are isomorphic.

Odd (5): How do you know X and Y are ismomophic?

Even (6): Because X is connected with E.

Now there's not much point in using the alleged isomorphism of X and Y (4) to prove X is connected with E (2) if we have to know that X is connected with E (6) to prove X and Y are isomorphic (4), is there?

NICKEL: No.

PENNY: Another way to see the flaw in the argument is to juxtapose 1 and 6, dropping out the intervening sentences.

1. Does X have a connection with E?

6. (Yes) Because X is connected with E.

NICKEL: Isn't 6 a good answer to 1?

PENNY: If true, it's a perfectly good answer, but if it is a good answer, there isn't much point in having brought in reference to Y, is there? The reference to Y is superfluous. Presumably we needed to look only to X itself; here the synonymity technique is shown to be useless.

Do you see why you needn't have been impatient? In clarifying the point about the lexicographer's presupposition, we've silently stolen into the philosophical tent show. We have painlessly advanced our notion of combinatory philosophy by glimpsing the fecund source of philosophic questions—doubt and/or disagreement about a combination.

NICKEL: I think I'm pretty clear about the lexicographer's synonymity substitution technique now, and I see the limitations of it. But now that we've seen the uselessness of the substitution technique, the only kind of linguistic rule we have left to the combinatory philosopher is the arrangement rule. This means that all his answers to combinatory questions will be in the form of arrangement rules.

PENNY: That would be true if substitution rules provided only for the substitution of one synonymous expression for another; however, we do have other kinds of substitution rules. You can see that by reflecting on Polish and Principia and their rules. What's the relation between α in $f\alpha\beta$ and Polish letters?

NICKEL: Alpha is a variable into which I can substitute a Polish letter.

PENNY: Is there any difference in the generality of two synonymous expressions?

NICKEL: No.

PENNY: What do you conclude from the fact that α is more general than p?

NICKEL: That they aren't synonymous. And that there is another kind of substitution rule than the synonymity rule.

PENNY: And it's a good thing there is another kind. Imagine giving combinatory rules for a language in which there are no synonymous expressions, a non-redundant language. If you allow the possibility of such a language and that the expressions in it have meaning, we have to give the rules of regularity for that language without the use of synonymity substitution. With regard to such a language the lexicographer's technique is completely useless.

NICKEL: I'm getting with you now, but only negatively. What you've said gives me only a negative idea of how the philosopher differs from the lexicographer. I still can't positively describe the difference between them, because I don't know how doubt or disagreement about a word's connections leads the philosopher to consider language as a system.

PENNY: That's because we haven't completely specified the nature of a philosophical question. Until we do, we won't know why its answer requires reference to a system.

NICKEL: Then our next step is to determine the nature of philosophical questions.

PENNY: We proceed. Hereafter, I'm going to use the phrases "philosophical question" and "combinatory question" interchangeably, and as short for "combinatory philosophical question."

So, suppose there is a combinatory question about E's connection with X. How do we go about answering it? Let's consider two possible kinds of answers.

It's always better to work with an example. We should be able to find one in a logic book. I think I know of a good one from Bennett and Baylis's *Formal Logic*. Yes, here it is, on page 239.

> It should be noted that concepts are definable only in terms of concepts and classes only in terms of classes. A class may be determined or identified by a concept but not defined by one. We never assert that a class is equivalent to any of its determining concepts.*

I'm primarily interested in the last sentence. Let's suppose that the class in question is the class of men, and that its determining concepts are rationality and animality. Here comes Abel and he says, "Men are equivalent to rational animality." A rough fellow, Cain, overhears him and comes over and says, "We never assert that a class is equivalent to any of its determining concepts."

They're disagreeing about the combination of "men," "equivalent," and "rational animality." How do we settle the disagreement? Do we settle it the way Abel wants to, were he to reply to Cain with, "What do you mean we never assert such a thing; I just got through making such a combination."?

NICKEL: I don't think so. Abel can't appeal just to what he says, or even what he hears others say, for they may speak incorrectly, just as your boy, Benny, did. It seems to me that a dispute about E's connection with X is a dispute about how we ought to talk, if we are to talk correctly, which is not the same as a dispute about how we do talk. So asking how people actually talk doesn't seem to me a way to settle such a dispute.

PENNY: Excellent. You've just indicated two possible natures for philosophical questions: "Do people in fact combine X and E in a sentence?" and "Is it correct for people to combine X and E in a sentence?"

NICKEL: And I think the second expresses the nature of philosophical questions. Further, if I follow you, the nature of philosophical questions

* Bennett and Baylis, *Formal Logic*, Prentice-Hall, Englewood Cliffs, N.J., 1939, p. 239.

being what it is, we have to see next why a philosophical answer containing a claim about the correctness or incorrectness of a combination can't be given without appeal to language as a system. Is that out of line?

PENNY: That's well enough put to show you know what has to come next.

NICKEL: There is something about the lexicographer still puzzling me, however.

PENNY: Give it air.

NICKEL: A lexicographer is supposed to report "standard" uses, isn't he? Anyway that's what we said before.

PENNY: Quite right.

NICKEL: Well, if that's so, then it appears he has the same problem as the philosopher.

PENNY: How so? The lexicographer, in reporting standard uses, reports uses upon which there is agreement, thus, avoiding disputes about correctness; whereas the philosopher's problems arise when there is disagreement.

NICKEL: But what if there is a doubt or disagreement about whether a use should be standard? The lexicographer can't ignore that, especially if his dictionary entries are to serve as rules for future use.

PENNY: No, he can't. I think you're just worried about lexicographers sometimes doing philosophy. Nothing wrong with that. So he does philosophy? But, of course, our previous point still holds. The substitution technique is of no use even for the lexicographer who mucks in disagreement and does philosophy.

NICKEL: Say, that's right!

PENNY: Sure. Besides, dictionary definitions are generally vague enough to evade controversy; they hardly ever get specific enough to be philosophically interesting. That's why recourse to a dictionary seldom settles philosophical disputes. Differences about the use of "good" can't be resolved simply by referring to the definition of "good" in the OED. But don't knock lexicographers for that. Dictionaries aren't meant to be philosophical treatises.

Now that you, as many other philosophers, have renounced word substitution and all its sins, I believe you are ready for rebirth.

NICKEL: I am ready to take up my first point now and be enlightened about linguistic systems, m'lord.

PENNY: Consider the parrot, that highly regarded bird, for a moment. Although he comes close to human speech, he does have linguistic limitations. What would you say they were?

NICKEL: We say someone is "parroting" when he merely repeats a phrase without understanding.

PENNY: And what can be meant by "without understanding"?

NICKEL: Well, for one thing, a parrot doesn't know in what circumstances his phrase or sentence is appropriate. There must be lots of jokes about parrots breaking into conversations and saying their piece in appropriate places; of course, the joke depends on its being a surprise that it was appropriate. You remember the one about the sailor's parrot in the minister's house when ——

PENNY: Uh, Nickel, we're on the air. Heh, heh. So you realize that sentences or phrases aren't isolated; they are related to other phrases and sentences.

NICKEL: I see. Whenever we have some items, for example, sentences, between which there are relations, we have a system.

PENNY: That's not strong enough. The presence of relations is a necessary condition for the existence of a system, but not a sufficient one. It is possible to have a non-systematic collection of items all of which have relations to each other. This scattering of numbers is an example of that.

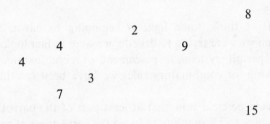

We can specify their left to right relations, or their above and below relations; but it doesn't follow that they are systematic. Instead of having been systematically arranged, they could have been randomly thrown from a hat.

NICKEL: Example B* would be another random case wouldn't it?

PENNY: It could be. I'm still not saying, Trapper. You used a key word just now in reference to the parrot jokes: Appropriate. In using that word you acknowledged the distinguishing feature of any collection of items that is systematic. The way you used it is similar to the way we used "correct" before. Thus, you could have said there are correct and incorrect places for the parrot to utter his sentence, instead of having said there are appropriate places.

NICKEL: I feel the pangs of rebirth, I think. We said the general form of a philosophical question is, "Is it *correct* for people to combine X and E in a sentence?" And now I find that if we can say of any item

* Reader: See page 8.

Eleventh conversation 309

of a collection that it is correctly, or incorrectly, placed, we can say the collection to which it belongs is systematic. It looks to me as if the notion of correctness is the link between philosophical questions and systems.

PENNY: Splendid. Now bear down some more. In order to judge whether or not an item is correctly placed, we have to have recourse to a rule or rules.

NICKEL: You're ahead of me. I'm not sure I follow that leap.

PENNY: Put the number 11 in its correct place in the scattering of numbers.

NICKEL: I can't.

PENNY: And why not?

NICKEL: I can't give a better reason to put it to the left of and below 7 than I can for putting it above and to the right of 9. Ah, in short, Sir, I see I lack a rule, without which, as you said, an item can't be correctly placed.

PENNY: Thus, as far as you are concerned, the scattering is random, not systematic.

NICKEL: Heh! I think some light is beginning to dawn. Right from the start, when we were trying to decode, we were in fact looking for rules that would permit *systematic* placement or combination. This whole time in looking for combinatory rules we have been treating language as a system.

PENNY: It should be clear now that at least part of the parrot's lack of understanding is due to his inability to judge the correctness of sentence placement in a conversation system. The parrot simply does not have the mental equipment necessary to grasp the combinatory rules which make such judgments possible.

Besides his incapacity for correct sentence placement, the parrot is also "without understanding" about correct word placement. A child is born into a society whose members combine words into sentences. The child listens to them doing it. He learns to repeat the combinations he hears, just as the parrot learns to repeat them. But soon the child outstrips the parrot, and in a profound act becomes human. That profound act, Nickel, is the expression of a correctly combined sentence he never heard before.

NICKEL: And this, too, implies that language is a system.

PENNY: Indeed it does. And so does your being able to understand sentences you have never heard before.

Let me relate this achievement to the Star of Meaning. Suppose we had a word-Star with twenty rays. The child's achievement has been this: On the basis of listening to, let's say, ten rays, he has grasped the combinatory rule which gives him possession of the other ten rays without having heard them.

Furthermore, in learning the language, the child hasn't enough knowledge of the language to utilize a synonymity substitution rule.

NICKEL: Birth and rebirth are similar then. Neither need utilize the synonymity technique.

PENNY: Indeed not.

NICKEL: And the poor parrot doesn't have the mental capacity to complete the Star. In short, it is incapable of either birth or rebirth.

PENNY: In short, the parrot doesn't have a soul.

NICKEL: Is this what you had reference to when you said earlier that the study of logic would be for the good of my soul?

PENNY: Are you not now, in the pangs of your rebirth, discovering your soul? And do you not see it is your great capacity for system? And do you not see that logic is the study of system? And are we not now discovering the relation between philosophy and logic? We have fallen on new days, Nickel.

NICKEL: At least I have.

PENNY: Guard them well. Be careful always to separate things of the body from things of the soul. The philosopher is not interested in the psychological or physiological facts that distinguish the parrot from the child. The philosopher is interested in the logical conditions of language which make the child's soul possible.

NICKEL: I can't tell how serious you are about this soul and rebirth business.

PENNY: Nor can you tell how literal I am.

NICKEL: Anyway, the philosopher is interested in those things about language which make it systematic. He is interested in combinatory rules.

PENNY: "Regular" was the word we used in place of "systematic" at first. Now is the contrast between the philosopher and lexicographer ——

NICKEL: It's beginning to clear up. Now that we've discovered the relation between philosophical questions and language systems, I guess we should pass on to the relation between language systems and inferences. When I grasp that last relation, I should understand why the philosopher needs to make use of inferences. It was this requirement that you said distinguished him from the lexicographer.

PENNY: You are with me. We still have our dialogue. That is good, Pilar. The philosopher, being a man of soul, is interested in language's lawful fertility. Having had certain combinations exhibited we, the child, come to see that additional combinations may be generated which are consistent with the exhibited ones. It's this consistent, correct, extension of the given for which the philosopher must account.

This point we've been making about the child is directly relevant to philosophical doubts and disagreements. For those combinatory rules of language systems which permit the child to generate additional correct combinations are the same ones to which we must refer to decide whether or not "X is E" is a correct combination, one consistent with other known and agreed upon combinations. Obviously, an intuitive grasp of those rules is not enough; for two such "grasps" are frequently in disagreement. Our rebirth depends upon our finding out and making fully explicit those combinatory rules of language; unless we do that, we have no controlled way of settling philosophical disputes to our mutual satisfaction. We want to find a decision procedure for combinatory philosophy.

NICKEL: Wouldn't my map-dictionary be sufficient?

PENNY: It would be, if complete. Do you think there are any English sentences that have never been uttered?

NICKEL: Yes.

PENNY: Will your map-dictionary have a line between the proper pair of points showing that there is such an English sentence?

NICKEL: If the map is complete, there will be such a line.

PENNY: For every possible English sentence there will be a line between the appropriate points on a complete dictionary map?

NICKEL: Yes.

PENNY: You agreed with me before when we noted that persons sometimes disagree about the correctness of combining some words into sentences.

NICKEL: I did and still do; and I believe this is the source of one kind of philosophical disagreement.

PENNY: Since you have also said there is a one-to-one correspondence between English sentences and line-connected points on your dictionary map, won't the same disagreements arise about drawing lines between points on your dictionary?

NICKEL: Oi. The burning question is: How can I ever lay out a correct map-dictionary? Until we get a means of settling philosophical questions we won't be able to write my map-dictionary. In fact, because of the one-to-one correspondence, it appears that the aim of combinatory philosophy is the writing of the map-dictionary.

PENNY: Now we are at the beginning of all soul-birth, eh, Nickel?

NICKEL: You have tricked me, Mr. Penny. That carefully nurtured enthusiasm for my dictionary map that was on the wing has plummeted. I can see that my map is completely inadequate. An evil fate shadows it, an evil fate that has flown all the way here from the first day. I remember you warned me then not to produce a description rather than a cipher when working on the binary numerals.* At that time you remarked that every attempt to find a set of rules requires a general description of the seen and the unseen.

PENNY: You find that remark—which, incidentally, began with you, Nickel—applicable to our present problem, I take it.

NICKEL: I do. To write a dictionary, map type or otherwise, is to write linguistic rules, rules which govern our language system. My map-dictionary is neither general nor descriptive of the unseen. It contains no rules for judging the correctness of a never-before-uttered sentence —or for the correctness of a sentence in dispute. It's own nature allows no inference from it to the new case.

Hey! I said it! I said "inference!"

PENNY: You have fallen, as Thales did, into the well of philosophic profit while looking at the Stars of Meaning.

NICKEL: Not all is lost?

PENNY: Not if we follow up our advantage. Though your map may be inadequate, at least we realize that an adequate map should reflect the systematic structure of our language and should be general enough to provide us with a criterion for judging the new combinations and for resolving disagreement about doubtful combinations. At the hub of inference lie systematic arrangement rules and general substitution rules.

NICKEL: Arrangement and substitution again. We're never far from them when we study logic, are we?

PENNY: We'd better not be, for they are logic.

I think we will soon be ready to start reaping philosophic profit.

NICKEL: Are we going to bring together now combinatory philosophy and logic in the narrow sense?

PENNY: We are going to lay a path for their confrontation. And a parrot shall lead us. Actually, Nickel, this will be in the nature of a summary.

Do you remember how we spelled words with "Yes" and "No"?

NICKEL: By a series of cuts in the alphabet, the cuts being made after a "Yes" or "No" answer to "Is it in the first half of the alphabet?"

PENNY: What did you have to know before you could make the cut?

NICKEL: I had to know the alphabet.

PENNY: Suppose we picture similar activity by a line and a cut such as this: _____/_____.

We're trying to decide if parrots talk. Let the following line represent the totality of sounds made by a parrot. _____/_____ Let cut
/1.

* Reader: See pages 21–22.

l come at a place where it separates word sounds from sounds that aren't words, the latter lying to the left of the cut. Before one could make such a cut, what would he have to know?

NICKEL: He would have to know the vocabulary of some language, say, English.

PENNY: This is what we did in Po-1, the first rules for Polish, the ideal language we developed for a portion of logic in the narrow sense.

So far our parrot can talk. Now we make a second cut.

$$\frac{/\ \ /}{/1.\ /2.}$$ Cut 2 comes at a place where it separates

combinations of words which are gramatically correct from those which are not. To the left of cut 2 are such combinations as "Cracker Polly a wants" and to its right are such combinations as "Polly wants a cracker" and "Space began to toll."

NICKEL: Shouldn't "Space began to toll" be to the left of cut 2?

PENNY: No, for there is nothing wrong with the grammar.

What would you have to know in order to make cut 2?

NICKEL: The grammar of the language; I'd have to know what kind of vocabulary items go where. This amounts to knowing some arrangement rules, it seems.

PENNY: This is what we did in Po-3, the *wfe* rules for Polish, the ideal language we developed for a portion of logic in the narrow sense.

Still, there is some evidence our parrot can talk. Now we make a

third cut. $\dfrac{/\ \ /\ \ /}{/1.\ /2.\ /3.}$

Cut 3 comes at a place where it separates sensical combinations of words from those which, though grammatically correct, are not sensical combinations. "Space began to toll" is to the left of 3, as is "The grass is hungry" and "The proposition is thirsty" and "The color is moral."

What would you have to know in order to make cut 3?

NICKEL: More than I do now. I'd have to know the kind of inferences you say the combinatory philosopher must use in order to have a decision procedure for doubtful combinations. I'd have to have "sense" rules.

And I don't think there is anything comparable in the Po- and Pr-rules.

PENNY: Do you mean that we have no Polish sense rules to make such a cut as 3?

NICKEL: Not exactly. I mean we make no such cut at all. If we had a cut in Polish similar to 3, then there would be some Polish *wfes* that are not sensical combinations. For example, vqr is a *wfe*, and if we made a cut such as 3, though q can go to the right of v and to the left of r by the $f\alpha\beta$ grammatical rules, we would have to say some such thing as "q when combined with v and *r* is not sensical." We haven't said that kind of thing about Polish and Principia so far. Wherever one letter can go, any other letter can go. Maybe I can make myself clearer. Take a subject-predicate sentence form: The *S* is *P*. Whatever is a noun can be substituted into *S* and whatever is an adjective can be substituted into *P*. That is a grammatical rule and makes your example, "The grass is hungry," an English *wfe*. But not every word which is an adjective can be substituted into *P* when "grass" is in *S*; some substitutions, such as "hungry," result in nonsensical sentences. We have no such restrictions on Polish as I tried to illustrate with v*qr*. Every permissible substitution instance of *f*, α, and β when combined in *f*$\alpha\beta$ is a Polish expression. But not every permissible substitution instance of *S* and *P* when combined in "The *S* is *P*" is an English sentence. It's harder to be an English sentence than it is to be a Polish expression. I guess Polish is more primitive than English. Have I made myself at all clear?

PENNY: You have to me. It seems, however, that you're forgetting the Po-6 rules for *wfe*10s. Now you and I both know that 1 or 0 may be substituted into γ, α, and β and binary functors into *f* in $\gamma f\alpha\beta$, but we also know there are restrictions on combinations of them. For example, 1v00 is not a *wfe*10. For *wfe*10s we have restrictions similar to the sense restrictions of English.

NICKEL: I had forgotten *wfe*10s and the fact that we had brought referential meaning into Polish and Principia.

You know, you're getting through to me with your reminders about the similarity of the Polish rules to the English rules we need in order to make our cuts. At last I can see how the logic in the narrow sense we've studied so far is starting to pay off. Having learned the kinds of rules we need for Polish and Principia, we can use those rules as models for constructing a new ideal language, the language which should contain the inference schema rules we need to make cut 3 in English.

Am I getting there?

PENNY: Encouragingly well.

NICKEL: As I see it, we want a new logical symbolism that will help us make cut 3 just as Polish and Principia help us make cut 5.

PENNY: Say, you are moving along. What are cuts 4 and 5, Emory?

NICKEL: $\dfrac{/\ \ /\ \ /\ \ /\ \ /}{/1.\ /2.\ /3.\ /4.\ /5.}$.

Cut 4 separates all those correct sentences which are true or false from those which aren't, that is, it separates propositions from other sentences. Cut 5 separates true sentences from false ones.

PENNY: You look satisfied with yourself.

NICKEL: I am, because today I learned never to become impatient when doing philosophy. A person can't predict a dialogue; philosophy must wend where it will. I suspect a philosopher's whole life is like our days have been.

PENNY: Except for committee meetings. I must confess we have covered quite a lot of ground today.

NICKEL: I'll say we have. We have found out the limitations of the lexicographer's synonymity technique, discovered the nature of philosophical questions, gotten some hints about systems, revealed why philosophy is good for our soul, and, best of all, been reborn in soul again. What more can one ask for in a day?

PENNY: Exercises and review questions.

11.1: As you noticed in working out Mrs. Hurlbutt's problem, 2 in 10.9, her premises suffered from the defect of contradiction. (a) What is the least thing you could do to eliminate the contradiction and (b) what added information would allow you to deduce that Mr. Hurlbutt did not come home late?

11.2: The premises supplied in 3 in 10.9 allowed you to deduce only that McNitt should get the contract. (a) Suppose you were a lawyer for Osterloh and wanted him alone to get the contract. By using only the bar functor, what changes in the premises would you have to make with it in order to deduce that Osterloh alone should get the contract? (b) Perform the same function for Ricklin.

11.3: Here's a dialogue between Odd and Even.
1. When we play chess we ordinarily use the Queen-shaped piece to make Queen moves and Pawn-shaped pieces to make Pawn moves.
2. Yes.
3. But we could reverse it and use a Pawn-shaped piece to make Queen moves and Queen-shaped pieces to make Pawn moves.
4. Yes.
5. If a piece can be used to make either Queen or Pawn moves, how can we tell which way a player is using it?
6. By watching to see how he moves it across the squares on the board.
7. Almost every word has several meanings. We could give each of those meanings a different word shape. As it is, we don't. So they have the same word shape. The number of combinatory concepts, therefore, is greater than the number of expressions in a language. How do we distinguish the different concepts from each other when they wear the common guise of the same inscription?

NICKEL: I suppose by the different moves people make with the common word.

PENNY: You can tell one kind of move from another in chess by observing how the piece moves on the squares. What in language plays the background role that the chess board squares play in chess?

11.4: Suppose a player is moving a Pawn-shaped piece. You are passing by and only have time to see him make that one move. Would that one move be sufficient to tell you whether the player was using the Pawn-shaped piece as a Pawn or Queen?

NICKEL: Not necessarily. For he might simply move the piece straight ahead one square. Both a Queen and a Pawn can do that. It might take several moves to determine the piece's role.

PENNY: Quite right. Now consider a somewhat analogous linguistic case. Suppose you are reading a book and there is a word which occurs in the book only once. As we said before, a word may have several uses or meanings. Can we tell from the single occurrence of this word in the book which one of its several uses is the correct one to select? Or is there the same problem as with the double-roled chess piece?

NICKEL: I don't think so. For the context will tell us which one is intended by the author.

PENNY: I didn't ask for the intended meaning; I asked for the correct meaning. Let me push you a little. The term "context" trips as lightly off your tongue as it does most linguists and philosophers. What I want you to do is to analyze the context into the relevant details we have to observe to be able to make such a judgment. Simply saying "context" doesn't tell me anything definite. Work with examples.

11.5: Here is a quotation from David Pole's *The Later Philosophy of Wittgenstein.* I want you to relate it to what we've been talking about.

> Our concern is with language, not reality. In some sense, experience is clearly private; one person cannot be said literally to feel another's feelings. To say that is to notice a point in grammar; and we might teach the use of the word in this way, by saying "Experience is private." It would be like saying that a rod necessarily has a certain length, or that colours are visible.* These terms "physical object" and "experience" are grammatically different.† And this difference requires to be stressed, for the dualist error is to assimilate them. Grammar allows us to say that two people see the same table; it forbids us to say that two people have felt the same pain. Again it forbids us, in the case of mathematical entities, say of numbers, to talk of our seeing or feeling

* Ludwig Wittgenstein, *Philosophical Investigations*, Basil Blackwell, Oxford, 1953, pp. 251–253; 295.
† *Ibid.*, p. 293.

them at all. Numbers are not invisible objects as some perfectly transparent stuff might be invisible; for the notion of seeing them is absurd. That is the kind of difference we are concerned with.*

Review Questions

1. What kind of substitution rule does a conventional dictionary use most? How does such a dictionary give us arrangement rules?

2. What advantage does Nickel's proposed King *M* dictionary have over a conventional dictionary?

3. What presupposition does the lexicographer make in his investigations that the philosopher cannot make? Why does the nature of philosophical questions prevent the philosopher from making that presupposition?

4. What other kinds of substitution rules are there besides a synonymity rule?

5. How is the fact that dictionary entries are rules rather than predictions related to Abel's reply to Cain about the equivalence of a class to its determining concepts?

6. What is the general form of a philosophical question of the variety which a combinatory philosopher seeks to answer?

7. How is a child's learning to utter a sentence it has never heard before related to a decision procedure for combinatory philosophy?

8. Why does Nickel say the aim of combinatory philosophy is the writing of a map-dictionary?

9. What is the importance of cut 3 for the philosophic profit of logic in the narrow sense?

10. Which concept is the link between philosophical questions and a linguistic system?

11. Why is the map-dictionary as conceived by Nickel inadequate for the purpose of answering philosophical combinatory questions?

* David Pole, *The Later Philosophy of Wittgenstein*, Athlone Press, London, 1958, pp. 68–69.

Twelfth conversation

THE CONSTELLATION: A LOGIC OF COMBINATORY CONCEPTS

Ther was att mye frend's howse a numbr of uss gatherrd tawking
of Stars and wun of them, a lernd mann told of beeholting
ina Hevin a nu tracerry of lynnes, wherupon a lyttl ladde, a
vysitore whos nayme I lerned latr was John Locke sayd, "Perhaps
if ideas and words were distinctly weighed and duly considered,
they would afford us another sort of logic and critic than what
we have hitherto been acquainted with."   Wee awl laffed in
delyght at this keene lyttl felow.—Fanebius Perlyng

D IME: Hello, Mr. Penny?
PENNY: Yes. Speaking.
DIME: This is Hillary Dime calling, Emory Nickel's friend.
PENNY: Oh, yes. Nickel has spoken of you.
DIME: I suppose he's told you of my disagreements with you.
PENNY: Yes, he has. You've been kind of a disembodied respondent
—but strong, nevertheless.
DIME: I felt disemboweled rather than disembodied afterward, which
shows I'm not as strong as I thought I was. Anyway, despite our differ-
ences, I'm enjoying what Emory and you are doing. That's why I'm
phoning. In the last exercises you gave Emory you included a quotation
from David Pole.
PENNY: The one about the privacy of experience?
DIME: That's it. That whole issue escapes me. I was wondering if
you could work it into your discussion in some way today. I won't be
able to come along, but naturally I'll read Emory's report.
PENNY: Maybe I can work it in.
DIME: It shouldn't be too hard to do that. You'll have to talk about
inferences today and the role they have in philosophy. You always use
examples, so I thought maybe you could use that privacy of experience
topic as your example.
PENNY: Perhaps we can, but without you're being here, our conversation may not take that turn. You'll have to come along some time when
you can.
DIME: I'd like that. Thanks for the invitation. Good-bye.
PENNY: Good-bye. I'll be out in the gazebo in a minute, Nickel.
NICKEL: Did Dime call you on the telephone?
PENNY: Yes, he did. I hope we'll get around to satisfying his request
about the quotation from Pole. Well . . .
NICKEL: I'd like to begin by trying to state where our last conversation deposited us, so we can start today from a common point.
First, philosophical questions arise out of doubt or disagreement
about the correctness of combinations of the cut 3 variety, where cut 3
separates sensical from nonsensical expressions. Secondly, we can't
decide about such correctness without reference to a system governed by
rules general enough to cover the doubtful cases.
PENNY: Good, and where do we go from here?
NICKEL: On to my theory about the role that inference plays in
settling philosophical disputes. It's my theory about how logic in the
narrow sense when applied to combinatory philosophy produces philosophic profit. I'm going to try and fill that last gap in my chart, the one I
showed you at the beginning of our tenth conversation.

320

PENNY: Proceed, Emory.

NICKEL: My first point is that the kind of rule we need in order to decide about doubtful combinations is an inference rule.

My reason for saying that comes from something I've learned about inference in general. Every use of a valid inference schema produces a conclusion of a certain nature which augments a given set of premisses having the same nature.

PENNY: "Of a certain nature" isn't clear to me.

NICKEL: You gave me a lot of English arguments in the exercises the other day. Assuming that the premiss expressions had the nature of being true, we wanted to know if we could augment them with the conclusion expression. We could augment them only if the conclusion had the same nature; that is, if it too were true.

In order to make a decision about the augmentation, I had recourse to rules; those rules were the transformation and argument schemas. They were general rules, for they contained variables.

PENNY: How does all of this apply to doubt about the correctness of combinations?

NICKEL: I analogize from the truth of expressions to the sensicalness, the meaningfulness, of expressions. We can state a question about the sensicalness of an expression this way: Can I augment the class of English sensical expressions with this one?

I learned I can augment a class of true expressions with a conclusion if it is a substitution instance of a truth schema because the truth schema assures me that the truth of the conclusion follows from the truth of the premisses. In other words, the schema assures me that the conclusion has the same nature as the premisses.

Similarly, if I had sense schemas which assure me that the sensicalness of a conclusion follows from the sensicalness of the premisses, then I could decide that the doubtful sentence can be used to augment the class of sensical English sentences I already know. Sense schemas would assure me that the conclusion has the same nature as the premisses; they would assure me that the conclusion is sensical.

Thus, I would use inference rules to make cut 3 as well as cut 5, though the rules would be different, of course.

PENNY: Let me summarize and generalize your remarks.

The decision to augment a corpus of given expressions of a certain nature with an additional expression of the same nature can be known to be correct if we make use of an appropriate schema rule of inference.

NICKEL: I guess that summarizes my remarks. Do you mean by a "corpus" simply a "collection" of expressions?

PENNY: I do. A set of premisses can be a corpus, or part of a corpus, for example.

Let me be sure I've got you straight. You are saying that cut 3 in the English language, for example, is the cut that separates all sensical English sentences from nonsensical English sentences.

NICKEL: I am.

PENNY: And that if we are in doubt about whether a combination of words is sensical, we first should find some English sentences we know to be sensical as premisses; then, if from them, with the use of sense inference schemas, we can derive the doubtful combination, we would know that the doubtful combination is sensical.

NICKEL: How does that sound to you?

PENNY: Pretty good, though it's not a foolproof method of settling our doubts, for failure to derive the doubtful combination doesn't prove it's nonsensical.

NICKEL: For the, by now, familiar reason: We might not have been clever enough to find a proof or the needed premisses. I don't feel too bad, though, for at least we're no worse off than the mathematician. He sometimes despairs of ever finding a proof for an expression he suspects is a theorem.

PENNY: That's some solace, isn't it, being compared to the strictest of the sciences?

NICKEL: Yes, I find it is. Though, and this is the second point in my theory of philosophic profit, we still have to find sense schemas. We have to find general rules containing variables. Once again, I say that the truth schemas won't do; they apply to expressions belonging to cut 5. But before I can make cut 5, I must have made cut 3. Cut 5 presupposes already having made cut 3, already having decided that an expression is sensical.

PENNY: You've been thinking about philosophic profit since I saw you last.

NICKEL: I have, though I am near the bottom of my barrel, having only one more point to make.

My third point is that arguments in combinatory philosophy should utilize sense schemas, if we can find them, and that these rules, not being synonymity rules, distinguish the philosopher from the lexicographer and show how he utilizes the system of language—if it has one.

PENNY: It had better have one, if we are to be able to give reasons why we believe that certain combinations of words are correct or incorrect.

NICKEL: That's what chiefly worries me. I can see we have to find sense schemas in order to show that philosophy is a rational enterprise. That's about all my "theory" comes to; the next step is one I haven't been able to take.

PENNY: What step is that?

NICKEL: Actually finding some sense schemas. I don't really know how to proceed to find them.

PENNY: Sense schemas are no different than any linguistic rules; they are simply substitution and arrangement rules. An argument schema consists of an arrangement of functors and variables into which we are allowed to substitute.

You first learned how to extract linguistic rules when you found a cipher between the binary numerical system and the decimal system. Extracting sense schemas is no different in nature.

NICKEL: Well, that makes sense. In that case, I'll first have to find some expressions from which to extract the rules.

But how can I be sure they're not just my rules? I've been worrying about that question ever since our sixth conversation.* Remember? We were talking about a "pleasant shout," and I suggested there were rules for non-combination. You asked me if my rule of non-combination was just my rule or if it was more general.

PENNY: I remember that—sort of.

If you're worried about verifying that you have extracted the correct rules, that's not a new problem. You had to worry about that when you tried to find the correct cipher between Polish and Principia and between the binary and decimal systems. You simply had to make sure that you didn't use the total corpus of expressions from which to draw the rules; you had to leave part of the corpus against which to check your hypothesis.

The same goes for sense schemas; we have to leave a corpus of expressions against which to check them for corrections.

NICKEL: I realize that. But that's not what I'm worried about. I don't know quite how to say it. Maybe this will do. How do I know that the rules I extract are standard rules? That they are the same rules other persons use? Or are willing to use?

PENNY: I get what you're driving at. Suppose that you extract from a corpus of expressions the rules which if followed would in fact have produced that corpus.

NICKEL: OK.

PENNY: Those rules won't be standard rules if that corpus isn't a standard corpus. A person drawing rules from a non-standard corpus will end up with non-standard rules. Suppose someone claims that the non-standard rules are English rules. What will be the result if someone tries to produce English expressions with them?

NICKEL: He will utter non-English expressions.

* Reader: See page 142.

PENNY: What will have been the original cause of this?

NICKEL: Picking non-English expressions from which to extract the rules.

PENNY: So, what had we better be sure of before we begin to extract sense schemas?

NICKEL: We'd better be sure that we begin with expressions most people will grant are English expressions.

PENNY: "Most people" or most English-speaking people?

NICKEL: Most English-speaking people, of course.

PENNY: Before we try to extract the rules which will allow us to make cut 3 in English we'd better come to some understanding about the rules which allow us to make cut 1 and cut 2 in English. The rule for cut 1 will be vocabulary rules just as Po-1 and Pr-1 consisted of vocabulary rules. Finding the vocabulary rules seems like a rather enormous task for us to carry through double-handed in our summer gazebo, doesn't it?

NICKEL: Rather. May I suggest we just take the OED as our vocabulary list rule?

PENNY: Excellent suggestion. Whatever inscription occurs in the OED will be an English written word and whatever inscription doesn't occur will not be; with OED we make cut 1 in the English language—except for one thing: dirty words.

There are, after all, dirty English words, some of which don't appear in the OED; and some of them are quite old. Or will you stolidly and implacably follow the OED and rule that **** isn't an English word?

NICKEL: Let me chicken out, Mr. Penny, and simply say that the OED shall serve us as the vocabulary list for clean, standard English.

And please don't ask me about new words that don't appear in the latest edition. You can't step twice into the same dictionary.

PENNY: And what shall we do about cut 2?

NICKEL: Make that as simple as possible.

PENNY: An excellent suggestion. Especially since I have it in mind to alter the geometry of your map-dictionary in such a way that we'll be able to use it as a criterion for the correctness of a never-before uttered sentence.

NICKEL: Plucking up my enthusiasm for my dictionary map again, I hope not falsely!

PENNY: I hope not either. That's why I want to keep our *wfe* rules for cut 2 as simple as possible. Burden me with as little grammar as we need, Emory. Keep the geometry simple.

NICKEL: Why not confine ourselves to simple subject-predicate sentences?

324

PENNY: Fine.   Though if we so restrict our corpus, the sense schemas we produce will not cover the whole of English.   But, then, we only have an introductory course here, not the whole of logic, so we shouldn't feel too inadequate about that.

Do you agree that all of the following sentences are instances of a subject-predicate sentence: "This dog is dirty," "This dog is not dirty," "All dogs are dirty," "Some dogs are not dirty," "The dog is dirty," "Most dogs are dirty," "A dog is dirty," "Dogs are dirty," "Few dogs are not dirty," "No dogs are dirty"?

NICKEL: I agree.

You've said you plan to revive my dictionary map.   Are we going to drop all the auxiliary expressions, such as "this," "not," "some," and "is," from it as we decided we should the first time we talked about the map?*

PENNY: Yes, and we can give a reason for being consistent with our former decision if we consider that the rules for auxiliary expressions more properly belong to the grammatical rules for cut 2.

NICKEL: What kind of rules do you have in mind?

PENNY: Substitution rules.

Suppose we consider this, "_____α_____β", as the general form of a subject-predicate sentence, where we substitute auxiliary expressions into the blanks and such expressions as "dog" and "dirty" into alpha and beta.

NICKEL: That general form looks like an English *wfe* rule, for there is an arrangement of variables with rules for substitution into them, just as *f*$\alpha\beta$ is a *wfe* rule.

PENNY: The very thing.   In order to produce an English subject-predicate sentence, we have to take two steps, both of them substitution steps.

NICKEL: We produced Polish expressions by substituting into *f* and into alpha and beta; so, I guess one step is the substitution of auxiliary expressions into the blanks, a grammatical step, and the other is the substitution of pairs of words into alpha and beta.

PENNY: Good.   For which substitution do we want to find rules today?

NICKEL: The second.   We want to find rules of regularity governing the substitution of pairs of words into alpha and beta, sense rules.   Such rules would tell us which words may be combined and which may not, the information I originally thought my dictionary map would give us.

* Reader: See page 241.

_____

Twelfth conversation   325

PENNY: Let's call such pairs of words sentence cores. Some sentence cores are sensical and some are not. "Dog" and "dirty" is a sensical sentence core; "proposition" and "thirsty" is a nonsensical sentence core.

What do you think we should say of a sentence resulting from the substitution of "dog" and "dirty" into alpha and beta?

NICKEL: That it is a sensical sentence; and we should say a sentence with "proposition" and "thirsty" as its core is nonsensical. "Some dog is dirty" and "No dog is dirty" are both sensical sentences; but "Some proposition is thirsty" is a nonsensical sentence.

PENNY: By putting the substitution rules for auxiliary expressions among the grammatical rules, we have pinpointed the kind of rule we need to distinguish sensical from nonsensical sentences. Our sense schemas must enable us to distinguish sensical from nonsensical sentence cores.

NICKEL: That's a good reason for dropping auxiliary expressions out of the dictionary map.

PENNY: I have another reason. By dropping auxiliary expressions from our dictionary map, we keep them from carrying us too far. They might have carried us right up to cut 5, the cut that separates true sentences from false ones.

"Some dog is dirty" is true and "No dog is dirty" is false. Is that of any moment to our present purpose?

NICKEL: I don't think so. We're looking for sense rules, and the sensicalness of a sentence is independent of its truth value. I say that because, as you said, a sentence's sensicalness depends only on the sensicalness of its core, and we can't say of its core that it is true or false. "_____dog_____dirty" isn't true or false.

I get your other point about dropping auxiliary expressions from our dictionary map now that I've made that last remark. By leaving them out, we don't run the risk of confusing the truth value of sentences with their sensicalness; which it is important not to do, for questions of sensicalness come before questions of truth, cut 3 before cut 5.

PENNY: Good, Nickel. We don't care if all dogs are dirty, or none are, or if there are any dogs. We're doing logic, not natural science; our subject-matter is linguistic regularity, and, because it is, all we're concerned with are the pairs of inscriptions or sounds which may be substituted into alpha and beta.

NICKEL: Well, shall we begin to extract sense schemas? I am ready and eager for rebirth. My soul wants to know itself.

PENNY: Do you think we have considered everything we need to know to be able to say of a combination of inscriptions or sounds that they are a simple English subject-predicate sentence?

NICKEL: I think so. We have considered a vocabulary rule which allows us to decide if all the inscriptions are English words. By that rule we would know, for example, that "All fraldanobs are wispy" isn't an English sentence.

We have considered the grammatical rule governing the general form of simple, subject-predicate sentences, "_____α_____β"; and we have assumed grammatical rules governing the substitution of auxiliary words into the form. By those rules we would know for example, that "This all dog dirty" isn't an English sentence.

Now we need to find sense schemas governing sentence cores.

PENNY: I don't see how the rules you've cited so far help us decide that "This dirty is dog" isn't an English sentence. All the inscriptions are English words; they are arranged correctly; the auxiliary expressions are in the right places and right combinations; and we have a sensical sentence core.

NICKEL: Hmmm. The best laid plans and all that.

Obviously what's wrong here is that some words can be substituted into α and not into β, while others can be substituted into β but not into α. I can see we need to supplement our rules to prevent improper substitution of sentence core words.

Now that I think of it, I'm not surprised we need such a rule. After all, our Polish rules prohibited us from substituting functors into α and β, and from substituting letters into f in $fαβ$. Our Polish vocabulary rule made this prohibition possible by dividing vocabulary items into letters and functors.

Maybe we can solve our problem the same way. How about dividing all the vocabulary items that can be in a sentence core into S's and P's; S's can go into the subject place and P's can go into the predicate place. Thus, S's may be substituted into α but not into β, while P's may be substituted into β but not into α.

PENNY: On what grounds will you make the S-P vocabulary division?

NICKEL: You pointed out once* that the dictionary gives us arrangement rules by telling us a word's part of speech. "Dog" being a noun is an S and goes into the α place. "dirty" being an adjective is a P and goes into the β place.

We could use the OED not only as our vocabulary rule but also as our S-P vocabulary division rule. Naturally, my map-dictionary will have to contain the S-P information just as the OED does.

PENNY: To give us a rule enabling us to decide that "This dog is dirty" is an English sentence and that "This dirty is dog" is not an

---

* Page 300.

English sentence, you're proposing adding the *S-P* vocabulary division rule as a grammatical rule?

NICKEL: I am. My rule requires that an English subject-predicate sentence have an *SP* core; it can't have a *PS* core. I'm saying that the two words (or phrases) constituting a sensical core must be in a certain order, the *SP* order, before we can have an English sentence.

PENNY: You're able to rule out "This thirsty is proposition" as an English sentence even before you consider whether or not "thirsty" and "proposition" constitute a sensical core?

NICKEL: I am. Grammatical decisions precede sense decisions. This means that by purely grammatical criteria "This proposition is thirsty" is an English sentence; it isn't until we make a sense decision that we can finally say it isn't an English sentence. Let me put it this way: To be grammatical each sentence must have an *SP* core, but not all sentences with *SP* cores are sensical.

PENNY: Then no sentences with *PS*, or *SS*, or *PP* cores are grammatical?

NICKEL: Right. We ruled out *PS* cores when we ruled out "This dirty is dog." The left-hand list I'm going to make up clearly shows we should rule out *SS* cores also.

All balls are color.	All balls are colored.
Some widows are dole.	Some widows are doleful.
These pictures are color.	These pictures are colorable.
All players are score.	All players are scoring.
This plant is nymph.	This plant is nymphaceous.
Yon woman is bitch.	Yon woman is bitchy.
This butcher is friend.	This butcher is friendly.
Our daughter hawk.	Our daughter hawks.

The strings on the left are ungrammatical, those on the right grammatical, because of a purely grammatical criterion, a suffix criterion. Words which take such suffixes as -ing, -ful, -able, -ed, -aceous, -y, -ly, and -s are (to play safe) generally *S*'s; when we add the *P*-making suffixes they are generally *P*'s.

Would you like me to make up a list of strings with *PP* cores that are clearly ungrammatical?

PENNY: Why not?

NICKEL: The last list showed how *S*'s, such as "color," "dole," and "score," turn into *P*'s when we add the suffixes, thus giving us *SP* cores. This list will show *P*'s such as "doleful" and "free" turning into *S*'s by the addition of *S*-making suffixes, thereby turning ungrammatical *PP* cores into *SP* cores.

Doleful is unattractive.	Dolefulness is unattractive.
Free is precious.	Freedom is precious.
All run are swift.	All runners are swift.
Some propose are accepted.	Some proposals are accepted.
An opt was honored.	An option was honored.
The create is proud.	The creator is proud.

PENNY: Almost convincing, Nickel.

NICKEL: What do you mean, "almost?"

PENNY: Is there anything wrong with this sentence: "A bitch is a dog?"

NICKEL: No.

PENNY: Are "bitch" and "dog" both *S*'s?

NICKEL: I guess so. Neither of them has a *P*-making suffix on the end.

PENNY: Why then we have a perfectly grammatical and sensical English sentence with an *SS* core.

NICKEL: What do we do now?

PENNY: Give you another shocker. Is "scarlet" in "W. C. Fields' nose was scarlet" a *P*?

NICKEL: Yes.

PENNY: And is "red" in "The barn is red" a *P*?

NICKEL: Of course.

PENNY: Then we must have a *PP* core in "Scarlet is a red."

NICKEL: My *SP* core bites the dust once more. Once again, what do we do now?

PENNY: Bow to the facts. Allow that English sentences with *SP*, *SS*, and *PP* cores may all be grammatical.

NICKEL: But that means an *S*, such as "dog," can be a grammatical predicate, and a *P*, such as "scarlet," can be a grammatical subject.

PENNY: That shouldn't bother us. Bend with the winds of grammar as the reed does rather than being blown over as a resistant oak. Aesop would advise it.

NICKEL: But how can some *SS* and *PP* cores be ungrammatical while others are grammatical?

PENNY: Are you sure it's the grammar which is at fault when you find some sentences with *SS*, or *PP*, cores unacceptable? After all, if some sentences with *SS* cores are grammatical, then it must be the case that *SS* sentences are grammatical. Other things can go wrong with a sentence, you know.

NICKEL: You're maintaining that sentences with *SP*, *SS*, and *PP* cores are grammatical.

PENNY: I am. Let me put it this way: *SP*, *SS*, and *PP* are *wfcs* (well-formed cores).

NICKEL: Are you hinting that what I find unacceptable about "All balls are color" is not the grammar but the sense?

PENNY: That might be one fault, though it may not be the only one. That's not what's wrong with this sentence, "A bitch is dog."

NICKEL: There an auxiliary term, "a," is missing, right?

PENNY: Uh huh. Apparently some sentences with an *SS* core require an "a." But does "A bitch is brown" require an "a"?

NICKEL: No, it doesn't.

PENNY: How about a sentence with a *PP* core?

NICKEL: "Scarlet is a red" requires it.

PENNY: I suggest that the English subject-predicate sentence form is perfidious, that it hides two different logical forms. One form, which I will call the descriptive form, requires an *SP* core, the other, which I will call the subsumptive form, requires either an *SS* or a *PP* core; sentences with the indefinite article preceding the grammatical predicate ordinarily take *SS* or *PP* cores.

The important consequence for a logic of sense is that there may be different sense rules for *SP* cores than for *SS* and *PP* cores.

NICKEL: It's pretty crucial that we be able to distinguish between *S*'s and *P*'s, isn't it?

PENNY: It is, and the job of formulating the criteria for distinguishing them isn't easy. The perusal of such a book as Jespersen's *The Philosophy of Grammar* will show you just how hard it is. You had a start at the distinction with your suffix criteria. But a sentence such as "The beautiful is harrowing" shows it frequently requires supplementation. For our purposes today, which is only to get a start on some sense schemas, we don't need water-tight criteria. And the fact that we may be in doubt about whether a sentence is of the descriptive or subsumptive form won't vitiate what we have to say.

We'll rely on the OED and our grammatical intuition for deciding whether a sentence is descriptive or subsumptive and whether a word is an *S* or a *P*.

NICKEL: Will we decide that a sentence is descriptive or subsumptive before or after we decide that its core words are *S*'s or *P*'s?

PENNY: Do the forms of these two sentences look different: "All dogs are hungry," "All dogs are animals"?

NICKEL: No, and they're both grammatical.

PENNY: What kind of cores do they have?

330

NICKEL: *SP* and *SS*, respectively.

PENNY: Since their forms are similar, it seems we have no other basis for deciding whether they are descriptive or subsumptive than the nature of their core words.

NICKEL: Then the first is descriptive and the second subsumptive.

PENNY: You look doubtful.

NICKEL: On that basis, we can't say a sentence is ungrammatical because of the nature of its core.

PENNY: We ruled out "The dirty is dog" on the basis of its having a *PS* core.

NICKEL: Oh, yes, I'd forgotten. Is that all we've gotten out of the *S-P* vocabulary division?

PENNY: No. We've seen that in looking for sense schemas we have to keep our eyes peeled for two kinds of subject-predicate sentences, descriptive and subsumptive sentences.

The *S-P* division can't do everything; we do want to leave room for other grammatical things to go wrong. Take the sentence "A dog is a hungry"; it strikes us as being subsumptive.

NICKEL: Because of the indefinite article preceding "hungry."

PENNY: But we notice that it has an *SP* core; that means it is descriptive. Thus, nothing is wrong with the sentence on the basis of its core. But having an *SP* core, it can't be subsumptive, and not being subsumptive, it shouldn't have that indefinite article preceding "hungry." Put the blame on "a," Mame, not on "hungry."

NICKEL: Are we ready to have a go at sense schemas now?

PENNY: After I'm sure that you have clearly in mind all the points we've made.

NICKEL: You want a summary, I see. Well, we have the OED as a vocabulary rule; the "_____α_____β" *wfe* rule; the substitution rules for auxiliary words; the OED and our intuition for making the *S-P* vocabulary division; the *wfc* rule requiring an *SP* core for descriptive sentences; the *wfc* rule requiring *SS* and *PP* cores for subsumptive sentences.

PENNY: Excellent. We set off now to find schema rules for sentence cores, rules which will help us to decide which pairs of words substituted into the *SP*, *SS*, and *PP* general *wfc*s are sensical.

Notice that our rules for a sense logic parallel our rules for the truth logics, Polish and Principia. We have a vocabulary list, a vocabulary division rule, and *wfc* rules. *S* and *P* are variables just as *f* and *α* and *β* were; and *SP*, *SS*, and *PP* are general expressions which exhibit an arrangement and require substitution of particular kinds of vocabulary items just as *fαβ* did.

What do you expect we should do next to carry out the parallelism?

NICKEL: We should find which combinations of general *wfcs* constitute valid sense schemas. This is parallel to finding that $*\alpha\beta$, α, and β when combined as $\dfrac{*\alpha\beta \quad \alpha}{\beta}$ constitute a valid argument schema.

PENNY: Here is a corpus of words to which you may apply the rules we've outlined so far.

ball	weighs-4-pounds	ostrich	envy	degree	weighs
blue	figure	mild	cube	bird	anger
emotion	green	violent	chicken	strong	weighs-5-pounds
goose	pyramid	red	love	colored	weighs-6-pounds

NICKEL: First, I'll make the *S-P* division. There seems to be no doubt that they are all English words or phrases.

S		P		
emotion	bird	blue	red	weighs
goose	anger	green	strong	weighs-4-pounds
pyramid	cube	mild	colored	weighs-5-pounds
ostrich	ball	violent		weighs-6-pounds
chicken				

"Envy," "love," "degree," and "figure" could be either an *S* or a *P*, depending on how they are used. The same inscription can play a double role in English; "figure" is an *S* in "Some figure is red" while it is a *P* in "I figure you owe me one dollar".

PENNY: Good observations, Nickel. Certainly a logic of sense should give us a means of distinguishing the various senses an inscription or sound may have, and give us a means of deciding which sense it has on a particular occasion of its use.

Does the following remark fit in with anything else you notice about the corpus? "Figure" is used in the sense in which balls, pyramids, and cubes are figures.

NICKEL: I think it does. It seems that the words can be grouped into families, families which determine one of the senses of each of the terms "figure," "envy," "love," and "degree."

"Figure," "bird," "emotion," "colored," "weighs," and "degree" are words which have their offspring; they are, so to speak, parent words.

	figure			bird	
ball	pyramid	cube	goose	chicken	ostrich

	emotion				colored	
anger	envy	love		blue	red	green

	degree				weighs	
strong	violent	mild		weighs-4-pounds	weighs-5-pounds	
				weighs-6-pounds		

PENNY: Do you see any relation between word families and *SS* and *PP* cores?

NICKEL: Now that you mention it, I do.

PENNY: Now, Nickel, using the words in our corpus, I want you to write all the sensical *SS* and *PP* cores you can.

NICKEL: I'll write the sensical *SS* cores first.

figure	figure	figure	figure	figure	figure	figure
ball	cube	pyramid	bird	goose	chicken	ostrich

emotion	emotion	emotion	bird	bird	bird
anger	love	envy	goose	chicken	ostrich

PENNY: Why did you write the parent word on top and the offspring word below?

NICKEL: I wanted to write a subsumptive sentence's grammatical subject below and the grammatical predicate above, as in "Envy is an emotion."

PENNY: Then these cores, ball chicken, aren't sensical?
figure bird

NICKEL: No, they aren't. Their order is reversed.

PENNY: "This ball is a figure" is sensical while "Some figure is a ball" is nonsensical?

NICKEL: Obviously, both are sensical. I guess that both ball
figure
and figure are sensical *SS* cores. The same point can be made about *PP*
ball
cores; "Blue is a color" and "Some color is a blue" are both sensical sentences.

PENNY: It seems clear that the order of *SS* and *PP* cores can be reversed—unlike *SP* cores. The order offspring is as sensical as parent
parent offspring
If we let the general form for *SS* and *PP* cores be S_m and P_m, then we'll
S_n P_n

allow that either a parent or an offspring word may be substituted for S_m and P_m; similarly for S_n and P_n.

NICKEL: I'm kind of uncomfortable about the symmetry of SS and PP cores. Maybe this is why. "All balls are figures" seems acceptable to me, but "All figures are balls" doesn't.

PENNY: Maybe you're confusing truth value with sensicalness.

NICKEL: That could be. "All balls are figures" seems obviously true to me while "All figures are balls" seems obviously false.

PENNY: The last sentence needn't be false; if there were a universe in which there were no other figures than balls, it would be true.

We can't be too careful to keep truth value and sense distinct. If a core is sensical, then every grammatical sentence in which it occurs is sensical; and we can expect some of the sensical sentences to be false and others to be true. Auxiliary expressions change the truth value of sentences without affecting their sensicalness. For example, substituting "no" for "all" in the true sentence, "All balls are figures," we get the false, but still sensical, sentence, "No balls are figures."

NICKEL: But I can't imagine "All balls are figures" as false, nor "No balls are figures" as true. Surely that's not unrelated to the order of figure.

ball

PENNY: You're quite right. The truth value of those sentences is related to the order of their core. The very meaning of "ball" and "figure" guarantees their truth. An entity emplaceable in "ball" will also be emplaceable in "ball's" parent, "figure." That guarantees the truth of the sentence, but, once more, that is a question of truth value, not of sense.

This fact about the relation between the truth value of SS and PP sentences and their order is important to note, and we may wish to give some precedence to figure over ball in our search for sense schemas.

ball   figure

NICKEL: Even though the SS cores formed by writing the offspring above and the parent below will also be sensical?

PENNY: Yes, but let's usually write SS and PP cores as parent

                                                         offspring

NICKEL: A touching bit of filial piety.

Here are the PP cores, written in the pious way.

color	color	color	degree	degree	degree
blue	red	green	strong	violent	mild

weighs		weighs		weighs	
weighs-4-pounds		weighs-5-pounds		weighs-6-pounds	

PENNY: Now write some nonsensical *SS* and *PP* cores.

NICKEL: figure ostrich color   red
      love   envy   weighs-4-pounds mild

PENNY: Is goose   a sensical core?
    weighs-6-pounds

NICKEL: Tricky. It's not a sensical *SS* or *PP* core, but it is a sensical *SP* core: goose:weighs-6-pounds. Shall I list all the sensical *SP* cores now?

PENNY: Do something more interesting. List only the sensical *SP* cores composed of parent words. Then give us directions for how to use them to produce some more sensical *SP* cores. What we should move to is a rule, not enumeration.

NICKEL: figure:color, figure:weighs, bird:colored, bird:weighs, and emotion:degree.

You also want a rule for producing other sensical *SP* cores. How about this? Whenever I have an *SP* core composed of parent words, any *SP* composed of offspring of either or both of them is an *SP*. Thus, since "ball" is an offspring of "figure," I can substitute ball for "figure" in figure:colored and get a new sensical *SP*, ball:colored. Also I can substitute the offspring "red" for "colored" and get ball:red.

PENNY: Your rule is a linguistic substitution rule, then.

NICKEL: That's right.

PENNY: Can you do the reverse? Will you get a sensical *SP* if you substitute a parent word for an offspring word in a sensical *SP*?

NICKEL: I don't see why not. The order of parent and offspring words is reversible. Chicken:weighs-4-pounds is a sensical *SP*, and substituting "bird" for "chicken" certainly gives me a sensical *SP*, bird:weighs-4-pounds.

PENNY: Do you think you're on the trail of a sense schema, Nickel?

NICKEL: Huh? Do you think so?

PENNY: Sure. You purported to give me a rule for augmenting some sensical cores with another sensical core, for augmenting the *SP* core, figure:color, and the *SS* core, figure*r*ball, with the *SP* core, ball:color.*

To get a schema you have to generalize. You've generalized before. You've practiced replacing Polish expressions in Polish arguments with

---

* When I typed my notes, I thought it would ease the reading of *SP* cores if its words were separated by a colon. That explains figure:color, as you've probably figured out by now. To save space I decided to write *SS* and *PP* cores horizontally and to separate the words in them with an italic *r*. The *r* is an abbreviation for "rests on," the significance of which will be clear to you in a few pages. That explains figure*r*ball.

variables in order to produce schema rules. Try doing a similar thing with this last inference.

NICKEL:
$$\frac{\text{figure} \quad \text{figure:color}}{\text{ball:color}}$$
$$\text{ball}$$

is the inference which, when I replace the words with variables ($S_1 =$ figure, $S_2 =$ ball, and $P_1 =$ color) yields (1) $\dfrac{S_1 \quad S_1 P_1}{S_2 P_1}$.
$$S_2$$

PENNY: Excellent, Nickel. You've just produced the first sense schema. We now have a sense schema for deriving a sensical SP core from sensical premiss cores.

Are there any other sense schemas which yield SP cores?

NICKEL: Of course.

$$\frac{\text{figure:color} \quad \text{color}}{\text{figure:red}} \quad \text{yields (2)} \quad \frac{S_1 P_1 \quad P_1}{S_1 P_2}$$
$$\text{red} \qquad\qquad\qquad\qquad P_2$$

and $\dfrac{\text{figure} \quad}{\text{figure:red}}$ ball ball:red yields (3) $\dfrac{S_1 \quad}{S_1 P_2}$ S_2 $S_2 P_2$

and $\dfrac{\text{ball:red} \quad \text{red}}{\text{ball:color}}$ yields (4) $\dfrac{S_2 P_2 \quad P_2}{S_2 P_1}$.
$$\text{color} \qquad\qquad\qquad P_1$$

PENNY: Given bird^{r}chicken and weighs^{r}weighs-4-pounds and chicken:weighs-4-pounds, how would you prove that bird:weighs is a sensical SP?

NICKEL: I could use two of the above schemas.

$$\frac{\text{bird}}{\frac{\text{chicken} \quad \text{chicken:weighs-4-pounds}}{\text{bird:weighs-4-pounds}}} \quad \text{by (3)}$$

$$\frac{\frac{\text{weighs}}{\text{weighs-4-pounds}}}{\text{bird:weighs}} \quad \text{by (4)}$$

Neat! We can construct chains of inferences with those schemas.

PENNY: Wouldn't it be nice if we could generalize over those four argument schemas, reduce them to a single principle?

NICKEL: It would be. We'd have less schemas to remember.

PENNY: Let's look for a regularity among the four schemas you just gave us, then.

(1)	(2)	(3)	(4)

$$
\begin{array}{llll}
\text{(1)} & \text{(2)} & \text{(3)} & \text{(4)} \\
\begin{array}{l} S_1 \quad S_1 P_1 \\ S_2 \\ \hline S_2 P_1 \end{array} &
\begin{array}{l} S_1 P_1 \quad P_1 \\ \qquad P_2 \\ \hline S_1 P_2 \end{array} &
\begin{array}{l} S_1 \\ S_2 \quad S_2 P_2 \\ \hline S_1 P_2 \end{array} &
\begin{array}{l} \qquad P_1 \\ S_2 P_2 \quad P_2 \\ \hline S_2 P_1 \end{array}
\end{array}
$$

which can be condensed to

$$
\begin{array}{llll}
\dfrac{\begin{array}{l} S_1 P_1 \\ S_2 \end{array}}{S_2 P_1} &
\dfrac{\begin{array}{l} S_1 P_1 \\ P_2 \end{array}}{S_1 P_2} &
\dfrac{\begin{array}{l} S_1 \\ S_2 P_2 \end{array}}{S_1 P_2} &
\dfrac{\begin{array}{l} P_1 \\ S_2 P_2 \end{array}}{S_2 P_1}.
\end{array}
$$

Perhaps you can see the regularity and generalize over it now.

NICKEL: I could use some help.

PENNY: Look at this square arrangement: $\begin{array}{l} S_m P_m \\ S_n P_n \end{array}$. It contains six possible cores, four of them SP cores: S_m, $S_m P_m$, $S_m P_n$, $S_n P_n$, $S_n P_m$, and $\begin{array}{l} S_n \\ P_m \\ P_n \end{array}$.

NICKEL: The four arguments I worked out all fit into that square arrangement except that one of their corners is empty.

PENNY: Correct. Now look at the conclusion. Do you notice anything there that you can relate to the empty corner?

NICKEL: Sure. The conclusion is the SP core that results from filling that empty corner with the S or P above or below the empty corner. In (1), we bring the P_1 down, and the resulting new expression, $S_2 P_1$, is the conclusion. In (4), the empty corner is filled with the S_2 below it, giving us $S_2 P_1$ as the conclusion.

PENNY: We need to generalize over those four now.

NICKEL: To do that, I guess I'd better use the $_m$ and $_n$ subscripts in place of the numerical subscripts.

Here's a try. If we have any three of the corners of the square, $\begin{array}{l} S_m P_m \\ S_n P_n \end{array}$, filled, as in $\begin{array}{l} S_m \\ \ \\ S_n P_n \end{array}$, we can fill in the fourth, the empty, corner with the expression above or below the empty corner; in the example, we fill in the empty corner with P_n. That yields the new core $S_m P_n$, which is one of the six cores contained in the square.

PENNY: What new core would you get from $S_m P_m$?

$$P_n$$

NICKEL: $S_m P_n$.

PENNY: Good. We can put what I'll call the Square schema in this way:

$S_m P_m$

$\dfrac{S_n P_n}{S_i P_k,}$ where S_i is S_n or S_m, and P_k is P_n or P_m.

If one of the corners of that square is empty, it may be filled in with the expression above or below the empty corner; the resulting SP *wfc* is a valid conclusion.

NICKEL: We're really coming along, aren't we? Shall we find schemas for deriving SS and PP cores now?

PENNY: We have to add other kinds of *wfc*s before we do that.

Sometimes two similar inscriptions or sounds are used with the same sense and sometimes with different senses; and sometimes two different inscriptions are used with the same sense and sometimes not. We make judgments about sameness and difference of sense whenever we read or listen to someone talking. You, for example, probably believe that I've used the sound "different" with the same sense every time I uttered it in my last speech.

NICKEL: I do. Since similarity of sense is such an important factor in communication, you're suggesting we have a general *wfc* for sentences in which we claim that two expressions have the same meaning.

PENNY: "'Pyramid' means the same as 'pyramid'" can be written as pyramid = pyramid, or in general, $S_n = S_n$.

NICKEL: Do similar subscripts, as in $P_n = P_n$, require the substitution of similar inscriptions into both P's?

PENNY: They yearn for identity.

We may also claim sometimes that two dissimilar inscriptions are synonymous, for example, fast = swift. What would be the general *wfc* for such cores?

NICKEL: Being different inscriptions, they would require different subscripts, such as $P_m = P_n$.

PENNY: That gives us three different kinds of general *wfc*s now: descriptive cores, SP; subsumptive cores, SS and PP; and synonymity cores, $S = S$ and $P = P$.

NICKEL: Don't we also have to allow that a pair of words don't mean the same?

PENNY: Thank you for bringing up negation.

NICKEL: You're welcome.

PENNY: When we substituted 1's and 0's into the letters in Polish *wfe*s, the result was that the *wfe*s meant 1 or 0. A *wfe* meaning 1 could be

338

changed into a *wfe* meaning 0 and *vice versa* with the use of a bar on the *wfe*. The bar was Polish negation. The English equivalent of the Polish bar is "not." With "not" added to a true English sentence, the sentence becomes a false one, and *vice versa*. "Not" is the English negation.

NICKEL: So, the logic of sense should have negation as well.

PENNY: That's right. When we substitute words into the general *wfc*s, the result is either a sensical or a nonsensical core. The addition of negation to our symbolism will make it possible to change the sense value of a core, and a sentence.

NICKEL: But it can't be equivalent to bar and "not," for they are truth value negations.

PENNY: Perfectly correct, Nickel. To help us keep the concept of sense negation distinct from truth negation we'll give it the name of "cover"; and we'll write it like this: $\overline{\text{bird}^r\text{envy}}$ and $\overline{\text{pyramid:violent}}$ and $\overline{\text{pyramid}=\text{cube}}$, or, more generally, $\overline{S_mP_m}$, $\overline{S_m}$, $\overline{P_m}$, $\overline{S_m=S_n}$ and $\overline{P_m=P_n}$.

$$\frac{S_n}{} \quad \frac{P_n}{}$$

All of these general *wfc*s with covers on them are also general *wfc*s.

NICKEL: Is a sensical core such as pyramid:blue nonsensical with a cover on it?

PENNY: That's the power of the cover functor; $\overline{\text{pyramid:blue}}$ is a nonsensical core. The cover changes the sense value of a core; it changes a sensical core to a nonsensical one and a nonsensical core to a sensical one. Double cover, or double negation, on a sensical core results in a sensical core.

The introduction of cover reminds me that we should be careful how we read such cores as $\overline{\text{bird}^r\text{chicken}}$, bird^{r}envy, bird:red, ball=ball, color^{r}blue.

A core without the cover, for example, bird^{r}chicken, is to be read as "The core 'bird^{r}chicken' is sensical."

Those claims may be true or false. Bird^{r}chicken is a true claim; bird^{r}envy is a false claim, for bird^{r}envy is not a sensical core. However, $\overline{\text{bird}^r\text{envy}}$, read as "The core 'bird^{r}envy' is nonsensical," is a true claim.

Our subject matter is the arrangement of inscriptions and sounds; we are engaged in an empirical investigation when we try to find the rules of regularity governing the substitution, the emplacement, of inscriptions into the *wfc*s. Our statements about which inscriptions may be so emplaced are true or false.

This seems like the opportune moment to turn to the map-dictionary. I think we're in a position to say how it must look if it is to exhibit combinatory rules.

In turning to the map-dictionary now, we're reversing the Cartesian procedure. Descartes, you may remember, discovered how to give discursive, algebraic, formulations for geometrical figures when he discovered analytic geometry. We, instead, are going to give a geometrical model for what we have done discursively with cores.

NICKEL: That means the map-dictionary has to reflect the *S-P* vocabulary division, provide for descriptive, subsumptive and synonymity cores, and be so arranged geometrically that by looking at it we can decide which cores are sensical and which are nonsensical.

This last point seems particularly important, for that was the reason for the failure of my initial map-dictionary. The Stars of Meaning couldn't help us to decide whether a sentence which had never before been uttered is sensical, nor could it help settle disagreements about a sentence's sensicalness.

PENNY: I'm glad you remembered the pivotal item. Our map-dictionary has to provide at least what the Square schema provided.

To do this we have to arrange the map-dictionary, not as you first suggested, with a star as the model, but with a constellation as the model. We are interested in a regulated geometry.

Here is the general model, a double pyramid, which satisfies those demands.

S_1				P_1			
S_2		S_3		P_2		P_3	
S_4	S_5	S_6	S_7	P_4	P_5	P_6	P_7

You understand that this is a "digest" model. The number of levels in a pyramid has no limits; we have three levels here for that will serve most of our purposes. Also, the number of offspring for each parent is two in our model; there may be an infinite number of them as you can realize if you consider "weighs-4-5-6-7-8 . . . pounds."

NICKEL: "Bird" had three offspring, "chicken," "ostrich," and "goose"; we could list many more.

PENNY: The seven places in the *S* pyramid and the *P* pyramid are places, variables, where words may go. The map-dictionary will consist of many of these double pyramids. Whether ultimately the map-dictionary can be one single large double pyramid with sub-pyramids is unknown to me. At any rate, the map will be made by substituting words into the variable places; it will then exhibit which cores are sensical and which are nonsensical. But, of course, we shall have to give directions for knowing what geometrical features to look at to tell which cores are sensical and which are nonsensical.

340

NICKEL: I can see that the double pyramid gives us the S-P vocabulary division; vertical direction looks to me to mark the SS and PP cores; and horizontally we have the SP cores. Very nice. But I don't quite see what feature of the model provides us with the Square sense schema.

PENNY: I think you can figure it out by looking at the positions occupied by the six possible cores we can get by substituting into the Square, S_1P_1. They are: S_1, S_1P_1, S_1P_2, S_2P_1, S_2P_2, and P_1.

$$S_2P_2 \qquad\qquad S_2 \qquad\qquad\qquad P_2$$

NICKEL: The S and P of S_1P_1, and also S_2P_2, have matching locations in their pyramids; so I guess an SP core is sensical when its two members have matching locations.

S_1 and P_1 are sensical because S_1 rests on S_2 and P_1 rests on P_2. Any

$$S_2 \qquad P_2$$

SS or PP core is sensical if one of them rests on the other. Also, our map reflects our decision about the way to write SS and PP cores putting the parent word on top and the offspring word below, or the parent word first and the offspring last, as in bird^{r}chicken.

S_1P_2 can be gotten from S_1P_1 by moving down from P_1; I can do that, I guess, because P_1 rests on P_2. And I get S_2P_1 from S_1P_1 because S_1 rests on S_2.

It appears that a combination of matching locations and resting on are the spatial features which do what the Square schema did. The relation of resting on, or being rested on, shows us which S's may be substituted into other S's and which P's may be substituted into other P's.

PENNY: It would be useful to generalize the map-dictionary. I'm going to give you some *wfc*s and you tell me how we could tell if they are sensical by citing a spatial feature of the map.

NICKEL: I hope I'm going to be reborn with a caul.

PENNY:	NICKEL:
S_mP_m is sensical because ——	S_m and P_m occupy matching positions in the double pyramid.
S_m and P_m are sensical ——	if either S rests on the other and if
$S_n \qquad P_n$	either P rests on the other.
S_mP_n is sensical if ——	P_n rests on or is rested on by P_m.
S_nP_m is sensical if ——	S_n rests on or is rested on by S_m.
S_nP_n is sensical ——	because S_n and P_n occupy matching positions.

PENNY: Is S_2 sensical?

$$S_6$$

NICKEL: No, for neither rests on the other. In other words, $\overline{S^2}$.

$$S_6$$

PENNY: Can you give us substitution instances for the double pyramid variables?

NICKEL: I'll try.

earth				earthy			
dirt		rock		dirty		rocky	
loam	clay	igneous rock	meta-morphic rock	loamlike	clayey	igneous	meta-morphic

I put in "igneous" and "metamorphic" under rock, though I know they are P's rather than S's, because I don't know the proper matching S word.

PENNY: Under the double pyramid supposition that for every place in the P pyramid there is a matching place in the S pyramid, and *vice versa*, we're not surprised that where "circle" is an S we find "circular" as a matching P; that where we find "dirt" as an S we find "dirty" as a matching P.

NICKEL: This comes from our former remarks about suffixes.

PENNY: It does. Sometimes, however, we find that for a matching place in the double pyramid we don't have an English word, or we don't know what it is, or we don't know what suffix to use to form a word. In that case, we do what you just did; we use a phrase made up of the S's matching P and the S's parent. Thus, igneous (P) rock (parent S).

Of course, sometimes the matching words use neither suffixes nor a phrase. The same inscription may be used in both the S and P place. "Square" is an example of that; we say "A square is square."

NICKEL: I don't always know a matching P word for an S either. For example, for the S "loam" I can only think of "loamlike," though "earthy" for "earth" and, of course, "dirty" for "dirt" come easily to mind.

A descriptive sentence with a core made up of a matching S and P sounds like what my speech class teacher called a tautology. "Dirt is dirty," "The rock is rocky," and "The clay is clayey" all sound redundant and uninformative.

PENNY: They are. Which isn't surprising. Make a redundant double pyramid and you inherit redundant SP cores.

Did your speech class teacher also talk about contrary terms and definitions?

342

NICKEL: He did.   Can we get those out of the dictionary map?

PENNY: Yes, we can.

S_1				P_1			
S_2		S_3		P_2		P_3	
S_4	S_5	S_6	S_7	P_4	P_5	P_6	P_7

The contraries in that map will account for the nonsensical cores. Words in the S_2 and S_3 places will not form a sensical core, that is, $\overline{\dfrac{S_2}{S_3}}$; and, similarly, $\overline{\dfrac{P_2}{P_3}}$.

NICKEL: Those expressions are not matching, nor does either rest on the other, two spatial arrangements which we said yielded sensical cores. It occurs to me that possibly $\overline{\dfrac{S_2}{S_6}}$, $\overline{\dfrac{S_2}{S_7}}$, $\overline{\dfrac{S_3}{S_4}}$, and $\overline{\dfrac{S_3}{S_5}}$, for in those cases neither word rests on the other.   I would say the same of the matching *PP* cores.

PENNY: Good, Nickel.   Would you care to venture a remark about contraries now?

NICKEL: A pair of words in an *SS* or *PP* core, neither of which rests on the other, are contraries.

PENNY: We need the additional restriction that both words are in the same pyramid.   After all, "red" doesn't rest on "weighs-4-pounds" nor does "weighs-4-pounds" rest on "red," but you wouldn't want to say they are contraries like "red" and "blue" are.

We can formulate a Contrary schema in our symbolism as follows:

(1)   (2)   (3); similarly for S: (1)   (2)   (3)

$$\dfrac{P_m}{P_n} \qquad \dfrac{P_m}{P_o} \qquad \dfrac{\overline{P_n}}{P_o} \over P_n/P_o \qquad\qquad \dfrac{S_m}{S_n} \qquad \dfrac{S_m}{S_o} \qquad \dfrac{\overline{S_n}}{S_o} \over S_n/S_o$$

NICKEL: The stroke in P_n/P_o is the sign of a contrary, I take it?

PENNY: Yes. P_n/P_o is a new *wfc*, a derived *wfc*.   It is equivalent to the three expressions above the familiar double line; thus, we could do without the contrary *wfc*, but it serves as a handy summary.

(1) and (2) in that equivalence schema show us that P_n and P_o belong to the same pyramid, the restriction we placed on contraries just now.

NICKEL: And (3) shows that P_n does not rest on P_o, nor does P_o rest on P_n.

PENNY: You'll notice that each larger pyramid contains sub-pyramids. For example, P_2, P_4, P_5 in our standard pyramid make up a sub-pyramid within P_1's larger pyramid. (3) states that P_n and P_o belong to different sub-pyramids.

To make sure you understand contrary *wfc*s, give me examples of contraries.

NICKEL:

color			
red		blue	
scarlet	crimson	cobalt	navy

This pyramid and its two sub-pyramids give us the following:

(1)	(2)	(3)
color	color	red
red	blue	blue
	red/blue	

It appears to me that red/cobalt, scarlet/crimson, scarlet/blue, scarlet/navy, scarlet/cobalt, crimson/blue, crimson/cobalt, and crimson/navy.

PENNY: We might distinguish between strong and weak contraries. If two words at the same level have the same word directly above them, they are strong contraries.

NICKEL: "Red" and "blue" being at the same level under "color" are strong contraries then. And so are "scarlet" and "crimson"; and "cobalt" and "navy."

PENNY: Otherwise, they are weak contraries. "Red" and "cobalt" are weak contraries for they are at different levels, and "scarlet" and "navy" are weak contraries for, though they are at the same level, they have two different words, "red" and "blue" respectively, directly above them.

Contraries are a particular class of nonsensical *SS* or *PP* cores; they differ from arrowʳhedgehog.

NICKEL: Some *SS* cores, such as arrowʳhedgehog, are nonsensical because the words don't belong to the same pyramid, while dirtʳrock is nonsensical even though both words do belong to the same pyramid.

PENNY: That may be right.

NICKEL: May there be *SP* contraries as well?

344

PENNY: Yes, there may. Care to venture some such nonsensical cores?

NICKEL: Sure.

S_1				P_1			
S_2		S_3		P_2		P_3	
S_4	S_5	S_6	S_7	P_4	P_5	P_6	P_7

S_2/P_3, S_2/P_6, S_2/P_7, S_3/P_2, S_3/P_4, S_3/P_5, S_4/P_6, S_4/P_7, S_5/P_6, S_5/P_7, among others, all seem to hold. I think I can summarize which SP cores are contraries. Every S in the S_2 sub-pyramid is contrary to a P from the P_3 sub-pyramid, and every S from the S_3 sub-pyramid is contrary to a P from the P_2 sub-pyramid. In short, if I may be so bold as to introduce a new piece of terminology, the S_2 and P_3 sub-pyramids and the S_3 and P_2 sub-pyramids are contrary sub-pyramids.

Of course, I'm not using "dirty" in rock/dirty, S_3P_2, in the sense in which it is sensical to say "A rock is dirty," that is, "A rock has dirt on it" and I'm not using "rocky" in dirt/rocky, S_2P_3, in the sense in which it is sensical to say "The dirt is rocky," that is, "The dirt has rocks in it."

PENNY: Those are good remarks, Nickel, but now I invite you to observe the following:

earth				color			
dirt		rock		yellow		black	
loam	clay	igneous rock	metamorphic rock	lemon	cadmium	coal black	cork black

I would say that the same relatively placed SP cores you said were contraries are all sensical here. Dirt:black, rock:yellow, dirt:coal black, rock:lemon yellow, and igneous rock:cadmium are all sensical, though some of them may be false. "Clay is coal black" is false. But its falsity shouldn't bother you since you know that the same sensical core can occur in false sentences as well as in such true sentences as "No clay is coal black."

NICKEL: I'll have to admit that those cores seem sensical, all right. What happened?

PENNY: I placed non-redundant S and P pyramids side by side. Your observations about contrary SP cores hold only when we have a redundant double pyramid. Clearly a double pyramid can be constructed from both redundant and non-redundant pyramids.

Twelfth conversation 345

Placing non-redundant pyramids side by side seems quite important if we want our map-dictionary to contain sensical *SP* cores which aren't purely tautological, for redundant pyramids led us to such tautological *SP* cores as dirt:dirty.

NICKEL: Incidentally, do such tautologous cores occur in false sentences?

PENNY: Sure. "No dirt is dirty" isn't true.

NICKEL: But how can tautologies be false? When we talked about tautologies in Polish and Principia we said they are expressions which always mean 1. When we substitute English sentences for the variables in Polish tautologies, the resulting English sentence necessarily must be true. For example, if I substitute "Primroses are red" into "*p*" in "v*p*–*p*," I get "Primroses are red or primroses are not red." Surely that is necessarily true.

PENNY: "Tautologous" could be used in two senses, you know. I think it is, and I also think the two senses are sometimes confused. When we use it of Polish and Principia expressions and substitution instances of them, we are using it in the truth sense. When we use it of dirt:dirty, we are using it in the sense sense. We have to remind ourselves occasionally to keep truth and sense distinct; this is one of those times. Thus, we should distinguish between truth tautologies and sense tautologies.

NICKEL: I take it that dirt:dirty is a sense tautology.

PENNY: Yes, it is. Because people do confuse sense tautology and truth tautology, they are also led to confuse self-contradiction in the truth sense with nonsensicalness. I have read philosophers who say that self-contradiction is a mark of nonsensicalness, of meaninglessness.

NICKEL: And you do not believe that?

PENNY: I do not have to, for I know the two uses to which a "not" may be put.

The "not" in "Cadmium is not a yellow" may be used in the truth negation sense. In that case the sentence is self-contradictory; that is, necessarily false, for we know that whatever is emplaceable in "cadmium" is emplaceable in "yellow."

NICKEL: Because of the sensical core yellow'cadmium?

PENNY: Of course, and that being a sensical core, the sentence containing it is sensical; so, "Cadmium is not a yellow" is a sensical sentence, not meaningless after all, though necessarily false.

Persons get themselves into the confused position of calling self-contradiction a mark of nonsense because they are dimly trying to use the "not" in such sentences as "Cadmium is not a yellow" as a sense negation, as a cover. What they're trying to say is "The sentence

'Cadmium is a yellow' is nonsensical," which, of course, is correct, for cover when applied to a sensical sentence changes that sentence's sense value from sensical to nonsensical.

Once again we see the importance of keeping the concepts of truth and sense distinct.

NICKEL: We know that "Cadmium is a yellow" is nonsensical because the SS core yellow‿cadmium is nonsensical. Putting a cover on that core claims "yellow" doesn't rest on "cadmium" in our map-dictionary, which goes counter to the uses standard English speakers give to those words.

PENNY: This distinction between sense negation and truth negation also saves us from making the following error. It is tempting to say that "A chicken is a goose" is necessarily false because "chicken" and "goose" are contraries. But we can't say that, can we?

NICKEL: Because chicken/goose shows us that "chicken" and "goose" don't form a sensical SS core?

PENNY: Sure. A grammatical string can't be false if it isn't sensical. What should be said instead of "A chicken is not a goose?"

NICKEL: Either chicken‿goose or chicken/goose.

PENNY: Good.

NICKEL: Do you think we should have a special term for sense tautologies?

PENNY: It might prove useful. I suggest we use "battological core" for "tautological sense core."

NICKEL: Do battological and contrary SP cores occur any other time than when we have redundant pyramids?

PENNY: Yes, and that brings us to the other kind of wfc I said I wanted to introduce, the definitional wfc. This occurs when we bring non-redundant pyramids together but bind them by definition.

Redundant pyramids, you'll recall, were those where a P pyramid was formed by adding suffixes to the words in the S pyramid, for example, "dirt" and "dirty"; or where an S pyramid was formed by adding suffixes to the words in the P pyramid, for example, "doleful" and "dolefulness"; or by using a higher S and a P to form a phrase, for example, "igneous rock" and "igneous."

You made a non-redundant double pyramid before when you placed the "earth" pyramid beside the "color" pyramid.

NICKEL: A non-redundant double pyramid doesn't contain SP battologies nor SP contraries.

PENNY: But non-redundant double pyramids bound by definition do contain something like SP battologies and do contain contraries; such cores are in the same relative positions they occupied in a redundant double pyramid. You can see that from the example of the double pyramid formed by defining various kinds of plane figures.

plane figure					a closed line		
curved figure		polygon			a closed curved line	a plane figure composed of n straight sides	
circle	ellipse	other	quadrilateral				a polygon composed of four sides
		other	parallelogram				a quadrilateral with opposite sides equal
			other	square			a parallelogram with = sides & = angles

The pyramid contains expressions which we can use to describe lines. If we can describe a line by saying "This line is closed," the double pyramid tells us the line is a plane figure. This is useful where redundant pyramids are not useful. For example, the S, "square," has a redundant P, "square," but in teaching someone the use of "square" as an S, the use of its redundant P, "square," would be nil. "A square is square" wouldn't be helpful. All battologies suffer from this defect.

NICKEL: But someone might learn the use of the S, "square," from "A square is a parallelogram that has equal sides and equal angles." That is not battological.

PENNY: Right. Definitions almost elude the defect of empty repetition. I say "almost" because you should notice that for purposes of economy, we often use in the definition of the S word we are defining the S which rests on that word. For example, "quadrilateral," an S which rests on "parallelogram," is used in the definition of "parallelogram." That gives us some battology, for upon being asked for the definition of "parallelogram," because "quadrilateral" rests on it, we are given a definition which uses "quadrilateral" as in "a quadrilateral with opposite sides equal."

NICKEL: That does sound repetitive, all right, or battological. But does a definition have to be battological?

PENNY: Not blatantly, for the S in the definition can be replaced by its definition.

NICKEL: If we eliminated "parallelogram" from the definition of "square," "a parallelogram with equal sides and equal angles," then we would have to replace "parallelogram" with its definition, wouldn't we?

PENNY: Yes, we would; and so on up the line. After all the S's are eliminated, the definition of square is seen to be the totality of PP cores from the bottom to the top, for the definition of "parallelogram" uses "quadrilateral," whose definition in turn uses "polygon," whose definition in turn uses "figure," all those S's being replaceable by the P phrase which is their definition.

We can show this schematically, taking this double pyramid as a definitional double pyramid.

S_1		P_1	
S_2	S_3	P_2	P_3
S_4	S_5	S_6	S_7	P_4	P_5	P_6	P_7

The definition of S_3 is given, in the economical fashion by S_1P_3, but in the full fashion by P_1; the economical definition of S_7 is given by $\genfrac{}{}{0pt}{}{P_3}{S_3P_7}$, but in the full fashion by P_1 and $\genfrac{}{}{0pt}{}{P_3}{P_7}$. Let's write definitional wfcs this way: $S_n\Big|\genfrac{}{}{0pt}{}{S_m}{P_n}$

NICKEL: S_m, in the definition, being higher than the S_n being defined, we know S_m is a sensical SS core, the higher S resting on the lower S, $\genfrac{}{}{0pt}{}{S_n}{}$ correct?

PENNY: Correct.

NICKEL: It looks to me as if the top S in a pyramid is without a definition then, for there is no S_m above it which we can use in its definition; and, naturally, there is no P to replace the S_m.

PENNY: It may have a definition, though its form may not be $S_n\Big|\genfrac{}{}{0pt}{}{S_m}{P_n}$; as you notice, not having an S_m above it, its form will have to be $S_n|P_n$.

There is something peculiarly interesting about the first kind of definitional wfcs. I can show it best by the Definition schema.

$$\frac{S_n\Big|\genfrac{}{}{0pt}{}{S_m}{P_n}}{\Big|\genfrac{}{}{0pt}{}{S_m \;\cdot\; S_nP_n \;\cdot\; S_mP_n}{S_n}}$$

All three of those expressions may be derived from a definitional wfc.

NICKEL: Why can't we put a double line in that schema?

PENNY: If we did, then we'd be saying that the wfc above the line is equivalent to the three *wfc*s below the line, and this schema would also have to hold:

$$\frac{S_m \qquad\qquad\qquad\qquad}{S_n \ \cdot\ S_nP_n \ \cdot\ S_mP_n}$$
$$S_n\Big|\begin{matrix}S_m\\[2pt] P_n\end{matrix}$$

You can see, for example, that a definition doesn't follow if we substitute into the top *wfc*s as follows:

$$\frac{\text{earth}\qquad\qquad\qquad\qquad}{\text{rock}\ \cdot\ \text{rock:red}\ \cdot\ \text{earth:red}}$$
$$\text{rock}\Big|\begin{matrix}\text{earth}\\[2pt]\text{red}\end{matrix}$$

"Rock" isn't defined by earth:red.

NICKEL: Definitions are pretty important and basic, aren't they?

PENNY: They are, but not as important or basic as they've been made out to be historically. After all, definitions are only one way of joining *S* and *P* pyramids together. We've seen that there are three kinds of double pyramids: Those made up of redundant pyramids, those made up of non-redundant pyramids, and those bound together by definition.

Excessive attention to such definitionally well ordered words as those used in geometry or algebra or biology or geology, where classifications have been well worked out and a theory is well-established, may lead us to believe there are more double pyramids formed by definition than there really are.

If you take a look in the dictionary at such a word as "chair," you'll notice that the entry really hedges; there's none of the precision which marks the definition of "parallelogram." This is so even though there isn't much doubt that furniture·chair is a sensical *SS* core.

With words such as "chair" most of our use is practical; we make everyday applications. Thus, its sense is acquired most often by such *SS* cores as this:

chair.

We're not much interested in furniture theory, so we don't have a clearly developed pyramid beyond furniture·chair, furniture·couch, etc., though I am hesitant to be so cavalier about it, for I'm sure the Chippendale

Society would want to beat me about the head with a Hepplewhite stool for my ignorance.

NICKEL: So that's where the world comes into my map-dictionary! It's the foundation for the pyramids; its objects are the lowest stones in the structure.

PENNY: Exactly, but should the lobjects be swept away, the pyramids would still stand, for the lowest inscription stones would then be the foundation. A pyramid of inscriptions is thus shown to be independent of the world's referents. The world's referents find their places in relation to the inscriptional pyramids and not *vice versa*. In the beginning was the inscriptional pyramid.

NICKEL: But the inscriptions, being physical entities, are part of the world.

PENNY: They are; that's why we're not floating through an idle dream, Emory. While doing sense logic, we're dealing with combinations of bits of the world. But we're dealing with them as physical entities governed by rules of regularity; it's their regularity that gives them the pyramidal arrangement.

And it's their pyramidal arrangement which generates rules for sensical cores; out of pyramidal arrangement can come schemas.

NICKEL: Are there more schemas than the Square,* Contrary,† and Definition‡ schemas?

PENNY: Many more. We've only scratched the surface. We have SP, SS and PP, $S=S$ and $P=P$, S/S and P/P, and $\begin{array}{c|c} S_m \\ \hline S_n & P_n \end{array}$ *wfc*s; descriptive, subsumptive, synonymity, contrary, and definitional *wfc*s; and all those *wfc*s with covers on them are also *wfc*s. In order to have a complete logic of sense, we need at least as many schemas as there are kinds of *wfc*s, for we want to be able to draw conclusions about all the kinds of cores there are. We want, for example, to be able to conclude that two inscriptions are used in the same way, $S=S$, or that they are not, $\overline{S=S}$.

NICKEL: It will take a long time to go through all of the schemas and find applications, won't it?

PENNY: It could, particularly if we wanted to make you as competent with sense logic as you've become with Polish and Principia.

NICKEL: I don't think we'll have time for that. I got a letter from my parents this morning. They've decided to go to Mexico for a vacation and want me to go along. The offer is too tempting to turn down, and if you don't mind, I think I'll accept. But that leaves us only one more meeting time, because they plan to leave Monday.

* See page 338.   † See page 343.   ‡ See page 349.

PENNY: This is a sudden development. But by all means have a change of scene. We can adjust our conversations to your sudden departure without unduly crippling them. Our long-range aim was to show how logic in the narrow sense can be philosophically fruitful. What with the schemas we've already worked up and the others I'll give you today, you'll have some notion of how logic in the narrow sense yields philosophic profit.

NICKEL: Learning the Polish and Principia rules of regularity finally did pay off, all right; by using them as models we knew what kinds of regularities to look for in our search for a logic of sentence cores. I'm right about a logic of sentence cores being our philosophic profit, am I not?

PENNY: You are, indeed.

We can speed up our search for schemas having *wfc*s with cover on them if we have a general procedure for getting such schemas. I hearken back to where I showed how to get schemas from **Twfes*.† Suppose **.αβγ* is a **Twfe*. We can go from **.αβγ* to $\dfrac{\cdot\alpha\beta}{\gamma}$ to $\dfrac{\alpha\ \beta}{\gamma}$. Now we transform

$$
\begin{array}{c}
\text{*.}\alpha\beta\gamma \\ \hline
\text{v-.}\alpha\beta\gamma \\ \hline
\text{vv-}\alpha\text{-}\beta\gamma \\ \hline
\text{v}\gamma\text{v-}\alpha\text{-}\beta \\ \hline
\text{vv}\gamma\text{-}\alpha\text{-}\beta \\ \hline
\text{vv-}\alpha\gamma\text{-}\beta \\ \hline
\text{v-.}\alpha\text{-}\gamma\text{-}\beta \\ \hline
\text{*.}\alpha\text{-}\gamma\text{-}\beta
\end{array}
$$

We can take the last expression in this transformation chain and get an argument schema from it. From **.α–γ–β* to $\dfrac{\cdot\alpha{-}\gamma}{-\beta}$ to $\dfrac{\alpha\ {-}\gamma}{-\beta}$.

How could we get $\dfrac{\alpha\ {-}\gamma}{-\beta}$ from $\dfrac{\alpha\ \beta}{\gamma}$ without having to go through all the transformation steps?

NICKEL: To get $\dfrac{\alpha\ {-}\gamma}{-\beta}$ from $\dfrac{\alpha\ \beta}{\gamma}$, the conclusion, γ, trades places with a premiss, β; and each of them acquires a bar when they trade places.

PENNY: Good. Apply that to this sense schema: $\dfrac{S_m\quad S_n\ S_nP_n}{S_mP_n}$.

† Pages 259–260.

NICKEL: $\dfrac{\begin{array}{c}S_m \\ \hline S_n \quad \overline{S_m P_n} \end{array}}{S_n P_n}$. I'd better check that against a standard corpus.

$$\dfrac{\begin{array}{c}\text{polygon} \\ \hline \text{square} \quad \overline{\text{polygon}:\text{envious}} \end{array}}{\text{square}:\text{envious}}$$

That figures okay.

PENNY: You might see some confirmation of the legitimacy of the procedure in the following schemas. $\dfrac{{}^*\alpha\beta \quad \alpha}{\beta}$ $\dfrac{{}^*\alpha\beta \quad -\beta}{-\alpha}$

NICKEL: I not only might see, I do see. Since that procedure when applied to the Modus ponens schema yields the Modus tollens schema, both of which are valid, the general application of that procedure to valid arguments should yield further valid arguments.

PENNY: Let's call this general procedure, inspired by the change in mode from ponens to tollens, a re-moding procedure.

Can you re-mode the Square schema?

NICKEL: I think so. Whenever the SP core that occurs in a Square schema has a cover on it, the SP core that I can derive from the premises also has a cover on it: $\dfrac{\begin{array}{c}\overline{S_m P_m} \\ S_n \end{array}}{S_n P_m}$.

PENNY: Excellent, Emory. Whenever we want to derive a particular kind of *wfc* with a cover on it, all we need do is find a schema with that kind of *wfc* among the premises, put that *wfc* below the single line with a cover on it and put that schema's usual conclusion among the premises with a cover on it.

Suppose you wanted an SS core with a cover on it.

NICKEL: I could take the same schema you used above, $\dfrac{\begin{array}{c}S_m \\ \hline S_n \quad S_n P_n \end{array}}{S_m P_n}$,

and put the SS core below and put the conclusion above, each with covers on them and voila! $\dfrac{\begin{array}{c}S_n P_n \quad \overline{S_m P_n} \\ \hline \overline{S_m} \end{array}}{S_n}$.

PENNY: There's a good exercise!

12.1: Find two substitution instances of that last schema.

NICKEL: Once we get valid sense schemas, then we reap philosophic profit when we find substitution instances of some schema. I am led to say that blindly, scarcely believing it, mainly hoping for elucidation.

PENNY: Your remark at least needs correction. Not all words, we said, are "philosophic" words, so not all substitution instances will be "philosophic cores," nor, consequently, philosophic profit. Secondly, we don't go about randomly substituting into schemas. We start looking for arguments when we run into some doubtful sentence. The doubtful core is the substitution instance of the conclusion of some schema for whose *wfc* premisses we then need to find substitution instances. Should we find some premiss cores to substitute which seem to all interested parties to be sensical, we have then resolved our doubts, for if the premiss cores are sensical and the sense schema valid, the conclusion core is necessarily sensical.

NICKEL: Will we substitute some "philosophic cores"?

PENNY: I plan to, but before we start that, we'd better complete our weaponry by setting up some more schemas.

12.2: (a) Write the general *SS wfc* conclusions for the following premisses that yield valid sense schemas. (b) Also give substitution instances of each. We'll call them Subsumptive schemas.

1. $\dfrac{S_m \quad S_n}{S_n \quad S_o \quad \overline{S_n/S_o}}$ 2. $\dfrac{\left|\begin{matrix}S_m\\S_n\end{matrix}\right.\quad P_n \quad \left|\begin{matrix}S_n\\S_o\end{matrix}\right.\quad P_o}{}$ 3. $\dfrac{S_m \quad S_m}{S_n \quad S_o \quad \overline{S_m/S_o}}$

Similar schemas can be made for *PP* cores. All we need to add are definitions for *P* words, which aren't hard to do: $\left.\begin{matrix}P_m\\S_n\end{matrix}\right|P_n$, or, if we replace P_m with the *S* in the matching place in the *S* pyramid, $\left.\begin{matrix}S_m\\S_n\end{matrix}\right|P_n$

I think it will be useful for you to check back on the schema we used in introducing a contrary core when you come to 3 in 12.2, and you may be able to draw more than one conclusion from the premisses in 2.

NICKEL: After I do 12.2, we'll have schemas for *SP*, $\overline{SP}$, and *SS* cores.

PENNY: You can also get schemas for $\overline{SS}$ cores if you re-mode either the Square schema or the Subsumptive schemas you're to complete in 12.2.

NICKEL: And I'll have Subsumptive schemas for *PP* and $\overline{PP}$ cores as well if I make suitable changes in the schemas in 12.2.

PENNY: How handy is the word "suitable"!

12.3: Make the suitable changes in the schemas in 12.2 that will (a) yield valid Subsumptive schemas having *PP wfc*s for conclusions and (b) having $\overline{PP}$ *wfc*s for conclusions.

NICKEL: I regret having to leave prematurely.

PENNY: Why?

354

NICKEL: Because only now have I gotten to the point where you can't surprise me; now I can anticipate what you're going to have me do next. You'll either have me find schemas for synonymity cores or definitional cores.

PENNY: What makes you think there are such schemas?

NICKEL: Huh?

PENNY: We saw before* that

$$\frac{\dfrac{S_m}{S_n} \quad S_n P_n \quad S_m P_n}{S_n \Big|^{\displaystyle S_m} \; P_n}$$

didn't hold because the definition cannot be derived from the three top expressions. Not all substitutions lead to a definition.

$$\frac{\dfrac{\text{emotion}}{\text{anger}} \quad \text{anger:violent} \quad \text{emotion:violent}}{\text{anger} \Big|^{\displaystyle \text{emotion}} \; \text{violent}} \quad \text{isn't valid.}$$

The reason for the invalidity lies in the different ways S and P pyramids may be joined together to form a double pyramid, which is what we do to get SP cores.

NICKEL: I remember we had three ways of joining S and P pyramids; there were redundant, non-redundant, and definitional double pyramids. Is that schema invalid because no definitional *wfc* may be derived from a set of premisses that doesn't come from a double pyramid joined by definitions?

PENNY: That's right. Only if we have a means of indicating the mode by which S and P pyramids are joined, can we tell if a definitional *wfc* can be derived from some premisses. We need a symbol in front of SP cores to indicate the mode by which the S and P pyramids are joined; we need some kind of modal symbol.

NICKEL: I'm good at this sort of thing. How about using a "D" for "definition" in front of SP cores to indicate they come from a double pyramid joined by definition, thus, DSP; and a "B" for battological pyramids, thus, BSP; and nothing for non-redundant pyramids?

PENNY: Okay by me.

NICKEL: Then

$$\frac{\dfrac{S_m}{S_n} \; \cdot \; DS_n P_n \; \cdot \; DS_m P_n}{S_n \Big|^{\displaystyle S_m} \; P_n}$$

is valid and

* Pages 349–350.

$$\frac{\dfrac{S_m}{S_n} \cdot BS_nP_n \cdot BS_mP_n}{S_n\Bigg|\dfrac{S_m}{P_n}}$$

isn't valid.

PENNY: I doubt whether the first schema is valid. Look at this substitution instance.

$$\frac{\begin{array}{l}\text{plane figure}\\\text{parallelogram}\end{array}\; D\; \text{parallelogram: opposite sides equal}\; D\; \begin{array}{l}\text{plane figure: opposite}\\\text{sides equal}\end{array}}{\text{parallelogram}\;\Bigg|\;\begin{array}{l}\text{plane figure}\\\text{opposite sides equal}\end{array}}$$

That is certainly not the definition of "parallelogram" for that definition also covers a regular six-sided figure.

NICKEL: What went wrong?

PENNY: We have too large a gap between the S and P in the definition. That gap exists in the subsumptive core. Between "plane figure" and "parallelogram" there are "polygon" and "quadrilateral."

NICKEL: To prevent invalidity then, the subsumptive core must be made of a word and another resting immediately on it.

PENNY: That's the restriction we need. To symbolize such a subsumptive core we could introduce a new *wfc*, an "immediate" subsumptive *wfc*, such as $\dfrac{S_m}{S_n}$.

NICKEL: What with the $\dfrac{S_m}{S_n}$ restriction and the *DSP* requirement, it's pretty tough to derive a definitional *wfc*; in fact, I can't really be said to derive it without knowing beforehand that some of the cores I derive it from are the results of the very definition I'm trying to derive. Some schema!

PENNY: Don't be so disappointed. Definitions are the products of self-consciousness about language. They are deliberate attempts to bring order where before we discovered there was not much order. They come when we move from the practical, everyday use of language to the theoretical use.

Although we may have a neat logic of sense, we may not always be able to utilize it to settle disputes, simply because some areas of language are not well enough ordered to provide the disputants with unassailably sensical cores for premisses. I recall a place in *Animal Farm* by George Orwell when after the animals have successfully revolted against the farmer and reduced their Seven Commandments to a single maxim, "Four legs

356

good, two legs bad," the birds objected to that maxim. Snowball then proceeded to "prove" that wings are legs and not hands. Now the area of language involving wings and legs and hands is not very well ordered. We could imagine a lot of indecisive arguments. Should the question about wings become an important one, as it did on the animals' farm, there is nothing left but to bring more order into that area of language, and this is the role definition plays. Definition may not be the only way to bring more order, but it is one way.

Definitions are needed because the lack of isomorphic double pyramids breeds misunderstanding between persons. Without isomorphic pyramids people won't mean the same thing by expressions.

NICKEL: In that case, were we to develop sense logic further, we could expect definitions to play their major role as premisses in schemas.

PENNY: I think that's the correct thing to say.

NICKEL: Now, on to synonymity cores?

PENNY: Isn't it about time?

What feature of your map-dictionary will show the knowing observer that two inscriptions have the same meaning, that the two inscriptions when substituted into either $S=S$ or $P=P$ yield a sensical synonymity core?

NICKEL: Those two inscriptions will occupy the same place in the same pyramid. Rather an inscription or inscriptions similar to them will occupy the same place, for those particular visible inscriptions won't be written in the dictionary map.

PENNY: And what feature will show that two inscriptions have different meanings?

NICKEL: Each will have an inscription similar to it occupying different places in the same pyramid or occurring in different pyramids; the latter is probably the most likely.

PENNY: Do the two inscriptions that may be substituted into a synonymity core have to be similar to each other?

NICKEL: No. They may be either similar or different. Sometimes we may wish to claim part=portion, $S_m = S_n$, is sensical, for in "This part of the money is mine" and "This portion of the money is mine," "part" and "portion," though they are dissimilar inscriptions, have the same meaning in those sentences.

And sometimes we have to claim part=part, $S_m = S_m$, is sensical, for "Your part is crooked" and "Your part is neat," said of the part in someone's hair, show we are using "part" in the same way in both sentences.

PENNY: Does the same thing hold of $\overline{S_m = S_n}$ and $\overline{S_m = S_m}$?

NICKEL: Sure. "Part" and "portion" aren't always used in the same way; "a part in the hair" doesn't mean the same as "a portion in the hair"; thus, $\overline{\text{part} = \text{portion}}$, $\overline{S_m = S_n}$, is sensical in that case. But neither is "part" always used in the same way; "a part in the play" and "a part in the hair" show $\overline{\text{part} = \text{part}}$, $\overline{S_m = S_m}$, is sensical.

PENNY: Then two dissimilar inscriptions sometimes may be synonymous and sometimes may not; and two similar inscriptions sometimes may be synonymous and sometimes may not.

NICKEL: Pretty clearly, yes, but if you had asked me if there are two dissimilar inscriptions which are always synonymous, I'm not sure I would have been able to answer you.

PENNY: That is an interesting remark. Do you have any reasons for thinking that?

NICKEL: I'm not sure I can give any examples of dissimilar inscriptions which always occupy the same place in the same pyramid and which occur in only one pyramid.

I suppose this reflects something I've learned this summer; namely, that it's much harder to prove a hypothesis than to disprove it.

PENNY: I'm glad to see you've learned the intellectual virtue of cautiousness about proof of hypotheses, but don't let it inhibit your vitality to start new hypotheses. I see it hasn't so far in view of your last remark, "and which occur in only one pyramid." Why do you so hypothesize?

NICKEL: Well, if I have two dissimilar inscriptions and one of them occurs in a pyramid where the other doesn't, then there will be at least one *SS* core which is sensical with one inscription in it and nonsensical with the other inscription in it.

Take "spheroid" and "ball"; both appear in the "figure" pyramid, but "ball" also appears in an "entertainment" pyramid; thus, entertainment^{r}ball is a sensical *SS* core where entertainment^{r}spheroid isn't; or where ball^{r}costume ball is sensical and where spheroid^{r}costume ball isn't.

PENNY: Here is an exercise that will entertain you, Nickel.

12.4: (a) Produce a schema with a $\overline{S_n = S_m}$ core for a conclusion, and (b) another, different schema with a $\overline{P_n = P_m}$ core for a conclusion, and (c) substitution instances for each of them.

NICKEL: The question you haven't asked me that interests me even more than 12.4 is this: Can we have a valid schema with $S_n = S_m$ as a conclusion?

PENNY: Only if we restrict what the schema is supposed to demonstrate. Clearly no schema will show either that two dissimilar inscriptions always occupy the same place in the same pyramid or that they occur in only one pyramid. Both facts, as you said, must be known before we can say that two dissimilar inscriptions are always synonymous; to know both facts we have to know the entire language; we have to survey all the pyramids that occur in the map-dictionary; this is a matter of enumerating all pyramids, something which none of our deductive schemas do.

NICKEL: What information can we expect from a "restricted" schema with an $S_n = S_m$ conclusion?

PENNY: There are occasions when two dissimilar inscriptions do mean the same thing, though they may not always do so; your example was "part" and "portion." We can find schemas which show that different inscriptions on occasion may have the same meaning. You know what has to be shown to prove that.

NICKEL: We have to show that the two inscriptions occupy the same place in the same pyramid.

PENNY: All you have to do now is find the schema or schemas which express that.

NICKEL: I don't see how we can get a schema which expresses that, short of one which gives the whole pyramid. This seems analogous on a smaller scale to the problem of finding out whether two dissimilar inscriptions are always synonymous; we have to look at all the relevant inscriptions but once we've done that, the conclusion doesn't come as new information to us.

PENNY: There are two schemas we can have whose premisses contain less than the whole of a pyramid. Here's one of them:

$$S_m \begin{vmatrix} S_o \\ P_m \end{vmatrix} S_n \begin{vmatrix} S_o \\ P_m \end{vmatrix}$$
$$\overline{ S_m = S_n }$$

NICKEL: I'd forgotten about definition.

PENNY: There's another schema we can give, but it requires level-ordered pyramids before it is usable. The premisses use immediate subsumption. Between the top and bottom inscriptions in a pyramid there might be a lot of levels, and unless we know the inscriptions immediately above and below the two dissimilar inscriptions, we don't know they occupy the same level; and if we don't know they occupy the same level, we don't know if they occupy the same place in a pyramid. At any rate, here is that schema:

$$\frac{S_o}{S_m} \quad \frac{S_o}{S_n} \quad \frac{S_m}{S_p} \quad \frac{S_n}{S_p}$$
$$\overline{ S_m = S_n }$$

This schema enables us to locate S_m and S_n in both dimensions of a pyramid—vertically by level and horizontally to prevent them from being contraries.

NICKEL: Then there aren't any other schemas besides those two which yield synonymity conclusions for two dissimilar inscriptions?

PENNY: You might try these out.

12.5: (a) Determine if the following schemas are valid, and (b) give substitution instances of each of them. Here's a hint: The solution may lie in non-redundant double pyramids.

$$\text{A.} \quad \frac{\overset{P_o \quad P_o}{S_m P_m \quad S_n P_n \quad P_m \quad P_n}}{S_m = S_n} \qquad\qquad \text{B.} \quad \frac{\overset{S_o \quad S_o}{S_n P_n \quad S_m P_m \quad S_n \quad S_m}}{P_n = P_m}$$

I now invite you to consider Horace Homophone and Harry Homograph.

NICKEL: Who are they?

PENNY: Homophone is the vocable that sounds like another vocable but means something different; "bare" is a homophone with respect to "bear." Homograph is the inscription that looks like another inscription but means something different; "part" in "The part in your hair is straight" is a homograph with respect to "part" in "He has the leading part in the play."

For brevity I'll refer to both homophones and homographs as homonyms.

NICKEL: Don't we also have to consider synonymous similar inscriptions and vocables? They seem terribly important if we are ever to demonstrate that we use or have used an inscription or vocable the same way twice—or more.

PENNY: That's true; it's important to find schemas with that kind of synonymous conclusion, $P_n = P_n$ and $S_n = S_n$, as well as that kind of homonymous conclusion, $\overline{S_n = S_n}$ and $\overline{P_n = P_n}$.

In contemplating our probable success in finding schemas with synonymous and homonymous conclusions containing similar inscriptions, we have to consider the same four possibilities that we considered for dissimilar inscriptions: Every use may be synonymous with every other use or only some uses may be synonymous; every use may be homonymous with every other use or only some uses may be homonymous.

NICKEL: Surely inscriptions can't always be homonymous, for if they were, we couldn't learn a language. Learning a language requires repetition; without it we can't confirm a stab at a rule. Thus, I would say a schema with a homonymous conclusion is directed toward two particular occurrences of similar inscriptions; they may be homonymous on occasion with respect to each other.

Naturally, from the possibility that similar inscriptions may sometimes be homonymous it follows that there can't be valid schemas demonstrating they are synonymous on every occasion; this forces us to say a schema can only demonstrate that two particular occurrences of similar inscriptions are synonymous.

PENNY: What feature of the map-dictionary shows a language contains homonyms?

NICKEL: The presence of similar inscriptions in two different pyramids.

But what feature of the map shows that similar inscriptions may be synonymous?

PENNY: Just the fact that more than one inscription similar to those appearing in the dictionary may occur. Tell me, Emory, are the two inscriptions similar to "bank" used homonymously in these sentences, "The bank is steep," and "The bank forecloses"?

NICKEL: Of course they are.

PENNY: Does saying they belong to different pyramids help explain how you knew they are used homonymously?

NICKEL: Well, the first "bank" belongs within a "geodetic" pyramid and the second belongs within a "business" pyramid. The "geodetic" S pyramid can be joined with certain P pyramids that the "business" S pyramid can't be joined with, and *vice versa*. If they could be joined with the same P pyramids, then we'd have, so to speak, synonymous instead of homonymous pyramids.

I can tell both times "bank" is used homonymously because "steep" belongs to a P pyramid that can't be joined with the S "business" pyramid, the pyramid in which the second "bank" occurs.

PENNY: Sometimes, however, we get such sentences as "The bank is sold." Here "sold" belongs to a P pyramid which can be joined with both the "geodetic" and "business" S pyramids.

NICKEL: Naturally, from just that sentence alone, I can't decide which use of "bank" is intended. If the speaker is careful, he will add a word such as "river" to more clearly reveal his intent. I wouldn't be puzzled by "The river bank is sold."

PENNY: Frequently people deliberately wish to conceal their intent, just for laughs. Wouldn't the world be a poorer place without *double entendres*? Consider "The woman is fast."

NICKEL: That sounds like a line from a college novel of the twenties, and all because "fast," similar inscriptions of which occur in two different P pyramids, may be combined with "woman." And now for jolly songs at the Pretzel Bell.

PENNY: Softly, Emory. We may be near the lair of Metaphor, and we don't want to rouse him before we are ready to throw our net over him, else we may find ourselves the captives.

NICKEL: Can't we just peek into his lair for a moment?

Twelfth conversation   361

PENNY: I'm afraid not; we've got to get you to Mexico and we've not yet reached the end of our sense schema trail, which I can see we had better do soon, for you're beginning to get circles under the eyes.

NICKEL: And my tongue is getting thick and there's a ringing in my ears.

PENNY: Quickly, then, what is wrong with this argument?

Some pineapples are ripe.
All pineapples are steel.
_____
Some steel is ripe.

NICKEL: A Venn diagram shows the argument form is valid, but the conclusion is nonsensical even though both premisses are true, because there is equivocation or homonymy in that argument. "Pineapple" is used as in a "fruit" pyramid in the first sentence, and as in a "weapon" pyramid in the second sentence, as another name for a hand grenade.

PENNY: Re-state the argument using only the sentence cores.

NICKEL: pineapple:ripe   pineapple:steel
$$\overline{\hspace{2cm}\text{steel:ripe}\hspace{2cm}}$$

PENNY: The addition of one more core to the premisses, a premiss assumed in all valid arguments, will give you a clue to schemas with $\overline{S_n = S_n}$ conclusions. The additional premiss, if true, guards us against equivocation.

NICKEL: Is the additional premiss a synonymity core? Such as pineapple = pineapple?

PENNY: It is. Now when we have two sensical premiss cores and a nonsensical conclusion core and two similar inscriptions occur in the premisses, what do you suspect?

NICKEL: I suspect equivocation.

PENNY: The issue we face is this: If you suspect equivocation, or homonymy, then to be able to prove that it occurred, the very thing we need is a sense schema with this sort of conclusion: $\overline{S_n = S_n}$ or $\overline{P_n = P_n}$.

Work with our "pineapple" example and see if you can come up with something.

NICKEL: We've developed a pyramid-oriented notion of meaning, where the pyramid, rather than the word, is the minimum unit of meaning. If similar inscriptions belong to two different pyramids, then they have two uses, or two senses, or two meanings. So if we want to know whether "pineapple" is equivocal, we have to know if one of the "pineapple" inscriptions belongs to one pyramid and the other inscription belongs to a different pyramid.

Let me think out loud some more. If the inscriptions belong to different, homonymous S pyramids, then there is at least one P pyramid that will join with one of the S pyramids that won't join with the other. Using our example, there is some P pyramid, for instance, the "metallic" pyramid, that will join with the "weapon" pyramid that will not join with the "fruit" pyramid. We can then expect that one of the S's from the "fruit" pyramid, perhaps "fruit" itself, will be nonsensical when it occurs in an SP core with a P from the "metallic" pyramid.

I'm satisfied that pineapple:ripe shows me "pineapple" is used in the "fruit" sense. That gives me an SS core, fruit^{r}pineapple. How about this schema? It seems to work.

(a)
fruit (b) (c)
pineapple pineapple:steel pineapple$=$pineapple
————————————————————————
fruit:steel
(d)

(d) follows from (a) and (b) by the Square schema; (c) states a necessary condition of univocality if the argument is to be valid. Since we are led to a conclusion, (d), which is nonsensical, and since we know that (a) and (b) are sensical and that the argument is valid, the other premiss, (c), must be nonsensical. We have nothing left but to re-mode that argument as follows:

(a)
fruit (b) (d)
pineapple pineapple:steel $\overline{\text{fruit:steel}}$, providing fruit$=$fruit and
————————————————————————   steel$=$steel
pineapple$=$pineapple
(c)

This shows us that the two "pineapple" inscriptions are not being used in the same sense; "pineapple" in (b) is not being used in the fruit sense.

PENNY: Excellent, Nickel. Now all you have to do is generalize over the argument to get a sense schema.

S_m
NICKEL: S_n $S_n P_o$ $\overline{S_m P_o}$ $(S_m = S_m$ $P_o = P_o)$
——————————————————————————
$S_n = S_n$

The schema for $\overline{P_n = P_n}$ is analogous, I guess.

PENNY: Righto. You can bring it tomorrow as an exercise.

12.6: (a) Write the valid schema for $\overline{P_n = P_n}$ that is analogous to the schema we just finished. (b) Use it to prove that "fair" is being used homonymously in character:fair and complexion:fair. (c) And bring in your own substitution instance of the $\overline{P_n = P_n}$ schema.

It's just occurred to me that we can probably get another schema showing homonymy. Although different uses may be expressed by similar inscriptions, contraries of the uses frequently are expressed by dissimilar inscriptions. For example, "partial" is a contrary of the "moral" sense of "fair" while "dark" is a contrary of the "hue" sense of "fair."

NICKEL: You mean fair/partial and fair/dark show that "fair" has two different uses because one "fair" inscription appears in the same pyramid that "partial" does and the other appears in the same pyramid that "dark" does.

PENNY: Exactly. Suppose we substitute

$$S_m = \text{complexion}$$
$$S_n = \text{character}$$
$$P_m = \text{fair}$$
$$P_n = \text{partial}$$

into this schema:

$$\begin{array}{ccccc} \text{(a)} & \text{(b)} & \text{(c)} & \text{(d)} & \text{(e)} \\ S_m P_m & S_n P_m & P_m/P_n & S_n P_n & \overline{S_m P_n} \end{array}$$

$$\overline{P_m = P_m}$$
$$\text{(f)}$$

We may be in doubt about the synonymity of the P_m inscriptions in (a) and (b). P_n, "partial," a contrary of P_m, (c), exposes the "moral" use of P_m, which is the use "fair" has in (b). But since we see by (e) that P_n isn't sensical with both the S's with which "fair" is sensical, for complexion:partial isn't sensical, (e) shows us that "fair," P_m, isn't being used in the "moral" sense in the complexion:fair core, and that, consequently, P_m is being used in two different senses in $S_m P_m$ and $S_n P_m$.

NICKEL: This resolves our doubt about the synonymity of the P_m inscriptions in (a) and (b). And we can chalk up another schema.

PENNY: Chalk isn't a permanent enough medium. Carve it on the cave wall.

NICKEL: I'm not going to have a surplus of time to do my packing for the trip, what with all this carving. Understand, Mr. Penny, I don't mind. This is so interesting that I want to get as much of it as I can.

PENNY: I'm glad you feel that way, Nickel. Just a couple more things, then.

Consider this argument, which when spoken, involves homophony:

All capitals are letters.
Some cities are capitols.
_____
Some cities are letters.

NICKEL: Isn't it like the "pineapple" argument? The form of that argument is valid by the Venn forms, and it has sensical premises and a nonsensical conclusion.

PENNY: It does involve equivocation again, but it has different kinds of cores.

NICKEL: It has SS cores, doesn't it?

$$\frac{\begin{array}{cc} \text{letters} & \text{cities} \\ \text{capitals} & \text{capitols} \end{array}}{\begin{array}{c} \text{cities} \\ \text{letters} \end{array}}$$

PENNY: Yes, and since it does, we can handle the proof of homonymy in a different way. Do you see why we can?

NICKEL: The "pineapple" argument involved SP cores; this argument doesn't. Can we prove homonymy by confining ourselves to SS or PP cores?

PENNY: Let's see if we can. If capitals = capitols, what do we know about their location in an S pyramid?

NICKEL: They are in the same place in the same pyramid.

PENNY: If that's so, and if letters⌐capitals and cities⌐capitols are sensical SS cores, what do we know about "letters" and "cities"?

NICKEL: Well, if those SS cores are sensical, then either "letters" rests on "cities," that is, letters⌐cities, or *vice versa*.

$$\begin{array}{ccc} \text{(a)} & \text{(b)} & \text{(c)} \end{array}$$
$$\frac{\begin{array}{cc} \text{letters} & \text{cities} \\ \text{capitals} & \text{capitols} \quad \text{capitals} = \text{capitols} \end{array}}{\begin{array}{c} \text{letters} \\ \text{cities} \\ \text{(d)} \end{array}}$$

Since we know, however, that $\overline{\text{letters⌐cities}}$, by re-moding that argument, exchanging (d) for (c) and placing covers on both, we get what we want,

$$\begin{array}{ccc} \text{(a)} & \text{(b)} & \text{(d)} \end{array}$$
$$\frac{\dfrac{\overline{\begin{array}{c} \text{letters} \\ \text{cities} \end{array}}}{}}{\begin{array}{c} \text{capitals} = \text{capitols} \\ \text{(c)} \end{array}},$$

a proof that "capitals" and "capitols" are homonymous; they don't occupy the same place.

PENNY: There's one possibility not accounted for by your argument with (d) as the conclusion, a possibility which renders that argument invalid.

NICKEL: What is that?

PENNY: You conclude letters^{r}cities, (d) in your argument. It's possible that neither rests on the other, for it's possible that cities/letters. Look at this S pyramid. If "capitals" and "capitols" were both in S_2, and "cities" in S_4, and "letters" in S_5, then cities/letters. This arrangement is possible because of the reversibility of SS cores.

S_2		
S_4	S_5	

In that even letters^r cities even though letters^r capitals and cities^r-capitols, which shows your argument with (d) as a conclusion is invalid. That means your re-moded argument is also invalid. We get valid arguments by re-moding only if we re-mode valid arguments.

NICKEL: In that case, I can just add (e) $\overline{\text{cities/letters}}$ to my premises. Wouldn't that take care of the objection?

PENNY: It would. Now, give me the re-moded schema.

$$\text{NICKEL:} \quad \frac{S_m \quad S_o \quad \overline{S_m}}{\dfrac{S_n \quad S_n \quad S_o \quad \overline{S_m/S_o}}{\overline{S_n = S_n}}}$$

PENNY: Good.

12.7: Give me a sense proof of the core $\overline{\text{letters}=\text{cities}}$. You can use your answer to 12.4, (a), to do that.

That will be a relatively simple proof, only requiring you to find premises that substitute into a single schema.

Let's consider a sense argument now whose proof requires two steps.

(a)	(b)	
puzzles	puzzles	(c)
construction puzzles	jigsaw puzzles	construction puzzles: difficult
	jigsaw puzzles: difficult	
	(d)	

NICKEL: Hmmmm. Would you give me a hint?

366

PENNY: Maybe something will occur to you after we symbolize the argument.

$$
\begin{array}{ccc}
\text{(a)} & \text{(b)} & \text{(c)} \\
S_m & S_m & \\
S_n & S_o & S_nP \\
\hline
& S_oP &
\end{array}
$$

NICKEL: Something does occur to me.   (a) and (c) are a substitution instance of . . . well, here is a proof.

$$
\begin{array}{c}
\text{(a)} \\
S_m \quad \text{(c)} \\
\text{Square} \dfrac{S_n \quad S_nP}{S_mP} \quad \text{(b)} \\
\qquad\qquad S_m \\
\text{Square} \dfrac{ S_o }{S_oP}
\end{array}
$$

$$
\dfrac{\begin{array}{c}\text{puzzles} \\ \text{construction puzzles} \quad \text{construction puzzles : difficult}\end{array}}{\text{puzzles : difficult}}
$$

$$
\dfrac{\begin{array}{c}\text{puzzles} \\ \text{jigsaw puzzles}\end{array}}{\text{jigsaw puzzles : difficult}}
$$

PENNY: Again, except for one possibility.   Suppose the following pyramidal arrangement were the case and that the double pyramid were redundant or definitional.

S_m					
S_n		S_o		P	

NICKEL: I guess the important possibility is the contrariety of S_n and S_o.   If the double pyramid were redundant or definitional, then we would have S_o/P, which means that S_oP, the conclusion of our argument, is nonsensical.

PENNY: By your two-step proof, using the Square schema twice, you proved S_oP is sensical; but since there is the possibility you just pointed out, S_oP could be nonsensical.   This is a serious threat to the validity of the Square schema.

NICKEL: I recall a Subsumptive schema that we might use in place of one of the Square schemas. It was one of the answers to 12.2:

$$\frac{S_m \quad S_m}{\dfrac{S_n \quad S_o \quad \overline{S_n/S_o}}{\dfrac{S_n}{S_o}}}.$$

In our "puzzle" argument, (a) and (b) are the first two premisses of this Subsumptive schema; the third premiss of this schema shows us that unless $\overline{S_n/S_o}$ were the case, we couldn't carry out the proof. And, of course, if $\overline{S_n/S_o}$, the possibility which invalidated the repeated use of the Square schema couldn't occur. With that additional premiss and the use of the Subsumptive schema our proof would look like this:

$$\text{Subsumptive} \ \frac{\dfrac{S_m \quad S_m}{\dfrac{S_n \quad S_o \quad \overline{S_n/S_o}}{\dfrac{S_n}{S_o}}} \quad S_n P}{S_o P} \ \text{Square.}$$

PENNY: That's very clever, Nickel. But I don't think it extricates us from our difficulty.

When we constructed Polish argument chains, did the order or combination in which we used our schemas make any difference to the validity of the chain?

NICKEL: No.

PENNY: Then your suggestion can't be a good one, for if two Square schemas give us the same conclusion that a combination of a Subsumptive and a Square schema does, then they should both be equally valid. But they aren't.

NICKEL: What do we do about that?

PENNY: Obviously we have to know the conditions under which repeated use of the Square schema is valid. Maybe you can figure out what they should be from this remark: The repeated use of the Square schema gets us into difficulty (1) when two S's or two P's are contraries and (2) when we have an SP core from a redundant or definitional double pyramid.

NICKEL: My solution was addressed to (1) only, which isn't adequate, is it?

PENNY: It's not that your solution is inadequate; it's irrelevant. You were to determine the conditions under which the repeated use of the Square schema is valid. To avoid drawing an invalid conclusion by that means, you suggested instead that we use a Subsumptive schema and a Square schema once. But, supposing we were to use the Square schema twice, you still have to spell out the conditions under which it yields a valid conclusion—which it sometimes does.

NICKEL: Well, as you said, we get into difficulty only when we have an SP core from a redundant or definitional double pyramid. If we know that the SP cores in an argument are not from such pyramids, then we can validly use the Square schema repeatedly. For in a non-redundant double pyramid such as this the fact that S_n/S_o doesn't make S_oP nonsensical.

S_m					
S_n		S_o	P		

I suggest that if the SP cores aren't prefaced by the modal D, for definitional, or the modal B, for battological, that the repeated use of the Square schema is valid; otherwise it isn't.

PENNY: That does it, Emory.

NICKEL: I hate to complicate matters for myself, but I am curious to know if *reductio ad absurdum* arguments are possible with sense schemas.

PENNY: Yes, they are. But before we take up that topic, I think we should be aware that we've got enough schemas to derive any kind of *wfc* now except BSPs and DSPs. Our struggle to save the validity of proofs in which the Square schema is used twice showed us they need separate treatment.

NICKEL: Can't the Square schema have BSP and DSP conclusions?

PENNY: No. The double pyramid (above) that invalidated the repeated use of the Square schema in arguments containing a DSP or BSP also shows the single use of the Square schema doesn't validly yield a BSP or a DSP conclusion. Consider this: Certainly S_m and DS_mP are
$$S_o$$
in that pyramid, right?

NICKEL: Yes.

PENNY: According to the Square schema we should be able to conclude DS_oP, then: DS_mP. But is DS_oP the case?
$$\frac{S_o}{DS_oP}$$

NICKEL: I'm afraid not, for S_o/P. And BS_oP couldn't be the case either.

PENNY: Here's another double pyramid.

<table>
<tr><td colspan="4">S_m</td><td colspan="4"></td></tr>
<tr><td colspan="2"></td><td colspan="2"></td><td colspan="2">P</td><td colspan="2"></td></tr>
<tr><td></td><td></td><td></td><td>S_n</td><td></td><td></td><td></td><td></td></tr>
</table>

If it were a battological or definitional double pyramid, would the Square schema hold here?

NICKEL: No. $\dfrac{\begin{array}{c}DS_mP\\ S_n\end{array}}{DS_nP}$ isn't valid, for S_n/P.

PENNY: I agree; it's invalid. But, forgetting that particular double pyramid now, would this be invalid? $\dfrac{\begin{array}{c}S_m\\ BS_nP_n\end{array}}{BS_mP_n}$

NICKEL: $\dfrac{\begin{array}{c}S_1\\ BS_6P_6,\end{array}}{BS_1P_6}$ a substitution instance of that schema, is certainly valid according to the arrangement of this double pyramid.

<table>
<tr><td colspan="4">S_1</td><td colspan="4">P_1</td></tr>
<tr><td colspan="2">S_2</td><td colspan="2">S_3</td><td colspan="2">P_2</td><td colspan="2">P_3</td></tr>
<tr><td>S_4</td><td>S_5</td><td>S_6</td><td>S_7</td><td>P_4</td><td>P_5</td><td>P_6</td><td>P_7</td></tr>
</table>

PENNY: Are $\begin{array}{c}S_2\\ BS_1P_3\end{array}$ substitution instances of the premisses of $\dfrac{\begin{array}{c}S_m\\ BS_nP_n\end{array}}{BS_mP_n}$?

NICKEL: Yes, they are, for we said we could write an offspring word, S_2, above a parent, S_1, in *SS* cores.

PENNY: Can you validly draw the conclusion BS_2P_3?

NICKEL: No, for S_2/P_3. And you want me to figure out why I can validly conclude BS_1P_6, but can't validly conclude BS_2P_3.

One difference between those two arguments lies in the fact that in the first one the parent word is on top and in the second the offspring word is on top. That shows us, I guess, that in Square schemas containing *BSP* and *DSP* cores, we have to make sure that in the *SS* and *PP* cores the parent word is always on top.

PENNY: That's one rule we need. To indicate that we are restricting the symmetricality of SS and PP cores, allowing only parent words on top, let's introduce another kind of wfc, $\left|\begin{matrix}S_m\\S_n\end{matrix}\right.$ and $\left|\begin{matrix}P_m\\P_n\end{matrix}\right.$, the Parent Subsumptive.

NICKEL: Then to have a valid Square schema with a BSP or DSP conclusion, the schema's SS or PP premiss has to be a Parent Subsumptive. And, of course, it must have a BSP or DSP premiss.

PENNY: So far, so good.

NICKEL: That seems sufficient to me.

PENNY: Park your eyes on this argument, then, and see if you still think so. It meets the two restrictions, having a Parent Subsumptive and a DSP premiss.
$$\frac{D\left|\begin{matrix}S_1P_7\\S_5\end{matrix}\right.}{DS_5P_7}$$

NICKEL: That's not valid, because S_5/P_7. But how about a return match, Coach?

PENNY: Only if you come out fighting, Nickel. The BD Square schema is a worthy opponent.

NICKEL: Here's the KO. I think one further restriction on the Square will yield a valid BD Square schema. If one of the upper corners of the Square is empty, it may be filled in with the S or P below the empty corner. The resulting DSP or BSP, for they can be treated alike, will be a valid conclusion.

PENNY: Not bad. Would the winner care to write the BD Square schemas?

NICKEL: $\dfrac{D\left|\begin{matrix}S_m\\S_n\end{matrix}\right|\begin{matrix}P_m\\P_n\end{matrix}}{DS_iP_k}$ and $\dfrac{B\left|\begin{matrix}S_m\\S_n\end{matrix}\right|\begin{matrix}P_m\\P_n\end{matrix}}{BS_iP_k}$, where ——

PENNY: —— if S_i is S_m, P_k is P_n, and where if P_k is P_m, S_i is S_n.

NICKEL: The big problem with redundant and definitional double pyramids is all the SP contraries we derive when we use the Square schema. The Square schema works on non-redundant double pyramids without trouble because there aren't any SP contraries in them. But I think the restrictions we've just placed on the Square schema, giving us the BD Square, prevents us from running afoul the SP contraries. By starting with a lower BSP or DSP and allowing ourselves to move only upward in a pyramid, we prevent the derivation of contrary SP cores.

PENNY: Yes, I know. Do you think that the form which our "puzzle" argument had, when we made the SP cores battological, $\dfrac{\begin{matrix}S_m & & S_m\\S_n & & S_o & BS_nP\end{matrix}}{BS_oP}$, can be shown to be valid by the repeated use of the BD Square schema?

NICKEL: I'm not sure. I remember I said that if the SP core is prefaced by the modal D or B, the repeated use of the Square schema wouldn't be valid. If our BD Square schema is all it's supposed to be, we won't be able to derive the conclusion with it either.

PENNY: That would be a good exercise for you.

12.8: Show that this argument, rewritten to conform to the restrictions imposed by the BD Square, $\dfrac{\begin{array}{c|c} S_m & S_m \\ \hline S_n & S_o \end{array} \quad BS_nP}{BS_oP}$, can't be proven valid by the repeated use of the BD Square schema.

12.9: Using the definitional double pyramid I gave you about "figure," * make a substitution into the argument in 12.8.

12.10: (a) Using that same "figure" double pyramid, give a set of premises and a conclusion which can be shown to be valid by at least two uses of the BD Square schema. (b) Using the collapsing procedure, write the new sense schema.

NICKEL: I'm pining to have you show me a *reductio ad absurdum* sense argument.

PENNY: You're getting quite adroit at diversionary tactics. Even so, I don't mind showing you one.

Let me take a simple case. Suppose we have this argument: $\dfrac{S_m}{\begin{array}{c} S_n \quad S_nP \\ \hline S_mP \end{array}}$ We'll add the conclusion with a cover on it to our premises, giving us the premises S_nP, S_m and $\overline{S_mP}$.

$$\dfrac{\dfrac{\dfrac{S_nP \quad S_m \quad \overline{S_mP}}{S_n}}{\overline{S_nP}}}{S_nP \cdot \overline{S_nP}}$$

A use of the re-moded Square schema gives us a contradiction, which is necessarily nonsensical. Any conjunctive expression containing both sensical and nonsensical conjuncts is nonsensical.

NICKEL: I knew I would complicate matters, because all of a sudden there's something new. We haven't talked about the conditions for the sensicalness and nonsensicalness of compound sentences, sentences constructed with our familiar functors, "or," "and," etc. That is what's involved in your last remark, isn't it?

PENNY: Yes, but it doesn't complicate matters much. We can use the

* Reader: See page 348.

same matrices for the functors that we used before, only instead of interpreting 1 as "true" and 0 as "false" we can interpret 1 as "sensical" and 0 as "nonsensical."

NICKEL: That means we are still making use of the logic in the narrow sense we learned in Polish and Principia; which also means that logic in the narrow sense yields still more philosophic profit.

PENNY: Sweet coin of the Realm, Emory; sweet coin of the Realm.

We have to stop minting sometime soon, for the natural lighting in the gazebo is failing quickly; besides, the natural light of reason also begins to dim with fatigue.

NICKEL: There is just enough of both kinds of light left to illuminate a summary of the *wfc*s and sense schemas, don't you think?

PENNY: Yes, and if I hurry, I may even get in some more exercises. But before I do that I'd better write out a table containing all the *wfc*s and one containing all our schemas.

TABLE OF *wfc*s

$S_m P_n$ Descriptive

$BS_m P_n$ Battological Descriptive

$DS_m P_n$ Definitional Descriptive

$\left.\begin{array}{c} S_m \\ S_n \\ P_m \\ P_n \end{array}\right\}$ Subsumptive

$\left.\begin{array}{c} \dfrac{S_m}{S_n} \\[6pt] \dfrac{P_m}{P_n} \end{array}\right\}$ Immediate Subsumptive

$\left.\begin{array}{c} |S_m \\ |S_n \\ |P_m \\ |P_n \end{array}\right\}$ Parent Subsumptive

$\left.\begin{array}{c} S_m/S_n \\ P_m/P_n \\ S_m/P_m \end{array}\right\}$ Contrary

$\left.\begin{array}{c} S_m = S_n \\ P_m = P_n \\ S_m = S_m \\ P_m = P_m \end{array}\right\}$ Synonymity

$\left.\begin{array}{c} S_n\Big|{}^{S_m}P_n \\[6pt] S_n{}^{P_m}\Big|P_n \end{array}\right\}$ Definition

$\bar{\alpha}$ is a *wfc* where we substitute for α any of the above *wfc*s.

$m\alpha f\beta m$ is a *wfc* where we substitute for f any binary functor, and for α and β any *wfc*.

Twelfth conversation

373

Square schema:

$$S_m P_m$$
$$S_n P_n$$
$$\overline{S_i P_k} \quad \text{where } S_i \text{ is } S_n \text{ or } S_m \text{ and}$$
$$P_k \text{ is } P_n \text{ or } P_m.$$

If one of the corners of that square is empty, it may be filled in with the expression above or below the empty corner; the resulting SP *wfc* is a valid conclusion.

BD Square schema:

$$\frac{D|S_m|P_m}{D|S_n|P_n} \qquad \frac{B|S_m|P_m}{B|S_n|P_n}$$
$$\overline{DS_i P_k} \qquad \overline{BS_i P_k}$$

where if S_i is S_m, P_k is P_n, and where if P_k is P_m, S_i is S_n.

If one of the upper corners of that square is empty, it may be filled in with the S or P below the empty corner; the resulting BSP or DSP *wfc* is a valid conclusion.

Subsumptive schemas: Similar ones for P's.

$$\frac{S_m \quad S_n}{S_n \quad S_o} \quad \overline{S_m / S_o}$$
$$\frac{S_m}{S_o}$$

$$S_n \Bigg|^{S_m}_{P_n} \quad S_o \Bigg|^{S_n}_{P_o}$$
$$\frac{S_m}{S_o}$$

$$\frac{S_m \quad S_m}{S_n \quad S_o} \quad \overline{S_n / S_o}$$
$$\frac{S_n}{S_o}$$

Contrary schemas:

$$\frac{P_m \quad P_m \quad \overline{P_n}}{P_n \quad P_o \quad P_o}$$
$$\overline{P_n / P_o}$$

$$\frac{S_m \quad S_m \quad \overline{S_n}}{S_n \quad S_o \quad S_o}$$
$$\overline{S_n / S_o}$$

Definition schema:

$$S_n \Bigg|^{S_m}_{P_n}$$
$$\overline{\Bigg|^{S_m}_{S_n} \cdot DS_n P_n \cdot DS_m P_n}$$

Synonymity schemas:

$$S_m \Bigg|^{S_o}_{P_m} \quad S_n \Bigg|^{S_o}_{P_m}$$
$$\overline{S_m = S_n}$$

$$\frac{S_o \quad S_o \quad S_m \quad S_n}{S_m \quad S_n \quad S_p \quad S_p}$$
$$\overline{S_m = S_n}$$

Homonymity schemas for different inscriptions (Similar schemas for homonymous P's):

$$\frac{S_n P_n \quad \overline{S_m P_n} \quad (P_n = P_n)}{S_n = S_m}$$

$$\frac{S_o \quad \overline{S_o}}{S_n \quad S_m} \quad (S_o = S_o)$$
$$\overline{S_n = S_m}$$

Homonymity schemas for similar inscriptions:

$$S_m$$
$$\frac{S_n \quad S_nP_o \quad \overline{S_mP_o} \quad (S_m=S_m \quad P_o=P_o)}{S_n=S_n}$$

$$P_m$$
$$\frac{P_n \quad S_oP_n \quad \overline{S_oP_m} \quad (S_o=S_o \quad P_m=P_m)}{P_n=P_n}$$

$$\frac{S_m \quad S_o \quad \overline{S_m}}{S_n \quad S_n \quad S_o \quad \overline{S_m/S_o}}$$
$$\frac{}{S_n=S_n}$$

$$\frac{S_mP_m \quad S_nP_m \quad P_m/P_n \quad S_nP_n \quad \overline{S_mP_n}}{P_m=P_m}$$

These last two schemas also have their analogues, the first one for $\overline{P_n=P_n}$, the last one for $\overline{S_m=S_m}$.

Re-moding

By re-moding a schema with an SP core in the premisses, we can generate a schema with an $\overline{SP}$ core for conclusion. We can generate schemas with $\overline{SS}$ and $\overline{PP}$ conclusions by re-moding schemas with SS and PP premisses. Similarly for all other wfcs.

NICKEL: Plenty of schemas and rebirth there. My soul runneth over.

PENNY: There are several schemas, all right, though if we took more time, we could produce others; but even if we produced others, I'm not sure when we would have "plenty." To have "plenty" means we would have enough to generate all possible sensical English cores. Certainly we would need to add schemas allowing us to generate cores containing relations, for we want to know if such a claim as "It makes sense to hold persons responsible only for what they do intentionally" is true. Here the relation is "responsible for."

NICKEL: That is an interesting claim.

PENNY: It's one made by my friend, the late Sidney Zink, in his book *The Concepts of Ethics*. If you're interested, you might take a look at his last chapter, "Intention." There's good reading material for your Mexican stay.

NICKEL: Thanks. It's growing dark, Mr. Penny.

PENNY: There's still light enough for a few exercises.

12.11: Fred Sommers in "The Ordinary Language Tree,"* a fine article dealing with the topic we've dealt with today, mentions the first three philosophical arguments below. Use our sense schemas on the arguments to check their validity.

1. The first argument is from Gilbert Ryle's *The Concept of Mind*, page 244. There Ryle claims an itch is not a mood. Does that follow from itch:locatable and $\overline{\text{mood:locatable}}$?

* *Mind*, April, 1959.

2. The second argument is also from Ryle, where Ryle claims seeing is not a process because process:takes time and seeing:takes time. Is that sense argument valid?

3. The third argument mentioned by Sommers is from Wittgenstein's *Philosophical Investigations*, page 59 n.

(1) Depression is a mental state.

(2) Depression lasts a whole day.

(3) Understanding lasts a whole day.

(4) Understanding is a mental state.

4. There is another argument from Ryle on page 244, an enthymeme, in which he argues perception⌐itch because "itches cannot be distinct or indistinct, clear or unclear." Complete the sense argument and decide on its validity.

5. (a) Plato argues in several places that good = pleasure. Can the following argument be re-moded to show that this is a defensible position?

$$\frac{good/bad \quad good = pleasure}{pleasure/bad}$$

(b) Does Plato's argument provide us with another sense schema? If it does, write it.

6. Margaret Macdonald in "The Language of Political Theory,"* calls attention to some terminology which is used in classical political philosophies, to such words as "contract," where citizens are said to have a contract with the government, to "organism," where the state is called an organism, and to "person," where the state is called a superior person.

She doubts whether those words are being used in their conventional sense, and suggests, for example, that "person" is not being used in a conventional sense because the state-person is something with which we never converse. Develop a sense argument along the lines suggested by Macdonald.

7. Ryle on page 204 of *The Concept of Mind* claims "it is nonsense to speak of either making or avoiding mistakes in sensation." What conclusion can be drawn from the following premisses?

(1) A twinge is a sensation.

(2) A twinge is mistaken.

(3) An observation is mistaken.

NICKEL: I guess there is enough philosophic profit there for me to go happily homeward and fill in the bank check.

* *Logic and Language*, First Series, edited by A. G. N. Flew, Basil Blackwell, Oxford, 1952.

Now that the ringing in my ears has turned to a roar and my tongue is so thick that I can't close my mouth, let me grunt out a request to end this conversation.

PENNY: You certainly deserve it. You also deserve my thanks for thinking this matter through with me, Emory, for up until our conversation today I hadn't done so. We have both discovered something today.

I'll work up some review questions and have Megan and Benjamin drop them off at your Aunt's house tomorrow.

Hurry off, or you'll have to drive home in your eyeless car.

NICKEL: Good night.

PENNY: Tell Dime I'm sorry we didn't get to privacy of experience arguments. We'll leave that to another summer.

Review Questions

1. Why do we need sense schemas in order to settle doubts or disagreements about the correctness of combinations?

2. What procedure do we use to produce sense schemas and how do we assure ourselves that our sense schema rules are standard?

3. What is a sentence core?

4. Why did we drop auxiliary, syncategorematic, expressions from consideration in looking for sense rules?

5. Give a reason for having made the *S-P* vocabulary distinction. What rules in Polish and Principia are analogous to that distinction?

6. Why was Nickel forced to acknowledge that there are *SS* and *PP* cores as well as *SP* cores?

7. What linguistic rules were needed before we could begin the search for sense schemas? How do they parallel Polish rules?

8. Explain word "families" and the distinction between "parent" and "offspring." (The Contrary schema is useful for this purpose.)

9. Are *SP* cores symmetrical? Are *SS* and *PP* cores symmetrical?

10. How is the truth value of sentences affected by auxiliary expressions? How is the truth value of sentences affected by the order of expressions in sensical cores?

11. Distinguish between sense negation and truth negation.

12. How are we to "read" sentence cores?

13. A dictionary map constructed according to the pyramidal constellation model differs from one constructed according to the Star model. Why are we able to use the former but not the latter to settle disagreements about the sensicalness of cores?

14. Does our account of sense schemas explain how we are able to utter and understand novel sentences, sentences we never heard or read before?

15. What spatial feature of the pyramidal dictionary map enables us to decide that an *SP* core is sensical? A *BSP* core? A *DSP* core? An *SS* and *PP* core? A contrary core? A synonymous core? A homonymous core? A definitional core?

16. Name and contrast the three kinds of double pyramids. Contrast them especially with respect to *S/P wfc*s.

17. In what two senses, sometimes confused, may "tautologous" be used?

18. How is the world related to the sense pyramids?

19. Why is logic in the narrow sense philosophically profitable?

20. Why is re-moding a valid procedure?

21. Why don't we have a schema with a definitional core as a conclusion?

22. Why don't we have a schema proving that two inscriptions are always synonymous?

23. What would be the consequence if all inscriptions were homonymous?

24. What are the conditions for the sensicalness and nonsensicalness of compound sentences formed with the use of the propositional functors?

Thirteenth conversation

THE TOWER OF BABEL

Hee who conntradycts mee is won wyth mee.—Fanebius Perlyng

I HAD told my friend Dime that I was leaving on Monday to go to Mexico with my parents and that Mr. Penny and I were to have our last conversation Sunday afternoon. He knew what our conversations were about so he thought his father's sermon that Sunday would interest Mr. Penny and me. The sermon was to be on the Tower of Babel; he invited us to come to church to hear it. Reverend Dime was kind enough to lend us a copy of his sermon which is here reproduced in part.—E. Nickel]

Dearly Beloved: The text for today's sermon is from Genesis, Chapter 11, verses 1 to 9, which reads as follows:

> And the whole earth was of one language, and of one speech.
>
> And it came to pass as they journeyed from the east, that they found a plain in the land of Shinar; and they dwelt there.
>
> And they said one to another, Go to, let us make brick, and burn them thoroughly. And they had brick for stone, and slime had they for morter.
>
> And they said, Go to, let us build us a city and a tower, whose top may reach unto heaven; and let us make us a name, lest we be scattered abroad upon the face of the whole earth.
>
> And the Lord came down to see the city and the tower, which the children of men builded.
>
> And the Lord said, Behold, the people is one, and they have all one language; and this they begin to do: and now nothing will be restrained from them, which they have imagined to do.
>
> Go to, let us go down, and there confound their language, that they may not understand one another's speech.
>
> So the Lord scattered them abroad from thence upon the face of all the earth; and they left off to build the city.
>
> Therefore is the name of it called Babel; because the Lord did there confound the language of all the earth: and from thence did the Lord scatter them abroad upon the face of all the earth.

So endeth the text.

I have heard doubters and skeptics argue in this way: If the Biblical story of Adam and Eve is true; if Adam and Eve were the first man and woman and the parents of us all, why is it that their children on earth don't all speak the same language as we and our parents do?

The Bible has an answer for the skeptic. That answer is found in today's text. First of all, it tells us that all Adam and Eve's children did speak the same language—"And the whole earth was of one language, and of one speech." And secondly, it also explains that the Lord deliberately "confounded" their language; he confounded their language and made many languages when he found them building the Tower of Babel. It is from this time on that there were many tongues. This is why people have different languages.

But now that we have seen how the Bible provides an answer to the doubter, we must ask why God did this thing.

God confounded the people's language to punish them. He could have punished them in other ways, but this was the most fitting way, for it was a punishment that fit their sin. Their sin was collective impiety.

I say their sin was one of impiety because they dared to set themselves on the same level as the Lord: They planned to build a tower that would reach to heaven, that would reach to the seat of the Lord. . . .

I say their sin was one of *collective* impiety because the fulfillment of their towering ambition required the consent and cooperation of all the members of their society. Men cannot accomplish great tasks without each other's aid.

Could you build a skyscraper without plans? You know you could not. The plans for such a building require acres of architectural drawings, endless and numerous conferences, detailed and precise coordination, not only of the draftsmen and the architects, but also of the architects and construction engineers. Could any of these things occur unless there was collective understanding?

Impossible.

And neither could any of the plans be executed without collective understanding. How can the foreman direct the workers by calling out, "Block!" "Pillar!" "Slab!" "Beam!" unless the workers understand him? Unless they know his language?

Common enterprises require cooperation, dearly beloved, and such complex cooperation requires a common language.

Now we can understand why God's punishment—the confounding of the people's language—fit the sin of which they all were guilty. A great impiety requires a great punishment; and since all were equally guilty, all must be equally punished. What terrible punishment to be cut off from your fellow men; how terrible to be forced to survive in the world without aid and comfort of others! And how equally the punishment applies to all. . . .

There is still another lesson to be learned from the text for today. "And the Lord said, . . . now nothing will be restrained from them, which they have imagined to do." This passage shows God's understanding of the consequences of collective sin. When all consent to participate as the people did in their act of impiety, there is no one left to say "Nay." When there is no one left to say "Nay," the people will do anything they imagine; sin may follow upon sin, for the consent to participate in an impiety of such magnitude shows they are lost to a sense of guilt and shame. There is not the least vestige of restraint left in them. They who have put themselves beside God imagine that their own moral authority is equal to God's. . . .

This shows us another way in which God's punishment fit this sin of impiety. Their own cooperative success led the people to believe they could do anything and that they were dependent on nothing but themselves. What more effective way to remind the people of their dependence upon God and his grace than to confound their tongues and throw each on his own poor resources? We can imagine how quickly the people must have then returned to God and prayed for help and guidance when they were forced to survive without the aid and comfort of their fellow men. . . .

And now let us apply this lesson to our present time and . . .

NICKEL: Thanks for the lunch, Mr. Penny.
What did you think of Reverend Dime's sermon this morning?

PENNY: Your friend Dime was certainly correct in assuming it would be pertinent to our topic, Nickel. I shan't make any comments on it other than those which apply to logic, though.

NICKEL: It does apply to logic, doesn't it? Especially that business about language being necessary for human cooperation.

PENNY: Yes, it does. Do you think we are still being punished? I'm thinking of you and me now, not all the people. Are we of one language, and of one speech?

NICKEL: That's the big question, the one we've been wrestling this summer, for you've continually been asking me how we know that two people mean the same thing by an expression.

I believe our answer has been that we can't be sure. We can get some evidence that we do mean the same thing, but it is always short of decisive; so, I guess we are still being punished, even unto the nth generation.

We can't even have a sense schema proving two terms are always synonymous.

PENNY: Do you think Reverend Dime's sermon should make us change our mind about logic being a civic virtue?

NICKEL: I don't think so. He thought there ought to be somebody able to say "Nay." And a knowledge of logic is supposed to make us effective critics, whose function, if it is anything, is to question and raise doubt about the adequacy of others' reasoning.

PENNY: That's true, but there is another, more profound aspect to logic as a civic virtue, besides the one we spoke of the third day, which has to be considered now that we have been introduced to a logic of combinatory concepts.

NICKEL: What is that?

PENNY: When we spoke earlier of logic as a civic virtue, we thought of it as a truth logic, not a sense logic. We now have to consider whether a sense logic is a civic virtue.

As a first step, let me remind you of response dictors and dia-logic.

NICKEL: "Response dictor" was the term we used to name the different ways we could respond to another person's sentence during a conversation. The intended effect of each response to a sentence in a conversation can be described in terms of a response dictor. As I recall, we said we could, for example, deny, doubt, assent to, or infer from sentences.

PENNY: Good recall, Nickel.

NICKEL: And dia-logic was discourse between persons who are mutually reasoning to a conclusion.

PENNY: By using the concept of a logical response dictor we can state a somewhat different description of dia-logic.

NICKEL: "A logical response dictor" is a new category.

PENNY: But not a difficult one. Logical response dictors are a sub-class of response dictors. They stem from the different kinds of logical relations between propositions. We've discussed three relations rather thoroughly this summer: entailment, which is a relation between premisses and conclusion; equivalence; and contradiction.

NICKEL: Entailment allows us to infer from propositions, and contradiction allows us to deny propositions, so inferring from and denying, two logical response dictors, are possible because of logical relations.

PENNY: That's true, though I think we should be careful to note that any of the logical relations allow us to infer. Denial is possible because the relation of contradiction allows us to infer. To make this clear, it might be a good idea to generalize on the notion of argument.

So far, when we've talked about arguments, we've had the logical relation of entailment in mind between premisses and conclusion. We've said that if an argument is valid, that is, if the logical relation of entailment is present, that the conclusion "follows from" the premisses.

NICKEL: And we also said that if the conclusion of a valid argument is false, one of the premisses must be false.

PENNY: We have said that, too.

If we know the argument is valid and at least one of the premisses is false, what do we know about the truth value of the conclusion?

NICKEL: Nothing.

PENNY: And if the argument is valid and the conclusion is true, what do we know about the truth value of the premisses?

NICKEL: Nothing.

Thirteenth conversation

PENNY: Let's summarize those remarks in the form of an argument table:

$$
\text{Entailment:} \quad \frac{\alpha}{\beta} \quad \begin{array}{cccc} \text{(a)} & \text{(b)} & \text{(c)} & \text{(d)} \\ \text{T} & \text{F} & ? & \text{F} \\ \text{T} & ? & \text{T} & \text{F} \end{array};
$$

and let's read the table this way: We'll let α and β have either single propositions or a conjunction of propositions as substitution instances; and (a) and (b) we'll read from top to bottom and (c) and (d) from bottom to top.

NICKEL: Then α is considered the premiss and β the conclusion? Because the single line is the "therefore" line?

PENNY: Correct. Allowing a conjunction of propositions to be substituted for α allows us to consider the conjunction of several premisses as a single premiss, the conjunction being true if and only if all the premisses are true.

NICKEL: "Entailment," in the front of the argument table, indicates the logical relation which holds between α and β, I suppose.

PENNY: Using that table, we can generalize on the notion of argument. Let this be the general form of an argument table:

$$
\text{Logical relation:} \quad \frac{\alpha}{\beta} \quad \begin{array}{cccc} \text{(a)} & \text{(b)} & \text{(c)} & \text{(d)} \\ \text{T} & \text{F} & & \\ & & \text{T} & \text{F} \end{array}.
$$

NICKEL: Then all we need to do to have a "contradiction" rather than an "entailment" argument is substitute "Contradiction" for "Logical relation" and fill in the empty places in (a)–(d).

PENNY: Want to do it?

NICKEL: Sure.

$$
\text{Contradiction:} \quad \frac{\alpha}{\beta} \quad \begin{array}{cccc} \text{(a)} & \text{(b)} & \text{(c)} & \text{(d)} \\ \text{T} & \text{F} & \text{F} & \text{T} \\ \text{F} & \text{T} & \text{T} & \text{F} \end{array}.
$$

PENNY: That's perfect. Do you see how the denial response dictor owes its existence to the logical relation of contradiction? And how contradiction allows us to infer?

NICKEL: I think so. If someone says to me in conversation, "Abraham Lincoln was the first U.S. President," I can deny that by saying "Abraham Lincoln was not the first U.S. President." My sentence is a denial of his sentence because if my sentence is true, and the relation of contradiction holds between our sentences, then by inference his sentence is false. I have inferentially denied the truth of his sentence.

384

PENNY: Very good.

NICKEL: Let me make the table for an equivalence argument.

	(a)	(b)	(c)	(d)
Equivalence: α	T	F	T	F
β	T	F	T	F

PENNY: Do any of those argument tables look alike?

NICKEL: No, they don't.   Nor should they look alike.

PENNY: Why not?

NICKEL: If they did, then the logical relation between α and β would be the same.

Are there any other relations between propositions?

PENNY: Several more.   I'll give the traditional list: Superimplication, subimplication, contradiction, equivalence, independence, contrariety, and sub-contrariety.

NICKEL: We've discussed two of those seven today; namely, contradiction and equivalence.

PENNY: We've discussed four of them, for we've already discussed superimplication and subimplication, though we've done so under the name of "entailment."   Superentailment is (a) and (b) and subentailment is (c) and (d) in the entailment argument table.   It's often broken up that way.   You'll see why when you do the first exercise I have in mind.

I'm going to add one more relation to the traditional list: identity. It's very important if we're to discover if sense logic is a civic virtue.

But before we go into that, here are the tables for the other relations.

	(a)	(b)	(c)	(d)
Contrary: α	T	F	F	?
β	F	?	T	F

NICKEL: Contrary propositions, I see, can't both be true, (a) and (c), though it's possible for both to be false, (b) and (d).

PENNY: Right.   Contrariety and contradiction are sometimes confused; you have to be careful with them.   "The ball is black all over" and "The ball is white all over," said of the same ball, are contrary, not contradictory, propositions.   Do you know why?

NICKEL: Because if the ball is white all over, it can't also be true that it is black all over, though if the ball were gray all over, both those propositions would be false.

PENNY: Good.

	(a)	(b)	(c)	(d)
Subcontrary: α	T	F	?	T
β	?	T	T	F

NICKEL: Subcontrariety looks like the reverse of contrariety. Here both propositions can't be false, (b) and (d), though they can be true, (a) and (c).

PENNY:

	(a)	(b)	(c)	(d)
Independence: $\dfrac{\alpha}{\beta}$	$\dfrac{T}{?}$	$\dfrac{F}{?}$	$\dfrac{?}{T}$	$\dfrac{?}{F}$

NICKEL: Apparently nothing can be inferred if two propositions are independent; the name for that relation seems fitting enough.

Are you going to give me an argument table for identity?

PENNY: It takes more than a table to specify identity, for its table is the same as the equivalence argument table. I want to delay discussion of identity until we've discussed relations between A, E, I, and O propositions and restated a description of dia-logic.

Let's render the general forms for A, E, I, and O sentences this way:

> A: All *A* are *B*.
> E: No *A* are *B*.
> I: Some *A* are *B*.
> O: Some *A* are not *B*.

NICKEL: *A* and *B* are variables just as the circles in Venn were variables?

PENNY: That's right.

NICKEL: Do logical relations hold between sentence forms as well as sentences?

PENNY: It shouldn't surprise you that they do. We said Venn argument forms were valid, that entailment held between premiss forms and a conclusion form. You also had a lot of exercises in which you had to determine the validity of argument forms by the Truth-table Method, and you had an exercise, 5.3, I believe it was, in which you had to determine which sentence forms were contradictory. And the transformation and argument schemas, after all, are forms. Shame.

In doing those exercises and in using the schemas there was an extremely important provision we had to observe, a provision which we'll see is crucial in determining the civic virtuousness of sense logic. That provision was concerned with substitution into the variables in the forms.

NICKEL: We had to substitute uniformly for similar variables.

PENNY: Hang on to that provision. It's crucial.

If you fail to substitute uniformly into the similar variables in two or more sentence forms, only the logical relation of independence will hold between the forms; that relation is useless for practical purposes, for you can't use it to infer to the truth or falsity of a proposition from another proposition. You can see that from the Independence argument table.

For example, what can you find out about the truth or falsity of the I sentence, "Some books are instructive," if you know the E sentence, "No tides are random," is false?

NICKEL: Nothing. But if you had substituted uniformly into "No *A* are *B*" and "Some *A* are *B*," giving me "No books are instructive" and "Some books are instructive," from the falsity of the E sentence I'd have been able to infer that the I sentence is true.

PENNY: One more example to set this provision firmly in your memory. What did you have to do to show that this Polish argument is valid by the Shorter Matrix Method? $\dfrac{*pq \quad p}{q}$

NICKEL: When I substituted 0 for *q* in the conclusion, I had to make a uniform substitution into the *q* in the premiss; and when, in my attempt to make all the premisses 1, I substituted 1 into *p*, the second premiss, I also had to substitute 1 into the *p* in **pq*.

PENNY: Keeping in mind that uniform substitution into the variables in sentence forms is necessary if there is to be any other relation than independence between the forms, I want you to do this exercise.

13.1: Assuming uniform substitution into the variables in the A, E, I, and O sentence forms, I want you to state for every arrow pictured and numbered in the "Square of Opposition" below which logical relation the arrow represents. The relation of equivalence is not represented, but contradiction, contrariety, subcontrariety, superentailment, and subentailment are represented. Let the odd-numbered arrows represent (a) and (b), going from α to β, in the argument tables, and the even-numbered arrows represent (c) and (d), going from β to α, in the argument tables.

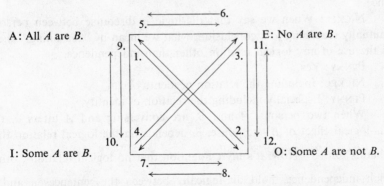

One assumption we'll make in determining the relations between A, E, I, and O sentence forms, the assumption of existential import, is that members of the class we substitute for A exist. If we don't make that assumption, only the relation of contradiction holds in that Square.

NICKEL: Would the whole answer to 13.1 be given away if you explained the effects of that assumption to me?

PENNY: Not if I don't explain all of it. Let's consider arrow 5, and suppose we have A: All books are instructive, and

E: No books are instructive.

What would make those sentences false?

NICKEL: General sentences are false if we find exceptions to them. The A sentence would be false if there were some book that is not instructive. And the E sentence would be false if we found a book that is instructive.

PENNY: Suppose there were no books in existence.

NICKEL: If no books existed, there wouldn't be any exceptions.

PENNY: And if there were no exceptions, what happens to the falsity of our two sentences?

NICKEL: They couldn't be falsified; so, they could both be true.

PENNY: There are those who say that arrow 5 is (a) and (b) in the contrary argument table. Would that still be the case if no books existed?

NICKEL: I think not, for (a) specifies that the A and E sentences can't both be true, but they both could be true if there were no books.

PENNY: So if there were no books in existence, those A and E sentences wouldn't satisfy the contrary argument table and, consequently, the logical relation of contrariety wouldn't hold between them. Such are the consequences of non-existence.

We're now in a position to state a new description of dia-logic. A conversation will be dia-logical if each response to a sentence is made with the intention of utilizing one of the logical relations other than independence.

NICKEL: When we say that dia-logic is discourse between persons mutually reasoning to a conclusion, what we mean by "reasoning," then, is the use of any logical relation other than independence.

PENNY: Yes.

NICKEL: Including the relation of identity?

PENNY: Especially including the relation of identity.

When two persons, A and B, are conversing and A utters α, the dia-logical effect of B's response, β, depends on the logical relation that obtains for $\frac{\alpha}{\beta}$. Now, it's my contention that no logical relations, other than independence, hold dia-logically between the sentences α and β unless the relation of identity holds between the meanings given by A and B to α and to the meanings given by A and B to β.

388

The provision that there are no logical relations other than independence between sentences unless there is an identity of meaning in the sentences' core and auxiliary terms is analogous to the provision that there are no logical relations other than independence between sentence forms unless we substitute uniformly into the forms' variables.

NICKEL: Wait a minute. I thought logical relations were supposed to hold between sentences, not meanings of sentences. And besides, you've got the relation of identity holding between two meanings of one sentence rather than between two sentences.

PENNY: Let me comment on your last remark first.

I was assuming a conversational context when I talked of the meaning given by A and B to a sentence, α. In effect, α is being used twice in the conversation, once by A when he utters it and once by B when he responds to it, even though the α inscription occurs only once. Unless B understands α the same way A does, he won't be responding dia-logically to what A intended to say when he uttered α.

The logical situation is no different there than the single use of each of two similar sentences in a non-conversational context such as this Modus ponens argument:

If psychedelic substances are legal (p),
then we can experiment without being   Psychedelic substances
arrested (q).   are legal (p).
———————————————————————————————————
We can experiment without being arrested (q).

In that argument two sentences, p and q, each occur twice, though each occurrence is used once only. Do you think that argument would be valid if the relation of identity didn't hold between the meanings of the first p and the second p, and between the meanings of the first q and the second q?

NICKEL: Probably not.

PENNY: Then entailment doesn't hold between the premises and the conclusion unless the relation of identity holds between the meanings of the relevant inscriptions.

In both the conversational context and the Modus ponens context, identity of at least two meanings is required; the fact that an inscription occurs once or twice doesn't alter that fact.

You know, I would have thought your answer to my question would be more positive than "Probably not." You can't have forgotten the havoc equivocation, homonymy, plays with entailment. Remember the argument we considered last time?

Some pineapples are ripe.
All pineapples are steel.
——————————————
Some steel is ripe.

NICKEL: I remember now.

PENNY: When we construct that argument's form by symbolizing the inscriptions and not their meanings, the argument is valid; but, as you pointed out, because each inscription of "pineapple" is used in a different way, the conclusion isn't entailed by the premises.

That shows us the relation of entailment can't be based on the relations between the bare inscriptions alone, but presupposes relations of identity between the meanings of the relevant inscriptions.

NICKEL: Isn't that inconsistent with what we've been arguing all summer, namely, that rules of regularity are rules about the relations between inscriptions or vocables, between marks or sounds?

PENNY: No, it's not. Perhaps the notion that logical truth relations hold only between meanings seems inconsistent with our views about the rules of regularity only because you're not clear about the relation between truth logic and sense logic.

The point of my remarks has been that the logical truth relations (other than independence) that we've been discussing today hold only on the condition that the logical sense relation of identity holds, for equivocation tolls the doom of truth relations. Thus, the valid employment of truth logic presupposes inscriptional knowledge acquired by the use of sense logic.

NICKEL: But just as sense logic is a logic of the relations between inscriptions, shouldn't truth logic also be a logic of relations between inscriptions rather than between meanings of inscriptions?

PENNY: It is. When we say that truth logic is the logic of relations between meanings of inscriptions, we mustn't forget all we've learned and conjure up the image of some kind of "meaning entities." "Meanings of inscriptions" is just a shorthand way of talking about inscriptions in so far as they exist in a linguistic system with its arrangement and substitution rules. So that truth relations hold between inscriptions, or sounds, all right, but only with respect to their occupancy in the pyramidal sense system of inscriptions and sounds.

NICKEL: Now I see the point of why you've always posed the question about meaning as "How do we know two persons give the same meaning to an expression?" Unless we have a means of deciding they do or don't mean the same, we won't know if the two persons are actually conversing dia-logically. Two persons can neither deny, infer from, agree with, nor doubt another's sentence if they don't mean the same by an expression.

PENNY: Exactly. So, it may turn out that a logic of sense is a civic virtue, for there is no community without common understanding.

And this above all, no one can say "Nay."

LOGIC: A DIALOGUE

NICKEL: Because the logical relation of contradiction doesn't hold between sentences unless there is a common meaning?

PENNY: Maybe it would be a good idea to consider an example which shows this clearly.

Suppose A says about one of Reverend Dime's parishioners " X is a good Christian," α, and that B responds with " X is not a good Christian," β. Which dictor would you say describes B's response?

NICKEL: Denial, for it appears that contradiction holds between α and β.

PENNY: But what if A meant by "good Christian," "tithes"; and B meant by that phrase "attends church regularly"?

NICKEL: Where the facts are that X does tithe but does not attend church regularly?

PENNY: The facts aren't relevant.

NICKEL: Then contradiction doesn't hold between α and β, because substituting the meanings A and B give to the phrase, "good Christian," into α and β, what we get is:

α': X tithes.

β': X does not attend church regularly.

Certainly β' doesn't contradict α'; so, B hasn't denied, said "Nay" to A's sentence.

PENNY: Do you see why identity of meaning is important to logical truth relations?

NICKEL: I believe I do. But I am still inclined to believe that, though sense logic is a civic virtue, we can't be sure we are no longer suffering the punishment of the Tower of Babel.

PENNY: So am I. Equivocation is the omnipresent natural enemy of logical discourse. We who have fallen from pre-Tower of Babel grace must continually struggle to find out if we are in the midst of logical babble.

NICKEL: And now I am off to Mexico, where by a constant search for regularity I shall attempt to transmute babble into understanding. But I do have one question to put to you before I go.

PENNY: You are welcome to it.

NICKEL: Are you sure you want to say that logical relations hold between meanings of sentences? When I say "I'm tired" and you say "I'm tired," we're uttering similar inscriptions, and it seems to me the two inscriptions have the same meaning. Now if they do have the same meaning, then identity holds between them, which means both sentences should have the same truth value.

PENNY: But clearly it may be true when you say it, but false when I say it, or *vice versa*.

NICKEL: Yes.

PENNY: Which seems to indicate, you think, that it can't be meanings that logical truth relations hold between.

NICKEL: It seems so to me.

PENNY: What makes you think "I'm tired" is a sentence?

NICKEL: Grammarians ordinarily say it is, and so do most of us.

PENNY: Now that we have spent a summer discoursing on these matters and have come to know better, perhaps we shouldn't continue to say so.

NICKEL: What else could "I'm tired" be but a sentence?

PENNY: I see you didn't read argument 6 in 10.4 very carefully. In that argument I claim that such an expression is not a sentence, but a sentential function, because "I" is a variable.

NICKEL: According to that argument, which I'm re-reading, we have a sentence only when we emplace a referent into "I."

PENNY: And since we don't substitute uniformly, for you are emplaced when you say "I'm tired" and I am emplaced when I say "I'm tired," we don't have any logical relation between them other than independence. Those "sentences" have different subjects.

NICKEL: Lack of uniform substitution dooms them to independence.

PENNY: Because the sentences that result after two different emplacements into the sentential function "I'm tired" are not identical, we haven't been forced to give up the view that logical truth relations hold between meanings. This is the advantage we get by having refused to bifurcate referential and combinatory meaning, by treating them as a single kind of meaning.

Let us not bifurcate again in the future, Emory.

NICKEL: I shan't.

PENNY: A happy stay to you in Mexico, then.

NICKEL: Hooray! I'm off, and scot-free!

PENNY: But you'll be logic free nevermore, and just to make sure of that, I want to place a wedge of logic in your consciousness by sending some more exercises with you. You can write them on onionskin if you like—so they won't weigh too heavily on your conscience.

13.2: Supposing the following compound expressions all mean 1, I want you to complete the argument tables by (i) filling in the empty places in (a), (b), (c), and (d), and (ii) filling the blank in the front of the table with the name of the appropriate logical relation. There is a table for contradiction, equivalence, entailment, contrariety, and subcontrariety.

I'll fill in the first one to show how it's done.

$$
\begin{array}{cccc}
 & \text{(a)} & \text{(b)} & \text{(c)} & \text{(d)} \\
\text{1. } v\alpha\beta\text{———} : & \begin{array}{c}\alpha \\ \beta\end{array} & \begin{array}{c}1 \\ \underline{}\end{array} & \begin{array}{c}0 \\ \underline{}\end{array} & \begin{array}{c} \\ \underline{1}\end{array} & \begin{array}{c} \\ \underline{0}\end{array}
\end{array}
$$

You know that if $v\alpha\beta$ means 1, and if α means 1 as in (a), that β could mean either 1 or 0 without changing the meaning of $v\alpha\beta$.

NICKEL: So I would put a question mark in the blank space in (a);

(a)
$\dfrac{1}{?}$·

PENNY: Right. And if you knew $v\alpha\beta$ meant 1, and that α means 0 as it does in (b), then β has to mean ——

(b)

NICKEL: 1; $\dfrac{0}{\underline{1}}$·

PENNY: Complete the table now.

$$
\begin{array}{cccc}
 & \text{(a)} & \text{(b)} & \text{(c)} & \text{(d)} \\
\text{NICKEL: } v\alpha\beta\text{———} : & \begin{array}{c}\alpha \\ \beta\end{array} & \begin{array}{c}1 \\ ?\end{array} & \begin{array}{c}0 \\ \underline{1}\end{array} & \begin{array}{c}? \\ \underline{1}\end{array} & \begin{array}{c}1 \\ \underline{0}\end{array}
\end{array}
$$ I don't know which

logical relation to put in the blank.

PENNY: Take a look at the argument tables I gave you before, and see which one it most resembles.

NICKEL: If the cipher between true (T) and 1, and false (F) and 0 still holds, it resembles the subcontrary argument table.

PENNY: So you can fill in the logical relation blank with "Subcontrary."

NICKEL: Then the logical relation of inclusive disjunction, the relation expressed by the English "or," is a subcontrary relation?

PENNY: Why not?

Now, here are the other argument tables I want you to complete as I specified.

$$
\begin{array}{cccc}
 & \text{(a)} & \text{(b)} & \text{(c)} & \text{(d)} \\
\text{2. } {}^{\ddagger}_{\ddagger}\alpha\text{-}\beta\text{———} : & \begin{array}{c}\alpha \\ \beta\end{array} & \begin{array}{c}1 \\ \underline{}\end{array} & \begin{array}{c}0 \\ \underline{}\end{array} & \begin{array}{c} \\ \underline{1}\end{array} & \begin{array}{c} \\ \underline{0}\end{array}
\end{array}
$$

$$
\begin{array}{cccc}
 & \text{(a)} & \text{(b)} & \text{(c)} & \text{(d)} \\
\text{3. } {}^{*}\alpha\beta\text{———} : & \begin{array}{c}\alpha \\ \beta\end{array} & \begin{array}{c}1 \\ \underline{}\end{array} & \begin{array}{c}0 \\ \underline{}\end{array} & \begin{array}{c} \\ \underline{1}\end{array} & \begin{array}{c} \\ \underline{0}\end{array}
\end{array}
$$

4. $/\alpha\beta$ —————: $\dfrac{\alpha}{\beta}$ $\dfrac{1}{-}$ $\dfrac{0}{-}$ $\overline{1}$ $\overline{0}$

5. $\overset{*}{*}\alpha\beta$ —————: $\dfrac{\alpha}{\beta}$ $\dfrac{1}{-}$ $\dfrac{0}{-}$ $\overline{1}$ $\overline{0}$

13.3: Here are four expressions: (1) $.pq$, (2) $.-p-q$, (3) vpq, and (4) $v-p-q$. I want you to place them at the appropriate corners of the Square of Opposition.

NICKEL: I will have to do 13.1 before I know the "appropriate corners of the Square of Opposition," won't I?

PENNY: Correct. You'll have to know, for example, where the contrary relation is supposed to go on the Square. Then you'll have to find out which of those two expressions satisfies the contrary argument table when one of them is α and the other is β.

NICKEL: From what you've given away earlier about the Square, the contrary relation holds between the top two corners. So the two expressions which satisfy the contrary argument table presumably go to the top corners.

PENNY: How quick you are. So quick that one more exercise won't harry your breakfast trip to Xochimilco.

13.4: Take each sentence below and state its logical relation to at least one other sentence, assuming identity of meaning for all expressions which occur more than once.

(1) A trip across the Styx is not one-way or Charon is a miser.
(2) Some trips across the Styx are not one-way.
(3) If Cerberus guards the shore of the Styx, then Charon is a miser, and Cerberus does guard the shore of the Styx.
(4) Either a trip across the Styx is one-way or Charon is not a miser.
(5) No trips across the Styx are non-one-way trips.
(6) All trips across the Styx are one-way trips.
(7) Either a trip across the Styx is not one-way or Charon is a miser.
(8) Charon is a miser.
(9) A trip across the Styx is not one-way and Charon is a miser.
(10) No one-way trips are trips across the Styx.

I hardly have the heart for it, but I feel bound to give you some review questions.

Review Questions

1. (a) What provision must be satisfied before logical truth relations hold between sentence forms? (b) Between sentences?
2. Why is it possible to use every logical relation other than independence to make inferences?
3. What is dia-logical discourse?
4. Why does truth logic presuppose sense logic?
5. Why is sense logic a civic virtue?

NICKEL: I don't mind review questions. I'm grateful for them; they have been very helpful.

PENNY: Speaking of gratitude, I think we ought to speak more of it.

ACKNOWLEDGMENTS*

If a person has a $500 debt, he knows what he has to do to repay it.

NICKEL: Give $500 to the person who lent it him.

PENNY: How do you repay persons who have given you time, effort, and advice?

NICKEL: Do the same for them. Repay them with time, effort, and advice—but with advice only when they ask for it.

PENNY: It can't be repaid with a public expression of gratitude?

NICKEL: No. That's only like signing your name to an I.O.U., a public performance committing you to repayment.

PENNY: Well, then, I would like to express my gratitude to some people who have made our summer conversations possible and in part what they are.

Naturally, you aren't the first student to whom I've talked about logic. I am grateful to all my former students who have furthered my logical education and were willing to take whatever sufferings and pleasures came our way.

One former student to whom I am particularly grateful is Günter Hiller because he saw in the early approximations to our conversations something useful and said so.

You should be as grateful to Professor Francis Seaman as I am, Nickel, for without his sensible and direct observations you wouldn't have gotten as good as you gave.

* When typing up my notes, I thought it fitting that the last part of our conversation be set apart as I have done.

And to Professor Frank Dollard we both owe much, for it is because of him that there are fewer stilts to prop our tongues from nature's bent.

NICKEL: I hereby acknowledge my share of our debts.

PENNY: Here are a couple of acknowledgments due from me alone, one to Professor Irving Copi, the other to Professor Donald Kalish. I'm grateful to them for saving me from some errors.

Nickel, will you forgive me for those errors that remain?

NICKEL: You are forgiven.

PENNY: You know our typing of your notes recording our conversations weren't as good as they might have been, so I think we should both be grateful to Mrs. Ann Steadman, Mrs. Sandra Hart Hansen, Mrs. Judy Hansel, Miss Audrey Lum, the beautiful Miss Chinatown of 1962, and Mrs. Anita Hotchkiss for their cheery-tempered accuracy.

NICKEL: M'ladies.

Let me put in an unprompted word here for your wife, Susan. I'm grateful to her for the brownies, cookies, ice cream, iced tea, and cold beer she served in the social gazebo; and to your children, Megan and Benjamin, for not bothering us too much while we talked.

PENNY: You think you're grateful to them! Listen! The possibilities of your gratitude are far less, for your debt to them is as nothing compared to mine. It took me a long time to prepare for our conversations; they had to forgo all the things that we normally would have done— playing, talking, taking week-end trips, going to the movies—if I hadn't been studying. And you know, they never complained much.

And now, Nickel, let us put ourselves in the hands of Miss Jean Swift, Robin Dwyer, and Fate.

NICKEL: Ta-ra-ra-boom-te-ay.

PENNY: No sad songs for us. Good-bye, Emory, and thanks for the conversations.

NICKEL: You're welcome, Fanebius. Good-bye.

Appendeletters

Mr. Emory Nickel
702 B———St.
Lincoln, Nebraska

Dear Emory,

Thanks for the post cards from Mexico, especially the enciphered one from Xochimilco—or were those marks answers to exercises?

Now that you're back in school, it's possible you have been following up our summer conversations by reading other logic books—or might do so in the near future. One of the first things that will strike you is the variety of symbolism, particularly for functor shapes.

You might already have noticed that we used my own variety of Polish symbolism. The arrangment rules are identical to standard Polish, but the functor shapes differ from standard Polish. I varied them because I believe my variety is easier to read; by making the letters larger than the functors, which is the reverse of standard Polish, the blocks of expressions stand out more prominently.

The right-hand column in this cipher is standard Polish.

$$-p = Np$$
$$.pq = Kpq \text{ (German spelling for "K"onjunction)}$$
$$\lor pq = Apq \text{ (Alternation or inclusive disjunction)}$$
$$*pq = Cpq$$
$$/pq = Dpq$$
$$\overset{*}{*}pq = Epq$$
$$Jpq \text{ (Exclusive disjunction)}$$

As Polish becomes more widely used, I expect there will be an increase in alternative notations.

The symbols we used for Principia were identical to those used in *Principia Mathematica* except that we used a bar, -, instead of a tilde, ~, and *Principia Mathematica* used dots for punctuation marks.

Here are some other symbols for the various functors.

$-p$ $\neg p$ $\neg p$ $\bar{p}$ The bar above the letter is not a cover, but a truth negation.

$.pq$ $p \land q$ $p \& q$ Sometimes no symbol for this functor is used; the absence of a binary functor where there ought to be one if the expression is to be well-formed is an indication that "and" is the functor. Of course, this is permitted only in Principia symbolism, a symbolism which uses punctuation marks, for in Polish symbolism we need all the binary functors because they also serve as punctuation marks.

$*pq$ $p{\rightarrow}q$
$\overset{*}{*}pq$ $p{\leftrightarrow}q$ $p{\sim}q$
$/pq$ $p|q$
vpq

This functor mark is the most stable, being used almost universally in Principia symbolisms; however, sometimes no symbol for this functor is used, which is analogous to those symbolisms noted above where no symbol for "and" is used. One could choose, of course, to "symbolize" $\supset$ by not using a symbol, or $\equiv$, though I know of no one who does. For an obvious reason, no more than one functor can be "symbolized" by using no mark.

The gazebo wasn't used much after you left. Perhaps we might enliven it with conversation again next summer by talking further on combinatory logic.

Cordially,
Max P.

Mr. Max Penny
San Francisco, Calif.

Dear Mr. Penny,

Thanks very much for the letter on alternative symbolisms. I have done some more work in logic since I got your letter and found your cipher useful.

For that kind service I would like to repay you in kind.

I've indexed the meta-Polish rules strung throughout our conversations and exercises, giving the page number where they occur in their most complete form. You'll notice that some rules occur in the answers to exercises which I've also sent along because they might be useful to other students.

I've left blanks in all of the rules that are answers to exercises.

And don't worry Mr. Penny, if anyone writes and asks me how to fill in the blanks in those rules, I won't answer them other than to say that there is so much pleasure to be gained in trying to complete the meta-Polish rules oneself that it would be masochistic of me to fill in the blanks for them.

I often think back fondly to those loquacious days we spent in your gazebo and hope we can meet there again next summer to add to the calculus of combinatory concepts.

Respectfully yours,
Emory

P.S. The knicker-clad calculus of combinatory concepts is displayed on pages 373–375.

Answers to exercises

1.6. 1. $\times 15\ 9$

3. $= \times 5\ 4 \div 40\ 2$

5. $= \times 7\ 2 + 6 \times 4\ 2$

$1'.\ (4 \div 2)$

$2'.\ [7 \times (4 + 2)]$

$5'.\ \{9 = [(3 + 3) + 3]\}$

1.8. 1.d.   3.a.

1.9. 1. $(-p \cdot q)$

3. $[-(q \cdot p) \supset r]$

5. $[(p \supset q) \equiv (q \supset p)]$

7. $\{(p \vee q) \cdot [(q \supset r) \cdot p]\}$

$1'.\ *pq$

$3'.\ \overset{*}{*} \cdot pq \cdot qp$

$5'.\ \overset{*}{*} - p \cdot qp$

$7'.\ \cdot \vee pq \vee r \vee pq$

2.3. (Expressions on page 25)

1. 100

   $*pq$

3. 1000

   $*-qp$

7. 1100

   $-\overset{*}{*}rp$

9. 20100

   $*q \vee pr$

12. 2210000

   $-\vee \vee pr - q$

13. 2100100

   $\vee \cdot pq * qr$

$2'.\ 110\ 1\ 01$

   $-(p \supset q)$

$4'.\ 110\ 1\ 001$

   $-(p \supset -r)$

$8'.\ 210\ 1\ 01202$

   $[(q \supset r) \vee p]$

$14'.\ 22110101210\ 1\ 0012$

   $-[-(q \cdot p) \vee (q \supset -r)]$

Po-2

2.4. 1. Letters: Each letter has an expression strength of (a)_____.

2. Bar: A bar has the (b)_____strength as the vocabulary item immediately to its (c)_____.

3. Binary functors: A binary functor has a strength (d)_____ greater than the (e)_____strength of the (f)_____vocabulary items immediately to its (g)_____that have not previously been (h)_____to determine a (i)_____'s strength.

Pr-2

1. Letters: Each letter . . .

2. Bar: A bar has . . .

3. Binary functors: A binary functor has a strength (d)_____ greater than the (e)_____vocabulary item immediately to its (f)_____or (g)_____.

4. Punctuation marks: The (h)_____vocabulary item to the (i)_____ of a (j)_____functor and the (k)_____vocabulary item to the (l)_____of (m)_____functor that have not previously been assigned a strength shall each be assigned a strength (n)_____to the strength of that (o)_____functor, providing that the (p)_____ functor has not previously been used to (q)_____any vocabulary item's strength.

2.5. 1. $\{[(p \supset r) \vee q] \cdot [-(p \cdot q) \cdot r]\}$

4. $-(p \cdot -[-\{-[(p \equiv q) \cdot r] \supset p\} \vee q]])$

$2'.\ -*-p**qp*pr$

$4'.\ -\vee *\vee \vee pq - qrp$

3.1. 1. 321000211000
    . v*prq.−.pqr

4. 550443322100000
    −.p−v−*−. ⚹pqrpq

1′. 3210 1 01 2 110 1 012 3 03
    { [(p ⊃ p) ⊃ −(q ≡ q)] ⊃ p}

3′. 4210 1 01202 4 303210 1 0 120234
    [[(q ⊃ p)∨r] ⊃ {p . [(q ≡ r) . p]}]]

3.3. Many of these sentences may be made unambiguous and true in several ways.

    a. "English" is a word in English.

    a. "English" is a word in " 'English'." (Literally in)

Remember that e. is to be so altered that it becomes a *true* sentence.

3.5. Argument a. is supposed to prove the invalidity of 5. But are all the premisses true?

Argument c. is supposed to prove the invalidity of 6. But do you *know* that all the premisses are true, or that the conclusion is false?

3.6. (i)

1. Some (____) are not / ____ /

    All) ____ (are / ____ /

    ――――――――

    (No)) ____ (are (____)

3. No (____) are / ____ /

    All / ____ / are) ____ (

    ――――――――

    No (____) are) ____ (

5. Some / ____ / are) ____ (

    No (____) are) ____ (

    ――――――――

    Some (____) are not / ____ /

4.2.

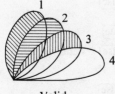

a.   Valid

c.   Invalid

d.   Invalid

4.3.

Valid

4.5. a. We see that in substituting the first premiss, the conclusion is given by one of its asterisks, the asterisk in the overlap of 1 and 3. But we have to get rid of the asterisk in 1.

This shading eliminates the unwanted asterisk and provides the other premiss.

d. To read the conclusion from a Venn form we need an asterisk. The substitution of our first premiss does not provide one; hence, our second premiss must be a "some" premiss.

This placement of an asterisk would give us our conclusion.

We could get an asterisk in that place and only that place by the following premiss, for the left-most asterisk is shaded out by the first premiss.

Remember that in a syllogism there are three possible relationships: 1 and 2; 1 and 3; 2 and 3. If the two premisses state, for example, the relationships 1 and 2, and 2 and 3, the conclusion will state relationship 1 and 3.

5.1. 1. /true/ if and only if (false) =)false(

   not (false) = {true} Valid

   _____

   not /true/ = [false]

3. If /false/ then (false) = {true}

   /false/ and)____(= [false] Valid

   _____

   (false) = (false)

8. If (true) then /true/ = {true}

   If /true/ then)false(= [false] Valid

   _____

   If not)false(then not (true) = ⟦false⟧

9. not (false) or /false/ $\qquad$ =)true(

   not /false/ $\qquad$ = {true} $\quad$ Invalid

   _____

   (false) $\qquad$ = (false)

5.3. 1. Contradictory $\quad$ 2. Contradictory $\quad$ 3. Contradictory

5.4. 1. Any of the following forms for the conclusion would constitute a valid argument from those premises.

   a. (⎯⎯⎯) $\quad$ b. ⟦⎯⎯⎯⟧ $\quad$ c. {⎯⎯⎯} and ⟦⎯⎯⎯⟧

5.5. 1. Even: If /true/ and (true), then)false($\quad$ = {false}

   Odd: (true) $\qquad\qquad\qquad\qquad$ = (true)

   Even: /true/ $\qquad\qquad\qquad\qquad$ = /true/ $\quad$ Valid

   Odd:)false($\qquad\qquad\qquad\qquad$ =)false(

   3. Even: /⎯⎯⎯/ and (⎯⎯⎯)

   Odd: If (⎯⎯⎯), then)⎯⎯⎯(

   Even: ⟦⎯⎯⎯⟧ $\qquad\qquad\qquad\qquad$ Valid

   Odd: If ⟦⎯⎯⎯⟧ and)⎯⎯⎯(, then {⎯⎯⎯}

   Even: /⎯⎯⎯/ and {⎯⎯⎯}

6.1. 1. $p*q$
   $\alpha f \beta$

1′. $(\supset pq)$
   $mf\ \alpha\beta m$

4. $*p\lor qr \cdot p$
   $\quad f\alpha\beta$
   $\dfrac{f\alpha\ \ \beta}{\alpha\ \ \ \ f\beta}$

4′. $[(p\cdot q)\lor rq]$
   $\quad m\alpha f\beta m$
   $\dfrac{}{m\ \ \alpha\ \ \ f\beta}$

7. $**pq\cdot qp$
   $\quad f\alpha\beta f\alpha\beta$
   $\dfrac{}{f\ \ \alpha\ \ \ \beta}$

5′. $[p\supset(\equiv p\cdot q)]$
   $\quad\quad \alpha f\beta m$
   $\dfrac{}{m\alpha f m f\ \ \beta\ \ m}$

9. $\cdot\lor*p\lor qr\lor\cdot* \ qr\cdot qq\cdot pr*pq$
   $\quad f\alpha\beta\ \ f\ \alpha\beta f\alpha\beta f\alpha\beta f\alpha\beta$
   $\dfrac{f\alpha\ \ \beta\ \ \ f\ \ \alpha\ \ \ \ \beta}{\dfrac{f\ \ \ \alpha\ \ \ \ \ \ \ \beta}{\dfrac{f\ \ \ \alpha\ \ \ \ \ \ \ \beta}{f\ \ \ \ \ \ \alpha\ \ \ \ \ \ \ \ \ \ \ \beta}}}$

7′. $\{\,[\,(p\supset q)\cdot(q\ r)]\supset(p\supset r)\,\}$
   $\quad m\alpha f\ \beta m\qquad\qquad m\alpha f\beta m$
   $\dfrac{m\ \ \alpha\ \ \ \ f\ \beta\qquad m\ \ \ \alpha}{\dfrac{m\qquad\quad \alpha\qquad\qquad \alpha\ \ f\ \ \ \ \ \beta\ \ m}{\beta}}$

6.3.   Po-3

1. α is a (a)_____where we (b)_____for α any Polish (c)_____.
2. *f*αβ is a *wfe* where we (d)_____for *f* any Polish (e)_____
   (f)_____, for α any (g)_____, and for β any (h)_____.
3. −α is a *wfe* where we (i)_____for (j)_____any (k)_____.

        Pr-3

1. α is a *wfe* where we (a)_____for α any Principia (b)_____.
2. *m*α*f*β*m* is a *wfe* where we (c)_____for *f* any Principia (d)_____
   (e)_____, for α any (f)_____, for β any (g)_____, and for
   the *m*'s (h)_____(i)_____, where the (j)_____(k)_____
   are

   (i) (l)_____if *f* has a strength which is a number belonging to the
       series 4n-3 (where we substitute for *n* the natural numbers);
   (ii) (m)_____if *f* has a strength which is a number belonging to
        the series (n)_____;
   (iii) (o)_____if *f* has a strength . . . . the series (p)_____;
   (iv) (q)_____if *f* has a strength . . . . the series (r)_____.
3. −α is a *wfe* . . .

Our rules for Principia would be simpler if we employed only
parentheses for punctuation marks. On the other hand, we would lose
some ease in reading when the expression gains in length; for example,
$(p \lor (((p \supset q) \cdot r) \lor (q \cdot p)))$.

Another convention for punctuating is found in some books; they
employ dots to distinguish *wfe*s. Here is a sample of two equivalent
expressions: $\dfrac{\{[\,(\,q \supset p)\lor r\,]\,\supset p\}}{q \supset p \,.\, \lor \,.\, r :\, \supset :\, p}$. Here the number of dots on each side
of a binary functor is one less than the strength of the functor. In such
notations, the binary functor dot is usually not written; the strength of
the missing dot is indicated by putting in its place the number of
dots less one than the strength of the binary functor. This notation
is discussed in *Symbolic Logic* by C. I. Lewis and C. H. Langford,
Appendix I.

6.4. Cipher from Polish to Principia   Po-4

1. Substitution Rules
   a. Letters: "*p*" is substituted for "*p*"; . . .
   b. Binary functors: "⊃" is substituted for "*"; . . .
   c. Monary functors: . . .
   where substitution instances have the (a)_____expression strength
   as the expressions for which they are (b)_____.
2. Arrangement Rules.
   a. Every Polish expression whose form is *f*αβ becomes a Principia
      expression whose form is (c)_____.
   b. Every Polish expression whose form is −α becomes a Principia
      expression whose form is (d)_____.

Cipher from Principia to Polish   Pr-4

1. Substitution Rules

7.1.   Po-5
1. Referential meanings of letters: Every Polish letter means (a)_____ or (b)_____.
2. a. The referential meaning of a ∨ expression, ∨αβ, is (c)_____when α is 0 and β is 0; in all other cases the ∨ expression means (d)_____.
   b. The referential meaning of an ast expression, *αβ, is (e)_____ when α is 1 and β is 0; in all other cases the ast expression means (f)_____.
   c. The referential meaning of a dot expression, .αβ, . . .
   d. The referential meaning of a double ast expression, ⁑αβ, . . .
3. The referential meaning of a −α expression is (g)_____when α means 1, and (h)_____when α means (i)_____.

7.2. 1. .−pq   1'. (p⊃q)
            0011   1 1 1
            1101   0 1 1
            0010   1 0 0
            0100   0 1 0

3. *−.qpr   3'. [(p.q)≡(q.p)]   5. ⁑*pq*qp   5'. [−p≡(q.p)]
   101111   111 1 111   1111111   01 0 111
   110011   001 1 100   0101010   10 0 100
   110101   100 1 001   0010101   01 1 001
   110001   000 1 000   1100100   10 0 000
   101110
   010010
   010100
   010000

7.3.   Po-6
1. α is a Polish *wfe*10 where we substitute for α (a)_____or (b)_____.
2. γfαβ is a Polish *wfe*10 where we substitute for f a Polish (c)_____ (d)_____, for α and β (e)_____, and for γ a (f)_____or (g)_____in accordance with Po-(h)_____.
3. γ−α is a Polish *wfe*10 where we substitute for α a (i)_____and for γ a (j)_____or (k)_____in accordance with Po-(l)_____.

7.5. (a) #pp   (c) $rq   (e) %qr   (f) ⁑pq
         ∨p−p   ∨r−q   ∨−∨q−q−r   .*pq*qp   } Reduce further.
                                             ∨.pq.−p−q

7.6.   1. T   8. C   15. T   21. T
                      2. T   9. T   16. T   22. T
                      3. C   10. T   17. C   23. T
                      4. T   11. I   18. C   24. T
                      5. T   12. C   19. T   25. C
                      6. T   13. I   20. T   26. T
                      7. T   14. T

8.2.

$$\begin{array}{l} p \\ \text{Double Bar—16:} \quad \overline{\overline{\alpha}} \\ \qquad \overline{--\alpha} \\ \qquad --p \end{array}$$

$$\begin{array}{l} \text{Vee Com—3:} \quad \begin{array}{l} \text{v}pq \\ \overline{\text{v}\alpha\beta} \\ \overline{\text{v}\beta\alpha} \\ \text{v}qp \end{array} \end{array}$$

$$\begin{array}{l} \text{.}p\text{.}qr \\ \text{Dot Assoc.—8:} \quad \text{.}\alpha\text{.}\beta\gamma \\ \qquad \text{..}\alpha\beta\gamma \\ \qquad \text{..}pqr \end{array}$$

$$\begin{array}{l} \text{.}p\text{v}qr \\ \text{Dist—19:} \quad \text{.}\alpha\text{v}\beta\gamma \\ \qquad \text{v.}\alpha\beta\text{.}\alpha\gamma \\ \qquad \text{v.}pq\text{.}pr \end{array}$$

$$\begin{array}{l} \text{*}pq \\ \text{Double Ast—22:} \quad \text{*}\alpha\beta \\ \qquad \overline{\text{v.}\alpha\beta\text{.}-\alpha-\beta} \\ \qquad \text{v.}pq\text{.}-p-q \end{array}$$

$$\begin{array}{l} \text{*.}pqr \\ \text{Exp—14:} \quad \text{*.}\alpha\beta\gamma \\ \qquad \text{*}\alpha\text{*}\beta\gamma \\ \qquad \text{*}p\text{*}qr \end{array}$$

8.3.

$$\begin{array}{l} \quad\;\; 32\; 1 \\ \text{D Com} \;\; \text{.*}q\text{v}rpr \quad \alpha = \text{*}q\text{v}rp \\ \qquad \overline{\text{.}r\text{*}q\text{v}rp} \quad \beta = r \end{array}$$

$$\begin{array}{l} \qquad\quad 3\; 21 \\ \text{Dot Assoc} \;\; \text{.}q\text{.v}pqr \quad \alpha = q \\ \qquad\quad \overline{\text{..}q\text{v}pqr} \quad \beta = \text{v}pq \\ \qquad\qquad\qquad\qquad \gamma = r \end{array}$$

8.4. (a) No. (b) No. (c) Yes for Com, and yes for Assoc.

8.5. (a) (b)

$$\begin{array}{l} \qquad\qquad\qquad\qquad 3\; 21\; 1\;\; 2\; 1 \\ \text{DeM—1, 25; Ast—17;} \quad \text{DeM} \; \dfrac{-\text{.}-\text{*.}q r\text{v}-pr\text{.}-\text{*}-qr-p}{\text{v}\text{*.}q r\text{v}-pr-\text{.}-\text{*}-qr-p} \quad \begin{array}{l} \alpha = \text{*.}q r\text{v}-pr \\ \beta = \text{.}-\text{*}-qr-p \end{array} \\ \text{Trans—24} \end{array}$$

8.7.
a. 1. Ast; 2. DeM; 3. D Com; 4. DeM; 5. Ast; 6. Trans.
d. 1. D Ast; 2. Ast; 3. Ast; 4. D Com.
f. 1. Exp; 2. Ast; 3. DeM; 4. V Assoc; 5. Ast; 6. Ast.

8.8. a. and b.; notice that the last *wfe* in each is equivalent to the other. How do we know they are equivalent? (Besides, c. and d. are substitution instances of an Association schema. Does Assoc hold for stroke?)

8.9. (i) a. 1. Ast; 2. Stroke.
c. 1. DeM; 2. Stroke; 3. Taut; 4. Stroke.
e. 1. Stroke; 2. Taut; 3. Stroke; 4. Taut; 5. Stroke.
g. 1. DeM; 2. Stroke; 3. Nob; 4. Taut; 5. Stroke

(ii) Step 6. in f is a substitution instance of a schema, Handy, which can be gotten by collapsing chain e.; the Nob schema, of which Step 3. in g. is a substitution instance, can be gotten by collapsing chain b.

8.10. (a)

$$\begin{array}{l} \text{.}p-q \\ \overline{\overline{-\text{v}-pq}} \quad \text{DeM} \\ \overline{\overline{-\text{v}q-p}} \quad \text{V Com} \end{array}$$

(which is the contradictory of vq–p)

(c)

$$\begin{array}{l} \overline{\overline{-\text{*}pq}} \\ \overline{\overline{-\text{.*}pq\text{*}qp}} \quad \text{D Ast} \\ \overline{\overline{\text{v}-\text{*}pq-\text{*}qp}} \quad \text{DeM} \\ \overline{\overline{\text{v}-\text{v}-pq-\text{*}qp}} \quad \text{Ast} \\ \text{v .}p-q-\text{*}qp \quad \text{DeM} \end{array}$$

(which is the contradictory of $-$v.$p-q-$*qp)

8.11. $\dfrac{p}{/pp}$ A substitution instance of a tautology schema for stroke. $\dfrac{/pp}{\dfrac{\text{v}-p-p}{-p}}$ Stroke Taut

8.12.   Po-7
A Polish transformation schema consists of a (a)_____line with (b)_____above and below it; the *wfe*s consist of variables (Greek letters) and Polish (c)_____, and are such that every substitution instance of the (d)_____above the double line is (e)_____to every (f)_____(g)_____below the (h)_____(i)_____when we substitute uniformly into the (j)_____s.

8.13.   Po-8
1. A transformation step in a transformation chain consists of two (a)_____which together are a (b)_____(c)_____of a transformation (d)_____, or two (e)_____such that a (f)_____of each together are a (g)_____(h)_____of a (i)_____schema.
2. A transformation chain consists of (a)_____or more (b)_____(c)_____s.

8.14. (a) $\dfrac{\text{v}-qp}{\dfrac{/q-p}{/q/pp}}$ St Nob   (c) $\dfrac{\text{v}.-p-qr}{\dfrac{\text{v}-\text{v}pq\ r}{\dfrac{/\text{v}pq-r}{\dfrac{///pp/qq-r}{///pp/qq/rr}}}}$ DeM St Handy Nob

(e) $\dfrac{[(p\supset q)\text{v}r]}{\dfrac{[(-p\,\text{v}q)\text{v}r]}{\dfrac{[(p\mid -q)\text{v}r]}{\dfrac{\{[p\mid(\overline{q/q})]\text{v}r\}}{[\{[p/(q/q)]/[p/(q/q)]\}/(r/r)]}}}}$ Ast St Nob Handy

9.1.
Modus ponens—2: $\dfrac{\begin{array}{cc}*pq & p\\ *\alpha\beta & \alpha\end{array}}{\dfrac{\beta}{q}}$; HS—15: $\dfrac{\begin{array}{cc}*pq & *qr\\ *\alpha\beta & *\beta\gamma\end{array}}{\dfrac{*\alpha\gamma}{*pr}}$; Conj—6: $\dfrac{\begin{array}{cc}p & q\\ \alpha & \beta\end{array}}{\dfrac{.\alpha\beta}{.pq}}$.

9.2. Modus tollens

(1) $\dfrac{\begin{array}{cc}3 & 21\\ *-.\text{v}qrp.r\text{v}qp & -.r\text{v}qp\end{array}}{\dfrac{.\text{v}qrp}{21}}$ (2) $\dfrac{\begin{array}{cc}4 & 321\\ *.*rp-\text{v}.qqq*.*-qrpp & -*.*-qrpp\end{array}}{\dfrac{-.*rp-\text{v}.qqq}{\begin{array}{cc}31 & 21\end{array}}}$

$\alpha = .\text{v}qrp \quad \beta = .r\text{v}qp$ $\alpha = .*rp-\text{v}.qqq \quad \beta = *.*-qrpp$
                                    etc.

9.5.

$\text{VS}\ \dfrac{\dfrac{\dfrac{q}{\text{v}-pq}\ \dfrac{p}{\dfrac{\text{v}rp}{\dfrac{-r}{\text{v}-*qp-r}}}}{\text{v}*qr\text{v}rp}}{} : \text{VS}$ $: \text{VS}$ $\overline{-*qr}\ \overline{--*qp} : \text{VS}$

9.6. Insert before the beginning of Po-13 and Pr-13 "Any number of (a)____ (b)____and . . . ."

9.7. This exercise raises a question about what is called the "completeness" of a system. The schemas we have used so far are complete if we can prove that every valid propositional argument can be shown to be valid by the use of those schemas alone.

Proving the completeness of a system lies outside the scope of our conversations, and, probably, outside the scope of your powers at this point in your study of logic. However, it is important to realize that completeness is an important property of a system, which is why I put this question to you.

To give you a hint about the completeness of our present list of schemas, you might try proving the validity of these two valid, single premiss arguments by the Substitution Method.

$$1.\ \frac{p}{vq-q} \qquad 2.\ \frac{*pq}{*p.pq}$$

9.8. 1. (3) DeM; (4) Simp; (5) Mt.

3. (4) VS; (5) Dist; (6) Simp; (7) Ast; (8) HS.

7. (3) Simp; (4) Ast; (5) HS; (6) Simp; (7) Trans; (8) HS; (9) Ast.

10. (7) HS; (8) HS; (9) Mt; (10) Conj; (11) Taut; (12) DD.

9.9.

1.

$$1(1 \supset 1) \qquad 0(0-1.t)$$
(1) $\dfrac{(q \supset p) \quad (2) \quad (-p.t)}{\begin{array}{c}(-qvs)\\0(0-1v0)\end{array}}$ Valid

3.

$$1v0.001*00 \qquad 1-0 \qquad 1*0s$$
(1) $\dfrac{v\ .qr\ *pr \quad (2) \quad -r \quad (3) \quad *ps}{\begin{array}{c}q\\0\end{array}}$ Invalid

7.

$$1*q1 \qquad 1(0 \supset 0) \qquad 1*0q$$
(1) $\dfrac{*qs \quad (2) \quad (p \supset r) \quad (3) \quad *rq}{\begin{array}{c}(s \supset p)\\0(1 \supset 0)\end{array}}$ Invalid

10.1.

2.

(1) $\dfrac{.*rmd}{(3)\ d}$ Simp (2) $\dfrac{..jg.mf}{(4)\ .mf}$ Simp

$\dfrac{}{(5)\ m}$ Simp

$\dfrac{}{(6)\ .dm}$ Conj

$(7)\ \overline{\overline{.md}}$ D Com

4.

(1) *vabm (2) $\dfrac{.bj}{(3)\ b}$ Simp

$(4)\ \dfrac{}{\overline{vba}}$ Add

$(5)\ \dfrac{}{\overline{\overline{vab}}}$ V Com

$(6)\ \dfrac{}{m}$ Mp

6.

(1) .*pr..mnj
(2) ..mnj   (2) ..mnj
(3) j   (5) .mn
(4) vj*lm   (6) m
    (7) vmp
(8) .vj*lmvmp

7.

(1) -.p-m (2) *rs (3) v-q-s (4) *-q-m
(5) v-pm
(6) *pm   (7) *q-s
    (8) *s-q
    (9) *r-q
    (10) *r-m
    (11) *m-r
    (12) *p-r
    (13) v-p-r
    (14) -.pr

10.2.

1.

(1) *-tr (2) *d-r (3) -r (4) vrd
(3) -r
(3) -r (4) t
(5) .-rt
(6) -vr-t

3.

(1) *.pq.rs (2) -*qr
(3) -v-qr
(4) .q-r
(5) -r
(6) v-r-s
(7) -.rs
(8) -.pq (4) .q-r
(9) v-p-q (10) q
(11) v-q-p
(12) -p

6.

(1) *si (2) *ui (3) *cvsu (4) c
(6) .*si*ui   (5) vsu
(7) vii
(8) i

10.3.

(1) (q⊃p) (2) (-p.t)
(3) -p Simp
(4) -q Mt
(5) (-qvs) Add

10.5.

2. (1) .*ab*bc (2) vd-c (3) -*-ab (R) -v-ad
(6) -va b (4) .a-d
(7) .-a-b (5) a
(8) -a
(9) .-aa

4.   (1) vcr (2) -.sc (R) -*-r-s
(8) vrc (6) v-s-c (3) -vr-s
(4) .-rs   (4) .-rs
(9) -r   (5) s
(10) c   (7) -c
(11) .c-c

6. (1) *si   (2) *ui   (3) *c∨su (4) c (R) –i

$$\frac{\text{(R) } -i}{\text{(6) } -s} \quad \frac{\text{(R) } -i}{\text{(7) } -u} \quad \frac{}{\text{(5) } \vee su}$$

$$\frac{}{\text{(8) } .-s-u}$$

$$\frac{}{\text{(9) } -\vee su}$$

$$\frac{}{\text{(10) } .-\vee su \vee su}$$

8. (1) *d*st (2) *dq (3) $\dfrac{\text{v.}dm.dr}{\text{(6) } .d\vee mr}$ (R) $\dfrac{-\text{v}-st}{\text{(4) } -*st}$ (1) *d*st

$$\text{(7) } \frac{d}{\quad} \qquad \frac{}{\text{(5) } -d}$$

$$\frac{}{\text{(8) } .d-d}$$

10.6. 1. $\dfrac{\text{(1) } \vee pq \quad \text{(2) } *q-r \quad \text{(3) } \vee r-s}{*-p-s \text{ (Valid)}}$ 3. $\dfrac{\text{(1) } *-p-q \quad \text{(2) } .rs \quad \text{(3) } *-u-t}{*.qtu \text{ (Valid)}}$

5. $\dfrac{\text{(1) } \vee -p*qr \quad \text{(2) } q}{\vee r-p \text{ (Valid)}}$ 7. $\dfrac{\text{(1) } *.pqr \quad \text{(2) } *s*tu \quad \text{(3) } p \quad \text{(4) } s \quad \text{(5) } \vee qu}{*-tr \text{ (Invalid)}}$

9. $\dfrac{\text{(1) } *.pqr \quad \text{(2) } s \quad \text{(3) } .pq \quad \text{(4) } *st \quad \text{(5) } *.utw \quad \text{(6) } u}{w \text{ (Valid)}}$

10.9. 2. (1) ∨–pq (2) *r–q (3) *–st (4) ∨–su (5) –u (6) .–w–t
p = Mr. Hurlbutt came home late.
3. p = McNitt; t = Osterloh; u = Ricklin
Ballard's remarks: Stephens' remarks:
(1) *–pq (2) –*–qr (3) ∨r–s (4) *.p–t–s (5) *∨–uq*ur

10.10. With the Reductio schema added to our set of schemas, we have a complete system.

12.1. Here's a sample answer: $\dfrac{\text{man:laughs} \quad \text{pilaster:laughs}}{\begin{array}{l}\text{man}\\\text{pilaster}\end{array}}$

12.2. (a) 1. $\dfrac{\quad}{\begin{array}{l}S_m\\S_o\end{array}}$ 2. $\dfrac{\quad}{\begin{array}{l}S_m\\S_o\end{array}}$ 3. $\dfrac{\quad}{\begin{array}{l}S_n\\S_o\end{array}}$

(b) $\dfrac{\text{animal} \quad \text{dog}}{\dfrac{\text{dog} \quad \text{dachshund} \quad \text{animal/dachshund}}{\begin{array}{l}\text{animal}\\\text{dachshund}\end{array}}}$

12.3. (a) 1. $\dfrac{\dfrac{P_m \quad P_n}{P_n \quad P_o \quad P_m/P_o}}{\begin{array}{l}P_m\\P_o\end{array}}$ (b) $\dfrac{\dfrac{\overline{P_m} \quad P_n}{P_o \quad P_o \quad P_m/P_o}}{\begin{array}{l}\overline{P_m}\\P_n\end{array}}$

12.4. (a) $\dfrac{S_nP_n \quad \overline{S_mP_n} \quad P_n=P_n}{S_n=S_m}$

(b) $\dfrac{P_o \quad \overline{P_o}}{\dfrac{P_n \quad P_m \quad P_o=P_o}{\overline{P_n=P_m}}}$

(c) $\dfrac{\text{monkey:chatters} \quad \overline{\text{telephone:chatters}} \quad \text{chatters}=\text{chatters}}{\text{monkey}=\text{telephone}}$

12.8.

$\dfrac{B\big|S_m}{B\big|S_nP}$ *BD* Square   This step is valid
$\overline{BS_mP}$

$B\big|S_mP$
$\big|S_o$

We can't derive the conclusion BS_oP from this pair of premisses with the *BD* Square schema, because it's a lower corner which is empty. The *BD* Square schema allows us to draw conclusions only when an upper corner is empty.

12.11. 1. Valid. $\dfrac{\overline{\text{Itch:locatable}} \quad \overline{\text{mood:locatable}}}{\dfrac{\text{mood}}{\text{itch}}}$ $\dfrac{S_nP_n \quad \overline{S_mP_n}}{\dfrac{\overline{S_m}}{S_n}}$ Re-moded Square

3. $\dfrac{\text{mental state}}{\text{depression}}$ $\overline{\text{depression:lasts a day}}$

$\dfrac{\overline{\text{mental state:lasts a day}} \quad \overline{\text{understanding:lasts a day}}}{\dfrac{\text{mental state}}{\text{understanding}}}$

Square $\dfrac{\dfrac{S_m}{S_n} \quad S_nP_n}{\dfrac{\overline{S_mP_n} \quad \overline{S_oP_n}}{\dfrac{\overline{S_m}}{S_o}}}$ Re-moded Square

5. (a) $\dfrac{\overline{\text{good/bad}} \quad \overline{\text{pleasure/bad}}}{\text{good}=\text{pleasure}}$ Yes. Plato claims $\overline{\text{pleasure/bad}}$ is sensical. If two different inscriptions, "good" and "pleasure," don't have the same contrary, then either they don't occupy the same place in the same pyramid or they occupy two different pyramids.

(b) Yes. $\dfrac{P_m/P_n \quad \overline{P_o/P_n}}{P_m=P_o}$

7. $\dfrac{\text{sensation}}{\text{twinge}}$ $\overline{\text{twinge:mistaken}}$

$\dfrac{\overline{\text{sensation:mistaken}} \quad \overline{\text{observation:mistaken}}}{\dfrac{\text{observation}}{\text{sensation}}}$

$$\frac{S_m}{\frac{S_n \quad \overline{S_n P_m}}{\overline{S_m P_m}}} \text{ Re-moded Square}$$

$$\frac{\frac{S_o P_m}{\overline{S_o}}}{S_m} \text{ Re-moded Square}$$

13.1. Arrows 1 and 2: Contradiction
Arrows 5 and 6: Contrariety
Arrow 9: Superentailment

13.3. (1) and (4) are contradictories
(3) and (4) are subcontraries

Index

LOGIC: A DIALOGUE